UNDERSTANDING
INTERPERSONAL COMMUNICATION

UNDERSTANDING INTERPERSONAL COMMUNICATION

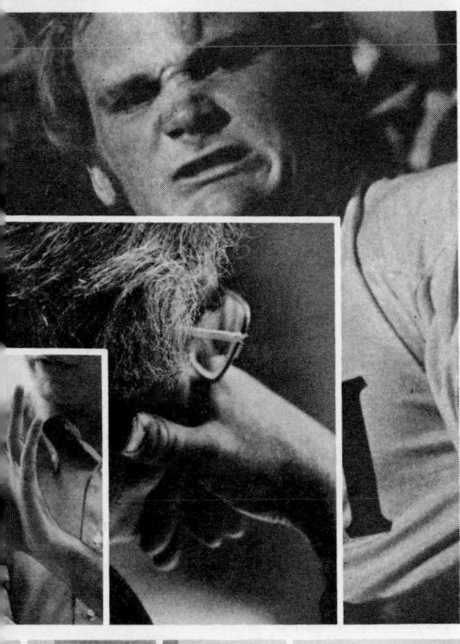

RICHARD L. WEAVER, II

BOWLING GREEN STATE UNIVERSITY

SCOTT, FORESMAN AND COMPANY GLENVIEW, ILLINOIS

DALLAS, TEX. OAKLAND, N.J. PALO ALTO, CAL. TUCKER, GA.
LONDON, ENGLAND

To Robert G. Gunderson and Edgar E. Willis—
teachers who have contributed to my growth and development

Line illustrations by Ron Bradford

Library of Congress Cataloging in Publication Data
Weaver, Richard L.
Understanding interpersonal communication.
Bibliographies
Includes index.
1. Interpersonal communication. I. Title.
BF637.C45W35 158'.2 77-24556
ISBN 0-673-15089-5

Printed in the United States of America.

2 3 4 5 6—KPK—84 83 82 81 80 79

ACKNOWLEDGMENTS

Chapter 1 Alinsky—From *Rules for Radicals* by Saul D. Alinsky. Published by Vintage Books, 1971. Classified ads—Reprinted with permission from *The New York Review of Books* 3/3/77. Copyright © 1977 Nyrev, Inc. Jong—From *Loveroot* by Erica Jong. Copyright © 1968, 1969, 1973, 1974, 1975 by Erica Mann Jong. Reprinted by permission of Holt, Rinehart and Winston, Publishers, and The Sterling Lord Agency, Inc. *Time*—From "The Bodacious New World of C.B.," *Time,* May 10, 1976. Reprinted by permission from *Time,* The Weekly Newsmagazine; Copyright Time Inc. 1976.
Chapter 2 Allen—From interview with Woody Allen by Ken Kelly, *Rolling Stone,* issue #216, 7/1/76. © 1976 by Straight Arrow Publishers, Inc. All Rights Reserved. Reprinted by permission. Coudert—From *Advice from a Failure* by Jo Coudert. Published by Stein and Day, 1965. Lee—From *Think Black,* Copyright © 1969, by Don L. Lee. Reprinted by permission of Broadside Press. McGrath—"As a Navaho" by James A. McGrath, *Arizona Highways,* August 1976. Reprinted by permission of the author. Thoreau—From "Solitude," *Walden* by Henry David Thoreau, 1854. Whitman—"Song of Myself" by Walt Whitman, 1855.
Chapter 3 Associated Press—From "Blue-collar sojourns of college president," *Chicago Daily News,* May 15, 1974. Reprinted by permission of The Associated Press. Reed—"Naming of Parts" from *A Map of Verona* by Henry Reed. Reprinted by permission of Jonathan Cape Ltd.
Chapter 4 Associated Press—From " 'Listen here!' Possible Motto for Man Who Is All Ears," *The Blade:* Toledo, Ohio, August 16, 1975. Reprinted by permission of The Associated Press. Egan—From *The Skilled Helper: A Model for Systematic Helping and*

Interpersonal Relating by Gerard Egan. Copyright © 1975 by Wadsworth Publishing Company, Inc. Reprinted by permission of the publisher, Brooks/Cole Publishing Company, Monterey, California. Harris—*Strictly Personal* by Sydney J. Harris. Reproduced through the courtesy of Field Newspaper Syndicate. Ignatow—"Two Friends." Copyright © 1963 by David Ignatow. Reprinted from *Figures of the Human,* by permission of Wesleyan University Press. Olds—From "Why Compliments May Make You Uneasy" by Sally W. Olds. Reprinted with permission *Today's Health* Magazine © February 1975—all rights reserved.

Chapter 5 Carlinsky—From "Waitress! Did I order THAT?" by Dan Carlinsky, *Chicago Daily News,* August 9–10, 1976. Reprinted by permission of the author. Harris—From "Yes, Harris Hasn't Changed a Bit," *The Best of Sydney J. Harris.* Copyright © 1975 by Sydney J. Harris. Reprinted by permission of Houghton Mifflin Company. Lacey—"Names Can Hurt" by Marj Frazer Lacey, *McCall's,* February 1974. Copyright © 1974 by The McCall Publishing Company. Reprinted with permission. Newman—From *Strictly Speaking* by Edwin Newman. Published by Bobbs-Merrill Company, Inc., 1974. Peter—Reprinted by permission of William Morrow & Company, Inc. from *The Peter Prescription* by Laurence J. Peter. Copyright © 1972 by Laurence J. Peter.

Chapter 6 Beier—From "Nonverbal Communication: We Send Emotional Messages" by Ernst G. Beier, *Psychology Today,* October 1974. Copyright © 1974 Ziff-Davis Publishing Company. Reprinted by permission of *Psychology Today* Magazine. Longworth—From "Standing Firm on the Rock" by R. C. Longworth, *Chicago Tribune Magazine,* March 6, 1977. © Copyright 1977 by Chicago Tribune Company. All Rights Reserved. Molloy—From *Dress for Success* by John T. Molloy. Published by Warner Books, 1975. Peck—From *How to Get a Teenage Boy and What to Do with Him When You Get Him* by Ellen Peck. Published by Bernard Geis Associates, Inc., 1969.

Chapter 7 Colson—From *Born Again* by Charles W. Colson. Published by Bantam Books, Inc., 1977. Harris—From "Reversing the Spool of Thought," *The Best of Sydney J. Harris.* Copyright © 1975 by Sydney J. Harris. Reprinted by permission of Houghton Mifflin Company. Jackson—From *Can I Poet with You?* Copyright © 1969 by Mae Jackson. Reprinted by permission of Broadside Press. Johnson and Goodchilds—From "How Women Get Their Way" by Paula B. Johnson and Jacqueline D. Goodchilds, *Psychology Today,* October 1976. Copyright 1976 Ziff-Davis Publishing Company. Reprinted by permission of *Psychology Today* Magazine. O'Connor—Reprinted with the permission of Farrar, Straus & Giroux, Inc. and Faber and Faber Ltd. from *Everything That Rises Must Converge* by Flannery O'Connor, copyright © 1961, 1965 by the Estate of Mary Flannery O'Connor.

Chapter 8 Andelin—From *Fascinating Womanhood* by Helen B. Andelin. Published by Pacific Press, 1965. Ginott—From *Between Parent and Child* by Haim G. Ginott. Published by The Macmillan Company, 1965. Lavin—From "Brigid," *Collected Stories* by Mary Lavin. Copyright © 1971 by Mary Lavin. Reprinted by permission of Houghton Mifflin Company. Nash—"Hush, Here They Come" from *Verses from 1929 On* by Ogden Nash. Copyright 1940, © 1959 by Ogden Nash. Reprinted by permission of Little, Brown and Co. and Curtis Brown, Ltd. Travis and Jayaratne—From "How Happy Is Your Marriage?" by Carol Travis and Toby Jayaratne. Reprinted from *Redbook* Magazine, June 1976. Copyright © 1976 by The Redbook Publishing Company.

Chapter 9 Baer—From *How to Be an Assertive (Not Aggressive) Woman in Life, in Love, and on the Job* by Jean Baer. Published by New American Library, 1976. Carmichael—From "For $5, she'll call your boss a jerk" by Carole Carmichael, *Chicago Tribune,* January 23, 1977. © Copyright 1977 by Chicago Tribune Company. All Rights Reserved. Korda—From *Power! How to Get It, How to Use It* by Michael Korda. Published by Ballantine Books, a division of Random House, Inc., 1976. Landers—From "Dear Ann Landers . . ." *The Blade,* Toledo, Ohio. Copyright © 1976 Field Newspaper Syndicate. Reprinted by permission. Maxine—From "Dear Maxine," *Chicago Daily News,* February 8, 1973. Reprinted by permission.

Chapter 10 Chapin and Chapin—From the song "Cat's in the Cradle" written by Sandy Chapin and Harry Chapin, © 1974 Story Songs Ltd. (ASCAP). Used by permission. All rights reserved. Emerson—From "Friendship" by Ralph Waldo Emerson, 1841. Hennig and Jardim—Excerpt from *The Managerial Woman* by Margaret Hennig and Anne Jardim. Copyright © 1976 by Margaret Hennig and Anne Jardim. Reprinted by permission of Doubleday & Company, Inc., and Marion Boyars Publishers Ltd. Stanat—From *Job Hunting Secrets & Tactics* by Kirby W. Stanat with Patrick Reardon. Published by Westwind Press, a Division of Raintree Publishers Limited, 1977.
Chapter 11 Crane—From "The Open Boat" by Stephen Crane, 1898. Golding—From *Lord of the Flies* by William Golding. Published by Coward, McCann & Geoghegan, Inc., 1962. Johnson and Johnson—From *Joining Together: Group Theory and Group Skills* by David W. Johnson and Frank P. Johnson. © 1975. Reprinted by permission of Prentice-Hall, Inc., Englewood Cliffs, New Jersey. Meir—From *My Life* by Golda Meir. Published by G. P. Putnam's Sons, 1975. Miller—From *Plain Speaking, An Oral Biography of Harry S. Truman* by Merle Miller, p. 95. Copyright © 1973, 1974 by Merle Miller. Reprinted by permission of Berkley Publishing Corporation and Victor Gollancz Ltd.

Photography Credits

p. 5, SF staff
p. 7, Richard Stromberg/Media House/Chicago
pp. 18–19, *The Key*
p. 25, Burk Uzzle/Magnum
pp. 34–35, Charles Gatewood/Magnum
p. 46, Peter Southwick—Stock, Boston
p. 51, SF staff
p. 52, George Lundskow
p. 57, Richard Stromberg/Media House/Chicago
p. 78, Richard Stromberg/Media House/Chicago
p. 88, Richard Stromberg/Media House/Chicago
p. 101, Photograph by Ken Heyman
p. 114, SF staff
p. 117, Kathy Borchers
p. 130, Kyle May
pp. 132–133, Patricia Hollander Gross—Stock, Boston
p. 137, Archie Lieberman
p. 148, Terry Stetler
p. 156, Richard Kalvar/Magnum
p. 167, SF staff
pp. 180–181, Thomas England
p. 188, Richard Stromberg/Media House/Chicago
p. 195, SF staff
p. 202, Inger McCabe—Rapho/Photo Researchers
p. 209, SF staff
p. 223, Maje Waldo—Stock, Boston
p. 229, Archie Lieberman
p. 234, Kathy Borchers
pp. 242–243, Archie Lieberman
p. 251, Archie Lieberman
p. 256, Richard Stromberg/Media House/Chicago
p. 264, SF staff
p. 278, *The Key*
pp. 282–283, Michael Marienthal
p. 289, *The Key*

Preface

Writing this book on interpersonal communication was, for me, very like the experience every student should have on encountering the subject for the first time: it increased my sensitivity to my own communication while strengthening my commitment to grow and improve as a communicator. I hope reading this book will mean some of the same things to the student.

In the Prologue, I say: "The goal of this book is to help you understand interpersonal communication, in general, and to help you improve your own skills, in particular." This dual emphasis on concepts and on skills underlies the overall approach in this book as well as the organization within chapters. Let me explain. I feel interpersonal communication is too often described as if it is something the reader observes or studies from the outside but does not actually practice. An important part of the course in interpersonal communication—and of this book—is teaching a body of information—concepts, principles, theory. This can be interesting in itself. But understanding the concepts, principles, and theory without putting them into practice has little value in the beginning course, in my view, and so I have emphasized throughout the book the practical skills needed to improve our communication with others. Each chapter begins with a discussion of concepts and concludes with a discussion of skills. The final chapters on communicating with family, friends, and co-workers and in small groups are an extension of this concern with both concepts and skills as they ask students to apply what they've learned in earlier chapters to the situations in which they most often find themselves.

The chapters can be used in different sequences to suit different course needs. For most instructors, the beginning chapters on the self and on perception will be the base on which the course builds.

While I believe Chapters 4–11 develop in a logical way out of each other, still they are written so that they can easily be taught in a different order.

I have tried to write a teachable book, one that will permit flexibility but cover essential content, and a readable book, one that will have an impact on the student. To these ends I have presented information in terms students will understand and have suggested skills that are commonsensical. The additional readings for each chapter list, for the most part, popular books of high interest to students, usually available in paperback. The "Consider This" readings scattered throughout the book are also high-interest materials. Sometimes these agree with and support the text, sometimes they disagree, but in all cases they should stimulate thought and discussion. The special "Try This" materials suggest exercises and projects that reinforce the concepts in the text. The photos and design, the informal writing style—all these are intended to engage the reader in what is a fascinating subject. An Instructor's Manual, available from the publisher, provides suggestions on how to use the "Try This" exercises and "Consider This" material to enhance students' understanding of the text. It also includes test and discussion questions, lists of important concepts and terms, exercises for the class to try as a group, and a list of references of special interest to the instructor.

Even though one author's name may appear on a book, seldom is a book the work of just one person. In the preparation and development of this one, I have had the pleasure of working with some fine individuals. My editors, JoAnn Johnson and Joanne Trestrail, have been fantastic. Their dedication and creativity inspired me at every step of the way. Writing this book has been a rewarding experience because of them.

The suggestions of manuscript readers are also important to the development of a book. For their care and frankness I thank James J. Bradac of the University of Iowa, Jo-Ann Graham, Bronx Community College of the City University of New York, and Theodore Hopf, Washington State University. These readers are not responsible for any errors but should be credited with strengthening the manuscript through their insightful observations.

For a good part of the supplementary material that appears in the sections labeled "Consider This," I thank Charles A. Wilkinson, Communication Counselor. His contributions have not only added variety to the text but have added a realistic base—examples of principles and concepts in action.

Special thanks are extended to *The Key,* the yearbook of Bowling Green State University, for permission to use photographs from their files.

Others who have contributed to the development of the manuscript are Cynthia L. Berryman, Stephen E. and Sherrell J. Earle, Gloria Gregor, Florence Miskovic, Paul Nelson, James Wilcox, Mary Lou Willmarth, and the assistant directors and teaching assistants connected with Speech 102, the basic communication course at Bowling Green State University. I also thank Delmer Hilyard, the Director, and the faculty and graduate students of the School of Speech Communication at Bowling Green—a group of beautiful human beings.

I must also thank my friends and the friends of my family. They often inspired examples I used to illustrate points in the text. Although the names have been changed, many of the illustrations in the book have come out of my experience with them.

Finally, and most importantly, I thank my family. They are the greatest. They have come to accept the comment, "I'm sorry, I have to write," even though they may not fully understand it or like it. Writing often becomes a family project, and I thank Scott, Jacquelynn, Anthony, and Joanna for their acceptance. I also express my deepest appreciation and love to my wife Andrea, not only for her continuing support and love, but also for her reading and typing of the manuscript and for her thoughtful, critical comments during each phase of manuscript preparation. Without the support and love of my family this book would never have been completed.

Dick Weaver

Contents

UNDERSTANDING
INTERPERSONAL COMMUNICATION

Prologue

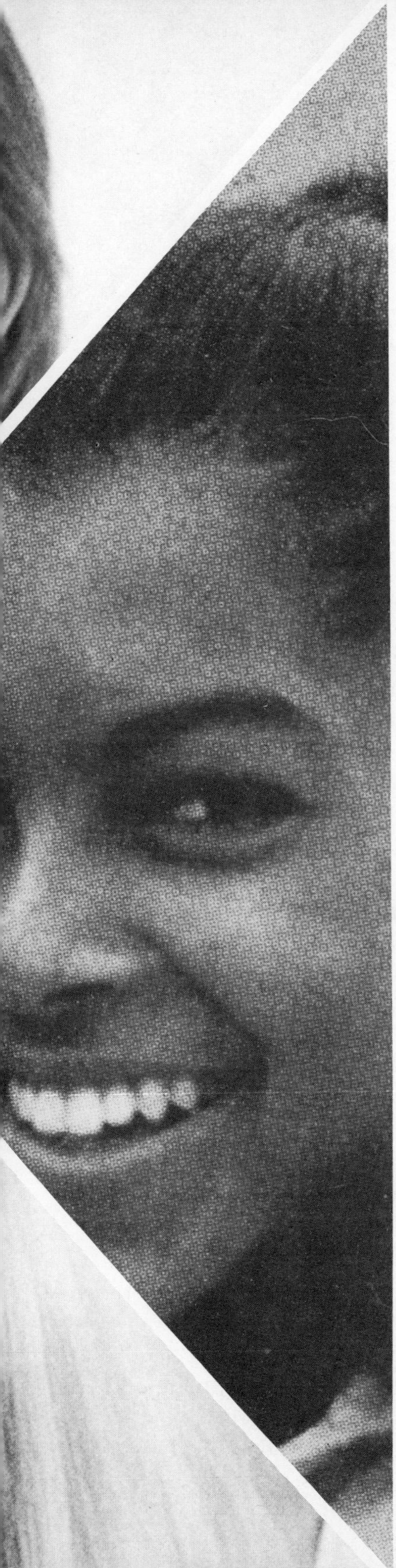

Finding Your Way: Values and Goals

You are beginning to read a book about interpersonal communication. This book and the course you are taking work toward two things: (1) increasing your knowledge about interpersonal communication and (2) improving your skills in interpersonal communication. You may say "I get along all right now" or "What difference does it make?" or "How can it possibly help me?" I can't answer for you. But I can speak for my self.

I am writing this book out of the belief that clear and open communication between people is generally a good thing. That's one of my values: clear and open communication. If you asked me why, I'd say because with clear and open communication I have a chance to build closer relationships with people. And close relationships—where we both give something of our selves—are something else I value. I could go on and say in relationships with other people I learn about my self and growth may take place. Self-knowledge, growth, and change are other values that are important to me. You know now some of the values that I bring to the writing of this book.

I cannot prove these values. You probably could not prove the truth of your values to me. Still, these ideas and beliefs shape how I live and determine how I communicate with others. Our lives and therefore our communication are guided by our value systems, and it's safe to say that no two people in the world have identical value systems. We learn and share our value systems through experience. Since no two people have identical experiences, no two of us have precisely the same set of values.

If you haven't already, I hope this book and this course will start you thinking about

—how you express your values when you communicate with others

—how your values control and shape the way you communicate

—how your values may change as a result of communicating with others

—how you can come to have confidence in the values you hold

You, too, have certain values that you consider important, even if you don't think or talk about them very much. What are some of these? Do you value cooperation? Love? Knowledge? Comfort? Play? Religion? Workmanship? Ambition?

Just for a moment, let's consider that last value—ambition. How might being ambitious affect a person's communication? Ambitious people tend to seek out other ambitious people in business and social relationships. They are goal oriented. They know what they want and have some idea of what direction they have to take in order to get there. We'll probably find this same orientation in their communications: they may be bored very quickly by information that doesn't pertain to their goal; they may put a high premium on efficient transmission of messages; they may be anxious to keep communications brief and to the point; they may show lots of energy and enthusiasm for anyone or anything that could help them reach their goals faster. The high value they place on ambition affects whom they talk to, how they talk, and what they say.

This works both ways. Even as our values affect our interpersonal communications, our communication skills affect how close we come to satisfying our values. If we are ambitious, weak communication skills can stand in the way of our ambition. We'll have a hard time moving toward any positive goals if we have trouble communicating with other people.

Although values and goals are not identical, they are related. The goals we set are often determined by our values. Satisfying a particular value can become a goal. We may value cooperation and want, as a goal, to become more cooperative. We may value knowledge for its own sake and yet want, as a personal goal, to become more knowledgeable. The goal is the ideal end. It is the reality of what we value—it is where we would like to be as a result of valuing certain things above others.

Only you know what your own goals are. The goal of this book is to help you understand interpersonal communication, in general, and to help you improve your own skills, in particular. I hope that your goals and this book's will coincide, at least temporarily! Each chapter in this book includes concepts and skills that should help you achieve the goal of effective interpersonal communication.

In the course of the book I'll be making some assumptions about your desire to grow—growth is important to me and I'm hoping it's important to you. Growth hardly ever takes place in total isolation. It takes communicating with people—understanding them and being understood by them. People who want to grow often have certain other motivations, things they hope to accomplish along the way. James L. Jarrett has identified these motivations and I think they describe the intermediate goals of any serious student of interpersonal communication.[1] As you read them, think about how well or how poorly they describe your own goals:

To Learn

The desire to learn cannot be instilled in us from the outside. It must come from within. As children we had a natural desire to explore, to find out about things. To the very young child, learning and playing are the same thing—any new discovery is exciting. As growing adults, we need to recapture that excitement of discovery.

To Broaden Range of Experience

Our routine—how we think and behave—becomes a kind of security blanket. Few people are eager to leave their security blankets behind for something they do not completely understand. But it is only by breaking out that we will meet new people, confront new ideas, and discover new frontiers. The more experience we have, the more options we have open to us and the more flexible we become.

To Repeat Pleasant Experiences

We all know what it is to do something for no other reason than that it was enjoyable the last time. We'll talk to Pam because last time we talked to her she was friendly. We'll talk about our trip to Montana because last time we brought up the subject we got a good reaction. The better we understand interpersonal communication, the better we'll be able to control the variables in a communication situation and recreate pleasant experiences.

To Internalize Insights

It is one thing to be able to comprehend an idea; it is quite another to be able to internalize it, to know what it means to us. We need to make insights personal if we're going to grow through them. These insights determine how we look at things, feel about them, and respond to them. Learning empathic interpersonal skills will help us with the internalizing.

To Savor Feeling

When we have a good feeling, we want to hold on to it. To know what our reactions are made of and what stimulates them in us will help us to savor such feelings. It can help us to make the most of an otherwise unmemorable experience. Do you know what you like? Knowing what we like is the first step toward recognizing pleasure when we see it. Though of course we never seek them out, even painful feelings can be savored, in a way. That is, we can explore the pain and try to understand what brought it on and at least appreciate the fact that we are not numb to sensation. That's what savoring means—experiencing a feeling to the utmost.

To Intensify Sensation

Whenever we can, we're likely to try to control communication situations so as to intensify whatever sensation that situation produces in us. It's like the kind of ride in an amusement park that lets us control the speed or spin of our own car. We can go faster when *we* want to, slower when *we* want to. Having communication skills is like having our own controls; we can get the most of what *we* want out of interpersonal communication situations.

To Become Discriminating

It is rare to find a person who is totally undiscriminating. We learn in early childhood how to sort color, shape, and meaning—how to be

discriminating. This does not mean assigning value, saying one thing is better or worse than another. Discriminating simply means recognizing samenesses and differences. A good communicator will be discriminating in this way—not judging "up" as better than "down," but at least always being able to tell them apart.

To Recognize Relevance

In order to deal with the millions of stimuli we encounter every day, we must be selective. We usually base our selection on relevance, not "What difference does it make?" but "What difference does it make *to me*?" This is how we begin to make sense out of our environment and our communications. An effective communicator learns to choose and cope with only the most relevant of the many available stimuli.

To Increase Human Potential

It is not uncommon to hear someone describing his or her philosophy of life as "to be everything I *can* be" or "to do everything I am capable of." There is a strong motivation on the part of many of us to live life to the fullest. The effective communicator wants to explore all known possibilities and, when they are exhausted, to discover even more. This is really what growth is all about: reaching out, discovering how far we can go in any given direction.

To Create

There is a real excitement about the creative impulse, the irresistible desire to invent and to put things together in a new way. We don't have to be artists in the traditional sense of musicians and sculptors to want to and to be able to create. We have more opportunities to exercise our creativity in communication than in any other area simply because we communicate more than we do just about anything else. As we engage in interpersonal communication we need to find our own personally effective ways of getting along. And this takes real, creative imagination.

As you begin to read about interpersonal communication, think about which of these goals and motivations are important in your life. You undoubtedly have others not listed here and you might want to argue about some of the ones I did list. That's fine. The idea is for you to think about the interpersonal communication process in general and to see how it applies to you as a communicator. We can read and read and not really understand if something is important to us until we try it out. The skills section of each chapter should help you to reach your goals by suggesting how to put concepts into practice.

Now that you have some idea about where I am coming from—a values-growth approach to clear and open communication—we need to find out more about the communication process itself. Chapter 1 provides a perspective on interpersonal communication. It should give you an overview so that as we discuss specific concepts within the communication process you'll have a better idea of how the parts relate to each other and to the whole.

OTHER READING

Leo F. Buscaglia, *Love* (Thorofare, N.J.: Charles B. Slack, Inc., 1972). Love is discussed as it relates to people's daily lives. Buscaglia believes that love is the creative force for change. He supports the need to speak honest convictions and feelings. This book is full of warmth and sincerity.

Albert Ellis and Robert A. Harper, *A Guide to Rational Living* (North Hollywood, Calif.: Wilshire Book Company, 1975). Self-analysis can be useful. Here is a practical, straightforward, well-explained approach to help people become creatively and actively involved in the world around them. The thesis of this book is that the best way to achieve a highly satisfying emotional existence is through reasoning powers.

Reuel L. Howe, *The Miracle of Dialogue* (New York: The Seabury Press, 1963). A sensitive examination of communication. Presents practical guidelines for those who want to become dialogical—in communication with the environment and open to the communication that environment offers.

Robert M. Pirsig, *Zen and the Art of Motorcycle Maintenance* (New York: Bantam Books, 1974). The story of a man in search of himself. Pirsig challenges readers to work well and to care and to be aware. It will make you question what you are, your values, and the quality of your life. This is a book about feeling.

NOTE

[1]From *The Humanities and Humanistic Education* by James L. Jarrett, p. 147. Copyright © 1973 by Addison-Wesley Publishing Company, Inc. Reprinted by permission.

Chapter 1

Speaking Interpersonally: A Perspective

We are all interpersonal communicators—that is, we all communicate with other people. We have been communicating since we were born. And most of us are fairly good at it. At least we are usually able to share ideas when we need to and get information that is important to us. Then why read a textbook or take a class in interpersonal communication? The answer is: Just because we communicate a lot does not necessarily mean that we do it as well as we can. We can all improve.

We engage in interpersonal communication innumerable times every day. Whether it is conversing with our family, talking with teammates, discussing a problem with a teacher, talking with friends over a cup of coffee, or planning a party, we are sending and receiving messages and those messages are having some effect. Even when we wave at someone we know or tap a person on the shoulder in passing, an interpersonal transaction occurs. All the transactions we engage in have certain elements in common. The better we understand these elements, the more likely we are to improve our own communication and to change our behavior for the better.

In this chapter I will present an overview of the whole process. I'll discuss what interpersonal communication is and what it isn't. I'll look at nine communication principles that affect every interpersonal situation we are involved in. And I'll examine the human and environmental contexts in which communication occurs. Finally, I'll offer some general suggestions on how we can all improve our interpersonal communication skills.

Figure 1. The skeleton of the communication process.

ELEMENTS OF AN INTERPERSONAL COMMUNICATION SITUATION

Figure 1 shows the skeleton of the communication process. It describes in the most basic terms the three elements necessarily involved in any communication situation: people, messages, and effects.

People

At any point in an interpersonal communication situation we may be a sender of a message, a receiver of a message, or a sender and a receiver simultaneously. Although Figure 1 suggests that messages begin with one person and are received by another, the process can be reversed at any time. We send and receive messages simultaneously when the person we're talking to says or does something as we talk that influences what we say next. Even as we speak, we receive the verbal and nonverbal messages our listener sends us.

Messages

Messages may be verbal and/or nonverbal. Both kinds of messages are equally valid communications. A lot of the feedback we get—cues that tell us how our message is being received—is mostly nonverbal. We get it in the form of head nodding, eye squinting, large and small gestures, shifts in posture, and in many other ways.

When we think of messages, however, the first thing we usually think of is words, or verbal communication. An important thing to remember is that words mean different things to different people. Words are personal. Words depend for their meaning on the experiences, reactions, feelings, contexts, and ideas of the people using them. All words have these kinds of associations. It is vital to be aware always of the reactions other people have to the words we use.

Effects

Notice that in Figure 1 the "message" arrow penetrates the heads: this is to show that the message is having an effect. An effect may be a mental, physical, or emotional response to a message. We may say something that causes another person to reconsider his or her position on a subject: mental effects. We may say something that causes someone to break out in a sweat, run away, or fight: physical effects. Closely tied to these effects are emotional ones. Our message may cause the other person to feel angry, affectionate, or joyous: emotional effects.

A message that does not achieve an effect serves no useful purpose in interpersonal communication. However, we must remember that all effects may not be readily observable. A person might respond to a message with silence. Silence is an effect. It could be based on a mental, physical, or emotional response and it could mean any one of a number of things. The point is, just because another person responds to a message with silence does not mean no effect has occurred. The silence itself is the effect. Another response that may appear to show no effect is that of boredom or apathy. But just because people do not care about what we are saying does not mean there is no effect. They have chosen not to care. We have produced an effect. Sometimes, too, an effect occurs only after some

CONSIDER THIS “**One can lack any of the qualities of an organizer—with one exception—and still be effective and successful. That exception is the art of communication. It does not matter what you know about anything if you cannot communicate to your people. In that event you are not even a failure. You're just not there.**

Communication with others takes place when they understand what you're trying to get across to them. If they don't understand, then you are not communicating regardless of words, pictures, or anything else. People only understand things in terms of their experience, which means that you must get within their experience. Further, communication is a two-way process. If you try to get your ideas across to others without paying attention to what they have to say to you, you can forget about the whole thing.”

—Saul D. Alinsky, *Rules for Radicals*

time has elapsed—a delayed effect. Some effects that take a long time to appear are more significant because they have been thought out better. The point is, for communication to take place every message must produce some effect, even if that effect is not immediately apparent.

CHARACTERISTICS OF INTERPERSONAL COMMUNICATION

Having briefly examined the basic elements of interpersonal communication, let us look at some of the unique features of the interpersonal process that define it and distinguish it from other forms of communication. Interpersonal communication:

1. Involves two or three people
2. Involves feedback
3. Need not be face-to-face
4. Need not be intentional
5. Produces some effect
6. Need not involve words
7. Is affected by context
8. Is affected by noise

TRY THIS

Pretend that someone made each of the following comments to you. This person is someone you know but do not consider a close friend. Categorize the comments according to the effect they might have on you. Is the effect mental, physical, or emotional?

1. "Have you ever considered changing your major?"

2. "Why don't you grow up?"

3. "You know, you really have a lot of friends."

4. "You're always complaining."

5. "What do you like best about this class?"

6. "I would really like to get to know you better."

7. "For somebody taking interpersonal communication you sure don't know much about it."

Interpersonal Communication Involves Two or Three People

The fact that interpersonal communication involves people may seem too obvious to mention, but by saying it involves people we rule out the communication we have with our pets, with our car (especially when it's running poorly), with our plants, or with other objects of affection. Such communication may be important and healthy, but it is not "interpersonal" as the term will be used in this book.

To say that interpersonal communication involves at least two people rules out the kind of communication we have within our selves. *Intrapersonal communication* is the name usually given to these kinds of internal messages. In the next chapter we'll look more carefully at intrapersonal communication—communication within the self—as the self is the starting point for all messages we exchange with others. But for the most part, the primary focus of this book will be on communication situations involving two people.

For our purposes, we will think of interpersonal communication as involving no more than three people. Three is an arbitrary number here—it was selected because it is a likely and useful cut-off point between interpersonal and group communication. As soon as there is a

8. "Are you really cut out for college?"

9. "You can give advice, but you can't take it."

10. "I really hate the way you are acting toward me."

Effects differ. Just because these comments have certain effects on you does not mean they would have the same effect on others. A lot depends on who makes the comments and in what context. Can you think of other factors that might determine how you would react to them?

larger group of people interacting, we move into an area called small-group communication and a variety of new factors are involved. In Chapter 11 we will consider small-group communication as an extension of interpersonal communication. The problem in defining interpersonal communication in terms of the number of people involved is that (1) small-group communication is really an extended form of interpersonal communication, and (2) interpersonal communication may actually occur between two people who are part of a larger group.

Sometimes within a group of people, splinter groups of two or three participants occur. As groups increase in size, this becomes more likely. When two people in a larger group argue over a point, they are definitely engaged in interpersonal communication. We've all been in discussion groups where two members dominated the conversation until the discussion became simply an exchange of ideas between those two people. There is often this kind of interpersonal communication in a group setting.

CHARMING, SOPHISTICATED LONELY WOMAN, 40, (comfortable in Pucci gown, tennis dress, sneakers and patched jeans, on the ski slopes, at symphony, or curled by fireplace, wine, good book, someone special to share mood with). Seeks full relationship with gentleman of similar interests. Recently migrated to Ohio (prefer 50 mile radius of Akron, unless you have your own Jet). Hobbies, many and diversified. Gestaltist: basic needs; awareness, sensitivity, giving, sharing, receiving, spontaneous, and total enthusiasm to enjoy life. Please, only honest, mature, intelligent and emotionally together reply.

FARMER WITH BUSINESS INTERESTS, articulate, non-drinker, non-smoker, ambitions in left wing politics. Seeks liaison with compatible woman. No triflers or swingers.

WEST OF MILWAUKEE, single male, 50, tops mentally, physically, into Jung, Yoga. Want independent, confident, intelligent, educated woman in good physical condition for equal-sided relationship. Good manners fine, but turn-ons (unconscious) count. Seek replies from nearby, California and Southwest for trip in March.

FEMALE GOLF ENTHUSIAST, 42, wishes meet male counterpart. Am also tall, blonde, attractive, very feminine, gentle natured.

—*New York Review of Books*, March 3, 1977

Interpersonal Communication Involves Feedback

When we use the term "interpersonal" we do not include TV newscasters or radio disc jockeys, whose messages go from source to audience but do not return. (See Figure 2.) We do not include public-speaking situations either, where the message goes from a speaker to a large audience with only a limited amount of return. (See Figure 3.)

Feedback is the message sent by the receiver back to the speaker. Interpersonal communication involves direct feedback. It is often immediate, obvious, and continuous. (See Figure 4.) It is important to note that the process includes not only an arrow from the source to the receiver but also an equal arrow from the receiver to the source. This direct relationship between the source and the receiver is a feature unique to interpersonal communication.

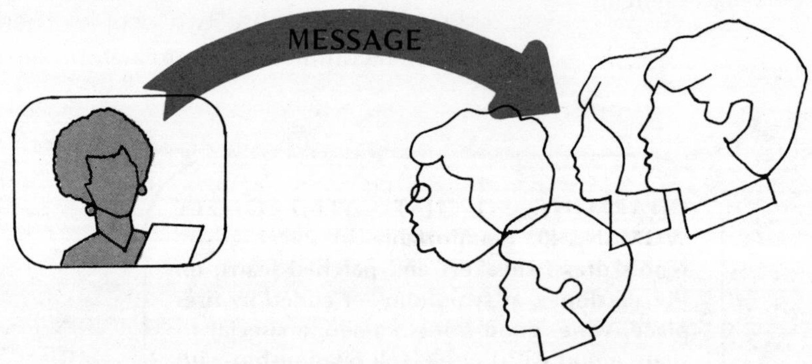

Figure 2. A no-feedback situation.

Interpersonal Communication Need Not Be Face-to-Face

Sitting on a bus, we may be affected by a noisy conversation between two people sitting in front of us (even though it does not involve us) and choose to move to another seat as a result. We may speak to a person on the telephone; we may pass nonverbal messages to a friend across the room by using facial expressions or gestures; we could even be in another room altogether and pass messages to another person by tapping on the wall. We need not be in a face-to-face situation to experience interpersonal communication.

It is true, though, that in a face-to-face situation we receive more information because we can see more of the other person. Communication is less likely to break down during a face-to-face encounter because we're more apt to catch each other's subtleties, special inflections, and emphases. We can perceive moods more accurately when we are face-to-face, and consequently we have a better chance of getting the whole message.

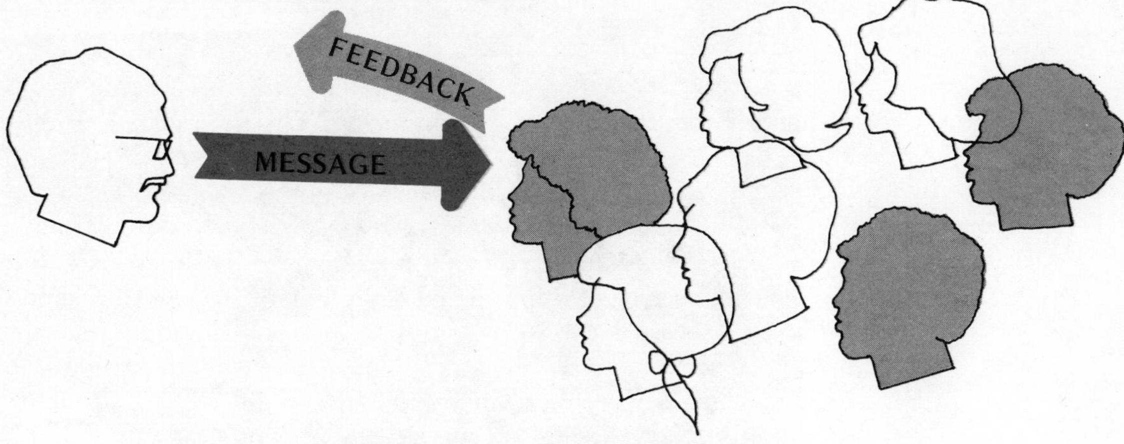

Figure 3. A limited-feedback situation.

Interpersonal Communication Need Not Be Intentional

Interpersonal communication does not have to be intentional. We might find out, for example, that someone has lied to us through a slip of the tongue. We could discover that a person is very nervous around us by the constant shifting of weight from one foot to another, continual fumbling over words, or by other nervous reactions. We might decide that we do not want to be around a person at all because of a certain abrasiveness or disagreeable manner. The person probably didn't intentionally communicate these things, but they are messages because they are signals that affect us.

Interpersonal Communication Produces Some Effect

To be truly considered interpersonal communication, a message must produce some effect. As we saw earlier, this effect need not be

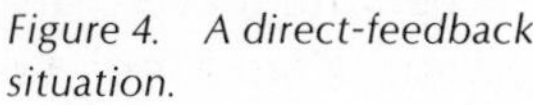

Figure 4. A direct-feedback situation.

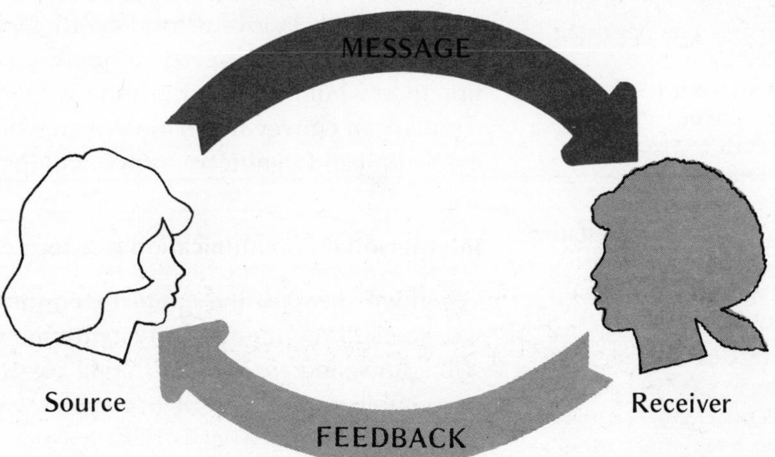

TRY THIS

Next time you have a long, chatty telephone conversation with someone, see how it affects the communication when you do the following things:

1. Let the other person talk for a while with absolutely no response from you.

2. See what kind of feedback works best to encourage the other person to talk:

A. No feedback
B. "Ummm," "Uh-huh," "Oh," "Ah"
C. Questions
D. Comments
E. Paraphrasing (restating the other person's words in your own words)

3. Instead of silence, engage in parallel talking: you talk on a subject parallel to your telephone partner's

immediately apparent, but it must occur. If we walk along the sidewalk toward a person we don't know, wearing our broadest, warmest, I-want-to-get-to-know-you-better smile, and the other person doesn't see us and walks on by, no interpersonal communication has taken place. A similar situation occurs if we are talking to someone while that person is listening to music on stereo headphones or using a hair dryer and doesn't hear us. These are not interpersonal communications if the messages are not received and have caused no effect.

Interpersonal Communication Need Not Involve Words

Though I've already mentioned some of the ways we can communicate without words, this characteristic needs a specific statement because nonverbal communication is so important. Picture two people secretly in love with each other who are standing on opposite sides of the room at a party. A quick glance between them can reaffirm their whole relationship and love for each other. Often a look or a touch can convey much more than words. Nonverbal messages are a powerful and significant form of interpersonal communication.

Interpersonal Communication Is Affected by the Context

When we speak of the context of an interpersonal communication we mean all the human and environmental factors which preceded, will follow, and are at work during the actual exchange of messages. Communication does not occur in a vacuum. There are countless stimuli that affect what is meant, what is said, and what is under-

but with no response to his or her communication.

4. Try to provide vocal responses only with no words. How many meanings can you provide without using words?

5. Try to affect the context of the message by your responses to your telephone partner's. Can you change business to pleasure? Can you change a serious message to a humorous one? Can you take the initiative in directing the conversation if your partner originally assumed it?

stood in a message exchange. Obviously, the people involved in interpersonal communication must be in a position to receive cues from each other; however, they could be two inches apart, two feet, or two miles. The kind of communication that takes place depends heavily on just such factors of circumstance.

Context often determines content. We usually talk about different kinds of things depending on whether we are alone with a friend or surrounded by people who can listen in on our conversation; on whether we're speaking over the phone at long distance or talking face-to-face; on whether we're both happy or depressed. These factors all make up the communication context and have great effect on the quality of the communication that takes place.

Interpersonal Communication Is Affected by Noise

In every communication situation noise is a factor. It can take two forms and in most cases, both forms are present. *Physical noise* is the kind we are most familiar with. We are talking to someone and a door slams, people walk by, a child yells, a car horn blows, and a stereo blares in the background. Our environment is filled with physical noise. There is another kind of noise, however, that often we do not think much about. Because it is hard to detect, because it is difficult to compensate for, and because we may not have thought much about it before, we tend to overlook it. It is *psychological noise* and it exists in the minds of both the sender and receiver.

We have all caught our selves thinking while another person was talking to us, "I wonder when this story is going to end?" or "I probably should get to class" or "Why is she telling me all this?" or any of a large number of other things. We are not listening to what is being said as well as we could because we are distracted by psychological noise. It could be a letter from home, how we did on an exam we just took, or how we are feeling that distracts us. It could also be a comment that the other person makes that triggers a specific response in us. The possibilities are endless.

As a speaker in an interpersonal situation we may have thought, "I wonder how he is going to take this?" or "Maybe she doesn't understand what I mean" or "Why did I say that?" We are communicating with our selves about a message we are sending and we are, in a sense, momentarily distracted from sending that message. Both physical and psychological noise interfere with the message. Both must be overcome, at least in part, if we are to communicate effectively.

SOME PRINCIPLES OF COMMUNICATION

There is more to understanding interpersonal communication than knowing its irreducible elements of people, messages, and effects. When we study this form of communication closely, we notice that there are nine principles operating that affect every interpersonal communication situation. They are inescapable. To understand these nine principles will help us to analyze, evaluate, and improve our own communication habits. They provide an important foundation. In the discussion of many of the concepts developed in later chapters, it will be assumed that these principles are affecting what takes place in any interpersonal communication situation. These nine principles are, then, the fundamentals on which other concepts depend:[1]

We Can't *Not* Communicate

Think of a time when you sat in the classroom waiting for class to begin, in a rotten mood, not wanting to talk to anybody, staring blankly ahead of you and not making a movement or a sound. Anyone coming into the room could see that you didn't want to talk. You may not have wanted to speak but you were communicating. Just as *you* were communicating, so were those people who decided not to speak to you. Communication is more than the exchange of words.

All observable behavior is communication and can be considered a message. No word, gesture, or mannerism is neutral. Even people who dress and speak inconspicuously do so for a reason. The fact that they choose anonymity communicates something about them. Knowing that we cannot *not* communicate should make us more aware of our behavior at all times. In the presence of others, we probably reveal far more about our selves than we realize.

Communication Can Be Verbal or Nonverbal

When we communicate with others we use either nonverbal messages, verbal messages, or a combination of the two. Words are either sent or not sent just as a light switch is either on or off. They have an all-or-nothing feature built in. Nonverbal cues are not as clear-cut.

Nonverbal communication includes such things as facial expressions, posture, gestures, voice inflection, and the sequence and rhythm of the words themselves. Just as a dimmer switch on a light can be used to adjust intensity, nonverbal cues often reveal shades or degrees of meaning. We may say, for example, "I am very upset," but *how* upset we are will be conveyed more by tears and frantic gestures than by the actual words.

CONSIDER THIS CONSIDER THIS CONSIDER THIS CONSIDER THIS CONSIDER THIS

You whom I hoped to reach by writing,
you beyond the multicolored tangle
of telephone wires,
you with your white paper soul
trampled in transit,
you with kaleidoscope stamps
& black cancellations,
you who put your finger on my heart as I slept,
you whom I jostle in elevators,
you whom I stare at in subways,
you shopping for love in department stores . . .

I write to you
& someone else answers:
the man who hates his wife
& wants to meet me,
the girl who mistakes me for mother. . . .
My strange vocation
is to be paid for my nightmares.

I write to you, my love,
& someone else
always answers.

—Erica Jong, "You Whom I Hoped to Reach by Writing"

Every Communication Contains Information and Defines Relationships

Imagine initiating a conversation with a woman by asking, "How about joining me for a cup of coffee?" The informational part of this message refers to what we expect of her—namely, that we want her to join us for coffee. The relationship aspect of the message is the meaning behind the words that says something about our relationship to her.

The relationship aspect tells her how to deal with the message. She recognizes, for example, that this is not a command, but a friendly invitation that implies no status difference between the two of us. What if this same suggestion were made to us by her and she happened to be one of our teachers? The relationship aspect of the message would be quite different. What if she commanded, "Come, have a cup of coffee with me!" The relationship implied here is one of unequal status.

The messages, "Please, won't you come and have coffee with me?" and "You are going to have coffee with me!" contain the same information but imply a different relationship. The message, "Could I please see your notes from yesterday's lecture?" has essentially the same relationship level as "Please, won't you come and have coffee with me?" but the content is very different. For people with whom we have an ongoing relationship, we tend to operate on the same relationship level for all our communication, no matter what information we're exchanging. This relationship level changes only when one of us perceives a change in status in relation to the other.

When we speak to another person we reveal something about how *we* see the relationship between our selves and that person, not necessarily how that relationship *should* be. In our simple opening comment, "How about joining me for a cup of coffee?" we have offered the woman a definition of our selves that implies we are her equal. She can make any of three general responses:

1. She may *confirm* our definition of self. She might say, "I'd love to," and verify our equality.
2. She may *reject* our view of self by saying, "I'm really not interested." This response implies that her view of the relationship is not the same as ours.
3. She may *disconfirm* by ignoring us—denying our right to definition of self. By ignoring our question, she could be saying she thinks we have no claim to a relationship at all.

True, these responses are extreme. There are many intermediate kinds of responses the woman could make. She could say no without rejecting our view of self by adding, "Could I take a rain check on it?"

But clearly, the kind of response she makes has significant implications for the definition of our selves and the relationship that we have offered.

Problems in communication most often occur in the relationship dimension rather than in the content dimension. Consider a situation where you have to do a major project and need to use your roommate's desk to spread out your materials. You do this without asking your roommate's permission first. He returns to find your things spread out all over the room and flies into a rage, saying, "What the hell do you think you're doing?" There is really no question about the content of that question or how you would answer it on that level: you are doing your project and you are using his desk. But that isn't really what he is asking. On the relationship level, he's saying, "You are taking advantage of me. You are acting as if I didn't matter. You think you are superior to me." To cope with the situation you need to address the fact that your roommate feels you have threatened the relationship of equality that existed before. To have asked his permission earlier would have acknowledged his equality with you—it would have said, "You are a person capable of helping me solve my problem."

TRY THIS

Plot several conversations you have had with other people recently. Put down the other person's name and a representative comment he or she made to you. Consider both the content and relationship aspects of the message. For example, let me transcribe part of a recent conversation:

Name
Wife

Comment
"Remember to write."

Content
Wants me to spend morning writing.

Relationship
Controlling (in this instance), as if she directs my life.

The trouble is not that the communication occurs on the relationship level—all messages imply something about a relationship. But problems occur when there is a discrepancy between the content and the relationship conveyed. In the above example, your roommate does not describe his feelings accurately. He asks an aggressive question (the literal answer to which he already knows) when what he really wants to do is reestablish the equal relationship that seems to have been threatened. There is a discrepancy between the content and relationship aspects of his message. The healthier a relationship is, the less discrepancy there is, because we are more likely to say exactly how we feel. And we will be more secure in our status regarding the other person, less likely to feel the balance is being threatened by the smallest word or action. Weak relationships are often characterized by constant struggles over the nature of the relationship.

This is not to say that arguments cannot occur over the information dimension of a message. But this kind of conflict tends to be more manageable because the content level of a message generally refers to something external to both parties. The content level refers to something that exists in the real world and can often be verified. An example of an argument on the content level is: "Did the newspaper come this morning?" "No, it didn't." "I thought I heard it hit the door." "Well, I didn't see it when I looked." "But I *heard* it." The content question raised in this argument can be resolved by both people looking to see if the paper is actually there. Either it is or it isn't. Relationship questions are not as easily resolved. Often the people arguing think they are arguing about content when actually it is the nature of their relationship that they are questioning.

We may find that questions of content can be raised and resolved using a minimum of nonverbal communication. Words and sentences are an effective medium for dealing with informational aspects of messages, both simple and complex. When questions of relationship arise, and particularly when these questions are buried in matter that is supposedly concerned with content, the intricacies of such questions are often better expressed nonverbally. That is, if all we care about is knowing where someone is going, we can simply ask, "Where are you going?" If we want to show what we see as our superiority over that person, we might say very loudly, "Where are *you* going?" with our hands on our hips and exasperation in our voice. We express the relationship aspect of our message nonverbally.

It's good to remember that every communication is a combination of content and relationship factors and is expressed with verbal and nonverbal elements together. If we're unsure about the information someone is trying to pass on to us, we should try not to be distracted by nonverbal messages. If we're trying to understand what that person is saying about the nature of our relationship, nonverbal cues might be more helpful to us.

TRY THIS

In the situations described here, do you see your self assuming an equal or an unequal relationship with the people indicated?

1. With your best friend: making plans for the weekend.

2. With your parents: deciding what you will do after you graduate.

3. With your roommate: determining when the record player or television will be on or off.

4. On a date: choosing where the two of you will go.

5. In working with another student on a project: deciding who does what part of the work.

Communication Relationships Can Be Equal or Unequal

The communication relationships we have with people are all based on whether we see our status as basically equal or basically unequal. This status depends on many factors—circumstance, personality, age, wealth, job position, and so on. We may, at different points in life, feel unequal with our parents, teachers, siblings, or authority figures. This can change at any time. We may find we feel equal or superior to people we once felt inferior to.

When we not only feel, but are, on an equal level with another person, the two of us tend to mirror each other's behavior—sometimes intentionally, sometimes not. We may discover we are depressed at the same time, cheerful at the same time. In relationships based on equality, both people usually try to minimize the differences and emphasize the similarities between them, whether or not they do this on purpose.

People involved in an unequal relationship do just the opposite. These relationships are often defined by social or cultural context. There are generally unequal relationships between doctor and patient, employer and employee, parent and child.

Unequal relationships also exist in more informal relationships. Two friends may slip into a pattern of one being the decision maker, the other less decisive; one levelheaded, the other scatterbrained; one the agitator, the other the soother. Sometimes there are very subtle arrangements where one person is the decision maker on matters of where to eat, but the other is the decision maker on matters of finance. One may be superior in matters of entertaining but the other is superior in matters of car purchase and maintenance. People sometimes work out an equilibrium or balance of unequal relationships. In each case it is important to note the interlocking nature of the roles; the superior behavior of one person often evokes and reinforces complementary behavior from the other person.

There can be problems in both equal and unequal relationships and one form is not being suggested as better than the other. Some people respond best in equal relationships, others in unequal relationships. Problems can arise in an equal relationship where partners mirror each other's negative behaviors, creating a vicious cycle. Trouble may surface in an unequal relationship when one person's inferior behavior reinforces superiority in the other person to such an extent that the superior person becomes unreasonably rigid or powerful. The nature of our communication relationship depends upon who the other person is, what position he or she holds, what message is being conveyed, and when and where the interaction is occurring.

We see these first four principles operating in every communication situation: We cannot *not* communicate, even when we choose not to speak. We use both verbal and nonverbal channels when we talk. Our communications with others relate information and define a relationship between us at the same time, and that relationship can be equal, unequal or both at different times. Knowing this may raise certain questions for us about our own interpersonal communication, such as:

1. Why am I having trouble communicating?
2. How much more am I saying than I mean to? How much more could I say that I am not?
3. How can I be certain my nonverbal communication agrees with and reinforces my verbal communication?
4. What kinds of relationships is my communication defining for me? Can or should this be changed?
5. Are the equal and unequal relationships that I have with others satisfactory, or should they be changed? How can I control the nature of the relationships I have with others?

If we are going to begin to question our own communication behavior, we do not need to stop with these first four principles. Dean Barnlund mentions five other characteristics that will help us gain a broader perspective of the interpersonal situation.[2] He says that our need to communicate "arises out of the need to reduce uncertainty, to act effectively, [and] to defend or strengthen the ego." To understand this, Barnlund suggests, we must view communication as a process that is circular, complex, irreversible and unrepeatable, and involving of the total personality.

Communication Is a Process

When we look at communication as a process we mean that we see each communication situation as part of an ongoing series of actions. To fully understand any single communication, we really need to know all that has come before. Each communication experience is accumulative—a result of what has preceded. And each experience affects all the ones still to come. For example, as we talk with another person, we may discover an attitude or prejudice that we hadn't known about. And that new information will change how we communicate with that person in the future. The present conversation is a point of development for all future conversations with that person. It is a point in a process.

Think about the kind of conversation you would have if you, at your present age, could talk to the person you were at sixteen, at thirteen, at eight. Each of the "you"'s would be a completely developed person *for that age*, yet each would be merely a developmental point for the "you"'s to follow. Communication builds on itself. It is a process that goes on as long as we are alive.

Communication Is Circular

To view each of our interpersonal communication situations as circular means that we are concerned not only with the effect of our initial message on someone else, but also with the effect of his or her response on us. We then respond based on this new message. This act of going around, back and forth in this way, is important to grasp. (See Figure 5.) Though this may sound as if we're going in circles, we are not. We are both constantly changing and making corrections in our thinking as we interact.

Although a minimum number of stimuli and responses are depicted in Figure 5, this figure reveals the cyclical nature of commu-

Figure 5. Communication is circular.

nication triggered by the first stimulus. For example, if your initial stimulus is, "How was the party last night?" I might reply, "Dull!" You might inquire, "Oh, how come?" and I would answer, "Nothing happened." You might follow with, "What do you mean?" and so on. The conversation builds on itself. Each remark makes sense only in terms of what preceded it. Remember that in real conversations, many stimuli can occur and be considered at once. Either person may, at any time, provide a new stimulus which can start off its own chain reaction.

Communication Is Complex

In every interpersonal communication we share with another person, there are at least six "people" involved:

1. the person we think we are,
2. the person our partner thinks we are,
3. the person we believe our partner thinks we are,
4. the person our partner thinks he or she is,
5. the person we think our partner is, and
6. the person our partner believes we think he or she is.

Even the most apparently simple interpersonal encounter is actually quite complicated.

Notice how many variables are operating in the relationship shown in Figure 6 when the six "persons" are described. With only four constants, mathematicians can come up with close to fifty possible relationships; thus, even in a simple communication situation the number of variables involved is large. When we talk with others, what we say depends on how we perceive each of the variables, just as what others say to us depends on the variables they perceive. The more honestly we talk, the more we can be sure that the variables we perceive are accurate. If the people in Figure 6 take the time to get to know each other, he may discover she's not as self-confident as she first appeared to be and she may find that his "enthusiasm" is nothing more than undirected nervous energy. She may start to appreciate his sincerity or ambitiousness instead, if those traits seem to apply to him. If our perceptions aren't accurate, we correct them. Thus, as open communication proceeds, it becomes better and better because:

1. It becomes grounded on perceptions that are more accurate—perceptions that are tested through actual interaction.
2. It becomes better adapted to the person we're talking to because we have a better idea of where he or she is coming from.
3. It becomes less open to chance. We need to do less guessing about the other person and less guessing about the nature of the message.

TRY THIS

Pretend you are doing poorly in a course and decide to go in to see the instructor who knows you are not doing well. Briefly describe the six "persons" that may be revealed at the beginning of your discussion with your instructor.

Figure 6. There are at least six "people" involved in every interpersonal communication.

4. There is less chance for breakdowns to occur. Breakdowns often involve simple misperceptions and misinterpretations. These can never be avoided completely. But big breakdowns based on gross error become less likely. We know better who and what we are dealing with.

Communication is complex. There is no way to control all the variables involved, but the more accurate our perceptions are, the better chance we will have of minimizing the complexity of the communication.

Communication Is Irreversible and Unrepeatable

Each interpersonal experience is totally unique. It can never occur again in just the same way under any circumstances. Sometimes we wish we *could* take back things we've said. Have you ever said, in the heat of an argument, "You're hopeless! You'll never amount to anything!" or something equally cruel? You can't ever take the sting out of a remark like that, no matter what you say or how you apologize later. The remark cannot be taken back.

It is impossible to recreate a communication situation because the knowledge, feelings, and impressions a person brings to an experience change with time, even within a matter of seconds. Saying "I love you" because we want to in a particular situation is quite different from repeating it because we are asked to, even if the words are the same both times. The communication can never be precisely repeated, no matter how many times we say the very same words, because both people are different as a result of the words' having been said in the first place.

Despite thorough organization and planning, most of what occurs interpersonally is spontaneous—open to chance. Every moment is, indeed, a once-in-a-lifetime moment, made unique by the once-in-a-lifetime set of circumstances that came together at that point in time. Have you ever tried to repeat a funny story or describe a hilarious incident only to have your listeners say, "What's so funny about that?" You end up saying, "I guess you had to be there." It is impossible to reconstruct past communication experiences. Even when we come close, new and different factors over which we have no control arise to change the situation and the communication.

Communication Involves the Total Personality

Our whole organism is involved in communication, not just our body or mind, reason or emotion. We find meaning in communication by involving our entire personality. Just as every message we send reveals, in a way, where we are, how we have developed, right up to that point, so we should look at the messages we receive from others as revealing the same things about them. From the various cues that others reveal to us, we construct a total picture of them. Whether the image is accurate or not does not matter as much as the fact that it is *our* configuration and we use it when we respond to them.

As we receive additional cues about people's whole personalities, we change our image of them. Communication provides information for this change. The fact that we depend on communication for the data we use to keep up with other people's development, and they with ours, is due to what is called the transactional nature of communication, or *communication as transaction.*[3] Communication is the tool used to gain the information. As the overlapping and interlocking circles in Figure 7 indicate, the personalities of the people become intertwined as they communicate.

Most of the communication we engage in is intended, consciously or unconsciously, to change the other person. The change need not be big. We might only want Sue to stop reading and listen to us. We might want Bob to consider our opinion on the upcoming election. Simply asking someone to focus his or her attention on us for a minute is asking that person to change, in a way.

Think of the last interpersonal communication you had where

you may have unintentionally tried to get the other person to accept your ideas or simply to understand where you were coming from.[4] Can you see how your interpersonal behavior was purposeful, even if you can't verbalize the purpose?

When we *consciously* set out to persuade or change another person, we will not only bring our total personality to bear in order to effect the desired change, but we will summon even greater resources—more effective language, stronger evidence, and more powerful delivery—to create the change. In analyzing any interaction, we must consider the purposes of those involved; that is, the reason they are bringing their total personalities into the relationship.

CONTEXTS

Human communication does not occur in a vacuum. It *always* takes place in a complicated context and the context *always* influences the kind of communication that occurs. Interpersonal events cannot be

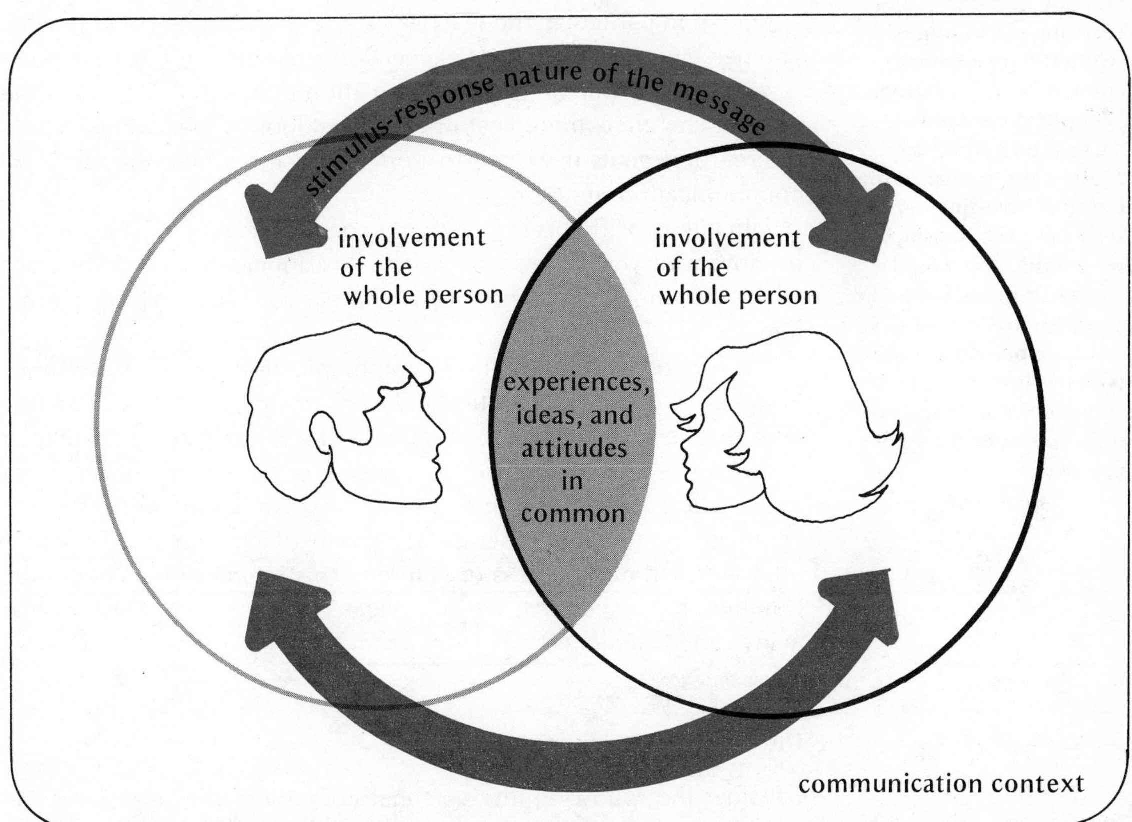

Figure 7. The transactional nature of communication.

CONSIDER THIS

The macho world of CB is part soap and part horse opera. Says Amitai Etzioni, the eminent Columbia University sociologist: "A CB allows you to present a false self: to be beautiful, masculine, tall, rich, without being any of those things. Like the traveling salesman who drops into a singles bar and says he's the president of his company, a person can project on the air waves anything he wants to be." The person who installs a CB set and adopts a "handle" (nickname) and starts "modulating" on the air, is creating a character and reaching out to others while still maintaining anonymity. Adds Etzioni: "People in our kind of society, torn from our roots, want to relate without fully investing ourselves in a relationship, as we would if we joined a church group or worked on a campaign. With a CB, you can have personal contact with the turn of a dial. It is very controllable and protects you from getting too involved."

—*Time*, May 10, 1976

understood by looking just at each individual in isolation, or by looking at the people but ignoring the environment. Who, what, when, where, and how are all important variables and the way these variables interact with each other is also important.[5] Unfortunately, it is impossible to be aware of *all* possible contextual elements, much less the way they affect each other. Some elements, like very personal and private feelings, are never revealed overtly. And always it seems there are so many elements at play at one time that we could never sort them out. Here, we will examine the human context and the context of environment.

The Human Context

Picture this: You are talking to a teacher in his office about the grade you think you ought to get for a course. Your communication is affected, simultaneously, by what your friend Karen told you about this teacher, your own past experience with him, your feelings about teachers in general, your feelings about education in general and your own in particular, the teacher's actual expectations of you, what you perceive as the teacher's expectations of you, etc., etc. The point is, we cannot separate the communication that is occurring from the people who are communicating. We must look at their wants, needs, desires, and goals if we are to understand the whole interpersonal communication situation.

In talking with this teacher, your communication will be affected by how well you know him. Just as his appearance, clothing, language, posture, and mannerisms will affect you, yours will also affect him.

It is people who give life to communication, and how well they know each other helps define the context. If you feel comfortable with teachers, you may not be affected by the role teachers play. If you've never known a teacher as a friend (or a friend as a teacher, for that matter) you might find the situation awkward and artificial. There are hundreds of other human context factors that will contribute to the ultimate success or failure of this interpersonal encounter. Communication contexts are complicated because they consist of so many varied elements.

The Context of Environment

Consider the following interpersonal communication encounter, as described on the left, and the specific environmental variables that bear on the situation, on the right:

Encounter	Variables
You are studying in the library late one evening and are ready to call it a night when in walks a friend who has just finished studying and is headed back to the dormitory. He asks, "Care to go for a walk?" You decide to walk across campus together.	Location: Library (sterile and cold) Time: 11 p.m. Light: Bright fluorescent lights Persons: Two friends Furniture Arrangement: Uncomfortable and awkward (large table, straight chairs) Temperature: Cold and damp Physical Space: Comfortable but distant

How would this encounter be different if it took place at noon on a crowded public beach on a hot summer day? Would you say different things? Talk louder? Laugh more? Walk slower?

All human communication is affected by the physical circumstances under which it takes place, whether it be a job interview, a pizza party, a formal cocktail hour, a classroom speech, a public lecture, or whatever. People's words and behavior change according to the context. Having a phone conversation with someone is not the same as talking to that person face-to-face. Each situation has its own set of variables and cues that may determine whether an exchange is friendly and comfortable or cold, hostile, and tense.

IMPROVING SKILLS IN INTERPERSONAL COMMUNICATION

The overall goal of this book is to help you to understand interpersonal communication and to become a more effective sender and receiver of interpersonal messages. Each chapter includes a list of specific skills that are tied to the concept developed in that chapter. There are some general skills, too, that relate to interpersonal communication as a whole. Developing these skills will make it easier to master those listed at the end of each chapter. They are practical. They can be started at once:

Broaden your experience. We should actively search out new relationships and not shy away from potential encounters just because they appear to be unlike what we've dealt with before. Interpersonal communication must occur between people—between us and someone else—and often this means reaching out for new relationships.

We can take steps toward forming new associations rather than waiting to let them simply happen to us. Growth will not necessarily be immediate, but there is no doubt that we will open up to many new kinds of experiences. Willingness to reach out requires risk but exciting relationships are often built on just that kind of risk.

TRY THIS

Think about the last communication you shared with the person you consider your closest friend. What contextual variables affected your communication? How many can you remember? Try to be specific. Here are several variables that may have affected it:

time of day
noise or distractions
how you met (at this time)
furniture
weather
smells
what you talked about

Realize that growth takes time. Wonderful, satisfying relationships don't develop overnight. Like getting to know one's self, really getting to know another person takes time. Give it time. It's a good idea, if we have known someone in one way only—in the college context, for example—and would like to know more about that person, to try interacting in different social settings, talking about different things, and sharing reactions to the new things we have experienced together.

People are often quite different in the context of their own families than they are in the context of college. We may discover a new side of a person by observing him or her in a setting other than the one we're accustomed to. Traveling, shopping, eating, or simply spending hours at a time with a person can be very revealing if the two of us usually don't do these things together. Only through time can we become familiar enough with the feelings and motivations of another person to really understand him or her. The key to relationship building at this stage is simply patience.

what you wore

touch

location

other people present

Explain the significance of each variable and how it affected your communication.

Use existing relationships in new ways. We might try using existing relationships as a testing ground for the information we'll be picking up about interpersonal communication. Try things out with a friend. Practice new patterns of sending and receiving messages. Create hypothetical situations similar to some of the ones described in this chapter and develop other ways of coping with these situations. Allow "communication" to be the subject for conversations and discussions. (Don't give up if this feels strange at first!) Talk about communication with reference to the principles discussed in this chapter. Be specific about how to improve skills.

Develop openness. Skill development in any area begins with an awareness that something can and should be done. We need to be open to change. We can start by simply trying to become more aware of the kinds of things we do, the feelings we have toward our selves and others, the way we view life and what we want our place in it to be. We should learn to monitor our own behavior and feelings as objectively as possible, becoming more open and responsive to our internal experiences.

Openness also means being receptive to all that goes on around us. As we open up to our environment, we will begin to be more sensitive to the small details of things that we may once have overlooked. This sensitivity will increase our ability to recreate situations in our mind to better analyze and dissect their parts. Our new behavior may be more carefully considered than before in light of our past successes and failures. This is growth, change, development—maturity. A lot of people would discover a great deal more if only they would pause and look and feel and care just a bit more than they do.[6]

Improve the exactness of your communication. We could all stand to improve the exactness of our communication. It's a great help to be able to convey to others just what we mean to convey and to receive from them just what they mean to send to us. This has been labeled *fidelity.* Improving the exactness of our communication is a skill. If we're aware of the need for fidelity, we will become more sensitive to those situations where some of the fidelity is lost. We will be better able to detect when meaning is becoming distorted. And, it is hoped, we'll be able to take steps to correct the situation.

In this chapter we have examined the three basic elements of interpersonal communication: people, messages, and effects. I have tried to show how interpersonal communication is unique by describing some of its characteristics. We looked at nine principles—things that occur in every communication situation. We mentioned two important contexts that must be considered whenever we communicate: the human context and the context of environment. Finally, I talked about goals and skills. In the next chapter I will discuss the self and self-disclosure as starting points for becoming more effective interpersonal communicators.

OTHER READING

Erving Goffman, *The Presentation of Self in Everyday Life* (Garden City, N.Y.: Doubleday Anchor Books, 1959). A description of how people present themselves as characters who wear masks which others acknowledge, like performers before an audience. The author illustrates how people often form teams to help define and support their roles, how inconsistent roles are enacted, and how people manage impressions.

Thomas A. Harris, *I'm OK—You're OK: A Practical Guide to Transactional Analysis* (New York: Harper & Row, Publishers, 1969). Provides practical methods for understanding and analyzing the complicated and destructive games people play. Helps those who are bound by the past to become free to respond to the needs and aspirations of others in the present and, thus, to become responsible people.

Muriel James and Dorothy Jongeward, *Born to Win: Transactional Analysis with Gestalt Experiments* (Reading, Mass.: Addison-Wesley Publishing Company, 1971). Straightforward methods concerned with discovering and fostering awareness, self-responsibility, and genuineness. A useful study guide for people who want to increase their awareness, direct their own lives, make decisions, and enhance the lives of others. Encourages people to see their uniquenesses.

Jess Lair, *I Ain't Well—But I Sure Am Better: Mutual Need Therapy* (Garden City, N.Y.: Doubleday & Company, 1975). The thesis of this book is that people will come to a greater appreciation of life once they see their mutual need for each other. Lair challenges readers to establish relationships with a few intimate friends they can trust—people they care about and who care about them.

Alan Lakein, *How to Get Control of Your Time and Your Life* (New York: New American Library, 1973). Practical, sensible suggestions on how to get more accomplished each day by setting goals and establishing priorities and getting organized. Tips include how to achieve better self-understanding, how to build willpower, and how to keep oneself on target.

John Powell, S.J., *Why Am I Afraid to Tell You Who I Am?* (Niles, Ill.: Argus Communications Co., 1969). An interesting, enjoyable, and basic approach that offers insights on self-awareness, personal growth, and interpersonal communication. Chapters on how to deal with emotions and the games and roles people play are realistic and down-to-earth.

Leonard Zunin and Natalie Zunin, *Contact: The First Four Minutes* (New York: Ballantine Books, 1972). The authors examine the way people meet and relate during the initial phase of interaction. They offer suggestions for developing more control over the first four minutes which will make relationships warmer, closer, and more significant.

NOTES

[1] Paul Watzlawick, Janet Helmick Beavin and Don D. Jackson, *Pragmatics of Human Communication: A Study of Interactional Patterns, Pathologies, and Paradoxes* (New York: W. W. Norton & Company, Inc., 1967). See Chapter 2, "Some Tentative Axioms of Communication," pp. 48–71.

[2] From "Toward a Meaning-Centered Philosophy of Communication" by Dean C. Barnlund, *Journal of Communication*, Vol. 12:4 (1962), pp. 202–203. Reprinted by permission.

[3] John Stewart, "An Interpersonal Approach to the Basic Course," *The Speech Teacher* 21 (1972): 10.

[4] Dean C. Barnlund, "Communication: The Context of Change," in *Perspectives on Communication*, Carl E. Larson and Frank E. X. Dance, eds. (Milwaukee: University of Wisconsin Communication Research Center, 1968), p. 27.

[5] See Harold D. Lasswell, "The Structure and Function of Communication in Society," in *The Communication of Ideas*, L. Bryson, ed. (New York: Harper & Row, 1948), p. 37.

[6] Arthur Gordon, *A Touch of Wonder* (Old Tappan, New Jersey: Spire Books, 1976), p. 11.

Chapter 2

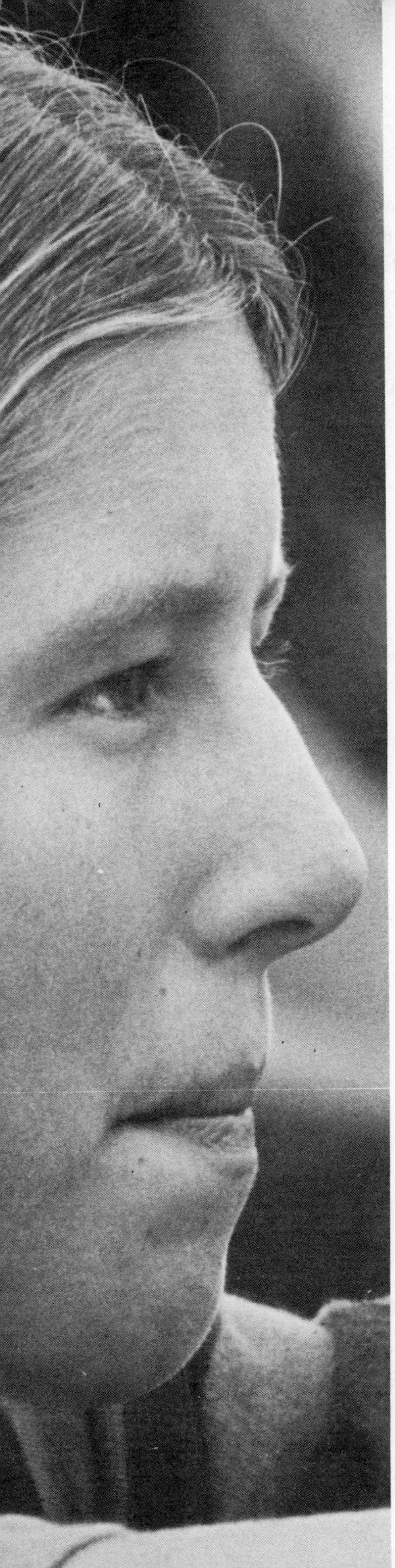

Getting in Touch:
The Self and Self-Disclosure

I am going to begin the discussion of how we can improve our skills in communicating with others by discussing how we communicate with our selves. This may sound contradictory, but before we can really be in touch with someone else, we must be in touch with our selves. This process of communicating with our selves is called *intrapersonal* communication. The interesting thing is that the way we learn most about our selves is through communicating with others. Let's look at an example of how this works.

If you grew up with strong-minded parents or siblings who made all the decisions, and if the only interpersonal contacts you ever had were with your own family, you could end up thinking of your self as an indecisive person. But among your friends you may be very opinionated and action oriented. Your friends may look to you for leadership and decisions. Conceivably, other communication contexts could bring out even more strongly the bully or the shrinking violet in you. You may be more or less decisive depending on if you're talking to a small child or to a salesclerk or to a police officer. The point is, you would have no way of evaluating your own decision-making ability if it weren't for the communication contacts you had with other people.

The starting point for all our interpersonal communication is our concept of self and that is why this is the first concept I will consider. After discussing the development of self-concept and the importance of disclosing that self to others, I will outline the skills necessary for improving our ability to self-disclose. This ability is the key to discovering the self and continuing to grow.

YOUR SELF-CONCEPT: WHO ARE YOU?

If you had to use *one* word to characterize your self, what would that one word be? Shy? Enthusiastic? Loving? Confident? Your characterization of your self will probably involve more than one word. You may think of your self as interesting and friendly once people get to know you; you may think you are intelligent, attractive, and generally concerned about other people and what happens in the world. Whatever words you select, this idea of your self—your self-concept—is directly related to how you behave. It works both ways. If you've always had the knack for making new friends, you've probably come to think of your self as friendly and outgoing. And if you think of your self as basically outgoing, it can actually make meeting other

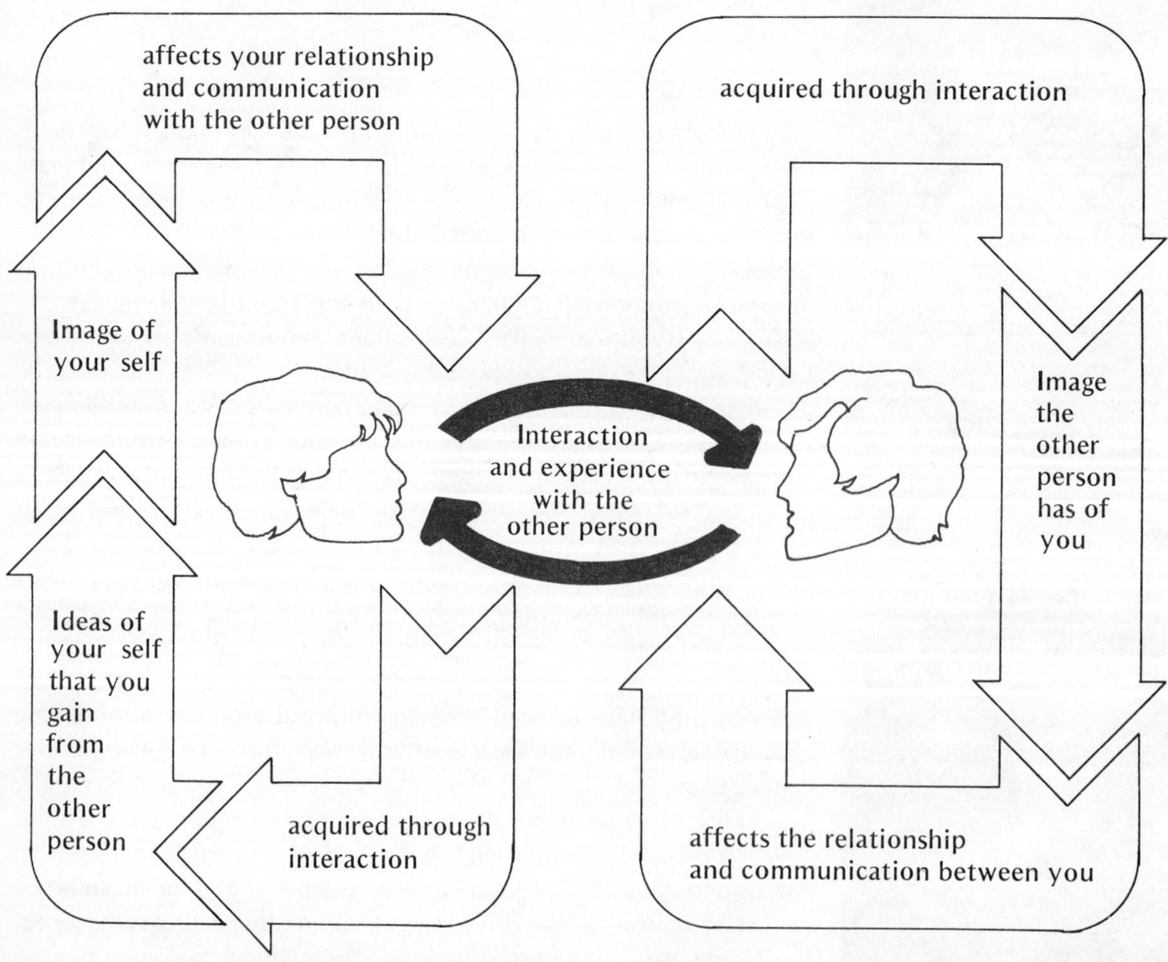

Figure 1. We derive information about our selves from our interactions with others.

people and making new friends easier. Your behavior reflects the opinion you have of your self.

Your success in college and in life may depend more on *how* you feel about your self and your abilities than on your actual talents. And your self-concept will affect your skill in dealing with other people. You can see how your communications with people could go haywire if all the time you are thinking of your self as a friendly, warm person, people around you see you as a loud, offensive boor. What you consider a concerned inquiry into a friend's health could be perceived by that person as nosy prying into something that is none of your business. Interpersonal communication, to be effective, depends upon a realistic perception of self.[1]

HOW DID YOU GET TO BE THIS WAY?

Think back to the word or words you used to describe your self just now. Chances are you arrived at that self-concept ("I'm popular") by the reactions other people have to you ("Glad to see you!"). But then you had to think about those reactions and decide what they meant to you ("They like to have me around. They appreciate my sense of humor."). In other words our self-concept is created through both interpersonal and intrapersonal communication. Much of this goes on without our being really conscious of it. There are four processes we all more or less unconsciously engage in as we build our self-concepts. By becoming more aware of the processes and working at them, we will gradually be more in touch with our true selves. Those processes are: (1) *self-awareness,* (2) *self-acceptance,* (3) *self-actualization,* and (4) *self-disclosure.*

SELF-AWARENESS

You have some understanding of your self—how attractive, intelligent, influential, and successful you are. You derive these perceptions from experiences and interactions with others. (See Figure 1.) Not all your beliefs about your self are realistic—some are beliefs about what you would *like* to be rather than what you are.

For example, if you would like to be chosen as the leader of a certain organization, you may behave the way you feel will get you the leadership role. It is what you would *like* to be—a leader—that causes you to be more careful about your clothes, your speech, your associates. Both what you are and what you would like to be are important factors in making up your identity. Self-awareness involves comprehending the sum total of beliefs you have about your self.

As another example, a woman who thinks of her self as fragile, elegant, and sophisticated may avoid anything that does not match her self-concept. She may avoid things that require physical effort, like a touch-football game or backpacking, activities that could force a compromise in her ideal self. Toward these activities she builds defenses. Getting dirty or injured wouldn't fit her image of her self. Activities more satisfactory to her might be going to the theatre, belonging to social organizations, or playing bridge.

Different experiences have different impacts on her self-image. She can accept more easily experiences consistent with her values; she will probably reject those that don't seem to fit. We all do this. Some experiences may be rationalized to fit our needs if they are inconsistent with our perceptions of our selves. For example, if at a club meeting the woman is asked to do something she considers inappropriate, like sitting on the floor, she may do it because she needs to be accepted by the members of this club. She may rationalize the activity as one that is novel or amusing—even though it is inconsistent with her values.

The Self-Fulfilling Prophecy: Like a Dream Come True

If the woman in the example above acts fragile, elegant, and sophisticated, others will respond to her as if she is. This is not to say the woman is not *genuinely* fragile and sophisticated—she may well be. The feedback or responses of others will help confirm her perception of her self. And she will feel more comfortable behaving in accordance with her self-image. This is what we call a self-fulfilling prophecy: your behavior reflects feelings you hold about your self, others respond to your behavior, and the original feelings are confirmed.

Now, think what might happen to this same woman if everyone she met thought of her as tough, vulgar, and simple. Her self-image would be compromised or threatened. She might react in several ways: she might change her self-image; she might reject the people who provided negative feedback; or she might seek out people who give her only positive reinforcement. Faced with a similar situation, most of us would be unlikely to change our self-image. More probably, we would seek confirmation by associating with people who reinforce our own feelings about our selves and by avoiding people who give us negative messages.

Your self-concept is developed over a long period of time. Periodic and regular reinforcement from others is necessary to help confirm your feelings about your self. You can see the obvious problems if you have negative feelings about your self. The self-fulfilling

THIS CONSIDER THIS

CONSIDER THIS CONSIDER THIS CONSIDER

I celebrate myself, and sing myself,
And what I assume you shall assume,
For every atom belonging to me as good belongs to you.
I loafe and invite my soul,
I lean and loafe at my ease observing a spear of summer grass.
My tongue, every atom of my blood, form'd from this soil, this air,
Born here of parents born here from parents the same, and their parents the same,
I, now thirty-seven years old in perfect health begin,
Hoping to cease not till death.
Creeds and schools in abeyance,
Retiring back a while sufficed at what they are, but never forgotten,
I harbor for good or bad, I permit to speak at every hazard,
Nature without check with original energy.

—Walt Whitman, "Song of Myself"

prophecy can work to strengthen both negative and positive self-concepts. If you want to change some quality in your self, the best way to begin is by believing in the characteristic you want to possess. For example, if you want to be considered dependable, begin by thinking that you *are* dependable.

This sounds easy but it isn't. You might have to get rid of some self-defeating ideas about your self you didn't even know you had. This kind of change requires hard work.

Negative Self-Concepts: The Power of Negative Thinking

What happens when your feelings about your self are weak or negative? Since you tend to act consistently with the feelings you have about your self, this can be a damaging or destructive situation. For example, what if you perceive your self as a failure in school? This attitude about your self may be a result of something as insignificant as misunderstanding directions for an assignment, or it may have developed over a long period of time: having to compete with a very successful brother or sister, having a string of unsympathetic teachers, or not gaining enough positive reinforcement at home for schoolwork. Whatever the cause, it is likely that once you start seeing your self as a failure, you will begin to act the part. Poor study habits, inadequate reading, lack of participation in class, and, in the end, a poor grade may result, reinforcing your feeling. You can see how such negative feelings feed upon themselves and become a vicious, growing cycle,

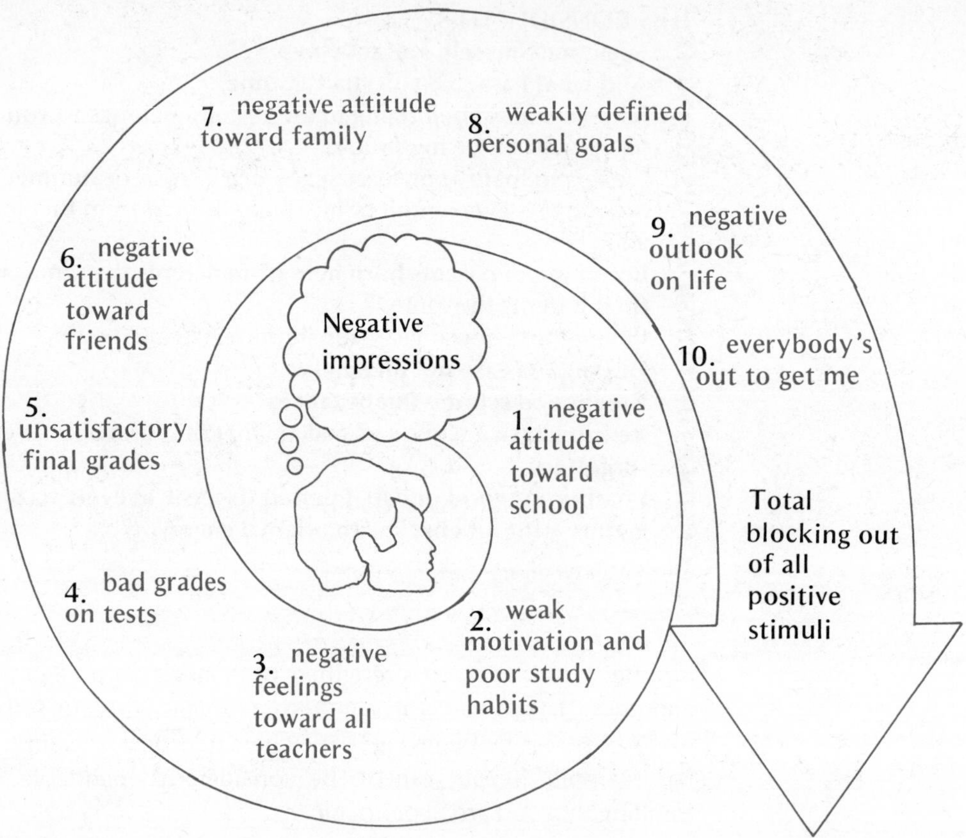

Figure 2. A negative cycle.

a cycle which will begin to encompass all of your thoughts, actions, and relationships. (See Figure 2.)

You may know people whose negative cycle is already well developed. It may be the person, for example, who can't accept criticism or who is over-responsive to praise. It may be someone who complains constantly, or someone who withdraws into self-imposed isolation. We all know people who couldn't think of a self-promoting thing to say if their lives depended on it. Why a person behaves this way, or how the feeling came about is too complex a topic to go into here. We are concerned with changing negative self-concepts to positive ones because of the effect such a change can have on interpersonal communication.[2]

Positive Self-Concepts: You Can Do It

We all know people who are confident about their ability to deal with problems. Given a difficult situation, they seek answers or ways of approaching it. They feel equal to other people and have self-respect. These people accept praise simply and graciously. They can admit to a wide range of feelings, behaviors, and desires, some of which are socially approved and others of which are not. They are realistic in their assessment of self.

People with a positive self-concept can accept as normal, negative feelings, behaviors, and desires if they are balanced and kept in perspective. They recognize that nobody is all good. Finally, these people are also capable of self-improvement. When they see they have an unlikable aspect or a negative quality, they find ways to change it.[3] And they are *likely* to discover personal faults because they are open and responsive to the way they behave and do not expect perfection. A positive self-concept creates a framework that is stable and well-balanced so that mistakes and failures can be successfully integrated into the behavior pattern without a shattering effect.

Few of us have entirely negative or entirely positive self-concepts. Either would be unrealistic and difficult to maintain. You probably fall into some middle-ground position. It would be healthy for all of us if we could be aware of our negative self-concepts and move away from them as well as we are able. Our self-concept affects how we view life, how we want to be viewed, how we view others, and how we interpret messages. Our self-concept holds a controlling influence on our life.

How you view life. Do you see the world as generally threatening and unfriendly? Or does it seem basically a friendly place where you feel at home? Your images of your self, whether positive or negative, form the framework for your intrapersonal and interpersonal communications. If you have a positive self-concept and rewarding and enjoyable relationships with others, you probably will hold a generally positive overall view of life. You'll be able to sort out what is important and what is irrelevant to you. To have a warm, open, and significant relationship with even one other close person often makes you look on *all* others with a more positive outlook.[4]

How you want to be viewed. If you think of your self as a "super salesman" or as a "terrific storyteller," then you want that view confirmed by others. You're going to try to live up to the label, whether you chose that label yourself or someone else chose it for you. Labels can be limiting if you don't think beyond them. It's not a good idea to let them come to *define* who you are and what you want to be. But on the other hand labels can be a useful tool for providing direction, for helping you make choices.[5] If you decide to aim for the label of "popular," you will want to behave in such a way that certain people will admire you. If the people whose esteem you're after insist on a neat and fashionable appearance, non-stop smiles, and sociability, then you will choose to carefully comb your hair, wear stylish clothes, smile a great deal, and seek the company of others. Your self-concept determines how you wish to be responded to and will encourage you to seek that response.[6]

How you view others. Your view of other people also will be affected by how you label your self. If you chose the label of "popular," you might suddenly become very aware of the relative popularity of other people. You'll be more anxious to keep as friends those people who are generally considered popular. You'll be more likely to avoid people who seem to be unpopular. Because the label is important to you, you'll see other people in terms of it. If you view your self as reliable, you are likely to judge others according to how reliable or unreliable they are. If you're very conscious of how well

TRY THIS

How aware are you of your self? Write ten statements that begin with the words "I am." We'll get back to your statements later in this chapter.

CONSIDER THIS

CONSIDER THIS

BLACK	PEOPLE	THINK
PEOPLE	BLACK	PEOPLE
THINK	PEOPLE	THINK
BLACK	PEOPLE	THINK
THINK	BLACK.	

—Don L. Lee, "Awareness"

dressed you are, you'll become extra aware of how other people dress. How you view others often results from how you view and label your self.[7]

How you interpret messages. Your self-concept also affects the kinds of messages you accept and the way you interpret them. If you see your self as "popular," you are likely to see people around you in terms of how they respond to your label. You'll probably keep as friends those people who accept you on your own terms. If it's popularity you're after, then your friends will be not only friends but also admirers. You're likely to see people you don't get along with as non-admirers—they do not help you cultivate your "popular" self-image. You accept messages that confirm your popularity. You might distort, misinterpret, or ignore messages that don't confirm your popularity in order to protect your self-image.

I've been taking a long look at self-awareness here because if we want to be more effective in our communications, this is where it all must start. It starts specifically with coming to grips with a realistic view of our selves. We've seen the control our self-image has in our intrapersonal and interpersonal communications—this image had better be realistic. We've seen how the self-fulfilling prophecy works, and we'd all like it to work for us rather than against us. It makes sense to be careful about the labels we assign our selves because we're probably going to live up to them sooner or later. This might sound like warnings to you, but think of it as encouragement. We all face similar problems in this respect. Realistic self-awareness is difficult to come by, but it is crucial if we want our communications to matter.

SELF-ACCEPTANCE

You begin by being aware of your self, but you must also be satisfied with your self. You must accept your self. By this I do not mean you are smug or uncritical of negative qualities, but rather that you see your shortcomings for what they are, making neither too much nor too little of them. Accepting your self means seeing how your positive and negative qualities are equally valid, equally *you,* equally normal to have. It means building on those qualities you're satisfied with and working to change the ones you're not happy with.

Like self-awareness, self-acceptance doesn't come easily. It isn't easy to accept your self when you are constantly being measured by other people's standards. There are the standards of your parents ("Your friend Jimmy Bentley has been accepted by both Harvard *and* Yale. Have you heard from any schools yet?"), your teachers ("If you don't love *Moby Dick* you might just as well give up on American literature because you'll never understand it"), and even of advertisers ("Use *Whammo* lemon-herbal-avocado shampoo and get out there and have fun like you're supposed to"). If you are unsure of your self and doubtful about how acceptable you are to others, if you cannot accept your self much of the time, your communication will suffer. Accepting your feelings, beliefs, goals, and relationships with others provides the base for a healthy, integrated self. What are some of the things that stand in the way of your accepting your self?

Living Up to an Image

If you are always trying to live up to the image of a perfect or all-A student that your parents expect, you may have difficulty with your self-concept. Whenever someone else tries to impose an image on you, it may be an unrealistic one or one that demands things that simply are not important to you. Setting your own goals too high, in much the same way, may cause you to have a negative self-concept if you can't achieve fulfillment or satisfaction.

Teachers sometimes have a habit of setting students' goals for them. Have you ever been told, "You know, you're not working up to your potential"? With little or no positive reward, or with little or no definition about specific expectations, students often feel frustrated, confused, or depressed, which may result in low self-esteem. Parents, teachers, employers, and friends all seem to have goals for you—standards they want you to or think you should meet. Living up to someone else's goals or image of you will make it more difficult to accept your self.

Living Without Answers

Add to these pressures the ones imposed upon you because of your age, your family situation, the decade, the place you live. There are pressures on you to make personal decisions, many of which seem to conflict with each other. These conflicts can make it difficult to accept your self.

At probably no other time in life will you be faced with so many momentous decisions about who you are, what to do with your life, what to believe, what principles to value highly, what standards to follow. Increasingly, most of us have to face and answer these questions without the answers family, school, and church once provided. Such a barrage of questions can make decisions, interaction, and life itself difficult.

CONSIDER THIS

"There is an assumption here that perhaps should be argued out rather than taken for granted. This is that the self is worth being. There is a philosophical dialogue that turns on the question of whether people are born good and become corrupted or are born evil and become civilized. My own opinion is that each is equally true. Thus, I cannot claim that if you strip yourself of the encrustation of attitudes and defenses, you are going to expose an angelic, euphoric, and expansive person. But, certainly, neither are you going to find the cretinous and willful monster that most of us fear is lurking underneath. There will be a human being, with the assets and limitations inherent in the definition of human being but, for the first time and most importantly, with the choice not to be ugly and cruel and stunted. If I look back at my own life, the hurtful things I have done have been out of defensiveness or an effort at adaptation or toward the end of becoming more comfortable with myself. Never once was the hurt of someone else gratuitous and unmotivated. Deliberate, yes, and wrongly motivated, but never gratuitous. Very, very few people are vicious without cause; and the cause, when the usual person is vicious, is archaic fear and defensiveness. It is the things that are not self, the pulp of notions around the self, that are the source of what we deplore and fear and long to change in ourselves. The dropping away of that pulp will not expose an ungovernable, reprehensible being but a self that can expand and afford to act with decency and generosity and courage. To give the self permission to be **the self, a leap must be taken across the chasm of dread that the self is little and mean and nasty to a certain faith that it is a good thing to be and that spontaneous behavior can be trusted."**

—Jo Coudert, *Advice from a Failure*

Living with Constant Change

In addition to having to cope with the high expectations of others and the struggle to find answers to important personal questions, you also live in a society where a great deal of rapid technological and social change is occurring. This makes self-acceptance difficult. How do you relate your self to things that are always changing? How can you accept your self when your own standards—and society's—change constantly?

Alvin Toffler labels as "future shock" our reaction to this "stream of change so accelerated that it influences our sense of time, revolutionizes the tempo of daily life, and affects the very way we 'feel' the world around us."[8] This pace, he says, creates in all of us a sense of impermanence which affects how we relate to other people, things, ideas, and values. And, assuredly, such rapid change affects the level of self-acceptance we are able to achieve. Change in our environment affects our work. Are you preparing for an occupation that will be obsolete ten years from now? It will affect your acquaintances. What kind of a permanent relationship can you establish with someone you may never see again after two or three years? It will affect your family. Will the ties in the family you form be the same as those in the family in which you were raised? What are the forces that cause a splintering of the family? It will affect your religion. Do you want rigid dogma or a philosophy that is adaptable to you and to a changing world? It affects your sexual relationships. How much stability do you want or need in your intimate associations? With all these changes, it's easy to become disoriented. How can you accept or measure the person you are when the measuring stick is different from one day to the next?

If these pressures and influences worry or upset you or make you uncertain, then you are normal. The adjustments you need to make to cope with the pressures of life end up changing your life and your concept of who you are. Self-acceptance will always be a problem when we are not certain of who we are. But actively working to accept our selves is an important step toward healthy interpersonal communication.

Putting It All Together

If we get our self-concept mainly from our interaction with the people and world around us, and if those people and that world are constantly changing, then you can see how difficult it is to get in touch with your self and feel confident in accepting it. It is very important to recognize the significance of change and its effect on your self-concept and on knowing your self.

THIS CONSIDER THIS

CONSIDER THIS CONSIDER THIS CONSIDER THIS CONSIDER THIS CONSIDER THIS CONSIDER THIS CONSIDER THIS CONSIDER

As a Navaho
I entered the Southwest
  on my striped blanket of rainbow
  in the 11th or 12th Century:
    may be earlier,
    may be later.

As a Navaho
Our rainbow stretched
  from the icy Northwest
  beyond the tallest trees
  to the desert Southwest
  among the tallest pinnacles
  of Monument Valley.
Our lands continually reach
  toward the sun—
    even when we sleep.

We Navahos
  are of all land and no land
  finding the canyons of our
  earth equalling the canyons
  of our travels.
  The canyon depths are as if
  carved by our moccasin
  feet walking and walking
  back and forth—

  always forward—
  across the earth
  again and again,
  sometimes herding
  sometimes schooling
  sometimes going to a Squaw Dance
  sometimes crossing the mountain over there. . . .

We Navahos
  carried with us our Yei
  who teach us from one end
  of the rainbow . . .
  who teach us all things.
  Who take us through
  all life in streams of beauty—
  flowing deeply in our rains
  flowing shallowly in our dry times.

  The Yei gives eyes and fingers
  and hearts to learn from Spider
  Woman,
  or learn from our grandfathers
  or learn from the many yous
  of the world.

We Navahos
  are always learning,
  it is our way,
  it is our eternal Transformation
  like a seed . . .
  we are seeds,
  and we plant ourselves.

—James A. McGrath, "As a Navaho"

The more realistic your self-concept is, the more value it will have for you. To make it realistic means to consider the expectations that others have of you, to answer or at least confront the most important personal questions you face, and to fit your self-concept with your current environment, not the high-school or grade-school world. These expectations others have of you, the questions you must answer, and your environment all are continually shifting, and if your responses do not change accordingly, you may develop an unrealistic picture of the world and of your relationship to it.

The part of your self-concept that evaluates your self is called *self-esteem.* The less distance between your ideal self and your real self, the higher your level of self-esteem. Your real self is the self you reveal as you function in daily life; your ideal self is the self you want to be. The greater the distance between ideal and real, the lower the self-esteem. This is nothing new—we all know we're much prouder of our selves when we act according to our best impulses than when our hopes lie in one direction and our behavior in another. (See Figure 3.)

How close do you come to measuring up to the standards you've set for your self as ideal? The closer you come, the more likely

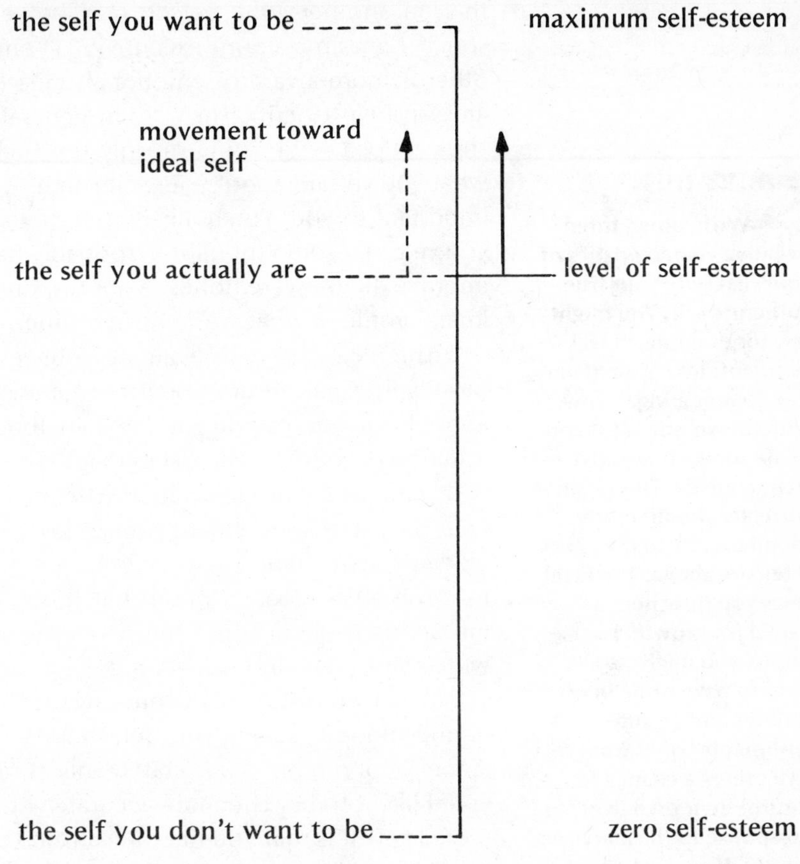

Figure 3. The less distance between the ideal self and the real self, the higher the level of self-esteem.

you are to respect your self.[9] Self-confidence, self-respect, self-esteem—these are words we hear all the time and they all mean pretty much the same thing. If your self-esteem is high, your behavior will reflect that.

Whether or not you can accept your self and feel that you are worthwhile may depend on your beliefs about who you are. Go back and briefly review your responses to the "I am" phrases you listed earlier. Having completed those statements, put each into one of the following categories: (1) Your *physical attributes*—such bodily characteristics as age, height, and weight; (2) Your *emotional attributes*—the feelings you possess: shy, happy, cynical, cheerful, frustrated, etc.; (3) Your *mental attributes*—your intellectual characteristics: smart, average, or dumb; (4) Your *roles*—functions you fulfill in relation to others: your class-level in school, whether you are single or married, your major, your profession, etc.; (5) Your *relationships with others*—the characteristic stance you take toward others such as whether you are accessible and open, closed and withdrawn, or neutral and moderate.[10]

You may find you tend to describe your self more in one way

than in another. One person may be very role conscious ("I am a son." "I am an account executive." "I am a sophomore.") while another is more aware of emotional traits ("I am often depressed." "I am sensitive to criticism." "I am generally optimistic."). While you should not take a listing of only ten such statements too seriously, what you've said about your self can give you a rough idea of what's important to you. You're likely to have listed personal attributes that you've given some thought to, possibly had doubts about, or tried to improve. If you were honest, your responses can give you an approximate profile of what we've been calling your real self.

TRY THIS

Write down three negative characteristics of your real self—your true, authentic self. You might say, for example, "I lack self-confidence" or "I am too domineering." Now, write down one ideal correlate for each negative characteristic. This positive correlate should correspond exactly to the characteristic above. The ideal gives you direction, a model for growth. For example, you might say, "I want to have pride in my abilities and accomplishments" or "I want to give others a chance to control their own lives" as a response to the above examples. How far from your ideal self (in these respects) are you? Do you think this is a good way to measure self-esteem?

The next step is to evaluate your responses either positively or negatively. Chances are, you listed some characteristics you feel good about having and some you feel bad about having. Put a plus (+) or a minus (-) next to each statement. The statements you've marked with a minus are probably areas where you feel you don't come up to your own standards, where you are less than your ideal self. If you've marked mostly minuses, it could be a sign of low self-esteem, at least in those areas. Bear in mind that this exercise is only a very crude measuring tool, and that the person who can label every response with a plus is rare indeed.

Check your statements once again for accuracy. Were you being unduly modest? Selling your self short is just as dishonest and useless as being pompous. Your statements should tell it like it is, not as you'd like it to be. The more accurate your observations are here, the more likely it is that you have a realistic self-concept. And only if you have a realistic self-concept can you fairly measure where you are in relation to your ideal self, and, consequently, your level of self-esteem. It could also reveal the distance between your ideal and real self, and could, thus, be reflective of the level of your self-esteem.[11]

Self-acceptance is always a difficult process, but it need not be painful. It's valuable for all of us to become conscious of and sensitive to the pressures that stand in the way of self-acceptance—the pressures of living up to an image, coping with environmental factors, and living with constant change. Acquiring such sensitivity is an important first step, but it is not enough. Learning to accept your self is an ongoing, lifelong process. It involves continuous awareness and evaluation of your self. Your standards and values are probably quite different from what they were five years ago. Five years from now they'll be even more different still. As you continue to re-evaluate your own standards honestly, you'll probably find some things you want to change.

This brings us to what I'm going to talk about next—self-actualization. What I've been talking about so far—self-awareness and self-acceptance—are pretty much internal changes. They do not involve taking positive action in your life. Self-actualization is a term for the change that comes when you really work at getting in touch with your self. This kind of change requires real commitment.

SELF-ACTUALIZATION

Self-awareness on some level and then self-acceptance are necessary prerequisites for self-actualization. Self-actualization is an important term to know because it is an important idea in interpersonal communication. To actualize means simply to make something (in this case, your self) *actual,* to make it happen. Self-actualization involves growth that is motivated from within you. It means willingness to pursue your ideal self on your own—to grow and change because *you* think it is important. If you see a need to change in your interpersonal relationships or communication with others, the motivation to do this, if you want positive results, must come from within you.

The self-actualized person is one who has taken steps to make things happen. Such people know their potential and actively strive to realize it. The question is, of course, how do you know what your potential is? The preceding discussions on self-awareness and self-acceptance should give you some clues. What it amounts to, again, is being completely honest about your real self, your real abilities. The real self is not some fantasized version—positive *or* negative—of your

CONSIDER THIS " **I find it wholesome to be alone the greater part of the time. To be in company, even with the best, is soon wearisome and dissipating. I love to be alone. I never found the companion that was so companionable as solitude. . . .**

Society is commonly too cheap. We meet at very short intervals, not having had time to acquire any new value for each other. We meet at meals three times a day, and give each other a new taste of that old musty cheese that we are. We have had to agree on a certain set of rules, called etiquette and politeness, to make this frequent meeting tolerable and that we need not come to open war. We meet at the post-office, and at the sociable, and about the fireside every night; we live thick and are in each other's way, and stumble over one another, and I think that we thus lose some respect for one another. Certainly less frequency would suffice for all important and hearty communications. Consider the girls in a factory,—never alone, hardly in their dreams. It would be better if there were but one inhabitant to a square mile, as where I live. The value of a man is not in his skin, that we should touch him. "

—Henry D. Thoreau, "Walden"

self, but a real picture of the you other people see, the you that functions in the real world, the you that has been proven by experience to be your true self.

People who have a good idea of their potential are likely to do things they know are right for them, to set and maintain personal standards, to become open to new experiences, and to trust themselves. That is, they have fairly assessed their own personal characteristics and have come to accept and believe in the self they discover. And, most important, they are able to act on that belief. They tend to realize the importance of change in their lives, and are willing to be forever in the process of "becoming."[12]

How might the behavior of a self-actualized student be different from one who is not self-actualized? Such a student is aware and accepting of his or her self. If this person consistently gets A's and B's it is likely to be more out of a belief in the value of learning than out of a desire to play the role of perfect student for parents, peers, or professors. Such a student will work chemistry problems and write English papers by acting on his or her own best judgment, without constant reinforcement or prodding or praise from other people. This student does not panic when a course in economics turns out to be tougher than expected, or a grade lower than hoped for. The self-actualized student interacts on an equal basis with the people he or she lives with and socializes with. This person might really enjoy belonging to a choir, working on the yearbook, and leading a Scout troop all at the same time, getting satisfaction from each activity. Such a student enjoys searching, seeking, and pursuing. This person might decide that after graduation he or she will live in California and work for a film-production company, taking college courses accordingly, at the same time remaining open to the possibility of living somewhere else and doing some other kind of work.[13]

TRY THIS

Have you ever simply recorded some of your personal goals so that you have a specific set of guidelines, a direction in which you want to move? Write down five of your most important personal goals—things you want to achieve and things you want to accomplish. Be as idealistic as you like. How do you want to accomplish these goals? For each of them, write three things you can do that will help you reach them. Be as concrete and practical as you can. Setting goals is one thing; working toward them is another. Are your methods realistic?

You probably already know some people who seem to have it all together, who know who they are and act on that knowledge. You may even know some for whom the whole process is pretty much unconscious, people who may have never even heard or considered the words "self-actualization." What would you add to our description of a self-actualizing person? It might be helpful for you to study such a person carefully and to try to pinpoint the kinds of things he or she does differently from you. Of course this person cannot and should not be a model for your own behavior; your goal, after all, is to be true to *your* self.

There are certain characteristics essential to the self-actualized person. If you are self-actualized, you:

1. Are willing to stand on your own two feet. This simply means appreciating and capitalizing on your own strengths and abilities.

2. Trust your self. You believe that you can make decisions for your self, and you trust that those decisions will serve your own (and others') best interests.
3. Are flexible. Flexibility is the willingness to broaden your own interests by experiencing as much as possible. It is also the willingness to change when you see certain decisions or alternatives are wrong.

Making What You Have Count

You may wonder why all this is so important. Why emphasize this phase of personal development we call "self-actualization"? The reason is that the self-actualized person is usually more capable of using interpersonal communication skills in an effective, healthy way. As I have said, the self is at the heart of intrapersonal communication, and it is also at the heart of interpersonal communication. How well you'll be able to apply the concepts treated in the following chapters of this book depends on how well defined your self-concept is. It will be to your benefit if you know your self well and are able to act on what you know.

Most of us are painfully aware of our shortcomings and failures. We can learn to be as *realistically* aware of our strengths. To do this, first find qualities you already possess that you can emphasize. These can be very simple qualities. You might begin with: I am good at tennis. I can make people laugh. I like animals. Make what you already have a starting place upon which you can build.

Then think about how often you act on your own likes and strengths. Do you play tennis often? Do you always wait for someone else to ask you to play? Try initiating getting together with someone the next time *you* feel like playing. Do all your friends think you have a good sense of humor or is it something you reserve for a few select people? Maybe you're holding back without knowing it. Do you own a pet? If you do, find out as much as you can about how to take care of it. If you don't or can't have a pet, join an animal welfare society. Make a small donation to a zoo. This is what your parents and teachers may have always encouraged you to do: Pursue your own interests! It makes sense. It can lead you to new, deeper interests and relationships. And it's the beginning of self-actualization.

TRY THIS

Write down some of your positive traits, characteristics, abilities, and accomplishments. What is there about your self that you would like to emphasize? For example, are you in good health? Are you comfortable meeting new people? Are you good at math problems and puzzles? Do you have a good memory? List as many things as you can think of—they don't have to be earth-shaking skills or accomplishments. Then, for each skill, write down the last time you can think of that you acted on that preference or ability. If it's been so long that you can't remember, list concrete steps

SELF-DISCLOSURE

Think of the last interpersonal communication you had with someone where you exchanged ideas and information freely and came away feeling the relationship had been strengthened, or at least better defined. What are the ingredients that cause one encounter to be memorable and another to be meaningless and forgotten? Perhaps one ingredient was the amount of self-disclosing that occurred. "Self-disclosure" simply means disclosing or revealing your self, showing what you know about your self. Isn't it true that when somebody reveals private, personal information you could acquire from no other source except him or her, that the quality of communication increases?

What probably made your latest encounter significant was that both of you shared information. It did not come from just one of you. The information, too, probably had to do with your feelings about

you can take to revive that particular skill. This can be as simple as talking to someone, writing away for information, looking something up in the library, joining a club or musical group. As you discover new preferences and skills, add to your list.

each other, the social situation, or about other people in your social situation. For example, you might say, "I feel great just knowing you" or "I'm glad I could do this with you" or "Can you imagine what Mike would say if he could see us now?" You would be revealing personal feelings that result from your interaction with the other person. These are potentially high-disclosure messages; that is, they say something particular about the circumstances of your relationship. Such messages need not be intimate exchanges, but they can be. They can also be quite simple. But they do depend for their complete meaning on your having shared certain experiences with the other person.

Potentially low-disclosure messages might relate to situations that the two of you do not share. For example, to reveal the name of a book you just read, or the fact that you did not like the eggs you had for breakfast, or that your roommate has a cold, is to share low-disclosure messages. They may, however, pave the way for high-disclosure messages. Self-disclosing is important because you need to know your self in order to do it, and because by disclosing your self you come to define your feelings toward your self more clearly.[14]

It's likely the last significant interaction you thought of involved a friend. It is in such close relationships that most self-disclosure occurs because revealing your self involves risk, and we are not as likely to take a risk with a new acquaintance. We do not want to share feelings with a person we don't trust. The interesting thing is that we cannot create trust in a relationship, and thus diminish the amount of risk in that relationship, without self-disclosure. And the more we trust another person, the more likely it is that we will self-disclose. Self-disclosure creates trust, and trust encourages self-disclosure. As in so much of what we talk about in interpersonal communication, a positive interacting circle creates growth.

What Happens in Self-Disclosure?

Before any further explanation of self-disclosure, we might consider some of the benefits to be gained. What happens when you self-disclose? One of the first things you might notice happening is *increasing accuracy in communication*. Because self-disclosure involves the expression of personal feelings, you not only pass along information ("Your philodendron died while you were gone") but you can also say how you feel about delivering that message ("I'm sorry to have to tell you your philodendron died while you were gone. I know how much it meant to you"). Otherwise, the other person would have to guess how you feel from your behavior. Feelings are often interpreted from behavior, and we hope that others interpret our feelings correctly. But we know from experience that other people do not always guess correctly how we feel unless we tell them. The first benefit of self-disclosure, then, is that it ensures a certain level of accuracy in communication.

Another thing that happens has to do with *getting to know others better.* Interpersonal relationships are built upon self-disclosure. If you want to deepen your friendships, discover more about how others think and feel, and increase the intensity of your associations, selfdisclosure provides one means. Think of the person you consider your closest friend. Chances are more mutual self-disclosure has taken place with this person than with anyone else you know. As you find out more about both your self and others, you will realize how little you know about both, and how much room there is for growth.

Self-disclosure also is a way of *increasing your number of contacts and enlarging your group of friends.* Getting to know a larger number of people can add knowledge, interest, and a degree of excitement to your present life. It might provide opportunities for you to experiment—to try out new attitudes, to experience new behaviors, and to encounter new relationships. It is not necessarily dishonest in your interpersonal encounters to be one thing to one person, something a little different to another. You have many sides. You are not composed of a single set of attitudes, behaviors, or relationships, but many times routine, habits, or laziness can prevent you from sharing certain aspects of your self. The self you reveal in every situation should be an honest one, but that does not mean it must be the same one exposed to everyone, or that it cannot change.

Perhaps the most important personal benefit to result from self-disclosure is simply the possibility of *gaining increased insight into the "real" you.* Self-disclosure is the window you use to see your self. The more self-disclosure you engage in, the more likely it is you will discover attributes, uniquenesses, and peculiarities you may not have been aware of, thus opening a window into your self.

The Johari Window: Here's Looking at You

Joseph Luft and Harrington Ingham created a diagram that looks at the self-disclosure process as a means of expanding what you know of your self. They called it the Johari Window (Joseph + Harrington).[15] (See Figure 4.)

The Johari Window identifies four kinds of information about your self that affect your communication. Think of the whole diagram as representing your total self as you relate to other human beings. Remember that for every person you relate with, a new window can be drawn. The panes of the window change in size accord-

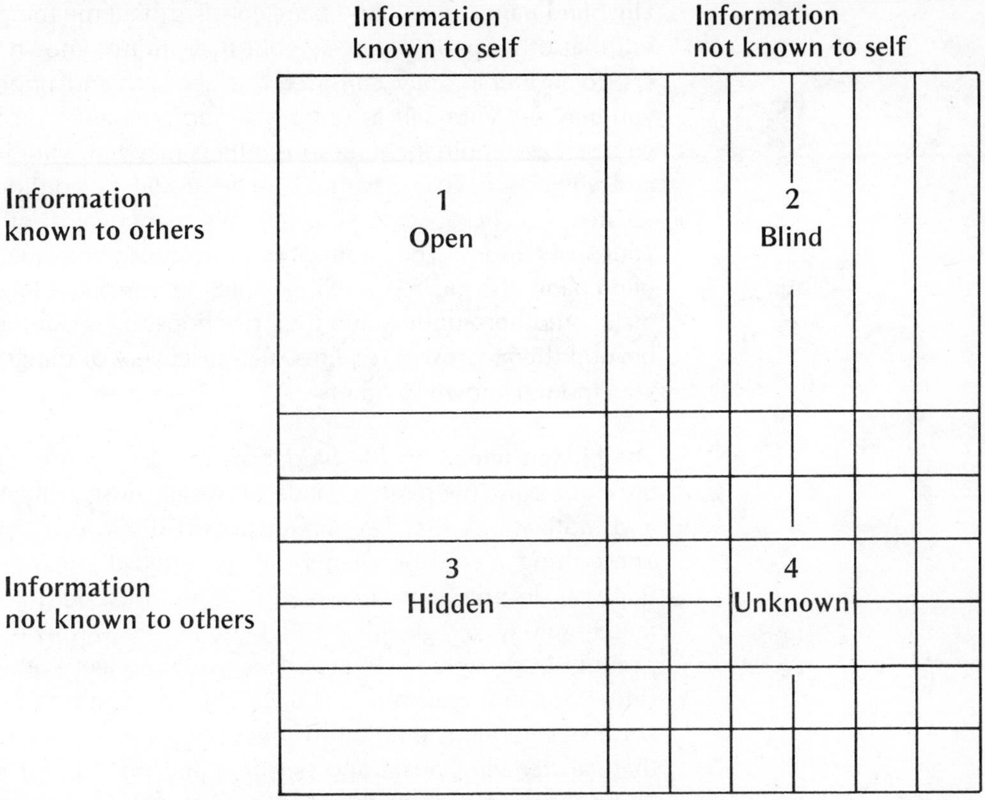

	Information known to self	Information not known to self
Information known to others	1 Open	2 Blind
Information not known to others	3 Hidden	4 Unknown

Figure 4. The Johari Window identifies different kinds of information about our selves.

ing to your awareness, and the awareness of others, of your behavior, feelings, and motivations. While the size of the panes can change according to different levels of awareness, the size will also be different for different people because your behavior, feelings, and motivations are actually different with them. Every relationship you have can be described by a Johari Window, and no two would be alike.

The open pane. The size of the *open* pane reveals the amount of risk you take in relationships. As relationships become deeper, the open pane gets bigger, reflecting your willingness to be known. This pane comprises all aspects of your self known to you *and* others. It includes such things as the color of your eyes, your sex, and whether you are standing up or sitting down at the moment. It may also include things you know and don't mind admitting about your self, such as the fact that you are married or a teacher or happy or depressed. Information included in this pane provides the substance for the biggest part of your communications with others. This is where everybody's cards are on the table.

The blind pane. The *blind* pane consists of all the things about your self that other people perceive but that are not known to you. Others, for example, may consider you abrasive and unpleasant while you may see your self as optimistic and pleasant. You may think of your self as genuinely humorous; others may find your humor forced and vulgar. Or you may think of your self as confident and self-assured, but because of your nervous mannerisms, others may see your insecurities. The more you learn about the qualities in your blind pane, the more you will be able to control the impressions you make on others, understand their reactions to you, and learn to grow beyond them. Growth requires such discovery of things unknown to you, though known to others.

The hidden pane. In the *hidden* pane, you are the one who exercises control. This pane is made up of all those behaviors, feelings, and motivations that you prefer not to disclose to someone else. These things could be events that occurred during your childhood that you do not want known. They could include the fact that you failed biology in high school, that you like soap operas, that you eat peanut butter with every meal. They could concern other people besides you, and need not be things you are ashamed of or think are wrong. Everyone is entitled to some secrets. There are certain things that can remain private and personal and need never be disclosed. These things remain in the hidden pane: things unknown to others but known to you.

The unknown pane. The *unknown* pane is made up of everything unknown to you and to others. No matter how much you grow and discover and learn about your self, shrinking the size of this pane, it can never completely disappear. You can never know all there is to know about your self. This pane represents everything about your self that you and other people have never explored. This pane includes all your untapped resources, all your potentials, everything that currently lies dormant. It is through interpersonal communication that you can reduce the size of this pane; without communicating with others, much of your potential will remain unrealized.

The interdependence of the panes. The four panes of the Johari Window are interdependent: that is, a change in the size of one pane will affect the others. For example, if through talking with a friend you discovered something you never knew before (something that existed in the blind pane), this would enlarge the open pane and reduce the size of the blind one. Your discovery could be of something rather insignificant, like the fact that your socks don't match, or it could be something crucial to your relationship, like the fact that Sam really doesn't care about you as much as you thought he did.

It can be rewarding and satisfying to add to your open pane, whether by revealing or by discovering things about your self. It can also be painful; enlarging the open pane involves some risk. You need to use discretion here, as inappropriate disclosure can be damaging whether you are giving it or receiving it. Be sure you are ready to cope with the consequences before you try to empty your hidden and blind panes into your open pane.

Generally, though, the more you reveal your self to others so that they can know you better, the more you will learn about your

IS CONSIDER THIS CONSIDER THIS

CONSIDER THIS CONSIDER THIS CONSIDER THIS CONSIDER THIS CONSIDER TH

Do you believe in reincarnation?

I certainly don't believe **in anything. It's conceivable, but I don't believe in it. Perhaps we come back as a deck reshuffling itself. Maybe we turn into birds. Who knows?**

What, then, is the meaning of life?

The meaning of life is that nobody knows the meaning of life. We are not put here to have a good time and that's what throws most of us, that sense that we all have an inalienable right to a good time.

It's in the Constitution—"life, liberty and the pursuit of a good time."

The pursuit is all right. We can pursue it, but we were not put here to have one. That anxiety is the natural state of man, and so I think it's probably the correct state. It's probably important that we experience anxiety because it makes for the survival of the species. It doesn't bother me that I'm not having a good time because I know I'm doing something right. Most people who are having a good time are paying an enormous price for it in some way. . . .

Are you a paranoid person?

I have a pessimistic view of people. Consequently, I have that view of myself. I think the worst in any given situation, so I think the other person is thinking the worst. The point is that paranoids are right a certain amount of the time. I guess that comes from my own feelings of hostility. I'm suspicious and negative. I feel others have to prove themselves to me, and I don't make it any easier on myself. I feel I'm not accepted and that I have to prove myself in any situation, that one can't take decency for granted, that you have to keep proving it to me.

—*Rolling Stone* interview with Woody Allen, July 1, 1976

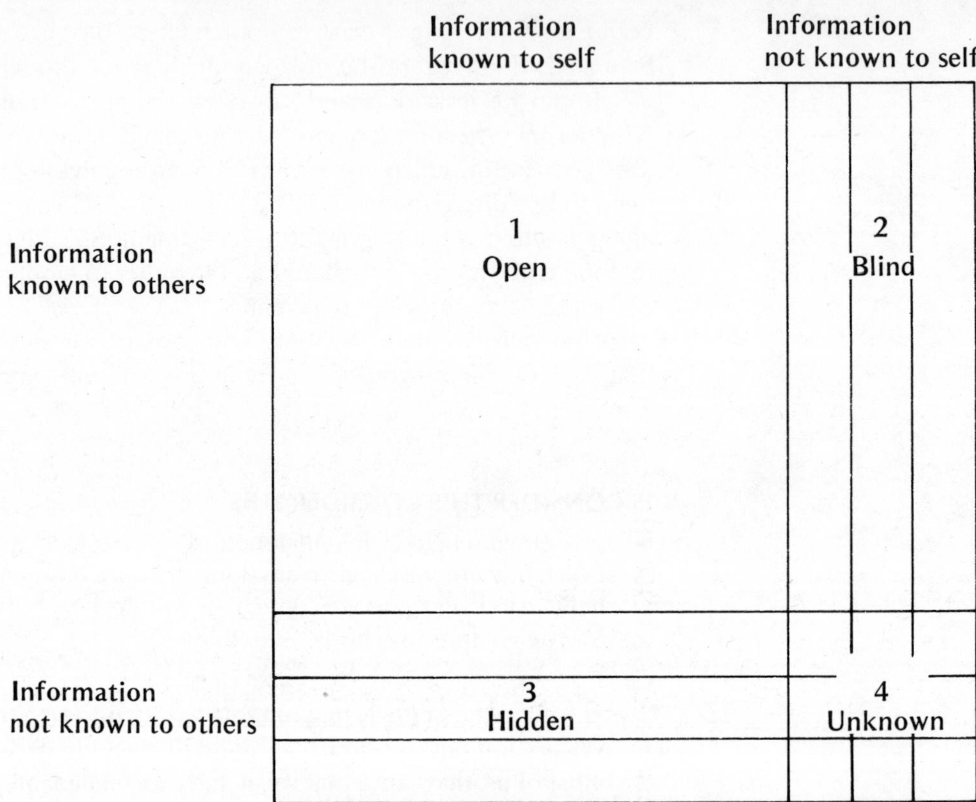

Figure 5. This window describes a relationship with a great deal of free and honest exchange.

self. And the more truth about your self you are willing to accept from others, the more accurate your self-concept will be. This increased knowledge of your self can result in greater self-acceptance. After all, if your friend is not shocked by your C average, perhaps you can accept it too. A Johari Window representing a close relationship between two people in which there is a great deal of free and honest exchange has a very large open pane. (See Figure 5.)

Sidney Jourard, a researcher, has concluded that humans spend an incredible amount of energy trying to avoid becoming known by other human beings. The acts of avoidance keep us from healthy human relationships. According to Jourard, allowing your self to be known to at least one other person who is important to you and whose opinions and judgment you value and respect highly is one characteristic of a healthy personality.[16]

What Are You Afraid Of?

Why are we afraid to reveal our selves to others? Why is it easier to hold back than to express our real being? In *Why Am I Afraid to Tell*

You Who I Am? John Powell suggests that one reason is that each of us thinks, "If I tell you who I am, you may not like who I am, and it is all that I have."[17] We fear rejection. We fear discovering that we might be not totally acceptable to others or that we are unworthy. Another reason is that we feel we may not get reinforcement. What if I open my self to you and you offer no support or positive feedback? Even the possibility of some slight negative reaction scares us. Or we might be afraid of hurting another person or making him or her angry. You may have wanted for a long time to tell someone that if she continues to treat her boyfriend callously she will lose him. Your fear of hurting her feelings may have kept you from telling her.

We may not self-disclose if we believe that no one else is interested in our thoughts, feelings, or view of the world.[18] Or we simply may not know how to self-disclose constructively. Since this disclosure is the primary channel for gaining information about our selves, some of the basic skills for successful, constructive self-disclosure will be outlined next.

IMPROVING SKILLS IN SELF-DISCLOSURE

How can we disclose our selves more successfully than we do now? Perhaps it would be more accurate in this chapter on the self to talk about improving attitudes rather than skills. Without the proper attitude, it is unlikely that our skills in self-disclosure will improve.

Commit your self to grow.[19] If we have no desire to grow or change, no commitment to improve our relationship with another person, we are not likely to self-disclose. We have to care about another person before taking the risk necessary to build a trusting relationship. The fact that we acknowledge the value of a relationship shows the other person our level of commitment and makes the self-disclosure even more useful.

It takes courage to let another person know he or she means something special to us. To say, "It has been fun talking to you," sounds superficial, but it may be enough to trigger further interaction. So, feeling a commitment to a relationship is part of it, but we also need to disclose that commitment to the other person. How often do we tell other people that we need them or appreciate them?

Share your feelings. Beyond sharing with another person what we consider the value of the relationship, it helps if we both agree to share feelings and awarenesses. This sharing often occurs naturally when the relationship is already comfortable and mutually supportive. Other times it might help if we simply make a comment like "I hope we can be honest with each other. I know I'm going to try." Self-disclosure operates best in a situation where both people know the value of sharing. Each should be willing to share feelings about the other person's actions, being careful not to confuse honest communication with thoughtless or cruel remarks.

We all need some reinforcement in our communications. Have you ever come out of a movie really excited and talking about it, wanting to share your enthusiasm, only to have your companions say nothing at all? You don't know if they agree with you or don't agree with you or are simply thinking about something else! Sharing is a two-way process and without give *and* take, one person might stop giving anything at all. To be ready and willing to share means each partner views the relationship from nearly the same viewpoint, lessening the feeling of risk.

Take a chance. We must be willing to take chances in self-disclosure. There is no guarantee that we will not get hurt or that we will not be rejected. If a relationship is important to us, it is worth risking being honest so that both people can learn and grow. One of us may become angry or defensive at something the other says, but if we aren't willing to express our real feelings, the result is superficiality and facade building.

If it bothers you that a friend always dominates conversations by griping about her parents, you might say, "Let's make any discussion of parents off-limits for tonight." This takes some courage, but it allows your real feelings to show. And your friend may not even have been aware that she *was* dominating the conversation. It's worth taking the chance of telling her how you feel as long as you have her best interests at heart and care about preserving an honest relationship with her. The habit of honesty in all matters, no matter how small, makes it easier to be honest in more difficult, personal areas. For example, to tell a friend that he seems to be feeling sorry for himself takes a lot of courage. But taking such a chance often pays off and the other person values us even more because of our honesty.

Don't manipulate. The best self-disclosure occurs when neither person tries to change or manipulate the other person. Despite the intense emotions that may surface, conversation should never turn to who is at fault but, rather, focus upon making the relationship more satisfying and productive for both parties. For example, if your friend does seem to be indulging in self-pity, it would be more helpful to simply point out to him that this seems (to you) to be so than to tell him to stop it. Stopping or not stopping is his choice to make. Any

"'Not the real you'? Well, of course it's not the real you. The real you is bald."

change that occurs in a relationship should result from one of us acting freely in response to information provided or acquired. This nonmanipulative atmosphere is created when we truly care for and accept the other person.

Watch your timing. It's a good idea to express our feelings and reactions as closely as possible to the time we actually feel them. Both parties must realize what behavior caused the reaction. Parents usually find a reprimand means more to a small child if they say "No!" just as the child is about to do something wrong than if the incident goes undiscovered for an hour and the "No!" comes late. This is true for adult interactions, too. Even disturbing reactions should be discussed at once. Sometimes feelings are saved up and then dropped on the other person; this does not aid healthy self-disclosure. Of course there are times when immediate expression of our reaction may be inappropriate. For example, we usually do not want to share highly personal reactions with a friend if we are in a crowded elevator. It's almost always better to wait until no one else is around.

Clarify, clarify. If we're not sure we understand what another person means, we should try stating his or her comments in other words. If we offer this paraphrase of the other person's remarks before supplying our own response, there's less chance of our misunderstanding each other. (Ralph: "I'm sick of taking this bus with you every day." Mike: "I hear you saying you're sick of riding to work with me. Is that right?" Ralph: "No, I just meant I'm sick of this bus. I wish we had a car.") Check, also, to make sure the other person understands your comments in the way you mean them.

As we respond to another person, we can try to eliminate any kind of personal judgments ("Don't you *ever* listen?"), name-calling ("You really are a hypocrite"), accusations ("You love walking all over people, don't you?"), commands or orders ("Stop running his life"), or sarcasm ("You really want to get to the top," when another person just flunked an exam). Instead, talk about things the other person did—actual, accurate descriptions of the action that took place. We can try to describe our own feelings, letting the other person see them as temporary rather than absolute. Instead of saying "I hate sitting next to you in class," we might try "I can't stand it when you crack your knuckles." We should make certain, too, that our assumptions about the other person are correct in the first place.

Your success in college and, indeed, in life, will depend on *how* you feel about your self and your abilities. Your self-concept is a product of intrapersonal and interpersonal communication. What you think about your self affects your behavior toward others. And it is what other people say about you and to you that is the information you use in thinking about your self. Thus, intrapersonal communication and interpersonal communication are intricately entwined. We see this especially in the process of self-disclosure. Disclosing your self is the key to discovering your self, but to engage in productive, worthwhile self-disclosure requires interaction with other people. Self-disclosure is an important method of acquiring information. Other methods of acquiring information will be discussed in the next chapter.

OTHER READING

Raymond Gale, *Who Are You? The Psychology of Being Yourself* (Englewood Cliffs, N.J.: Prentice-Hall, Inc., 1974). A challenging book for those concerned with expanding their awareness of who they really are. Comprehensive, well-documented, easy-to-read humanistic approach to becoming an authentic person. A book for those who want a thorough, well-organized presentation.

Sidney M. Jourard, *The Transparent Self* (New York: Van Nostrand Reinhold Company, 1971). Jourard describes how people can gain health and full personal development once they have the courage to be themselves. One of the best books written on the self and self-disclosure. It is lively, straightforward, interesting, and relevant.

Sam Keen and Anne Valley Fox, *Telling Your Story: A Guide to Who You Are and Who You Can Be* (New York: New American Library, 1973). Includes many simple and useful exercises to foster self-discovery and discover personal potential. Basic but enjoyable material. A good place to start.

Eugene Kennedy, *If You Really Knew Me, Would You Still Like Me?* (Niles, Ill.: Argus Communications, 1975). Kennedy develops a procedure through which people get to know themselves, identify strengths and weaknesses, and build self-esteem by building on their strengths. A simplified approach to achieving self-confidence.

Jess Lair, *I Ain't Much Baby—But I'm All I've Got* (New York: Doubleday & Company, Inc., 1972). Building on his own experience, Lair develops a philosophy of living based on getting in touch with the self. He discusses acceptance, trust, search, and change among other topics. This is an engaging, personal book that successfully holds the reader's attention.

Maxwell Maltz, *Psycho-Cybernetics* (New York: Pocket Books, 1960). The thesis of this book is that the self-image is the key to human personality and human behavior: to change personality and behavior, one must change the self-image. Maltz encourages the reader to experience.

Maxwell Maltz, *The Search for Self-Respect* (New York: Bantam Books, 1973). This is an expansion of *Psycho-Cybernetics.* In this book, Maltz tells the reader how to set and achieve goals, how to reinforce positive qualities and overcome negative ones, and how to gain freedom. He includes specific exercises and numerous examples.

Mildred Newman and Bernard Berkowitz, *How to Be Your Own Best Friend* (New York: Ballantine Books, Ltd., 1971). Light, easy, popular approach that suggests people will find themselves richer than they ever imagined if they can learn to love and nurture themselves. Readers are encouraged to make their own possibilities available to themselves.

John O. Stevens, *Awareness: Exploring, Experimenting, Experiencing* (New York: Bantam Books, 1971). Awareness experiments designed to help readers adjust to themselves and to discover their own reality, their own existence, and their own humanness. Enlightening and stimulating ideas.

NOTES

[1] Donald Washburn, "Intrapersonal Communication in a Jungian Perspective," *Journal of Communication* 14 (September 1964): 131–135.

[2] Paul Watzlawick, Janet Helmick Beavin, and Don D. Jackson, *Pragmatics of Human Communication: A Study of Interactional Patterns, Pathologies, and Paradoxes*

(New York: W. W. Norton and Company, Inc., 1967), pp. 98–99.

[3] D. E. Hamachek, *Encounters with the Self* (New York: Holt, Rinehart and Winston, 1971).

[4] Charles T. Brown and Paul W. Keller, *Monologue to Dialogue: An Exploration of Interpersonal Communication* (Englewood Cliffs: Prentice-Hall, 1973), p. 99.

[5] John C. Condon, Jr., *Semantics and Communication* (New York: Macmillan Co., 1966), p. 60.

[6] The following writers maintain that the self-concept is a direct result of the reactions of "significant others": Henry Stack Sullivan, *The Interpersonal Theory of Psychiatry* (New York: W. W. Norton and Company, Inc., 1953); John J. Sherwood, "Self Identity and Referent Others," *Sociometry* 28 (1965): 66–81; and Carl Backman, Paul Secord, and Jerry Pierce, "Resistance to Change in the Self-Concept as a Function of Consensus Among Significant Others," in *Problems in Social Psychology,* Carl Backman and Paul Secord, eds. (New York: McGraw-Hill Book Company, 1969), pp. 462–467.

[7] Experiments by Robert Rosenthal have confirmed that labels are lived up to as self-fulfilling prophecies. See Robert Rosenthal, "Self-Fulfilling Prophecy," in *Readings in Psychology Today* (Del Mar, Calif.: CRM Books, 1967), pp. 466–471.

[8] Alvin Toffler, *Future Shock* (New York: Bantam Books, 1970), p. 17.

[9] Nathaniel Branden, *The Psychology of Self-Esteem* (Los Angeles: Nash, 1969), p. 103.

[10] From *Personal and Interpersonal Communication: Dialogue with the Self and with Others* by John J. Makay and Beverly A. Gaw, p. 28. Copyright © 1975 by Bell & Howell. Reprinted by permission of Charles E. Merrill Publishing Co.

[11] Ibid.

[12] Earl C. Kelly, *Perceiving, Behaving, Becoming: A New Focus on Education,* 1962 Yearbook (Washington, D.C.: Association for Supervision and Curriculum Development, 1962), pp. 9–20.

[13] From *Encounters with the Self* by Don E. Hamachek. Copyright © 1971 by Holt, Rinehart and Winston. Adapted by permission of Holt, Rinehart and Winston.

[14] Sidney M. Jourard, *The Transparent Self* (New York: Van Nostrand Reinhold Company, 1971), p. 6.

[15] Adapted from *Group Processes: An Introduction to Group Dynamics* by Joseph Luft, by permission of Mayfield Publishing Company (formerly National Press Books). Copyright © 1963, 1970 by Joseph Luft.

[16] Jourard, *The Transparent Self,* pp. 32–33.

[17] John Powell, *Why Am I Afraid to Tell You Who I Am?* (Chicago: Argus Communications, 1969), p. 27.

[18] Jourard, *The Transparent Self,* p. 193.

[19] David W. Johnson, *Reaching Out: Interpersonal Effectiveness and Self-Actualization.* © 1972, pp. 37–38. Reprinted by permission of Prentice-Hall, Englewood Cliffs, New Jersey.

Chapter 3

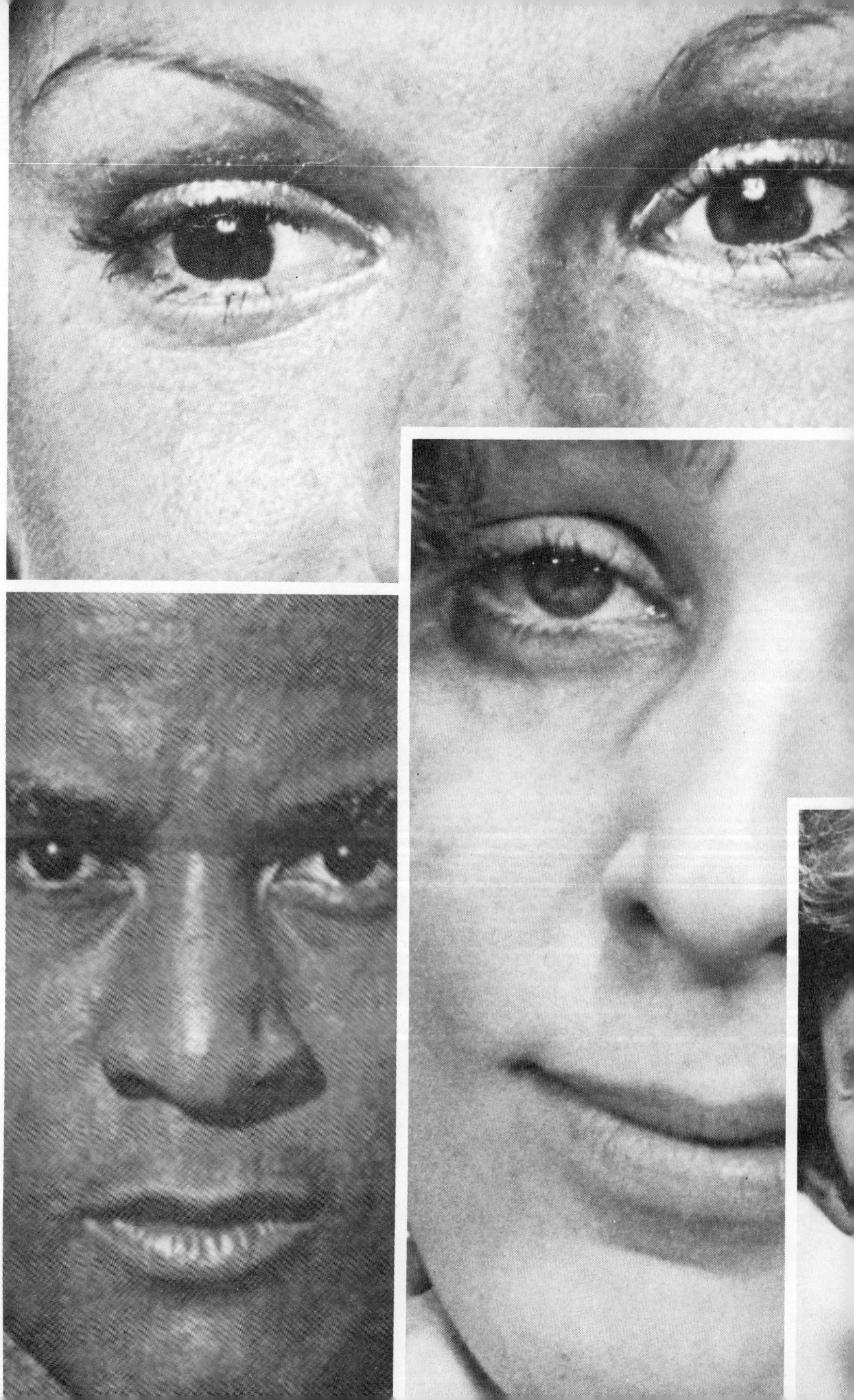

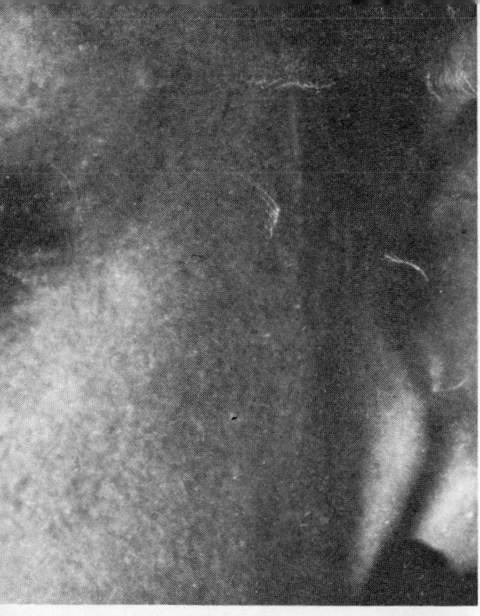

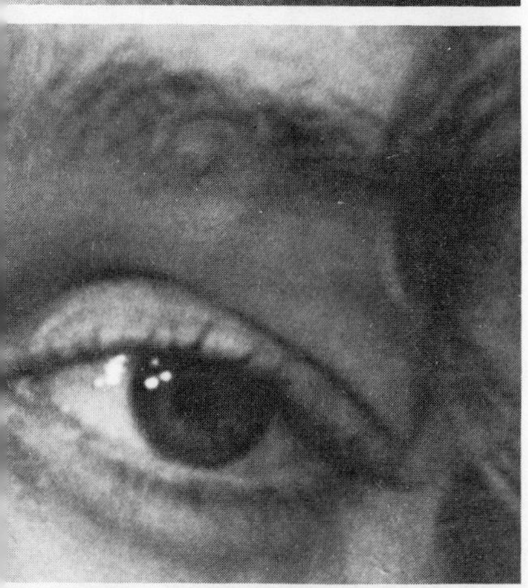

Creating Meaning: Perception

Have you ever thought about how people form impressions of other people? We do it all the time. If our perceptions of each other are correct, effective interaction can occur. But *how* do we form the impressions? Say a woman is at a party and she notices a man to whom she is at least superficially attracted. She is aware of his movements, his voice, his clothes. From her observations she draws conclusions about how this man thinks and feels. She may make inferences about his needs, goals, and attitudes. She will guide her action toward him and her prediction of future interactions by her perceptions. As she made judgments about him, he may also have been making judgments about her. If the observations and predictions being made are incorrect, communication between the two may get off to a bad start or may never start.

This chapter is about perception—how we create meaning. I'll talk about how we select, organize, and interpret information. I'll discuss some factors that affect what we perceive, such as our tendency to label things, physical and psychological distance, and the restrictive roles we sometimes play. Finally, I'll discuss how we can improve our skills in perception so that genuine, effective interaction is more likely to occur.

As you read this chapter, bear in mind what we just discussed about self-concept. We develop, create, and maintain our self-concept, in large part, by the information we process. At the same time, our self-concept helps to determine *what* we process. How we see our selves influences the kind of information to which we are likely to be receptive. The self-concept and the perceptive process are closely related.

WHAT YOU PERCEIVE IS WHAT YOU GET

You have just come out of a movie with a friend feeling that it was one of the best you have ever seen. You turn to share your exhilaration and quickly realize that your friend's reaction was completely different. You saw the same movie but your friend says that he was restless and bored, that the movie was too long and did not include enough action.

You have just completed your third week of the term and are walking away from class with a classmate who says, "Finally, I understand what is going on in there!" You look at her, surprised, and reply, "Not me. I have no idea what's happening. I'm more confused now than on the first day of class!"

These are normal, everyday occurrences, and they show that perceptions vary between people. What one person thinks is not necessarily the same as what another person thinks. Clearly, what each person perceives is a function of something unique and personal.

Perception is the process of gathering information and giving it meaning. We see a movie and we give meaning to it: "It's one of the best I've seen." We come away from class after the third week and we give meaning to it: "It finally makes sense." We gather information from what our senses see, hear, touch, taste, and smell, and we give meaning to that information. Although the information may come to us in a variety of forms, it is all processed, or *perceived,* in the mind.

Communication and perception are so closely related that we can't really talk about one without the other. To understand interpersonal communication we need some understanding of perception, for it is through perception that we give meaning to our world, become aware of our surroundings, and come to know our selves and others. Most of the time we engage in the process without paying attention to what we are doing. We rarely think of *how* it is occurring or how we could improve it. Perception is a complex activity, but by understanding the process we can improve our chances for more effective interpersonal communication. We will expand the perimeters of our own personal world.

THE PERCEPTION SIEVE: HOW YOU CREATE MEANING

One way to view the general process of perception is to visualize a large sieve with holes of different shapes and sizes. (See Figure 1.) Each hole represents a category we understand or with which we have some experience. The largest categories are those areas we're most familiar with or have given preference to—special needs and interests. The number of holes in the sieve changes constantly as we encounter new experiences, just as the size of the holes changes according to our changing values—what we consider to be most important.

Our perceptual categories develop as we grow. Our interests, experiences, and knowledge create them. Our culture, parents, religion, education, and peers are probably the strongest influences on how we perceive the world. As our interests change, we drop old categories and form new ones. As a child of six you may have wanted to be a firefighter; as an adolescent you may have wanted to be a veter-

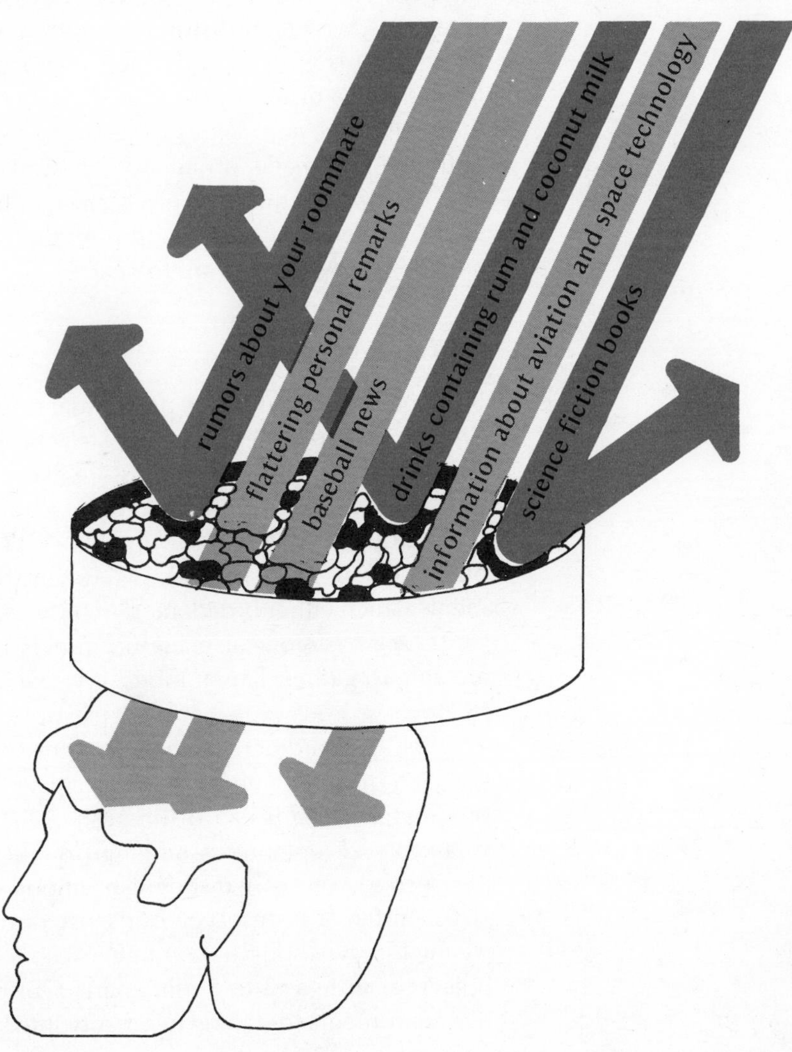

Figure 1. The perception sieve.

inarian; as a student you may want to be a lawyer; as an adult you may choose to become an electronics technician. Think of how many of your other interests have changed over the years. Sometimes we may expand a perceptual category to include a related piece of information; sometimes, when we can't relate the new information to the old, we create a whole new category.

Notice in the figure that certain holes are black. There are some areas where we make a determined effort *not* to gain any more information. We may no longer want to hear any more rumors about our roommate. We may no longer want to read science fiction. We might no longer want to taste any drinks containing rum and coconut milk. These are experiences we choose to close our selves off from.

Notice, too, that the sieve holes are irregular in size and shape. If information comes to us that does not exactly fit one of our present categories, we might distort that information so that it does fit. One function of our perceptual filtering process is to protect us from information we dislike or disagree with. We do not let that information through, or we adjust it as necessary. For example, if we heard some unflattering remarks about our roommate but one good comment like, "You must admit she has a sense of humor," we might hear only about the sense of humor and filter out all the other comments. We tend to hear what we want to hear.

No Two Are Alike

Every person has a unique perceptual filtering system, although there is some cultural overlap. If we are white, middle-class, urban eighteen-year-olds, our perceptions are likely to resemble those of other white, middle-class, urban eighteen-year-olds more than those of any other group in society. But ours still won't be exactly like those of any other person. Each individual's system depends on numerous elements which either broaden or limit the size of the categories.

Our physiological make-up affects how much information we are able to gather. The number of visual stimuli we take in is limited by how well our eyes work, for example. And although the number of stimuli we ordinarily sense is impressive, it is still little compared with the maximum amount of which we are capable. Most of us are physiologically able to distinguish 7,500,000 different colors.[1] Our ears can pick up sounds ranging from 20 to 20,000 vibration cycles per second. We can distinguish among 5,000 different smells and 10,000 different tastes. Even our sense of touch is more sensitive than we might have thought. Our fingers can feel the separations between objects as little as 3 to 8 mm apart.[2] Our bodies are extremely sensitive instruments for taking in sensory information.

IS CONSIDER THIS

CONSIDER THIS CONSIDER THIS CONSIDER THIS CONSIDER THIS CONSIDER THIS CONSIDER TH

Bows and flows of angel hair,
And ice cream castles in the air,
And feather canyons ev'rywhere,
I've looked at clouds that way.
But now they only block the sun,
They rain and snow on ev'ryone.
So many things I would have done,
But clouds got in my way.
I've looked at clouds from both sides now,
From up and down and still somehow
It's clouds' illusions I recall;
I really don't know clouds at all.
Moons and Junes and ferris wheels,
The dizzy dancing way you feel,
As ev'ry fairy tale comes real,
I've looked at love that way.
But now it's just another show.
You leave 'em laughing when you go.
And if you care, don't let them know,
Don't give yourself away.
I've looked at love from both sides now.
From give and take and still somehow
It's love's illusions I recall;
I really don't know love at all.
Tears and fears and feeling proud,
To say "I love you" right out loud,
Dreams and schemes and circus crowds,
I've looked at life that way.
But now old friends are acting strange,
They shake their heads, they say I've changed.
But something's lost but something's gained,
In living ev'ry day.
I've looked at life from both sides now,
From win and lose and still somehow
It's life's illusions I recall;
I really don't know life at all.

—Joni Mitchell, "Both Sides Now"

The kind of information we perceive is strongly affected by our expectations, attitudes, beliefs, interests, emotions, needs, language, experience, and knowledge. What is important to realize is (1) that what new information we pick up depends on the perceptual categories we have available, and (2) that each of our systems is unique. Although several of our categories may be similar to someone else's,

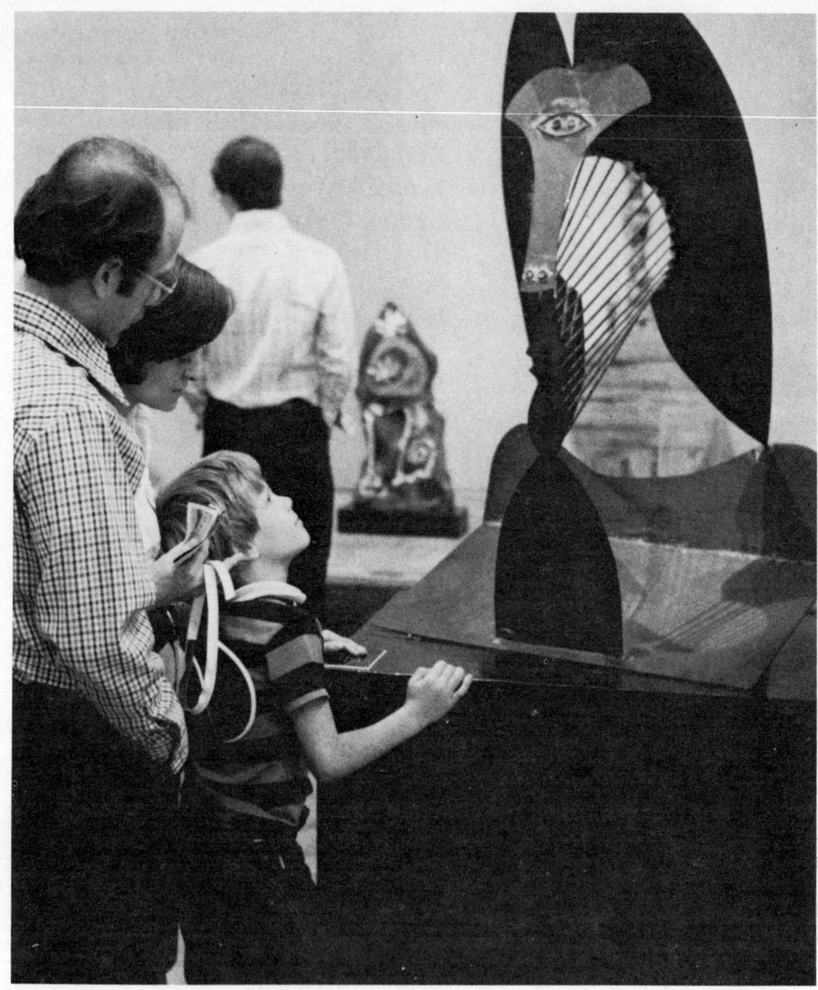

we must never assume that all of ours are like all of his or hers or even that *any* are identical.

Implications

What does this perception-sieve analogy imply? First, that perception is not a passive process. Our perceptions are our own and we have some control over them; we do not have total control because our culture, environment, and upbringing create categories we might not even be aware of. But because we have most of the control, we do not record everything our senses take in. Perception is selective. We block out some sights, sounds, and smells. For the most part, we actively apply our perceptual filter to incoming stimuli. Our perceptual system gives us a way of dealing with outside reality in terms of inside reality—our own thoughts, feelings, and attitudes.

Although our perceptions may be well established, they can and do change. The more open we are to new experiences, the more likely it is that our perceptions will change. If we aren't willing to try new things, we may not allow information through that does not correspond with established categories. We may adapt some of the categories to keep up with the times, but we are generally rather inflexible.

We can become less rigid if we realize we have a lot of room for new information and if we are willing to take in information unrelated to what we already know. We might develop conditional categories for information we consider risky, for information we're not sure what we're going to do with yet. We will have a hard time with information totally unrelated to our present knowledge and experience because we have no familiar way of processing it. But knowing that we do have room for new experiences, if we'll only let them in, is a good start toward flexibility. And sometimes just realizing how little we know is an education in itself.

Another implication of the perception-sieve analogy is that we do not accept stimuli just as they are presented. We hear a teacher talking; what is actually being said may *not* be what we hear. Just as we reject some information altogether, we also shape some to make it fit in with our existing perceptions. If we do not understand an assignment, we might make what the teacher says come as close as we can to an assignment we had in the past. We change what the teacher says to make it fit. We are actively involved in making things fit whenever we receive information from our senses. The more we adapt stimuli to fit in with what we already know, the less likely it is that our views will reflect what actually occurred.

CONSIDER THIS

In a class on the psychology of aging, students at the University of Michigan taped golf balls under their arms and tongue depressors to the joints of their knees and elbows. They wore ear plugs and placed tiny pellets of aluminum foil in their shoes.

"One of the things I learned from the experience," commented a coed, "was that outsiders seeing me probably thought that I didn't care that I was dropping things, that I had given up, when really it just hurt too much."

—*Christopher News Notes,* November 1976

Finally, whatever meaning we are left with is based on *how* we process the information rather than on what actually happened. When someone says she sat through a double header on a 90° day, what that experience means to us is a result of all our attitudes and feelings about baseball and hot weather. The experience could mean something quite different to her. (See Figure 2.)

Our interpretation of something is just that—an interpretation. Objects, events, and words don't *mean* in themselves. Their meanings are in us, in the way we evaluate them. When we talk with someone else, we make up what that person says just as when we see an object, we make up what that object looks like. Our filtering system determines how we view the world. The world exists for us as we perceive it. We cannot "tell it like it is," only "tell it like we perceive it." Understanding this is a big step toward more effective interpersonal communication: it will help us become more sensitive to reactions to experiences, both ours and others', as personal interpretations of

Figure 2. Our perceptions are based on our own attitudes and experiences.

events. It's useful to think in terms of how and why we respond to something rather than in terms of the "something" as an experience in itself. Experiences have meaning only as we respond to them.

THE PERCEIVER: DOING YOUR PART

To develop the concept of perception in greater detail, let's think in terms of *selecting, organizing,* and *interpreting* information. These steps occur simultaneously and often instantaneously. The perception process is complicated by the fact that each process depends upon and is affected by uncountable numbers of factors occurring within us and within our environment.

Selecting: Choosing the Pieces of the Puzzle

We perceive selectively. That is, we limit the quantity of stimuli to which we attach meaning. We are selective simply because we are exposed to too many stimuli each day to be able to deal with all of them. Notice, for example, how our selectivity works in reference to advertising messages:

> . . . the average American adult is assaulted by a minimum of 560 advertising messages each day. Of the 560 to which he is exposed, however, he only notices seventy-six. In effect, he blocks out 484 advertising messages a day to preserve his attention for other matters.[3]

We usually choose to focus on those messages we agree with or which are most meaningful to us. During an election campaign, we tend to recall acceptable comments made by the candidate we support and unacceptable comments made by the other person. And we tend to ascribe statements with which we agree to the person we support.[4]

We select what we will perceive on the basis of our experiences. The next time you go to a party, pay attention to what seems most important to the people there. One person may observe the "performance" of the host and hostess. Another person might be totally absorbed with what people wear. Only the handsome men might catch one person's eye, while somebody else is aware of all the vivacious women present. The pretzels and cheese dip might be the center of attention for a number of people.

Each person chooses what is most meaningful on the basis of his or her experiences. One person may have been brought up to believe that how a host behaves is an essential element at a party. Another person may have parents who attach great importance to clothes. We will usually select for perception stimuli related to matters we've already given some thought to or had memorable experiences with. The act of selecting stimuli is the first one in the perceptual process. Once we have it, what do we do with that information?

Organizing: Putting the Pieces Together

Because information comes to us in a random, unstructured manner, we must do something with it to make sense of it. We must determine relationships: how the new information relates to other information we are receiving and to information we already have. To get an idea of how we need to organize cues, stop reading and look at this page and the marks on it as if there were no structure to it. Look at the room you are sitting in right now as if it contained no structure, as if you didn't know that chairs were for sitting on, floors for walking on, lamps for providing light. How about the view from the nearest window? Can you look at nature as if there were no structure? Our world, for us to understand it, requires organization, and we organize our world by perceiving relationships.

If we see a swallow flying by, we know from experience that it is not the only bird in the world. We know there are many swallows like it and many other birds unlike it. We know that birds eat certain seeds for food, and that birds can be, in turn, eaten by larger forms of life. We know that birds are warmblooded as we are, and feathered as we are not. They walk as we do and fly as we do not. We organize our information about birds by noting relationships between this particular bird and all other birds of our experience. We organize information more or less consciously, in more or less detail, with all incoming stimuli. We can think of the organizational process as involving three steps—enlarging, simplifying, and closing—which occur simultaneously and instantaneously.

Enlarging. The information our senses receive is in small pieces. Think of words as tiny pieces of information. In any communication situation, we try to put the words we hear into a larger context so that we can understand them better. We call this enlarging, looking for a frame of reference for the message. We might start by observing the whole nonverbal picture—the facial expressions, gestures, and body movements of the person sending the message—placing the words into that picture.

Think of your self as you talk with George. You listen to his words for a moment, then shift to the sincerity in his face, then back to his words, then to the pleasantness of his voice, then back to his words, then, perhaps, to the hole in his sweater. As you focus on what seems to you the most important aspect of George's total communication, other aspects fade into the background. You enlarge on the one important aspect—which may be his sincerity—to try "to gain the big picture." You need all the pieces to the puzzle of George's message, of course, but it helps to have an idea what the completed puzzle is supposed to look like, so that you can better anticipate the meaning and significance of each piece. You want to understand the expressions and feelings George reveals in his nonverbal cues to better understand the words you hear.

Simplifying. Just as we search for a relationship between pieces of information and a larger framework into which we can place those pieces, we also look for ways to simplify complex or confusing stimuli. Complex stimuli are anything that we have difficulty understanding. We simplify them by finding patterns, an order that will help us make sense of the message.

For example, if we drove into a gas station to get directions, we might hear the attendant say something like, "You go up here to your first stoplight and turn left on Broadview. At your next light turn right. Then just after you pass Wiley High School, turn right, and the street you are looking for will be your next left." As a simplifying response we might reply, "So it's a left, two rights, and a left." We find order in the stimuli that will help us remember the essential information.

We do the same thing when we hear a teacher explaining an assignment or when we are taking notes in a lecture. We do not need, and we don't have time to record, all the teacher says. We simplify the message so that we have the essentials when it comes time to complete the assignment or to study our notes for a test.

Closing. Because we get information in scraps, we must also fill in gaps. We tend to think in unified wholes. That is, we tend to see things as complete rather than separate. For example, in Figure 3 we tend to see a triangle, a square, and a rectangle rather than a series of disjointed, unorganized lines.

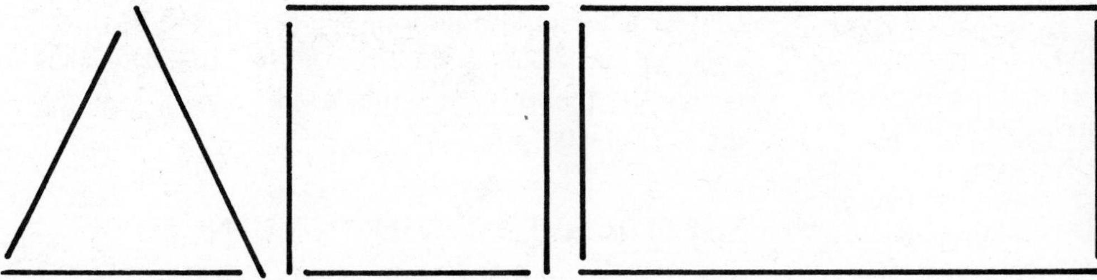

Figure 3. We tend to think in unified wholes.

We probably engage in closing (or closure) more often than we realize. For example, how often have you completed a sentence for the person you were talking to? The more we get to know people, the better we know how they think, and the more often we will find we think ahead and close their thoughts. Very close friends can say a great deal to each other with few words—without knowing it, they may depend on closure for their messages to get through. Another example of closing is when we overhear others talking but are able to pick up only fragments of their conversation. From the fragments we fill in the rest of the conversation. Have you ever sat in a bus station or airport and made up stories about the people you observed around you? From a minimum of cues we can put together a fairly complete story, making sense of the available information by closure.

Interpreting: Giving the Puzzle Meaning

Not only do we select and organize information, we also interpret it. That is, we assign some meaning to information, making evaluations and drawing conclusions about it to better predict future events and thereby minimize surprise.[5] Most of the interpreting we do takes either of two forms: *identification* or *evaluation.* Again, these processes occur rapidly and often simultaneously.

Stop reading for a minute and just listen. Can you label every sound you hear? Most of the sounds that go on around us are common ones and easily identifiable. Sometimes, however, there is a strange one—a scream, a bang, or an unrecognizable sound. After we identify the source of the noise, we evaluate it. Was it startling? Disruptive? Harmful? In identifying, but more significantly, in evaluating information, we bring to bear all of our experiences and knowledge. The interpretation of information is a subjective judgment; it is a product of our own creation and it may or may not be valid.

We should realize that in interpreting what we sense, we seldom stop with apparent, observable cues. We almost always infer other characteristics. Such things as a person's attitudes, values, beliefs, motives, personality traits, interests, or background are not directly observable. Identification can be fairly reliable—interpretation is usually open to some question. We need to remember that if appearances are deceiving and untrustworthy, then our own inferences are even more tenuous. They may be little more than guesses based on uncertain facts.

TRY THIS

In each of the following examples, make up a brief story about what happened, what is happening, and what is about to happen based on the clues provided:

A. An old woman rushes out from a store clutching packages to her chest, her face paled by terror . . .

B. A teen-ager looks both ways down the street and then quickly darts into a seemingly vacant alley . . .

C. As the teacher begins to collect the papers, one of your classmates gets up and runs out of the room crying . . .

The process you are engaging in as you complete the episodes above is closure, **and it is a process you engage in often. When messages you receive are incomplete, inaccurate, or incomprehensible, often you treat them in such a way that for you they become complete, accurate, and comprehensible.**

THE PERCEIVED: OTHER INFLUENCES

Although the perceiver has been the main focus of this chapter so far, there are other factors that directly influence our perceptions. In a sense, these factors—stereotyping, proximity, and role[6]—are restricting forces. To understand them will help us to detect, analyze, and cope with them as we engage in interpersonal communication.

Stereotyping: Labels Are Restricting

We can usually tell fairly quickly just by looking at another person whether or not we would like to strike up a relationship. How? The appearance of a person often provides us with just enough cues to stereotype him or her. Stereotyping is the process of assigning fixed labels or categories to things and people we encounter, or, the reverse of this, placing things and people we encounter into fixed categories we have already established. When we stereotype a person, we assume things to be true about him or her because that person reminds us of someone else about whom those things may really have been true. We assume that the pattern that holds for one person holds for another, even though these people may actually have little in common. Stereotyping simplifies our task of making judgments about things and people. It is a commonly used device; all human beings employ it to deal with the tremendous flow of events around them.[7]

It does, however, tend to distort our perceptions. Instead of recognizing what is unique in each person, stereotyping places people into categories, much as mail is pigeonholed according to route. She is not wearing a bra, thus she is "liberated" (a category); he has a full beard and glasses, thus he is an "intellectual" (a category); he plays football, thus he is a "jock" (a category). We do this with individuals, events, ideas—anything. To each category we attach an extensive set of corresponding labels, or stereotypes.

Take the man who plays football, for example. If we assign him the label of "jock," we may jump to the conclusion that he is insensitive, not very bright, and a male chauvinist. The man may or may not be any of these things. The point is, we can't know anything about him for certain simply by knowing he plays football. Many of our stereotypes are so conditioned into us that it is hard to see that we have them, much less get rid of them.

Besides the fact that stereotyping doesn't take into account the unique qualities of individuals, it also implies that all the people, events, ideas, or things we pigeonhole are static, when in reality they are ever changing. Nobody is witty or bright all the time. Everyone has his or her moments. And yet we tend to attribute static qualities and respond to others as if those qualities were appropriate *all the time*. Think carefully about the last time you made comments like, "Sam is really the life of *any* party," or "Carolyn *always* looks so nice." We use statements like these because they are the best predictors we have about how a person "should" act, if everything we know is right.[8]

If you were a job interviewer and had to decide between two applicants who were equally qualified for a particular job, would you spend hours agonizing over the decision if you could make it quickly on the basis of a stereotype, whether appropriate or not? If one applicant had long, straight hair, for example, and the other had short, styled hair? Or if one spoke with an accent and the other spoke as you do? If one applicant were a man and the other a woman? One stereotype, perhaps, would be enough to tip the scales.

Everyone stereotypes, to a degree that varies with the individual and with the groups to which the individual belongs. Take college freshmen as an example of a group: A study was done in which college freshmen, male and female, looked at photographs of men with different amounts of facial hair. The students were to rate the men in the photos on masculinity. The results? The more hair a man had on his face, the more likely the students were to see him as "masculine, mature, goodlooking, dominant, self-confident, courageous, liberal, nonconforming, industrious, and older."[9] The students didn't know anything about these men except what they looked like; they formed their judgments on the basis of a stereotype.

Physical attractiveness is another category by which we stereotype people and, unfortunately, we tend to give it disproportionate emphasis as we communicate with them. An attractive appearance creates a "halo effect": this appeal influences all other impressions a person makes on us. For example, research has shown that the defendant was given a harsher sentence in a criminal trial if either the victim was attractive or if the defendant was unattractive.[10] It has been shown, too, that an attractive female has a better chance of changing the attitudes of males than an unattractive one.[11] This is probably not news to anyone. And studies have proven that attractive people, regardless of their sex, will be perceived as having higher credibility.[12] How fair is this? Can you think of any situations where such stereotyping is justified?

Proximity: Distance Discovers/Distance Distorts

Proximity is simply nearness to something in place, time, or relationship. It can strongly affect the way we perceive. There are two types of proximity: physical and psychological.

An example of how physical proximity can influence perception is the experience of thinking one of our lecturers was quite young and not realizing the mistake until we went down to ask a question. Then the hair we thought was blond might turn out to be gray and the skin that looked unblemished might be crossed by age lines blurred by the distance at which we sat. Middle twenties might turn out to be late forties. Have you ever been in this situation, making judgments that later proved to be inaccurate because you were either too close to or too far from the object to perceive accurately?

Psychological proximity may have several effects on us. One is that the extent to which we are attitudinally similar to someone else may determine how well we understand him or her. You must know some people you feel you always have to be explaining your self to. You don't have psychological proximity with them—you don't understand each other. Then there are people with whom you just seem to get along; the two of you "click." With such people you rarely have

CONSIDER THIS "Dr. John Coleman has done a Horatio Alger in reverse. He went from college president to ditchdigger, restaurant salad-and-sandwich man and garbage collector.

But now he is back as head of Haverford College in Haverford, Pa., feeling enriched by having taken time off from the academic world to enter the world of the manual laborer. . . .

After a week spent toughening up at a friend's dairy farm in his native Ontario, Coleman got a job in Atlanta digging sewer ditches for $2.75 an hour and lived on his earnings.

"I knew which end of the shovel to use but I was not skilled and never would have been if I'd stayed there two years. Complicated machinery baffles me but I'm envious of those who can operate it," said Coleman. . . .

The next stop was Boston where Coleman, who has written seven books on labor and economics, found it difficult to find a job and had to settle for one as a dishwasher. An hour later the proprietor handed him $2 and said, "Sorry, you won't do."

"I was absolutely devastated when I lost that job," he recalled. "My salary check from Haverford was going to the bank each month, but I have never felt more worthless as a person. Because I deal in the world of words, always asking why, it was more frustrating because the boss didn't see the necessity of telling me why. I wouldn't do, and that was it.""

—(AP) *Chicago Daily News*, May 15, 1974

to say, "I *meant* that! I was serious" or "I was only kidding." They know without your telling them. Don't you feel you *understand* this other person? With this person you have achieved psychological proximity.

The second effect is that when we are attitudinally similar to someone, we give this person a more positive evaluation than if we are not. You probably like teachers you perceive as having tastes similar to yours—teachers you see buying your favorite record or wearing a parka very like yours. Research has been done that showed when teachers are attitudinally similar to the students, they are rated higher by them. Attitudinally dissimilar teachers are rated lower. The instructors in this test were rated on openmindedness, their ability to be stimulating and interesting, personal attractiveness, and desirability as instructors.[13]

A third effect of psychological proximity involves our readiness to respond in a specific way. For example, if we view an automobile accident along with some other people, although physical proximity is the same for all of us, viewpoints may differ. A police officer might look at the accident from the point of view of what driving violations were incurred. A doctor might be most concerned about the injuries sustained by the people involved. A highway worker might notice broken curbs or uprooted sewers. Each person would bring his or her own set of experiences or psychological set to the accident. Each would be psychologically near to a different aspect of the accident. Too, the testimony of each would be necessary to learn all important details of the accident. What we bring to an event such as this often influences our perceptions of it more than the actual facts of the event.

Role: A Limiting Point of View

The roles we play affect our perceptions strongly. Our roles are simply positions we assume in relation to someone or something else. In relation to your parents, your role is that of son or daughter. In a classroom, your role is that of student. A role is the stance we take or are assigned in a particular situation; the role we play affects our expectations, needs, attitudes, and beliefs about that situation; it restricts how we perceive that situation. There are job roles, family roles, sex roles, friendship roles, and many others.

Your father, for example, may have experienced some parental-role restrictions. He may have thought that he maintained open and harmonious relations with his children, welcoming their ideas on any problem that occurred. For him, in the position of father, it may really have seemed like that. It is possible, however, that his children, because of their role or position, did not see it the same way. Our own perceptions may be limited by our roles.

Each of us plays roles defined by our culture, by our upbringing,

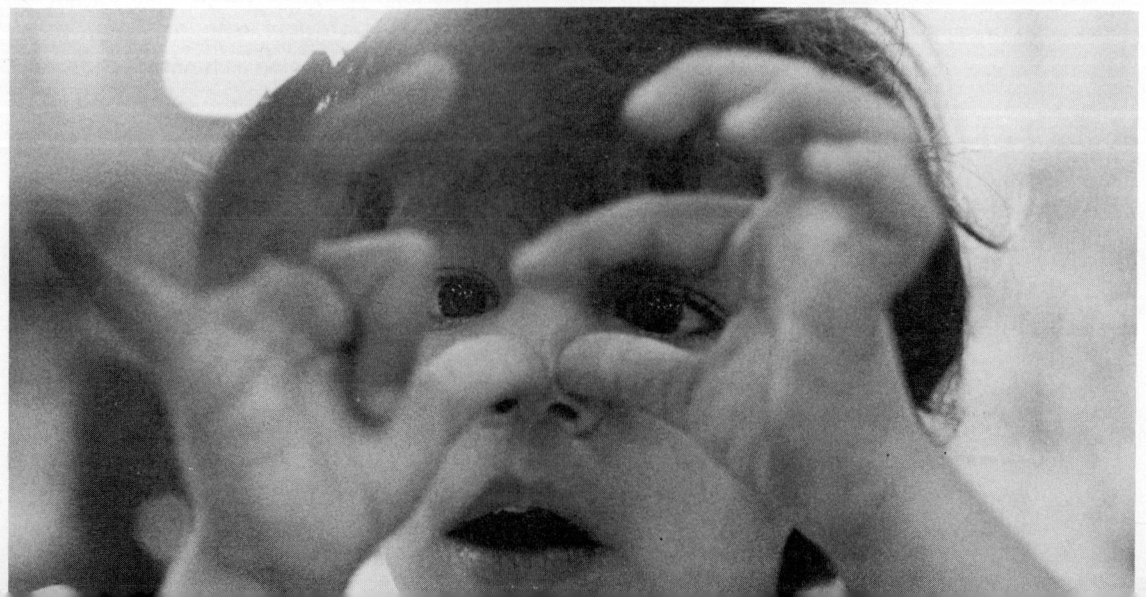

and by how we personally see those roles. We are all familiar with the sex roles that have come to be traditional in our society. Think of how our perceptions are affected by the degree to which we accept these traditional roles. A strong-minded man may be perceived as assertive and a natural leader while an equally strong-minded woman is perceived as pushy and castrating. An unpleasant woman may be called a bitch; an unpleasant man is a son of a bitch (he can't help it?). How often do we see male children dressed in pink? Our acceptance of traditional sex roles has a direct effect on our perception of the color pink as appropriate or inappropriate in certain situations. A woman wearing an apron at the kitchen sink is a natural and acceptable sight; we have been conditioned to squirm or laugh at a man in that same apron at that same sink. Our perceptions are affected.

We have learned to expect to hear a woman's voice in certain situations, a man's in others. Think of telephone operators, airplane pilots, and doctors' receptionists. Listen hard to television commercials. In how many of them is the "voice-over" provided by a man, even in advertising of products intended for use by women? Advertisers are banking on the fact that potential consumers will listen to a persuasive man's voice more closely than to a woman's. They know society has trained us to perceive men's voices as being more reliable and authoritative. How many other instances can you think of where acceptance of traditional sex roles affects perception in a directly observable way?

TRY THIS

What is the first image that comes into your mind when you think of the following people?

A. A gas-station mechanic.

B. Someone who walks with a cane and lives in a rest home.

C. A rock-musician.

D. A hairdresser.

E. Someone who sells vacuum cleaners door-to-door.

F. Someone who has five children and is on welfare.

G. A rapist.

H. A business executive for a large corporation.

I. A nurse.

J. Someone who is in the army.

What sex did you think of for each of these people? What age? What political persuasion? What ethnic background? What stereotypes are you aware of holding? What do your stereotypes simplify for you? What do they complicate?

Certain roles carry higher prestige or credibility than others. What we see as another person's role will affect our perceptions of that person in certain situations. The role of professor, for example, might carry higher credibility and prestige in a faculty meeting on curriculum than the role of student. On the other hand, any student would probably be better able to discuss the availability of drugs on campus than a professor. In this case, the role of student is perceived as the more reliable source of information. If we see a person in a certain position fulfilling the duties and responsibilities of that job and serving our own best interests, then we are likely to overlook what we see as that person's shortcomings. Our perceptions are affected by the fact that the responsibilities of the position are being satisfied. Anything else matters less to us.

IMPROVING SKILLS IN PERCEPTION

Because of the broad range of factors affecting our perception and because of the number of ways these factors interact, there are no universal rules that will guarantee improved, accurate perception. But there are several courses of action that might help. Some seem obvious and easy to put into practice; others may require more time to develop and use. All will contribute to the improvement of our perceptual skills. Since our perception influences and directs our reactions to others, improvement becomes crucial to improving our interpersonal communication.

Don't jump to conclusions. One error we may tend to make that affects the accuracy of our perceptions is generalizing or drawing conclusions based on weak evidence. Just because we see something happen once, we automatically tend to assume it happens that way regularly.

We may see a bus stopping at a new location and assume a new route was established to include that location. We may see a person go into a bar, and assume the person drinks heavily. Our perception will improve if we temper our thoughts and comments with conditional clauses like, "*I wonder if* the bus route has been changed to include . . ." or "*Maybe* he drinks heavily, because I saw him. . . ." Even better, stick strictly to the simplest facts: "I saw the bus stop at a new location today" or "I saw Ralph going into a bar downtown." If we are not reporting first-hand information, we should identify our source to indicate the potential believability of the observation. That is, if we have heard information from someone else or read it someplace, we should label what we report: "*Bill says* he saw Jane and Dave together downtown" or "*I read in the paper* that. . . ." This allows those who hear our information to gauge its believability without having our judgment interfere with it.

But often the problem is not in the labeling. Sometimes we believe our own judgments despite weak evidence. We convince our selves by phrasing the idea in a certain way, stating it to someone else, or repeating it. If we can learn to restrain our selves—suspend judgment—until we receive more evidence, we will improve the accuracy of our perceptions.

Maintaining a balance between openness and skepticism is difficult in our society. Forced to produce, make decisions, act, and respond quickly, it is hard to stand back and judge the worth of the information we hear daily. The point is not to doubt the validity of everything we hear; the point is to place new evidence into the context of other evidence we already have before drawing conclusions. If no other evidence exists, it is wiser to continue to have doubt than to make inferences. If a conclusion is necessary, the cautious skeptic will label the conclusion as a conditional one. We can never anticipate the decisions other people may make based on what we have

Drawing by Koren; © 1971 The New Yorker Magazine, Inc.

told them—all we can do is be responsible in reporting what we actually do know.

Give it time. Physical togetherness helps to increase the accuracy of our perceptions. We have all had the experience of being impressed by a person from a distance only to change our impression radically upon closer contact. The same phenomenon occurs after knowing people better or working with them.[14] Accurate perceptions of another person do not occur instantaneously like the picture on a solid-state television set. They require both time and spatial closeness. Give your self time to be with someone. Even so, long-term, face-to-face, physical togetherness provides only the opportunity to understand how another person interprets the world; it does not guarantee that we will understand it.

Make your self available. It's important to be available to other people, both physically and psychologically.[15] This means trying to get on another's "wave length" or "into another person's head." An old Sioux prayer stated it this way: "O Great Spirit! Let me not judge another man without first walking a mile in his moccasins." So often in this hurry-up, get-things-done society, we do not spend much time really making our selves available to others. Physical togetherness does not necessarily mean psychological availability.

Psychological availability requires an active commitment to openness on our part. We have to make time for other people—time not only to share but also to be aware. To improve the accuracy of our perceptions, we must be willing to go beyond cliché-level exchanges that require little time and demand no commitment from us.

Make a commitment. Any self-improvement requires active commitment, but it is especially important if we are truly seeking to in-

DER THIS CONSIDER THIS

CONSIDER THIS CONSIDER THIS CONSIDER THIS CONSIDER THIS CONSI

To-day we have naming of parts. Yesterday,
We had daily cleaning. And to-morrow morning,
We shall have what to do after firing. But to-day,
To-day we have naming of parts. Japonica
Glistens like coral in all of the neighboring gardens,
And to-day we have naming of parts.

This is the lower sling swivel. And this
Is the upper sling swivel, whose use you will see,
When you are given your slings. And this is the piling swivel,
Which in your case you have not got. The branches
Hold in the gardens their silent, eloquent gestures,
Which in our case we have not got.

This is the safety-catch, which is always released
With an easy flick of the thumb. And please do not let me
See anyone using his finger. You can do it quite easy
If you have any strength in your thumb. The blossoms
Are fragile and motionless, never letting anyone see
Any of them using their finger.

And this you can see is the bolt. The purpose of this
Is to open the breech, as you see. We can slide it
Rapidly backwards and forwards: we call this
Easing the spring. And rapidly backwards and forwards
The early bees are assaulting and fumbling the flowers:
They call it easing the Spring.

They call it easing the Spring: it is perfectly easy
If you have any strength in your thumb: like the bolt,
And the breech, and the cocking-piece, and the point of balance,
Which in our case we have not got; and the almond-blossom
Silent in all of the gardens and the bees going backwards and forwards,
For to-day we have naming of parts.

—Henry Reed, "Naming of Parts"

crease our perceptivity. If we want our perceptions to be accurate, we must make a conscious effort to search out as much information as possible on any given topic or question before we make a judgment or form an opinion. The more information we have, the greater the likelihood of accurate perceptions.[16] We should make a real effort to search out possibilities, asking "What if . . . ?" and "What about . . . ?" and "What else . . . ?" at every turn. We cannot hope to have reliable perceptions if we are indifferent and passive about acquiring information.

Establish the proper climate. Our perceptivity will improve if we establish a climate conducive to communication. This means maintaining an atmosphere in which self-disclosure is likely to occur. Where open communication can be sustained, the likelihood of accurate perception will increase simply because people will trust each other enough to exchange honest messages. The more we know about the needs and feelings of other people, the more likely our actions toward them and our prediction of future interactions will be accurate. We must establish an environment in which truth is free to surface, so that our perceptions may be based on that truth. Face-to-face encounters where both visual and vocal ingredients are part of the interaction help us gain the information we need.

Part of creating a proper climate also means recognizing our own uniquenesses; that is, recognizing that our view of the world is entirely our own. We need to acknowledge that the world does not revolve around us. If we see that everyone does not share our perceptions of the world, we will have at least acknowledged the need for a proper climate.

Be willing to adjust. Perception involves a perceiver, something perceived, and a context within which the process occurs. These components are so interwoven that they cannot be analyzed apart from each other. Changes in any one affect all others. The most we can do is to recognize that as these components vary, so must our perceptions. The flawless friend of two weeks ago may now be the most disliked and despised creature on earth. The arrogant and unfair teacher of yesterday may be the humble and helpful teacher of today. To be unwilling to change our perceptions, and righteous in our inflexibility, can only cause us perceptual problems. What we need is perceptual sensitivity: full recognition that our perceptions will change as our interests and experiences change. We cannot expect today's perceptions to be accurate if we are basing them on yesterday's attitudes.

Our own interpersonal communications will be a great deal more effective when we realize the role that perception plays. Each of us, in our own unique way, is responsible for our method of arriving at the meaning of things through selecting, organizing, and interpreting the information we receive. No one gives us meaning, and no one can control the meanings we determine for our selves. It is we who create meaning out of our own experiences.

The more accurate our perceptions, the more likely we are to communicate effectively with others. By acquiring more information, we increase the number of ways we can respond to other people and we strengthen our ability to grow in a positive direction. And since our first step in communicating with others involves forming some impression of them, how well we form those impressions becomes crucial to interpersonal success. One practical channel through which we acquire new information and broaden our perceptions is that of listening and feedback. These subjects are treated in the next chapter.

OTHER READING

Kenneth E. Boulding, *The Image: Knowledge in Life and Society* (Ann Arbor, Mich.: The University of Michigan Press, 1956). People's behavior depends on the image—the sum of what they think and what they know. The way that image grows tends to limit the direction of future growth. Boulding emphasizes communication and feedback as sources for orderly and organized growth.

Arthur Gordon, *A Touch of Wonder* (Old Tappan, N.J.: Pillar Books, 1974). The author challenges readers to look at things more closely—even the simple things. There is more to commonplace happenings than what normally meets the casual eye.

Edward T. Hall, *Beyond Culture* (Garden City, N.Y.: Anchor Books, 1977). Part of perception concerns increasing knowledge. This book may open up new dimensions of understanding and provide new capacities for perception. Hall challenges readers to rethink their values.

R. D. Laing, H. Phillipson, and A. R. Lee, *Interpersonal Perception: A Theory and a Method of Research* (New York: Harper & Row, Publishers, 1966). What kind of perceptions occur when two people meet? The authors present concepts which indicate both the interaction and interexperience of two people. They describe each person's own experiences and behavior within the context of the two-party relationship.

John Powell, S.J., *Fully Human, Fully Alive: A New Life Through a New Vision* (Niles, Ill.: Argus Communications, 1976). Powell argues that change in the quality of people's lives must result from a change in their vision of reality. Emotions, according to Powell, grow out of how people see themselves and out of their perceptions. He challenges readers to examine their perceptions. The book is written in a warm, personal style.

NOTES

[1] Frank A. Geldard, *The Human Senses* (New York: John Wiley & Sons, Inc., 1953), p. 53.

[2] Donald R. Gordon, *The New Literacy* (Toronto: University of Toronto Press, 1971), pp. 25–47.

[3] From *Future Shock* by Alvin Toffler. (New York: Random House, Inc., 1970).

[4] Hans Sebald, "Limitations of Communication: Mechanisms of Image Maintenance in Form of Selective Perception, Selective Memory and Selective Distortion," *Journal of Communication* 12 (1962), 142–149.

[5] J. S. Bruner, "Social Psychology and Perception," in *Readings in Social Psychology,* E. Maccoby, T. M. Newcomb, and E. L. Hartley, eds., (New York: Holt, Rinehart and Winston, 1958), pp. 85–94.

[6] Richard C. Huseman, James M. Lahiff, and John D. Hatfield, *Interpersonal Communication in Organizations: A Perceptual Approach* (Boston: Holbrook Press, Inc., 1976), pp. 28–32.

[7] George J. McCall and J. L. Simmons, "Identities and Interaction: An Examination of Human Association in Everyday Life," in *Speech Communication: A Reader,* Richard L. Weaver, II, ed. (Columbus, Ohio: Collegiate Publishing, Inc., 1975), p. 75.

[8] Ibid., p. 76.

[9] Robert J. Pellegrini, "Impressions of the Male Personality as a Function of Beardedness," *Psychology* 10 (February 1973), 29–33.

[10] D. Lancy and E. Aronson, "The Influence of the Character of the Criminal and His Victim on the Decisions of Simulated Jurors," *Journal of Experimental Social Psychology* 5 (1969), 141–152.

[11] J. Mills and E. Aronson, "Opinion Change as a Function of the Communicator's Attractiveness and Desire to Influence," *Journal of Personality and Social Psychology* 1 (1965), 73–77.

[12] R. N. Widgery and B. Webster, "The Effects of Physical Attractiveness upon Perceived Initial Credibility," *Michigan Speech Journal* 4 (1969), 9–15.

[13] Katherine C. Good and Lawrence R. Good, "Attitude Similarity and Attraction to an Instructor," *Psychological Reports* 33 (August 1973), 335–337.

[14] J. W. Shepherd discusses how people's conceptions of each other change as a result of working together. See J. W. Shepherd, "The Effects of Valuations in Evaluations of Traits on the Relation Between Stimulus Affect and Cognitive Complexity," *Journal of Social Psychology* 88 (December 1972), 233–239.

[15] For more on psychological availability, see John Stewart and Gary D'Angelo, *Together: Communicating Interpersonally* (Reading, Mass.: Addison-Wesley Publishing Company, 1975), pp. 99–103.

[16] See Frederick W. Obitz and L. Jerome Oziel, "Varied Information Levels and Accuracy of Person Perception," *Psychological Reports* 31 (October 1972), 571–576.

Chapter 4

Responding to Others: Listening and Feedback

You have just spent five minutes explaining to a friend the time and place of a birthday party and as you turn to go he asks you, "Oh, yes, where are we meeting and what time did you say?" You know he hasn't listened. And you know how it feels when someone hasn't listened to you.

Do I listen well? Chances are this is a question we never ask our selves. After all, listening is something we have done all our lives with no special training. We take it for granted. Everything I've said in this book about successful interpersonal communication describes it as a circular give-and-take in which we really tune in to the other person. An essential part of that give-and-take is listening. Not just putting on our "listening" expression and nodding and grunting agreement now and then while mentally planning our evening. But listening with our full and active attention—listening empathically. By this we mean trying to listen as though we are in the other person's place. We can never take this kind of listening for granted. It takes skill and constant practice, but the reward is greatly improved communication.

This chapter is about the importance of listening empathically and giving appropriate feedback. I'll talk about some of the bad listening habits we all have and ways we can improve our listening and feedback skills.

THE IMPORTANCE OF LISTENING

When we think of our selves in communication situations, we usually think more about getting our ideas to someone else than about receiving ideas from them. This is normal. We've come to think the word "communication" means a process that flows out from us rather than one in which we are the receiver. But communicating orally involves far more than just talking to a person. It involves sharing ideas, trying to exchange meaning with each other as perfectly as possible. In most interpersonal situations, we spend just as much time listening and responding to the other person as we do talking. Considering all the communication activities of a normal day—talking, listening, reading, writing—we probably spend more time in listening, on the average, than in any of the others.[1]

As I said, most of us do not think much about listening. We take it for granted until someone does not listen to us. We *do* get a great deal of experience in it. Think of all the things and people we listen to in an ordinary day: a clock radio to wake up, roommates or friends at meals, teachers and other students in classes, piped-in music in stores, radios and tape players in cars, television and stereo at home.

Because we spend so much of every day in listening we may think it takes no great effort. Not true. Listening is not the same as hearing. Hearing is done with the ears and, unless our hearing is impaired, goes on virtually all the time. We have no mechanism in our bodies that lets us shut our ears as we shut our eyes. Listening is done with the mind as well as the ears. If we want to improve our listening

ER THIS CONSIDER THIS

CONSIDER THIS CONSIDER THIS CONSID

I have something to tell you.

I'm listening.

I'm dying.

I'm sorry to hear.

I'm growing old.

It's terrible.

It is, I thought you should know.

Of course and I'm sorry. Keep in touch.

I will and you too.

And let me know what's new.

Certainly, though it can't be much.

And stay well.

And you too.

And go slow.

And you too.

—David Ignatow, "Two Friends"

we need to monitor our own listening habits and then actively work to improve. The kind of practice we get is important if we really want to get rid of bad habits.

The kind of listening we're concentrating on here is the most significant kind in interpersonal communication. We cannot and need not listen empathically to every gas station attendant or bank teller we exchange a few words with during the course of a day. Listening empathically—indeed, the kind of interpersonal communication skills this book is about—is appropriate in certain situations. There is also a place for the simple exchange of information and for small talk. But empathic listening is quite different.

Empathic listening involves integrating physical, emotional, and intellectual inputs in a search for meaning and understanding. It is an active, not a passive process. We cannot just make sure that our ears are alert or open and let the rest come naturally. Because empathic listening involves both emotional and intellectual inputs, it does not just happen. We have to make it happen and it's not easy. It takes energy and commitment. We have a lot going against us—there are many influences that practically conspire to make us poor listeners. Some of them we can control, some we cannot.

WHAT INFLUENCES YOUR LISTENING?

Being aware of the factors that affect listening will help us improve our own listening skills but will also help us become more considerate of people who listen to us. Knowing what factors operate increases our understanding of the whole communication process and can help explain why breakdowns and confusion sometimes result. Here are some of the things that influence how well we listen:

Physiological Differences Affect What You Hear

Listening is part of the perceiving process. As a means of perception its effectiveness is limited by the mechanics of the physical process of hearing—to be able to select from aural stimuli we must first be able to hear them. If we are hard of hearing our listening will be affected simply because we won't have as many stimuli to choose from, organize, and interpret as someone who hears well.

You Process Words Faster Than They Can Be Spoken

The average person speaks at a rate of 100 to 200 words per minute. But as listeners, we can easily process 400 words per minute.[2] Though our minds can absorb words very rapidly, in our ordinary listening we are rarely challenged to process them as efficiently as we can. Even the most skilled speaker pauses and stumbles occasionally; even the most polished speech contains words that are not essential to the actual message. These hesitations and extraneous elements add up to many precious seconds of wasted time *within* a message. What do we, as listeners, do with this time? Let our minds wander, mostly. Unless we purposefully make use of that time to concentrate on the speaker's message, we can find it very easy to be distracted.

Effective Listening Requires Active Commitment

If we believe that listening is a passive process in which we can simply monitor what we hear, we are likely to misinterpret information or overlook important cues. We'll hear only what we want to hear or only what grabs our attention startlingly. Productive listening involves real work. It takes emotional and intellectual commitment. It's possible that our TV-watching habits contribute to our tendency to listen passively. Television, after all, demands nothing from the viewer or listener. We don't have to respond to TV, we just let it happen to us. But in interpersonal communication, if we listen halfheartedly and passively we get only part of the message.

Those Hidden Messages . . .

Effective listening is listening with our third ear. By this I mean trying to listen for the meanings behind the words and not just to the words alone. The way words are spoken—loud, soft, fast, slow, strong, hesitating—is very important. There are messages buried in all the cues that surround words.[3] If a mother says, "Come *in* now" in a soft, gentle voice, it may mean the kids have a few more minutes. If she says, "Come in NOW" there is no question about the meaning of the command. To listen effectively we have to pay attention to facial expressions and eye contact, gestures and body movement, posture and dress, as well as the quality of the other person's voice, vocabulary, rhythm, rate, tone, and volume. These nonverbal cues are a vital part of any message. Listening with our third ear helps us understand the whole message.

Our ability to expand upon the obvious—to listen beyond words—allows us to really "see into" another person. People who seek us out for help and sympathy bear two messages—the one they speak and the one beneath the surface. To help them we need to "see through" what they say. You may know a person to whom everyone goes with problems, a person other people seek out for

counsel or just to share ideas. This person is probably an effective listener, someone who listens with the third ear.

Effective Listening Requires Empathy[4]

Another variable that works against effective listening is our tendency to evaluate what others say to us. We often want to judge, approve, or disapprove the statements we hear.[5] Then we act more on our evaluation than on what is actually said. There is a time for this kind of evaluative listening. The label "deliberative" has been given to the listening we do when we want "to hear information, to analyze it, to recall it at a later time, and to draw conclusions from it."[6] This is the kind of listening we do in a psychology lecture class or when we listen to a government official explaining a proposal to curb inflation. We judge the information we hear in these situations. We try to remember it and evaluate its significance—whether we think it is relevant or irrelevant to us, right or wrong.

Both empathic listening and deliberative listening are done in order to achieve accurate understanding. With deliberative listening we want to understand the message accurately because we want to make specific use of the information it contains; it's our evaluation of the information that matters most. But when we listen empathically, our first goal is to understand the other person, to see and feel what that person sees and feels. In deliberative listening, understanding of the other person is a secondary goal.[7]

The overall reason interpersonal communication improves when we listen empathically is that our own responses to the other person are based, ideally, on maximum understanding of what that person says. Specifically, this happens because:

1. There are more message channels available; we have a better chance of getting cues that will clarify communication;

CONSIDER THIS "**I happened to overhear some conversations of strangers on a plane not long ago, and it struck me that each of them was using the other as a sounding board and little else. One would speak about himself, the other would dutifully listen: then the second would take his turn, and the first would listen.**

But the "listening" was a matter of surface courtesy and nothing more. Each was going through a set of verbal gymnastics, a kind of exercise in self-disclosure, but no contact was really made. They were like golfers taking turns addressing different balls; they walked the same course, but no genuine transaction ever took place.

Mostly, they were seeking to reassure themselves that all was well; they were looking for identity and stability and acceptance, by means of constructing an image in the other person's mind. This is a futile and unsatisfactory way to do it—for in personal relations, the only structures that can stand are bridges, not skyscrapers. Unless we reach across, we are reaching out in vain."

—Sydney Harris, "Strictly Personal"

2. Our responses are more appropriate because we give our selves time to consider them carefully, and we are more likely to deal with the other person as he or she actually is instead of on the basis of a stereotype; and
3. We have a better picture of the other person's point of view, as a frame of reference for his or her remarks.

To understand where the other person is coming from requires a broader base than what we are probably accustomed to using. Empathic listening is one means to obtain that more comprehensive framework: the total image that is the other person.

WHY DON'T YOU LISTEN EMPATHICALLY?

If it is so important, and if there are so many advantages, you might wonder why more people are not empathic listeners. Actually, there are three reasons—all of them directly tied to each other. First, listening empathically is not easy. It is far more difficult than simply taking note of actual words spoken and responding to them literally. Second, empathic listening requires that we get outside of our selves by trying to share in the meaning, spirit, and feelings of another person. We're not always willing to do this. Our egos get tied up in our communication; we get involved in our own thoughts and problems. The next time you are involved in an interpersonal encounter, notice how hard it is to concentrate on what the other person is saying if you are preoccupied with your own next remark. Do you begin to plan what you are going to say before the other person even has a chance to stop talking? Instead of listening, you may find you are figuring out how to impress him or her with your next comment.[8]

The third reason we may not listen empathically is because of lifelong poor listening habits. We may listen too literally or too judgmentally by habit. We may habitually think of communication as a talking medium rather than as a listening medium. Here are some other habits we may have that get in the way of effective listening:

Tuning out. Habit may cause us to tune out much of the talk we hear. Our society is a talk-oriented one. We tune out to avoid listening, to protect our selves from the communication babble that sometimes seems to surround us. It is necessary to tune out some things. We must be selective or we would be inundated. But we cannot listen empathically if habit has caused us to avoid the very basics of the process—tuning *in!*

This does not mean we need to tune in to everything we hear. But good listeners do tend to discover interesting elements in almost all communications. They are able to cope with the bombardment of stimuli. Whereas poor listeners tend to find all topics uniformly dry and boring, effective listeners concentrate their attention well and learn efficiently through listening.

We can't expect to be fascinated by every subject. But if we too often find our selves bored by the communication in a certain situation—eating lunch with the same people every day, for example—we might ask our selves, "What were my reasons for going to lunch with these people in the first place? Do those reasons still hold?" We may remember we first started eating with these people because they are politically active and we wanted to discuss politics with them. If we still feel the same way, remembering our original motive can help us focus our listening in this group's communications. We may be able to pick out useful bits of information from conversations that would otherwise seem pointless.

Wanting to be entertained. Another habit that can affect our listening might be labeled the "Sesame Street Syndrome." We want to be entertained. We may mentally challenge a speaker: "Excite me or I won't listen." If we think ahead of time that the message we're going to hear will be dull, we're not likely to listen well. And if we expect to be bored, there's a good chance we will be. We generally prefer a lively, entertaining presentation to a straight, unembellished delivery. Think of the way local television news programs present the news. You may notice a real difference from one station to another in how many program elements are included mainly for their entertainment value.

Avoiding the difficult. Another version of the "Sesame Street Syndrome" is that we tend to stay away from difficult listening. That is, given a choice, we are likely to avoid listening that requires mental exertion. Any kind of communication that deals with subjects unfamiliar to us can seem tough to follow, especially if the speaker moves quickly from one point to the next. If we're not used to a speaker's reasoning, we may give up on the message rather than force our selves to follow his or her thought processes. Editorial comments on TV, panel discussions, and some lectures can be hard to follow if we're not used to really concentrating.

Criticizing the superficial. Think about a recent interpersonal encounter you had with people you do not know well. Can you remember what they looked like? What were they wearing? What did they say? We often let externals distract us from what the other person is trying to say.

Especially if we don't know someone well, we're likely to be diverted by that person's lisp or hairstyle or purple sweater. We may find our selves criticizing some unimportant characteristic of the person instead of listening to what he or she is saying. Think of how you and people you know size up a political candidate. Do you notice the candidate's hairstyle? Smile? Clothing? These nonverbal cues are important, but they shouldn't distract us from really listening to what the person is saying.

TRY THIS

Next time you catch your self being distracted by another person's clothes, mannerisms, or looks, stop **and try to:**

1. Refocus **your attention on the message.**
2. Paraphrase **what is being said.**
3. Review **the important elements of what has been communicated.**

The idea is to redirect your attention to the message and away from distracting elements.

Letting your emotions take over. Finally, we may habitually either (1) block things out; (2) distort things; or (3) agree too readily to everything. Often, when we hear things that don't fit in with our own beliefs, we put up a mental block so we don't get frightened or angry. Sometimes we hear just what we want to hear. We may have a conviction so strong that we twist whatever we hear to conform. Some words ("mother" "I love you") may appeal to our emotions to such an extent that we agree to anything that follows. If we loved every minute we spent at Barnwood High School, meeting someone else from old Barnwood automatically produces a favorable emotional climate for our conversation.

Our emotions may be triggered by a single word or phrase that seems to leap out at us. Suppose we meet a woman at a party who tells us, "I just got back from Colorado." Some emotional reactions we may have are "I never get to go anywhere" or "Colorado is overrun by crazy outdoor types. I wouldn't go there if you paid me" or "*Colorado!* I love Colorado! Mountains! Fresh air! Good times!" Any of these thoughts will color how we hear the rest of what the woman says to us. Once we hear that trigger-word ("Colorado"), we listen to nothing else. Instead we plan a defense, rebuttal, supportive example, argument, or other way to involve our ego. Effective listening means controlling emotional responses—trying to break old habits.

RESULTS OF EFFECTIVE LISTENING

When we are animated, cooperative, and responsive listeners, we help the person we are talking to because our reactions produce an immediate effect. We can influence what the other person will say next. And we, the listener, will benefit from the improved communication that results. (See Figure 1.)

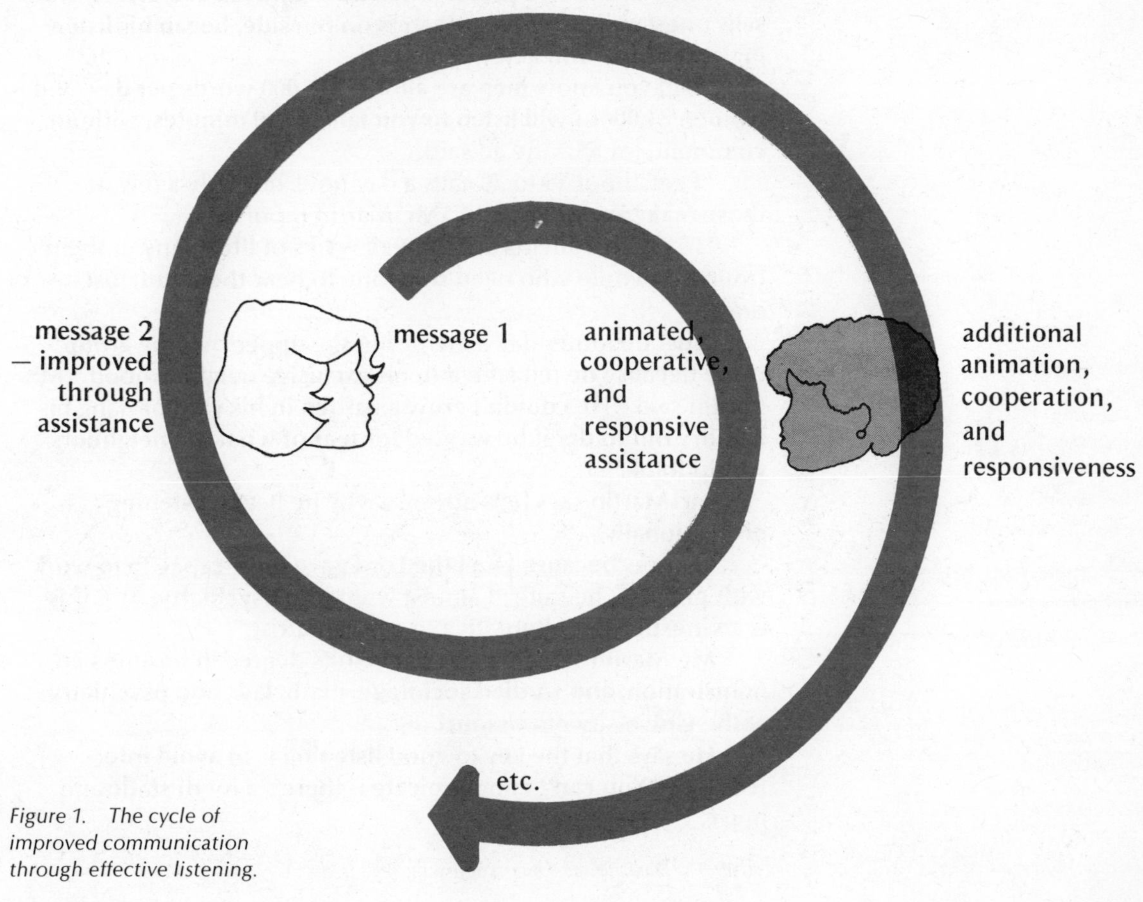

Figure 1. The cycle of improved communication through effective listening.

Specifically, what are the rewards to us of effective listening? The first is that we will get a more stimulating and meaningful message—the other person may subconsciously adapt the message specifically to our knowledge and background. The more closely we listen to a person and indicate what we do and don't understand, the more likely we are to end up with a message that makes sense to us. And we're more likely to remember it. By improving our listening habits we should be able to recall more than fifty percent of the information we hear, rather than forget it.[9]

For example, if we respond to a friend's description of a recent trip with partial or complete silence, our friend will probably cut the

CONSIDER THIS

CONSIDER THIS CONSIDER THIS CONSIDER THIS CONSIDER THIS CONSIDER THIS CONSIDER THIS

Kirk Martin listens, in person and by appointment only.

"I will talk, if a customer asks me to, or if he looks like he wants me to," Mr. Martin explained. "I can talk eyeball-to-eyeball to anyone who comes through my front door."

Mr. Martin, 48, a professional truck and taxicab driver who sells one-family homes and farms on the side, began his listening enterprise with a newspaper ad.

"Did you know men are allotted 27,000 words per day, and women 31,000? I will listen to you talk for 30 minutes, without comment, for $5," the ad said.

"I get about 10 to 20 calls a day now, but only a few of those make appointments," Mr. Martin reports.

He says his clients are from all walks of life, many of them troubled people who need someone to hear them out, just once.

"Just the other day a man from the upper-income group came because he felt stilted in his exclusive neighborhood," Mr. Martin said. "He couldn't grow a garden in his yard or hang his laundry out to dry if he wanted for fear of what the neighbors would think."

Mr. Martin says he's not sure why he began listening professionally.

"I guess because I feel the Lord gave me a capacity to work with people," he said. "I almost went into psychiatry. And this is an inexpensive alternative to a psychiatrist."

Mr. Martin said he has a bachelor's degree in business administration, and studied sociology, math, law, and psychiatry at the University of Missouri.

He says that the key to good listening is to avoid interference—"You can't communicate if there's a lot of static and noise."

—(AP) *The Blade: Toledo, Ohio,* August 16, 1975

description short. But if we ask such questions as, "Where did you go?" or "What did you do?" or "Was it fun?" or "Who did you see?" he or she will be more interested in providing the details. Our understanding of our friend's experience will be far more complete. Of course, we can purposely cut short a conversation if we want to by showing no interest or involvement. But we will also miss out on what may have been a stimulating and meaningful message.

The second reward of effective listening is improvement in our own communication techniques. By paying closer attention to the communication of others and by observing their methods, we will be able to analyze our own efforts more completely.

For example, we may notice that a friend ends every other sentence with the words "you know." If we find that this interferes with our listening, we'll be more alert to certain phrases or words that *we* might overuse. Once we see how distracting such things are to us, we'll be more inclined to ask a friend to point out mannerisms *we* have that we don't seem to be aware of.

We may find that another reward of effective listening is an enlarged circle of friends. Good listeners are in great demand. People have an emotional need to be heard; the person who is willing to take the time to listen is often sought out.

Finally, in becoming effective listeners we are likely to become more open and involved human beings. The ultimate reward is more meaningful interpersonal relationships. Effective listening habits will increase our capacity to meet the demands of modern life. It is one of the most important communication skills needed for human interaction.

THE IMPORTANCE OF FEEDBACK

These benefits of good listening occur only when the cues we give back to a speaker allow that person to know how we received the message, permitting that speaker to adjust the message as needed.[10] This important process is known as *feedback*. Feedback consists of responses made *as* communication occurs. Feedback provides reinforcement for the speaker. It shows if he or she is being clear, accepted, or understood.

The heart of this feedback process is the adjustment or corrective function. Feedback can be words ("Yes, I get it") or physical messages (a smile) or responses that show the other person that we are, indeed, sharing in the spirit of what he or she is saying. It can also show if we do *not* understand or agree. Just as we know, by the response we get, whether or not we are being listened to, the other person is in the same situation. We recognize that mutual understanding has or hasn't occurred through feedback. An atmosphere which promotes honest feedback is a necessary condition for understanding and for being understood.

In any communication setting, each of us is both a source of messages and a receiver of messages simultaneously. This means that each of us is at all times responding and being responded to. Feedback exists when each of us affects the other—each is a cause and an effect.[11] Just as we cannot *not* communicate, we cannot *not* send some kind of feedback. We send messages even when we do not speak.

Receiving Feedback

Imagine your self, for a moment, as only a source of messages; you gain no feedback to any message you send out. You say hello and nobody answers. You ask, "How are you doing?" and nobody answers. You say, "It sure is a beautiful day" and nobody reinforces or acknowledges what you've said. You have no way of knowing if you were heard or understood. You have no way to gauge your effectiveness. It's understandable how someone in this hypothetically one-way communication situation could become frustrated, feeling unacceptable and unloved.[12] What's the use in talking if there is no one to respond? Receiving feedback is one of the best ways we have of modifying our behavior. Monitoring feedback is our way of assuring that the message we intend is as closely related as possible to the message received.

Think of some people with whom you enjoy communicating. Do these people provide you with honest feedback as you speak with them? Their feedback affects not only *how* you communicate with them, but *why* you express your self as you do when talking with them, and *why* you treat them as you do. The cues we receive may cause us to keep talking, restate our ideas, become silent, begin to stumble or stammer, or stop short. Whatever the case, we need feedback for insight into our own communication and to aid us in understanding the communication behavior of others.

Giving Feedback

Just as we need to receive feedback, we also need to give it. Listening attentively and giving appropriate feedback lets us know that we are coping successfully with our environment; we are active participants, not passive observers of life. We are able to act in direct response to a specific stimulus.[13] The feedback we give people can make them feel unique and worthwhile and heighten their sense of well-being—it's

MISS PEACH by Mell Lazarus. Courtesy of Mell Lazarus and Field Newspaper Syndicate.

personally rewarding to know that our reactions matter.

Communication does not exist for long when the direction of flow is one-way. A person who receives no feedback, whose feelings are not encouraged and reinforced, will look somewhere else for support. Effective communication assumes a two-way flow of information.

The Effects of Feedback

If you ever think that your feedback is insignificant and makes no difference, remember that in a two-person interpersonal situation, you are the *only* source of reactions for the other person. Without you, there is no one else. If you do not provide feedback, the other person can't know how well he or she is getting through. It's up to you to help the other person make the message as accurate as possible: your influence is felt strongly.

In a landmark study, researchers investigated how differing amounts of feedback affected how the message was conveyed.[14] In all cases, students were to draw geometric patterns according to directions given to them by the instructors. In one situation the researchers allowed no feedback between the instructors and the students. In a second situation, the students and teacher could see each other, but ask no questions. In a third environment, students could answer yes or no to the instructor's questions. In a fourth circumstance, students could ask any questions and get information—a free-feedback situation. The researchers discovered that as the amount of allowed feedback increased, it took students longer to complete their tasks but they also drew their geometric figures more accurately. And they felt far more confident about their success in drawing the figures in this condition of free feedback. We can conclude from this that feedback in an interpersonal communication encounter takes extra time but results in more accurate message transmission and more confidence in the message-transmission process.

Styles of Positive Feedback

Feedback begins within us. Internal feedback takes place all the time as we communicate with others.[15] As we speak, we anticipate certain responses from the other person; our process of getting set depends on internal feedback. As we receive feedback from another person, we adapt and correct our own message; the process of adapting and correcting depends on internal feedback.

As we look forward to an interpersonal encounter, we may even quiz our selves on how we should behave in this situation. This process of asking our selves questions is internalized feedback.[16] You have probably caught your self going over the message you want to give another person or rehashing his or her ideas long after you have received them. For example, what kinds of feelings might you have if you were planning to meet a close friend for coffee after class? A professor in her office to discuss your final grade? A friend for a drink in the evening? An interviewer for a job interview? In each case your expectations would be different. But you would be able to predict what behavior would be appropriate on the basis of similar experiences you've already had. You would use internal feedback.

CONSIDER THIS

Why am I so discomfited by a compliment? According to a recent sociological study, I am, in fact, very typical. Praise seems to make most of us uneasy. . . .

Why do so many of us accept a gift-wrapped word as gingerly as we might a beribboned time bomb? Usually, say Professors Turner and Edgley, for one of six reasons: the felt obligation to return the compliment; the need to keep up a modest front and avoid seeming conceited by agreeing with the praise; suspicion of ulterior motives; fear that commendation is but a prelude to criticism; resentment at being evaluated at all by someone else; or worry that we won't be able to keep up whatever we're being praised for at the moment.

Giving positive feedback to another person begins with our own internal feedback. If we want to give someone positive reinforcement as he or she speaks, we must first be very attentive to that person's communications. We can't give helpful feedback if we aren't listening effectively to start with. To be ready to respond appropriately we must be alert to the other person's overall message—we should try hard to see where he or she is coming from so that our feedback is not insensitive or confusing.

Positive feedback is supportive. Giving it may be as simple as nodding "yes" or smiling or saying, "Mm-hmm. Go on." It can be just enough to let the other person know we're there and tuned in. It should mean the message is being received and understood—it's pointless and not helpful for us to nod and smile and say yes if we don't mean it. Feedback that expresses agreement is not the only kind of positive feedback; in most open, honest exchanges there will be times when we disagree with the speaker. But we can still give positive feedback; that is, we can still show that we are there and receptive.

In a conversation where both parties give positive feedback, certain kinds of distractions are less likely to cause problems. Each person's meaning is likely to get through to the other in spite of jet planes passing overhead or small children interrupting to ask questions. Exchanging positive feedback is a way of saying, "I want to hear what you want to tell me." If both people have this attitude, meaning is likely to survive problems in message transmission.

David W. Johnson suggests three kinds of response styles for giving positive feedback to others.[17] The three styles are called *supportive, probing,* and *understanding.*

Supportive. If a friend comes to us with an upsetting problem, we probably want to reassure him or her that all is not lost. Pointing out alternatives he or she may not have thought of would be supportive. Our support should be calming. It is meant to reduce the intensity of our friend's feeling. Initially, our support may be no more specific than a look or a touch that says, "I'm on your side." Once our friend knows that we are feeling with him or her, the two of us can discuss actions to correct the problem.

In being supportive, we must be careful we aren't really trying to teach our friend a lesson. If we try to say what we think the problem means, or describe our friend's feelings for him or her, our response may have a negative effect.

No matter how much we have the other person's best interests at heart, it's a bad idea to start out with, "I *told* you that would happen . . ." or "Next time you'll know better . . ." or "You should be glad you found out when you did . . ." We don't want to suggest what he or she ought to think. Remember, what our friend does think is what we have to deal with. To provide support we should first reassure, pacify, and reduce the intensity of *that* feeling. A comment like, "That is a serious problem and I can see why you are upset . . ." is a good beginning point. Being supportive means acknowledging the seriousness of the other person's feelings. We don't want to argue or suggest that his or her emotions are inappropriate.

Probing. A probing response may also be supportive because it can draw out the other person. The point of probing feedback is to get him or her to discuss the problem. A probing response is a good beginning point, too, because it gives us information about the nature of the problem. It gives us a better base to act on and provides an emotional release for the other person at the same time. This response often takes the form of a question: "What makes this situation so upsetting to you?" or "What do you suppose caused this to happen?" An implied question might be phrased, ". . . and you expect the situation to get worse, not better. . . ."

In probing, we don't want to be threatening or accusatory. Phrasing our questions carelessly can cause more problems than we solve. For example, we would probably not ask our friend, "How did you ever get into this mess?" because we are placing a value judgment on the experience. Questions like, "Didn't you know that was

. . . Reciprocity is a fact of social life. Just as we feel obliged to "return" a dinner invitation or a Christmas card, the Turner-Edgley study shows that most people feel they must return a compliment. . . .

Many respondents felt extreme anxiety about returning kind words; some felt the very relationship depended upon it. Most however, didn't like the feeling that they were "beholden" to their complimenters and wanted to even out the relationship as soon as possible.

Sidney B. Simon, Ed.D., professor of education at the University of Massachusetts, calls this rush toward reciprocation the "compliment-flick" syndrome. "Many people get rid of a compliment as fast as they can by giving one back," he says. "They just can't stand hearing themselves praised. That's because so many of us have been trained from an early age to be humble and modest and not to toot our own horns. We can't even enjoy hearing anyone else toot them, either, because that might imply that we think something of ourselves."

—Sally Wendkos Olds, *Today's Health,* February 1975

CONSIDER THIS

An engaging example of the impact of attending behavior is given by Ivey and Hinkle. At a prearranged signal, six students in a psychology seminar switched from the traditional student's slouched posture and passive listening and notetaking to attentive posture and active eye contact with the teacher. In the nonattending condition, the teacher had been lecturing from his notes in a monotone, using no gestures, and paying little or no attention to the students. However, once the students began to attend, the teacher began to gesture, his verbal rate increased, and a lively classroom session was born. At another prearranged signal later in the class, the students stopped attending and returned to typical passive student's posture and participation. The teacher, "after some painful seeking for continued reinforcement," returned to the unengaging teacher behavior with which he had begun the class. In the nonattending condition, the teacher paid no attention to the students and the students reciprocated in kind. Both students and teacher got what they deserved: reciprocated inattention. But simple attending changed the whole picture.

—Gerard Egan, *The Skilled Helper*

wrong?" or "You really weren't thinking, were you?" create defensiveness in the other person. If we tell our friend that his or her action was good or bad, appropriate or inappropriate, right or wrong, we are making a judgment. Again we don't want to imply what that person should have done or ought to do.

Understanding. Our first comment to our friend could be, "I can see you're very upset about this problem. It must mean a great deal to you." In paraphrasing the other person's remarks we show that we understand him or her. When we show that we care about correctly understanding our friend's situation, we are making an *understanding* response. When we reinforce our remarks with nonverbal gestures—eye contact, facial expressions of sincerity, touching—this response is very supportive.

In all three positive response styles we avoid judging the other person and the situation. Our choice of words is not as crucial as is our honest effort to understand the other person's problem and feelings and to convey that understanding. The idea is to indicate acceptance and respect for the other person. As these feelings are reflected back to us, an atmosphere of mutual respect, support, and trust develops. And our interpersonal relationships are likely to become more satisfying.

IMPROVING SKILLS IN LISTENING

As I said earlier, improving listening skills requires time and energy. I hope I have convinced you of the need for effective listening and now will discuss some ways we can improve our listening skills. As you read the suggestions, you may realize how many seem to be based on common sense. Some may seem obvious. Even so, the most commonsensical ideas are often not put into practice. If you simply read these and do not incorporate them into your own listening behavior, they will serve little purpose. Perhaps these suggestions will also bring to mind other practical ideas you can put to use in listening settings.

Prepare to listen. In many cases we do not listen well because we are not physically or mentally prepared. Our attention span—how long we are able to attend to a single stimulus (like someone talking)—is directly related to our physical and mental condition. This is obvious if we recall that listening involves an integration of physical, emotional, and intellectual elements. Think how impatient or short-tempered we become when we are mentally run-down, or physically tired. We stayed up all night studying for an exam and now everyone around us pays for it! We do not want to listen to anyone!

Control or eliminate distractions. Anticipating situations where we might have to listen helps prepare us. There may be something we can do to improve the situation: turning off a television, closing a door, asking the other person to speak louder, or moving to a less distracting location. If we can't eliminate distractions, we'll have to concentrate with greater effort.

Anticipate the subject. Whenever possible, think ahead about the topics or ideas that might be discussed. The more familiar we are with the subject matter, the more likely we will learn, and the more interested we will be. Also, thinking ahead may prompt questions to ask. Becoming actively involved in interpersonal situations makes them more memorable and meaningful.

Anticipate the speaker. Anticipating the speaker means adjusting in advance (or being prepared to adjust) to the other person. We cannot control how the speaker will look or talk, but we can make sure, in advance, that distracting appearance or faulty delivery does not dominate our attention. Our aim should be to try to find out what the other person is saying. We should try to not be bothered by peculiarities or eccentricities. If we are always ready to adjust, we will find it becomes a natural part of our behavior when we *must* adjust.

TRY THIS

To practice your supportive, probing, and understanding responses, think of one response of each kind for each of the following situations:

1. Your best friend comes to you with the following information: "I just flunked my second exam in my psychology course. It's all over. I just don't care about anything anymore . . ."

2. Your roommate says: "Someone stole my books and notebooks. I left them on a table in the cafeteria and when I came back they were gone . . ."

3. A friend down the hall laments: "Oh, I can't stand it, I can't stand it anymore! My roommate leaves the room a mess, plays the stereo at full volume, and sleeps only during the day. It's driving me out of my mind . . ."

Create a need to listen. We do not enjoy listening to some people as well as to others. We do not listen as well to some topics as we do to others. We often know in advance that we may not listen as well as we might in a certain situation. To try to counteract this situation, become a "selfish listener."[18] What can the speaker do for *you?* The key to being interested in another person or in a topic is making it relevant or useful to us. How can the other person help you?

We might try to discover if the message has any personal benefits for us. Can it provide any personal satisfaction? Does it stimulate any new interests or insights? Good listeners are interested in what they are listening to whereas poor listeners find all people and all topics dry and boring. True, some topics are dull but we often decide this in advance and don't give the speaker a chance.

If the speaker or the material does not satisfy a need, ask your self, "Why am I here?" Try to remember the motive that caused you to be there and see if the motive is still active. We might also try to discover a reward—some immediate way that we can use the material that will make the experience personally profitable.

TRY THIS

As you are listening to someone or just after a conversation ask your self the following questions:

1. What did the other person do—as far as effective communication goes—that was particularly strong? What aspects of the other person's presentation were especially powerful or convincing?

2. What did the person do that was especially weak? What would you change in his or her presentation?

The purpose here is growth and change. Try to learn something from each communication experience that will help you improve your own communication patterns and behaviors.

Monitor the way you listen. Even if we are prepared to listen and need to listen, our listening will not necessarily be effective. We need to check occasionally to make sure our thoughts are not wandering and that we are keeping an open mind to the other person's ideas. Because of the time difference between speaking and listening rates, we need to use the spare time that results wisely.

Concentrate on the message. To keep your mind on the message, try to review what the speaker has already said so that you can keep ideas together and remember them. Listen for the main ideas. Try to go "between" the words. Listen with your third ear. Listen for words that may have more than one meaning and discover, if possible, how the other person is using the word. Try to anticipate what the speaker will say next and compare this with what he or she actually says. This keeps your mind focused on the message.[19] Concentrate on the message, not on the other person's blue eyes or Hawaiian shirt.

Suspend judgment. Some words, phrases, or ideas evoke an automatic reaction in us. We may overreact to bad grammar, ethnic slurs, or vulgarity. We must learn not to get too excited about certain words until we have the whole context. Suspend your judgment until you thoroughly understand where the speaker is coming from.

Think about those words you react strongly to. Why do they affect you like that? Often sharing our reactions with others will help us see that our reactions are entirely personal. Finally, try to reduce the intensity of your reaction by convincing your self that the reaction is extreme and unnecessary, that the word does not merit such a reaction.[20] Our listening will always be affected when certain words touch our deepest prejudices or most profound values. Knowing that such reactions can happen is the first step toward overcoming them.

Empathize. Attempt to see the other person's ideas from his or her perspective. If Sam is telling you how angry he is with his brother, try to discover why he says what he does. Listen for his reasons, his views, and his arguments. You needn't agree with him. Sam's brother may be a friend of yours. But just because Sam's feelings differ from yours does not mean they aren't valid. Since you differ from Sam as a result of different past experiences, search for the message he is *really* trying to communicate. Look for elements he may have left out. What is he basing his evidence on? How did he come by his opinion? Through personal experience? Other people's observations? Guesswork? Try to see the problem through Sam's eyes.

IMPROVING SKILLS IN FEEDBACK

Effective feedback is as important as good listening. As listeners, we have a duty to respond, to complete the communication cycle. Although we can't avoid giving some feedback even if we don't say a word, there are ways we can improve.

Be prepared to give feedback. Feedback can be verbal, nonverbal, or both. Nonverbal feedback usually can say more about our sincerity than words alone. Our verbal feedback is more likely to be believed if we support it with appropriate gestures, direct eye contact, and possibly touching. Be certain that you are close enough to the other person—face-to-face if possible—that your feedback will be perceived. We will discuss nonverbal communication in more detail in a later chapter.

Although we must be prepared to give feedback, we shouldn't enter a situation with our specific reactions already planned. Spontaneity is important. The best feedback arises naturally as a result of an immediate and specific stimulus. But being prepared to give feedback is not contradictory to being spontaneous; it simply means that we are alert and sensitive to the need for feedback and are ready to give it.

Make your feedback prompt. Our response to the other person should be clear and prompt. The more closely tied feedback is to the original message, the less ambiguous it will be. The longer the delay between message and feedback, the more likely we are to confuse the other person.

TRY THIS

The next time you are communicating interpersonally, do not respond to what the other person says until you do three things:

1. Wait until the other person finishes **what he or she has to say.**

2. You fully paraphrase **what he or she has said.**

3. You have received an affirmative response **to the question, "Is this what you mean?" directly following your paraphrase.**

Following an affirmative response, you may make any appropriate comment you wish to keep the conversation going. If the other person says your paraphrase was inaccurate, keep trying until you get it right.

Although in many situations we don't need to wait until the other person finishes talking before we respond, forcing your self to wait will indicate how often you do not **wait. Does this kind of communication seem awkward or labored to you? Do you think it is a good way to get at the other person's meaning?**

Make your feedback accurate. Accuracy means making feedback specific to a single message and not general to the whole conversation. You probably know people who continually nod and smile the entire time you're talking to them. In addition to being distracting, this also appears insincere. It makes you want to ask, "All right, what exactly do you agree with? How will I know when you disagree?" Try to provide only necessary feedback.

React to the message, not the speaker. Our accuracy in giving feedback will also improve if we remember to direct it to the message and not to the person communicating. In addition to being distracting, personal comments may create hostility or frustration and a breakdown in communication.

Oddly, both complimentary and critical feedback may be better received if we phrase our responses in a slightly impersonal way. If we wish to praise someone for playing a piano sonata well, saying "I've never heard that piece done so beautifully. I really heard it in a new way" may make the performer less uncomfortable than "Sarah, you really did that well. I didn't know you were that good." Too-personal comments can imply, however subtly, "That was good, for *you*" when what we mean is "That was good." Effective feedback is message-oriented.[21]

Monitor your own feedback. If our feedback is not interpreted by the other person as we mean it, it serves no purpose. Check the effect you're making. You might have to repeat or clarify a feedback response. If Louise says, "I can never think of what to say to Alvin," and our response is "I know," it can either mean, "I know. I've noticed you never have anything to say" or it can mean, "I know. Alvin is hard to talk to." We must monitor our feedback to make sure we're being understood. Like any message, feedback can be blocked or distorted.

Concentrate on exchanging meaning. Finally, our feedback will be perceived more accurately and sent more accurately if both parties are committed to the honest exchange of meaning. Think about how to help the other person express ideas more effectively. We are more likely to provide constructive feedback if we are motivated by a sincere desire to enhance communication.

Effective communicators respond to others through listening and feedback. We should work to increase listening and feedback skills. Try to develop sensitivity to the feedback and listening of others. We will be using our listening and feedback skills to learn more about the process of communication; applying what we learn to our own behavior will help us grow. Just as listening and feedback are essential in human communication, so are the words that make up a good part of the message. The words—verbal communication—are the subject of the next chapter.

OTHER READING

Edmond G. Addeo and Robert E. Burger, *EgoSpeak: Why No One Listens to You* (New York: Bantam Books, Inc., 1973). EgoSpeak is the art of boosting our own egos by speaking only about what *we* want to talk about. This is an entertaining and systematic catalog of the major types of this disease: JobSpeak, BusinessSpeak, NameSpeak, SpeakSpeak, and many more.

Larry L. Barker, *Listening Behavior* (Englewood Cliffs, N.J.: Prentice-Hall, Inc., 1971). A textbook, this is one of the most comprehensive and thorough investigations of listening and feedback currently on the market. It is short, well written, and carefully documented.

Gerard I. Nierenberg and Henry H. Calero, *Meta-Talk: Guide to Hidden Meanings in Conversations* (New York: Pocket Books, 1974). This is a popular, uncomplicated approach to listening and feedback. Many examples are included. The author cautions the reader that no meaning is absolute; meaning lies in the speaker or listener. The book is important for pointing out some of the meanings behind or beyond words.

Carl H. Weaver, *Human Listening: Processes and Behavior* (Indianapolis, Ind.: The Bobbs-Merrill Company, Inc., 1972). This textbook proves that listening is a type of behavior difficult both to understand and to change. By doing the exercises provided, one can learn how to improve listening skills.

NOTES

[1] Larry L. Barker, *Listening Behavior* (Englewood Cliffs, N.J.: Prentice-Hall, Inc., 1971), pp. 3–5. The studies Barker summarizes suggest that close to 40% of all time spent in communication activities is spent in listening.

[2] Ernest G. Bormann, et al., *Interpersonal Communication in the Modern Organization* (Englewood Cliffs, N.J.: Prentice-Hall, 1969), p. 197.

[3] G. Egan, *Encounter: Group Processes for Interpersonal Growth* (Belmont, Calif.: Brooks/Cole, 1970), p. 248.

[4] Based on "Empathic Listening" by Charles M. Kelly, published in *Small Group Communication: A Reader,* 2nd Edition, Wm. C. Brown Company, 1974. Reprinted by permission of the author.

[5] Carl R. Rogers, *On Becoming a Person* (Boston: Houghton Mifflin, 1961), p. 330.

[6] Kelly, "Empathic Listening," p. 340.

[7] Ibid, p. 342.

[8] This phenomenon is called "EgoSpeak." Edmond G. Addeo and Robert E. Burger, *EgoSpeak* (New York: Bantam Books, Inc., 1973), p. xiii.

[9] The retention rate of orally communicated messages is approximately 50% immediately after the message is communicated and only 25% two months later. Ralph G. Nichols, "Do We Know How to Listen?" in *Communication: Concepts and Processes,* Joseph A. DeVito, ed. (Englewood Cliffs, N.J.: Prentice-Hall, Inc., 1971), pp. 207–208.

[10] Norbert Wiener, one of the first persons to be concerned with feedback, defined it as "the property of being able to adjust future conduct by past experience." Norbert Wiener, *Cybernetics* (New York: John Wiley & Sons, 1948), p. 33, and Norbert Wiener, *The Human Use of Human Beings: Cybernetics and Society* (Boston: Houghton Mifflin, 1950). Also see discussion of the monitoring function of feedback in David K. Berlo, *The Process of Communication* (New York: Holt, Rinehart and Winston, 1960), p. 111.

[11] Arnold Tustin, "Feedback," in *Communication and Culture,* Alfred G. Smith, ed., (New York: Holt, Rinehart and Winston, 1966), p. 325.

[12] Warren G. Bennis, et al., eds., *Interpersonal Dynamics: Essays and Readings on Human Interaction* (Homewood, Ill.: Dorsey Press, 1968), p. 214.

[13] William C. Schultz, *The Interpersonal Underworld* (Palo Alto, Calif.: Science and Behavior Books, 1966), p. 13.

[14] Harold J. Leavitt and Ronald A. H. Mueller, "Some Effects of Feedback on Communication," in *Interpersonal Communication: Survey and Studies,* Dean Barnlund ed., (Boston: Houghton Mifflin, 1968), pp. 251–259.

[15] See Wendell Johnson, *Your Most Enchanted Listener* (New York: Harper & Row, Publishers, 1956), p. 174.

[16] See Richard L. Weaver, II, " 'Internalized Feedback': The Process of Asking Questions," *The Report* III (June 1970), 24–35.

[17] David W. Johnson, *Reaching Out: Interpersonal Effectiveness and Self-Actualization.* © 1972, p. 125. Reprinted by permission of Prentice-Hall, Inc., Englewood Cliffs, New Jersey.

[18] Barker, *Listening Behavior,* p. 74.

[19] Ibid., pp. 75–76.

[20] Ibid., pp. 76–77.

[21] Ibid., p. 124.

Chapter 5

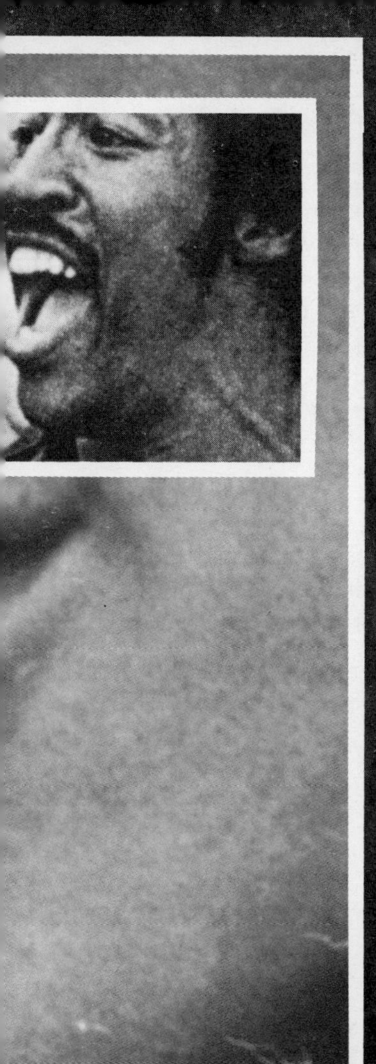

Creating Messages: Verbal Communication

Words, words, words! We live in a sea of words. If we are not talking, we are reading or writing or listening to others talk.[1] So many words—so much talk—it's no wonder we take most of it for granted. From birth we are confronted with people making noises at us trying to get us to do this, believe that, buy this, or think about that. Even so, sometimes we feel that not very much is being communicated. We rarely give the words themselves much thought.

Have you ever said something to someone and, in return, gotten an odd answer or none at all? You may have wondered, "What's wrong with me?" Words can be strange or, at least, can appear to be strange, but can you imagine a civilization without them? Their role and function in interpersonal communication is crucial. Understanding how language works will help us make sure we come across just the way we want to.

Think about the transactional nature of communication. In any communication transaction we are involved in constructing a mental image of the other person, just as he or she is constructing a mental image of us. We base all future communication with each other on these mental images. Our use of language, and especially the way we view each other's use of language, will affect how we construct those mental images. The closer we can make the other person's mental image of us conform to the one we have of our selves, the more effective our interpersonal communication will be. We use words to communicate ideas and describe feelings. We use them to reason and to transform experience into ideas and ideas into experience. Knowing how to use them well will increase our effectiveness in interpersonal communication.

In this chapter I will discuss language from the perspective of you, the language user. Since the problem of abstract language is major, I will spend some time talking about how we can modify our use of words for more precise meaning. I'll explore the way words shape our world by influencing our perceptions. Finally, I will suggest some specific things we can do to improve our language skills.

WHAT WORDS CAN AND CANNOT DO

If we see a series of stones lying across a stream, we know they will help us get across to the other side. But our experience with such stones tells us that some stones may be loose or covered with slime and could cause us to slip. Like these stones, words can help us to reach our goals or they can cause us to stumble and fall. Let's look at some characteristics of language that affect our interpersonal communication.[2]

What Did You Have in Mind?

When we talk to people we often assume too quickly that we are being understood. If we tell people we are going to put on some music, we probably don't think about whether they are expecting to hear the kind of music we intend to play—we just turn it on. But think about the word "music" and how many different interpretations there are of it. (See Figure 1.)

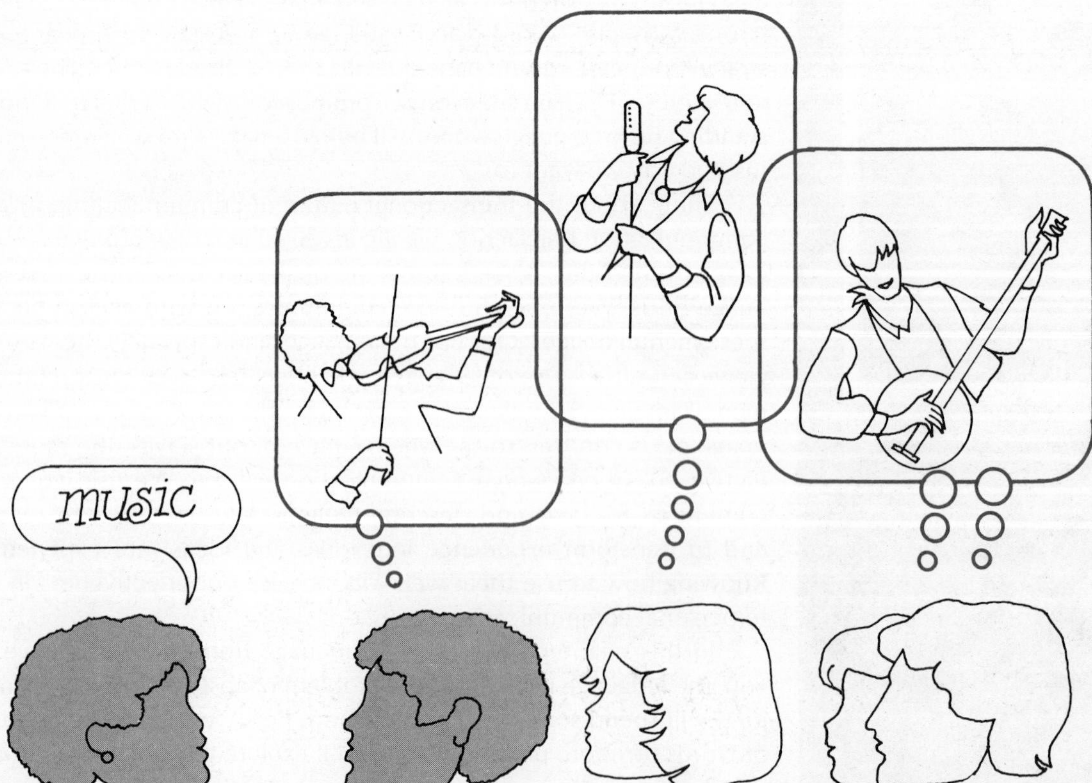

Figure 1. One word may have many different interpretations.

TRY THIS

Write down your definition of each of the following words:

bug
cool
pet
high
pot
make out
beat
gay
mod
speed

heavy
cop
chick
hip
swing
trip
gross
dude
love
smack

Words continually change meanings. The meanings we have for these words might result from how our peers use them, how our parents use them, how we hear them used on television, how a dictionary defines them, or in what context they are being used. We should (1) be aware that meanings change; (2) always be ready to ask for and provide definitions; and (3) try to use words with more stable meanings. Words chosen with care are less likely to cause confusion.

We depend on context and on nonverbal cues to give us the meaning of words. If we said we were going to put on some music, our friends might predict from knowing our taste and from nonverbal cues (our mood) what we might play. But they have a good chance of being wrong. In our daily conversation we use about 2,000 words. Of those 2,000, even the 500 we use most often have over 14,000 dictionary definitions.[3] Think of the possibilities for confusion! The problem of figuring out what a person means by a certain word is compounded by the fact that even dictionary meanings change and new words are constantly being added to the language.

Connotative meanings. Dictionary definitions would probably not help our friends predict the kind of music we would play or what we mean by "music." But their experience with us and with music will give them a clue as to what we mean. If "music" connotes the same thing to us and to our friends, there's less chance of misunderstanding.

When we hear a word, the thoughts and feelings we have about that word and about the person using it determine what that word ultimately means to us. This is the word's *connotative* meaning. Connotative meanings change with our experience. Just as we experience something different in every second of life that we live, so does everyone else. And no two of these experiences are identical! It's no wonder there are infinitely many connotations for every word we use.

If a word creates pretty much the same reaction in a majority of people, the word is said to have a general connotation. Actually, the more general the connotation of a word, the more likely that meaning will become the dictionary meaning, because most people will agree what that word represents. The more general the connotation of a word, the less likely people are to misunderstand it.

Denotative meanings. The denotative meaning of a word is its dictionary definition. Some words have relatively stable meanings. If several people were to define a particular word special to their discipline, they would probably use about the same definition—an agreed upon interpretation. In the legal profession, the word "estoppel" has one precise, *denotative* meaning. Doctors would probably agree upon the definition of a "myocardioinfarction." Many disciplines depend on certain words having precise, unchanging meanings in order to carry on their work. Denotative words give sharpness and accuracy to our ideas.

There is little likelihood of confusion with denotative meanings because there is a direct relationship between the word and what it describes. While every word must be processed by us if we're to understand it, connotative meanings depend a lot more than denotative meanings on our subjective thought processes.[4] (See Figure 2.)

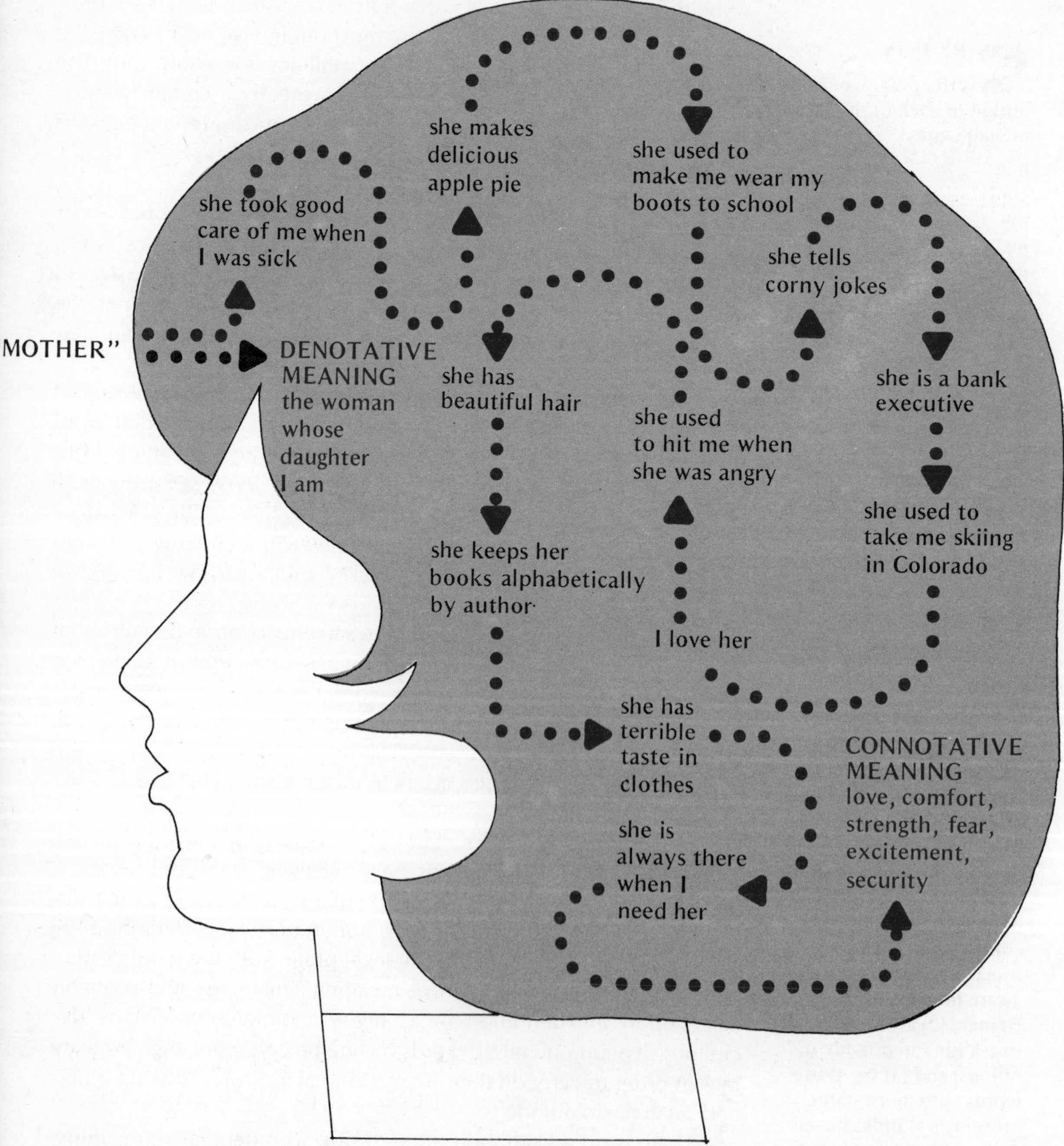

Figure 2. Connotative meanings depend a great deal on the perceiver's experience.

Problems in interpersonal communication increase as we use words with many connotative meanings. Because these meanings are so tied to the particular feelings, thoughts, and ideas of other people, we have a bigger chance of being misunderstood when we use them. On the other hand, richly connotative words give our language power. Note, for example, the differences between the following lists of words:

freedom	book
justice	piano
love	tree
liberty	teacher
music	fire

The words on the left have many connotations; the words on the right are more strictly denotative. "The teacher put the book on the piano" is a sharp, unambiguous statement. The sentence, "The love of freedom burns like a white flame in all of us" can be interpreted numerous ways.

What does all this have to do with our use of words? First, we should recognize that words evoke sometimes unpredictable reactions in others. We should try to anticipate the reactions of others to our words as much as we can. For example, if we are talking to an art major we may cause confusion or even produce a hostile response if we use English-major jargon we have picked up. If we anticipate this negative reaction, we'll leave the jargon in the English classroom.

Second, most words have both connotative and denotative meanings and we should recognize that these meanings vary from person to person. People will react to words according to the meaning *they* give them. An effective communicator tries to recognize different reactions and to adapt to them. Remember as you communicate that meanings do *not* reside in the words themselves. Meanings are in the minds of the people who use and hear the words.

Coping with Levels of Abstraction

Words vary in their degree of abstraction.[5] (See Figure 3.) The word "cow" means different things to different people. Think of experiences you have had with cows. It is considered a low level of abstraction when we perceive not the word "cow," but the cow itself as an object of our experiences. If we think of "Bessie," a particular cow, the name of this cow stands for one cow and no other. Or we may think of cows in general, all the animals that have the characteristics common to cows. This is a higher level of abstraction. At a higher level yet, we might think of "cow" as part of the broader category of "livestock." Going higher up the abstraction ladder, Bessie may be

Figure 3.[6]

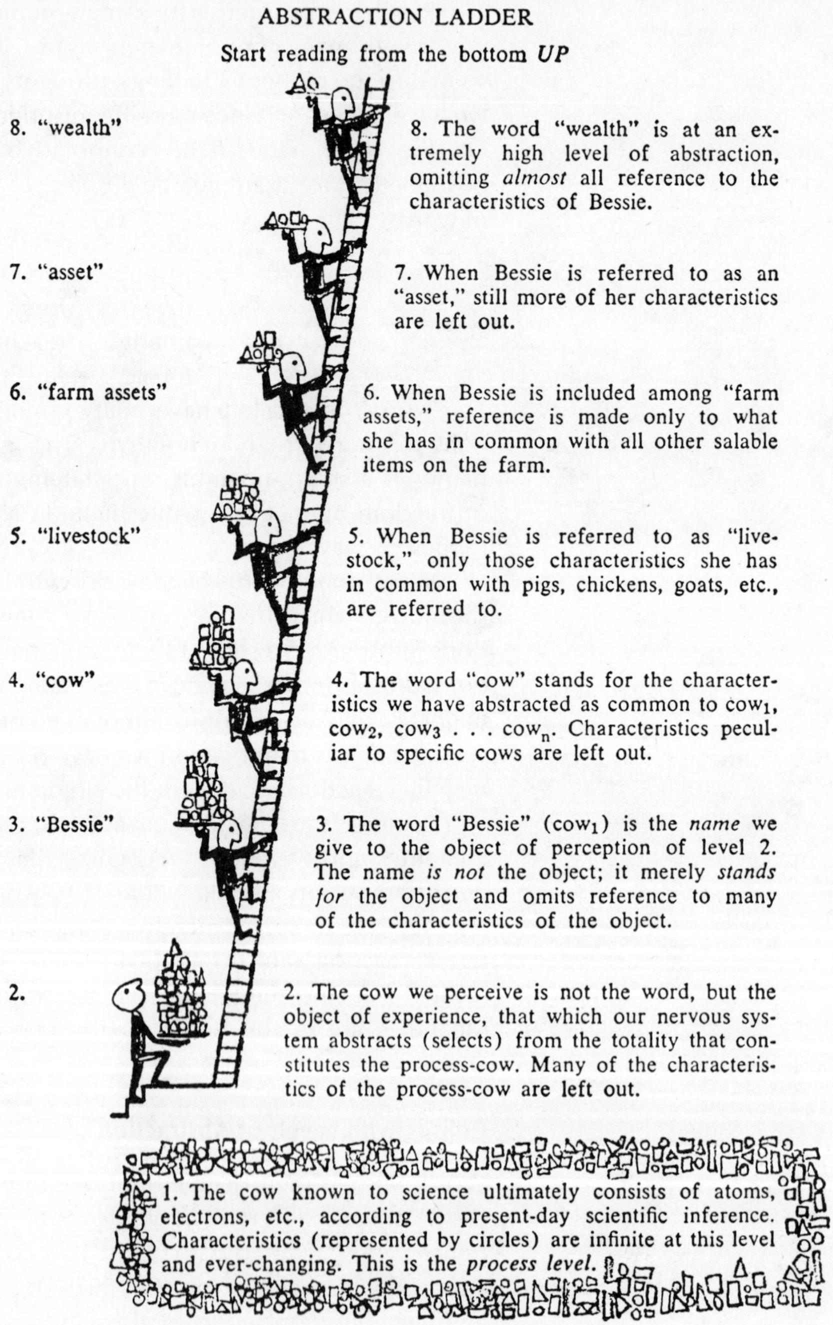

ABSTRACTION LADDER

Start reading from the bottom *UP*

8. "wealth"

8. The word "wealth" is at an extremely high level of abstraction, omitting *almost* all reference to the characteristics of Bessie.

7. "asset"

7. When Bessie is referred to as an "asset," still more of her characteristics are left out.

6. "farm assets"

6. When Bessie is included among "farm assets," reference is made only to what she has in common with all other salable items on the farm.

5. "livestock"

5. When Bessie is referred to as "livestock," only those characteristics she has in common with pigs, chickens, goats, etc., are referred to.

4. "cow"

4. The word "cow" stands for the characteristics we have abstracted as common to cow_1, cow_2, cow_3 . . . cow_n. Characteristics peculiar to specific cows are left out.

3. "Bessie"

3. The word "Bessie" (cow_1) is the *name* we give to the object of perception of level 2. The name *is not* the object; it merely *stands for* the object and omits reference to many of the characteristics of the object.

2.

2. The cow we perceive is not the word, but the object of experience, that which our nervous system abstracts (selects) from the totality that constitutes the process-cow. Many of the characteristics of the process-cow are left out.

1. The cow known to science ultimately consists of atoms, electrons, etc., according to present-day scientific inference. Characteristics (represented by circles) are infinite at this level and ever-changing. This is the *process level.*

thought of as a "farm asset," an "asset," or as "wealth."

You can see how these references to the word "cow" have become more and more abstract. At each higher level of abstraction, more items could be included in the category. The more that can be included in a category, the less possible it is for someone to know

CONSIDER THIS CONSIDER THIS CONSIDER THIS CONSIDER THIS CONSIDER THIS CONSIDER THIS C

EDUCATIONAL JARGON PHRASE INDICATOR

1	2	3
perceptual	maturation	concept
professional	guidance	process
environmental	creative	articulation
instructional	relationship	philosophy
homogeneous	motoric	activity
developmental	culture	resource
sequential	orientation	curriculum
individualized	cognitive	approach
exceptional	accelerated	adjustment
socialized	motivation	interface

To use the Indicator I selected at random one word from the first list, one from the second, and one from the third. This produced as many phrases as I needed. By sprinkling a few common Anglo-Saxon words among these phrases I was able to quickly compose answers to questions, speeches, letters to government agencies, and so forth.

—Laurence J. Peter, *The Peter Prescription*

exactly what we are talking about.

We may have been in conversations where different levels of abstraction were at work without being aware of it. We can see from the abstraction ladder how easy it would be, when dealing with something specific, to jump to a higher level and avoid answering or responding to the specific issue. If someone asked us, "What do you think of Dr. Smith as a lecturer?" we could say, "I do not like Dr. Smith's lecturing," which would be answering at the same level of abstraction. But if we think such a commitment is risky, we might respond that "lecturers just do not seem to care about the students in their audiences." By doing that, we move to a higher level of abstraction. If we respond that teachers at this institution just do not care anymore, we go to a higher level. Saying "education has sure gone to pot" is even more abstract. Teachers and politicians often try to avoid difficult questions by escaping to a higher level of abstraction when pressed on a specific issue.

As we escape to a higher level, we depend more on the connotative meanings of words than on the denotative meanings. Moving up the abstraction ladder causes the meanings of words to be less directly related to the thing they represent and more dependent upon the perceiver of the word. (See Figure 4.) If we actively work to keep our language at a low level of abstraction, there's much less chance for ambiguity and misunderstanding.

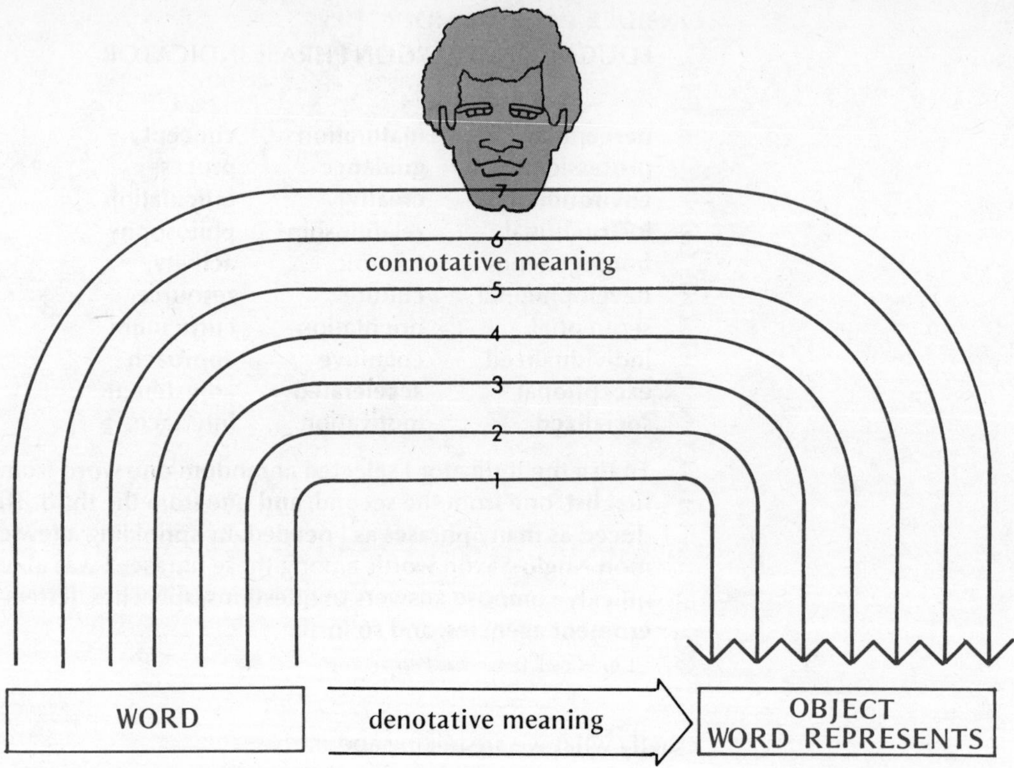

Figure 4. The more abstract a word is, the less directly related its meaning is to the thing it represents, and the more dependent that meaning is on the perceiver.

There are always some teachers who deal only in principles and theories and do not tie these abstractions to concrete reality. When we ask, "What does that have to do with me?" or "How can I apply that in *my* life?" we are asking to have the level of meaning brought down the abstraction ladder. We are asking for concrete particulars so that we can make sense out of the abstract principles.

Usually when we talk to people we go continually up and down the abstraction ladder. We adapt our words to each other's experiences. Knowing that certain words are more abstract than others will help us stay flexible. Words like "love" and "beauty" and "truth" are highly abstract and open to the possibility of confusion and error.

Limiting Your Horizons

In Chapter 3 we looked at how we select and organize incoming data and how we stereotype things. We process stimuli as they come to us, taking what we find meaningful and putting it into a form we can use. There are a number of bad language habits we get into that restrict the meaning exchanged in our communications:

"Have a nice day!" We simplify stimuli to make them understandable and we do this in our use of language as well. Since we depend on relatively few words to describe all our many experiences, we may find it hard sometimes to describe fine differences between experiences—our language loses precision.

One reason, for example, that some teachers insist that students not use the word "good" in speeches or papers is that the term is almost meaningless. What is good to one person can be so far from what is good to another that the term has no descriptive significance. When a word's meaning is restricted to the experience of the person who uses it, it will be difficult or impossible for listeners to understand that person. Codes are intentionally restrictive in that way, since only a few people know them. Our purposes are quite different; unlike the sender of a code, we *want* listeners to understand us.

"I know that." Another restriction on meaning shows up in the language of children. Children often get into the habit of saying "I know it" to whatever they are told—they assume that their experience is already complete. We cannot tell them anything they do not already

THIS CONSIDER THIS

CONSIDER THIS CONSIDER THIS CONSIDER THIS CONSIDER

There is no way to measure the destructive effect of sports broadcasting on ordinary American English, but it must be considerable. In the early days sports broadcasting was done, with occasional exceptions such as Clem McCarthy, by non-experts, announcers. Their knowledge of the sports they described varied, but their English was generally of a high order. If they could not tell you much about the inside of the game they were covering, at any rate what they did tell you you could understand.

Then came the experts, which is to say the former athletes. They could tell you a great deal about the inside, but—again with some exceptions—not in a comprehensible way. They knew the terms the athletes themselves used, and for a while that added color to the broadcasts. But the inside terms were few, and the nonathlete announcers allowed themselves to be hemmed in by them—"He got good wood on that one," "He got the big jump," "He really challenged him on that one," "They're high on him," "They came to play," "He's really got the good hands," and "That has to be," as in "That has to be the best game Oakland ever played."

The effect is deadening, on the enjoyment to be had from watching sports on television or reading about them, and, since sports make up so large a part of American life and do so much to set its tone, on the language we see and hear around us.

—Edwin Newman, *Strictly Speaking*

know! Some adults do the same thing. They respond to others with "I know" so as not to appear stupid or naive. When we do this we are not only lying to our selves and to others, we are closing our selves off to other people's insights, ideas, and feelings. The words "I know" can close the door to sharing. Often, too, they simply aren't true. We restrict our experience with the language we use in order to appear "in the know."

"Everybody knows that." When we assume everybody shares our experiences and feelings, we overgeneralize, which is another way of restricting meaning. We overgeneralize when our words imply that *our* interpretation is the best, right, or only one. We may say, "How can anyone think such a thing?" or "Who would ever want to see that movie?" We don't let other people possess their own meanings for their own experiences. Obviously, communication suffers when this happens.

"You've seen one, you've seen 'em all." Another way our language restricts the meaning exchanged in a communication is when we assume that everything stays the same. When we do this we don't allow for the possibility that things could ever be different. Time alone alters objects, things, people, and ideas—as well as the perceiver. To say, "Connie is like that" or "Bob always does that" or "That is just the way Sam is" allows for no flexibility or room for change in Connie, Bob, or Sam.

"What do you mean, what do I mean?" One of the most difficult barriers to successful human communication occurs when we assume that if something is clear to us, it is clear to everyone else. Even though few people are skilled in reading other people's minds, we still assume that because *we* said it, whoever is listening understood it! We sometimes assume this even when we have made no special effort to be clear: "You know *perfectly* well what I mean!" "What's wrong with you? *I* understand it!" We may even shout the same words again, assuming that repetition in itself is enlightening. It rarely is![7]

These problems are dangerous but we can't hope to completely avoid them since language itself is a body of generalizations. Perfect

CONSIDER THIS "**When I plead, as I often do, for greater precision in our use of words, perhaps it is because I am so prone to confusion. I remember as a little boy reading the signs on some highways and bridges: HEAVY TRAFFIC NOT PERMITTED.**

It puzzled me for a long time how the individual motorist was going to decide whether the traffic was too heavy for him to continue on the road or over the bridge. It was a year or more before I realized that the sign meant: HEAVY VEHICLES NOT PERMITTED.

And I may have been more stupid than most, but when I heard in fourth grade that a special class was being formed for "backward readers," I silently wondered how many of my classmates possessed that marvelous gift of being able to read backward.

A friend recently told me of an incident in a veterans' hospital. The physician in charge of the mental ward had a sign on his door: DOCTOR'S OFFICE. PLEASE KNOCK. He was driven to distraction by an obedient patient who carefully knocked every time he passed the door.

Youngsters, and people out of their right minds, are likely to take words more literally than they are meant. Unless we say exactly what we mean, youngsters will read another meaning into it.

I am not suggesting that everything should be spelled out in a-b-c fashion, thus reducing us all to the condition of children or savages. But words should be accurate **and** explicit; **except for poetry, they should say no more and no less than they actually mean.**

As Mark Twain remarked, "The difference between the right word and the almost right word is the difference between lightning and the lightning bug."

A lovely example I ran across in California last summer was a sign in a public park: PEOPLE WITHOUT DOGS ON A LEASH NOT PERMITTED. I wonder if the good aldermen realized that this banned everyone not owning a dog from entering the park? As you see, I haven't changed much since the fourth grade."

—Sydney J. Harris, *The Best of Sydney J. Harris*

interpersonal communication is virtually impossible. But to recognize that we are likely to be misunderstood because of the restrictive nature of language will help make us better communicators because it will make us more cautious about the words we select.

The restrictiveness of our language affects how we view the world as well as our ability to accept change. Our category system is fragile and sensitive and requires constant attention—once a category becomes rigid, it is difficult to ever relax it again. We must recognize that we'll always need to alter our views to keep pace with changing conditions. Failure to update our views will cause us to become "stalled on the periphery of effectiveness as a communicator."[8]

Speaking for Your Self . . .

Words are an indispensable mechanism of our lives. As our experiences accumulate, our vocabulary increases in size and in richness in order to describe those experiences. Although we probably spend little time thinking about language, unless to briefly consider a grammatical point, it reflects the basic features of our personality. Just as we adjust to changes in the physical climate, we also adjust our selves to changes in the verbal climate. We go from one type of discourse to another, from one set of terms to another, from listening habits for one kind of occasion to another kind, all without conscious effort. But we hardly ever acknowledge the relationship the words have to our personality or, for that matter, to our mental health or well-being.[9]

One thing we may not have thought about is that we describe our selves in some kind of language—words, mental pictures, idealizations. These descriptions are fairly clear: "I am an extrovert," "I am efficient," "I am self-motivated," and so on. These statements are more or less accurate descriptions of what we think of our selves. This self-concept determines how we dress, how we behave, what tasks we undertake, and even whose society we seek.

The language we use to describe our selves may have a direct effect on our self-concept. What kinds of self-concepts might develop in children who grow up thinking of themselves, variously, as "colored," "nigger," "Negro," or "black"? These are just words but they have come to connote a great deal about personal identity. Richly connotative words often acquire power beyond themselves. Such words can both draw meaning from, and lend meaning to, a person's sense of self.

What we think of our selves is also affected by the society we live in, the groups we belong to, the people we associate with, the family we were raised in, even the religious experiences we have had. There is no way we can escape from the values our environment imparts. Even if we reject them, they have influenced us—we have taken some action because of them. Language is designed and modified to meet the changing requirements of different cultures. That's why language differs from culture to culture. What we are, or even can become, is reflected in the language of our culture.

Language also differs among subcultures. Think about some of the subcultures that exist in our society. There are religious sub-

TRY THIS

We don't always realize the influence that a person's name, alone, may have on other people's reactions. What is your first reaction to the following names?

1. **Jonathan**
2. **Bernard**
3. **James**
4. **Curtis**
5. **John**
6. **Darrell**
7. **Patrick**
8. **Donald**
9. **Craig**
10. **Gerald**
11. **Thomas**
12. **Horace**
13. **Gregory**
14. **Maurice**
15. **Richard**
16. **Jerome**
17. **Jeffrey**
18. **Roderick**

The names next to odd numbers were considered desirable and the names next to the even numbers were considered undesirable in a study done at Tulane University.[10] If it is true that some names are more desirable than others, think about the effect that a name may have on a person's self-concept. Think about the psychological effect on a person who has the same name as a famous person or that of a television character.

cultures, ethnic subcultures, geographic subcultures, each with its own special vocabulary. Subcultures may form on the basis of disciplines of study, interests, and needs as well. A dormitory may have a code of its own that identifies other residents of the same dorm. One teacher who lectured to massive groups of students would give each term's group of students a way to identify each other or him if they met on campus. Sometimes they would use a code phrase like "spring-eight" for the spring term of 1978. In each case, the lecturer formed a subculture and gave it a unique way to let everyone else in the subculture know he or she belonged to it. Language can be used, as in this instance, to define who is in the in-group and who is not.

It is because of the common interests, needs, and conditions of individuals in subcultures that sublanguages come into being. These sublanguages help members communicate with each other. The statement, "A Quartimax rotated factor matrix will have very high and very low loadings in each *row*,"[11] may sound like a foreign language, but to the subculture known as "behaviorists," it is not unusual at all. Besides letting members communicate with one another, sublanguages provide a sense of common identity, a means of identification, and a specialized vocabulary for members to describe more accurately those things that concern them. A member of the prison subculture might not call a prison guard a prison guard but, rather, a *screw, roach, hack, slave driver, shield,* or *holligan.*[12] And there could be nuances of meaning to these words not apparent to the outsider.

As the words of a sublanguage come into general use outside the subculture, they no longer serve the purposes they were designed for and are dropped. New words take their place. This is one way that new words enter our language. This is also one reason why we must be flexible, adaptable, and open.

As words of sublanguages come into general use, they can cause problems if everyone doesn't understand precisely what the words mean. The meanings of words used by subcultures may include nuances not readily understood by the outsider. If we recognize the diverse ways in which people of different subcultures communicate, and then think about the people of different *world* cultures, we begin to understand the possibilities for misunderstanding and conflict. Despite the tremendous potential for breakdowns in communication, some consensus and predictability *are* possible if we are alert and sensitive.

Language Affects Your Perceptions

If we label something "attractive" or "pleasant," we are already predisposed to perceive it in a certain way, probably with interest and enjoyment. If we think of someone in terms of how much we like him or her rather than how little we hate him or her, we will probably respond more favorably to that person. Language shapes our ideas—the labels we attach to things are likely to affect the attitudes we hold. Doesn't a weather forecast of "partly sunny" make you feel better than "partly cloudy"?

CONSIDER THIS "**Maybe a rose is the same by any other name, but not a kid with a name like Hubert or Bertha. An unconventional first name can be a real burden to a grade-school child, marking him among not only his friends but his teachers as well. His teacher may actually discriminate against him by giving him lower marks.**

That's the conclusion of a recent experiment among 80 elementary-school teachers in San Diego, California. The teachers were asked to grade eight compositions written by some fifth and sixth graders on "What I Did All Day Last Sunday." They were average essays, all judged in advance to be of about the same quality. The researchers simply removed the real authors' names and attributed the essays to eight fake names, four popular ones—David, Michael, Karen and Lisa—and four unpopular ones—Elmer, Hubert, Adelle and Bertha.

The results: Michael and David came out a full letter grade higher than Elmer and Hubert in the grading done by experienced teachers. Karen and Lisa scored 1.5 letter grades better than Bertha.

What's the explanation? Dr. Herbert Harari, a professor of psychology at California State University—who, along with Dr. John McDavid of Georgia State University, conducted the experiment—says: "The name is a label. Teachers know by experience that students, especially boys, with unusual names haven't been their best students. So when a Sanford or an Elmer or a Rufus comes along, they don't demand much from him." The whole thing becomes a "self-fulfilling prophecy."

"Because he's taunted, he reacts by becoming belligerent, aggressive and antagonistic toward his teachers—and he doesn't study," Dr. Harari claims.

In real life, however, a name like Hubert doesn't have to be a handicap for a plucky boy. Senator Hubert Humphrey, for example, went to school as "Pinky" and he did so well he became valedictorian of his high-school class. "My name has never been a problem to me," he says. In fact, so unburdensome did he find it that he named his son Hubert (called "Skip" at school). And at last report his grandson Hubert Horatio Humphrey IV was doing well in kindergarten."

—Marj Frazer Lacey, *McCall's*, February 1974

To show how labels affect our responses, think of the possible confusion that might result if the person we label "professor" was also the person we label "best friend." If we are not accustomed to responding to "professors" in the same way as "best friends," conflicts occur and perceptual adjustments must be made.

Think about a person who seems to have a negative attitude toward life. Can you recall any conversations you've had with this person? What kinds of words did he or she use? Bob, a person with a pessimistic attitude if ever there was one, tends to label things as being different degrees of "awful." His perceptions cannot help but be reinforced by this labeling. Bob cannot approach a person he has labeled "abusive" without fearing emotional or physical injury. Think how often we describe things as "not bad" when what we really mean is "great." Changing the labels we use to describe things sometimes is the first step toward changing our attitudes.

TRY THIS

Next time you watch television, pay special attention to the advertisements. Notice, especially, the "weasel" words—words that allow the advertiser to evade or retreat from any direct or forthright statement or position. Weasel words are not only a retreat or an evasion, they make you hear things that are not being said, accept as truths things that have only been implied, or believe things that have only been suggested. How many of the following weasel words can you find in advertisements?

1. Help**—as in aid or assist. Examples: "Brand X** helps **keep you young." "Brand A** helps **prevent cavities."**

2. Like**—as used in comparison. Examples: It's** like **getting one bar free." "Cleans** like **a white tornado."**

3. Virtual **or** virtually**—meaning essentially, but not in fact. Examples:** "Virtually **trouble-free."** "Virtually **foolproof."**

4. Acts **or** works**—as used to bring action to a product. Example:** "Works **like new."**

Examples abound of how language shapes the way we perceive things. In a grocery store, labeling techniques can trick us into thinking an item is "first" or "A-number-one" when it is really a third- or fourth-quality item. How, for example, is a shopper supposed to identify different grades of beef? Jennifer Cross, in *The Supermarket Trap,* explains the dilemma:

> The fact is that "Blogg's Blue Ribbon-Gold Ribbon-Gourmet-Good-Better-Best" has no objective meaning at all. It bears no relation to any U.S. Department of Agriculture meat grade, though in high quality stores "Blogg's Finest" is mostly choice, and occasionally prime. Elsewhere it could be choice, or even a lower grade like good or standard.[13]

The problem is in identifying different levels of quality without making one level appear to be inferior.[14] When we buy "U.S. No. 1" fresh fruits and vegetables or "U.S. Grade A" butter, we are getting second grade, because "U.S. Fancy" is first grade for most fruits and vegetables and "U.S. Grade AA" is first for butter. When we buy "U.S. Extra" nonfat dry milk we get first grade but "U.S. Extra" dry whole milk is second grade, and "U.S. Extra No. 1" in cucumbers or peaches is also second grade.[15]

When we purchase clothes, we want labels that make us feel comfortable or good about our selves. We want a "Fine Linen Handkerchief," not a "Nose Rag." Schools that came under fire when they offered courses in "Sex Education" received fewer protests when the same material was taught as "Social Hygiene" or "Family Health." At work, most people will try much harder and be much happier if they have a title. Think how much more motivated you would be if you were called an "assistant manager" as opposed to a "sales clerk," or in a theater, a "ticket-taker."[16] Ever wonder why large corporations

5. Can be—**as used to indicate an ideal situation. Example: "Brand Y** can be **of significant value when used in . . ."**

6. Feel **or** the feel of—**as used to imply that it is a matter of opinion. Example: "So-and-so has** the feel of **real leather."**

For more examples and further explanation, see Carl P. Wrighter, I Can Sell You Anything **(New York: Ballantine Books, 1972), pp. 23–25. Can you find other weasel words not mentioned above?**

have so many vice presidents? The difference between "Vice President in Charge of Widgets" and "Widget Director" may sound slight to an outsider, but it can make a great difference to those involved. The way things are labeled leads us to respond to them in a certain way.

IMPROVING SKILLS IN LANGUAGE

A word is simply a vehicle we use to produce a certain response in another person. If our words do not accomplish their mission, we say there is a breakdown in communication. There is no guarantee that our language will produce the responses we want even if we apply all the suggestions mentioned here. Interpersonal communication can never be perfect. But learning language skills can help us move closer to the goal of effective, efficient communication. It will increase the chances for our success.

Make the message complete. Because there are so many ways for words to be misinterpreted, we must try to give listeners as much information as possible about our ideas, experiences, feelings, and perceptions so that they will know where *we* are coming from. There should be enough information so the other person can understand

our frame of reference. But don't go too far! Too much information can create a negative effect. We would very likely bore or overwhelm our listener with more details than are necessary or manageable.

Our message will be more complete if we repeat the message with some variation; that is, if we add details to the original message that make it more accurate. If the listener does not "get it" one way, he or she will have another chance the second time with the added information. To simply restate a misunderstood word or phrase in precisely the same way does not serve the listener's purposes and perpetuates confusion. What we want to make sure of is that our message is as complete and "on the mark" as possible.

Remember that meanings are in people. If we're going to use abstract language, it's extra important to monitor the reception of our messages to see that they are getting through. It often helps to move to a lower level of abstraction. Remember that as we talk we tend to project meanings into words just as much as our listener does. These projections are the result of our own experiences. The higher the level of abstraction, the more we must deal with our own and our listeners' connotations for words. If we remember that meanings are in people, not in words, we'll have a better chance of avoiding error and confusion. What another person brings to a word is usually more important than the word itself.

Stereotyping can also create breakdowns. Developing a sensitivity to labeling will help us avoid some of it. More importantly, it will help us to be conscious of labels used by others. We can't control what other people think when they either use stereotypes themselves or hear ours. But rather than take a chance that we hold the same stereotypes, we should try to avoid generalizations. Be specific and concrete instead.

It is impossible to know everything about anything. The mental picture we get of this world is incomplete; no matter how we describe the world, there will be distortion. To say that we "know all that" or that we "understand completely" is not recognizing that our picture of reality is partial. Too often we operate as if we know all the facts, and what's more, as if others see the facts as we do.

Talk the same language. If we can comfortably and naturally use words, including slang and jargon, that our listener understands, so much the better. If we adapt our language to the listener, very specifically, we will show concern for him or her—an attempt at genuine communication to reach honest understanding. But to litter our speech with fancy words, "cute" phrases, or inappropriate slang will do little to help create understanding (and can make us look ridiculous and phony).

There is nothing "wrong" with any word that we have in our vocabulary or that occurs in any dictionary. Words are only "wrong" if they are used inappropriately. We might not talk to our roommate as we do to our parents; the language we use with our roommate may be inappropriate for our parents. We may have all kinds of names and profanities we use for a teacher who seems to be doing us in, but we reserve them for our friends or for our selves, not the teacher. There are ways other than name-calling to express our dislike to the teacher. It would serve a negative purpose to use abusive language with the teacher; it would be "wrong" in that context.

To use different language in different contexts and with different people is not necessarily deceptive or hypocritical. Some language

You owe it to yourself to learn Hash House Greek, the peculiar American lunch-counter cant. It varies from town to town and even from diner to diner, but there are certain widely used numbers, words and phrases that can help you survive in the world of paper-napkin dispensers on the counter.

ADAM AND EVE ON A RAFT. Two poached eggs on toast.

BLOOD. Cherry flavoring: stretch one, let it bleed (or make it bloody) means a cherry Coke. Also refers to rare meat: a bloody burger is a rare hamburger.

BURN IT or BURNED. Well done.

DOWN. Toasted, as in BLT down. Also used as a noun, as in an order of down, smeared which means buttered toast.

HAIL. Ice. Hold the hail means without ice.

LET IT WALK. The order is to be taken out, to go.

SIDE. A side order that costs extra. A side of French means French fried potatoes in addition.

STACK. Hot cakes, as in a stack of wheat (which means wheat cakes); toast, as in a buttered stack; ice cream in a dish, as in a stack of van (a scoop of vanilla ice cream in a dish).

WRECK 'EM. Of eggs, scramble them, as in WRECK A PAIR.

—Dan Carlinsky, *Chicago Daily News*, August 9–10, 1975

may be more appropriate for a casual party with a group of friends, some language is better suited for dinner with our future mother-in-law. Hypocrisy and deceit do result from using language that is not our own, language that reflects a character or beliefs and principles that we do not really possess. We are being hypocritical when we try to appear as we are not or try to present a facade, when we are no longer adapting our language to the context in an honest manner. It is deceptive to manipulate others by using language that misrepresents who we really are.

Be flexible. Stereotyping paints an unrealistically black-or-white world because things either fit our categories or they do not. If we say, "Teachers are too tough," meaning *all* teachers are too tough, we

"I must say since we learned to talk, how well you express yourself in a crystalline and often aphoristic manner."

haven't allowed for variations among teachers. Statements like "Blondes have more fun" or "Professors are absent-minded" apply evaluations indiscriminately. If we think in terms of what is unique to a person or a situation, our language will become more accurate and flexible.

We increase our flexibility if we avoid extreme language. If we say, "I am totally happy," we allow no room for increased happiness. Happiness is seldom total, just as success and failure most often occur in degrees. Saying "I am a complete failure" is a rigid, inflexible response.

True, there are some things that *do* appear to be either-or, such as whether a woman is pregnant or not, whether we are here or somewhere else, or whether or not there is another person in the room with us right now. We can describe these things in black-or-white terms. But generally we tend to be too rigid rather than too flexible in our use of language.

It's a good idea to think in terms of "sometimes," "possibly," "normally," and "now and then." Such words as "always," "never," "all," and "none" can cause problems. "Allness" language makes us tend to think in set, rigid patterns. And in doing so, not only do we fail to distinguish what is unique in each case, but we do not allow for change.

Get others involved. If we assume that our communication has a good chance of being *un*successful and if we accept the fact that misunderstanding is *likely* to occur, we will be more cautious in our use of words. It will help if we can get others to share in our frame of reference. Ask your listeners what they think about what you have said. It is very easy to overwhelm another person with a verbal barrage and not realize we have caused that person to withdraw or become defensive. Saying "Do you understand?" or "You *do* see what I mean?" can seem accusatory or severe. But asking "Am I making sense?" or, simply, "What do you think?" involves the listener and can help us find out whether we really have been understood.

Using words well is not as simple as it might first appear. Trying to put our finger on the problems of using words is hard because so much depends on the users of the words and the contexts in which they are used. And we have to use words even to describe the problems of using words! There's no way around it. Even if we understood all about users and contexts, we wouldn't have all the answers because things would change. Words, we have seen, are flexible in meaning. Our effectiveness in using them depends upon our understanding how they can vary depending on different communication contexts.

Verbal communication has a tremendous impact on interpersonal relationships. Verbalizing our feelings can help us feel better about our selves and can strengthen our interpersonal interactions. Although verbal communication is important, it makes up only a fraction of our total communication with others. We communicate at least as much through nonverbal means as through verbal means, as we will see in the next chapter.

OTHER READING

Robert L. Benjamin, *Semantics and Language Analysis* (Indianapolis, Ind.: The Bobbs-Merrill Company, Inc., 1970). In this introductory textbook on language, the author examines *how* language, sentences, and words mean. He looks at the language of value, and, finally, offers the reader suggestions for clarifying language. This is a brief, readable approach.

Stuart Chase, *The Power of Words* (New York: Harcourt, Brace and Company, 1953). Enjoyable reading. A useful introduction to general semantics for the beginning student of language. An excellent place to begin.

Rudolf Flesch, *The Art of Plain Talk* (New York: Collier Books, 1951). Although over 25 years old, the need for this book is as great today as ever. Plain talk is colorful, precise, and easy to understand. This is a handbook that will help readers get across what they want to say.

S. I. Hayakawa, *Language in Thought and Action*, 3rd ed. (New York: Harcourt Brace Jovanovich, Inc., 1972). Semantics is the study of human interaction through communication. This is a study of semantics based on the assumption that cooperation is preferable to conflict. The principles explained here relate to thinking, speaking, writing, and behavior. Challenges are provided for undertaking actual semantic investigations and exercises.

Edwin Newman, *Strictly Speaking: Will America Be the Death of English?* (Indianapolis: The Bobbs-Merrill Company, Inc., 1974). Newman's underlying argument is that if words are devalued, so are ideas and so are human beings. This is an entertaining examination of the state of the English language.

Edwin Newman, *A Civil Tongue* (Indianapolis, Ind.: The Bobbs-Merrill Company, Inc., 1976). As in *Strictly Speaking*, in this book Newman supplies examples that prove we receive a smog of jargon from the press, television, schools, business, politics, advertising, public relations, military, and bureaucracy. He makes a plea to us all not to accept nonsense and to speak plainly.

Neil Postman, *Crazy Talk, Stupid Talk: How We Defeat Ourselves by the Way We Talk—and What to Do About It* (New York: Delacorte Press, 1976). An examination of talk that does not work (stupid talk) and talk that promotes purposes that are unreasonable, trivial, or evil (crazy talk). Written in down-to-earth, straightforward language.

NOTES

[1] S. Chase, *Power of Words* (New York: Harcourt Brace Jovanovich, 1954), p. 3.

[2] For their ideas on characteristics of language, see Kim Giffin and Bobby R. Patton, *Fundamentals of Interpersonal Communication*, 2nd ed. (New York: Harper & Row, Publishers, 1976), pp. 161–172.

[3] Ibid., p. 161.

[4] C. K. Ogden and I. A. Richards, *The Meaning of Meaning* (New York: Harcourt, Brace and Co., Inc., 1953).

[5] For the discussion on levels of abstraction I am indebted to S. I. Hayakawa, *Language in Thought and Action*, 3rd ed. (New York: Harcourt Brace Jovanovich, Inc., 1972), pp. 150–154.

[6] From *Language in Thought and Action*, Third Edition, by S. I. Hayakawa, copyright © 1972 by Harcourt Brace Jovanovich, Inc. Reproduced by permission of Harcourt Brace Jovanovich, Inc. and George Allen & Unwin Ltd. "The Abstraction Ladder" is based on a diagram originated by Alfred Korzybski to explain the process of abstracting. See Alfred Korzybski, *Science and Sanity: An Introduction to Non-Aristotelian Systems and General Semantics* (Lancaster, Pa.: Science Press Printing Company, 1933) especially chapter 25.

[7] Virginia Satir, *Conjoint Family Therapy* (Palo Alto, Calif.: Science and Behavior, 1968), pp. 65–70.

[8] Richard C. Huseman, James M. Lahiff, and John D. Hatfield, *Interpersonal Communication in Organizations: A Perceptual Approach* (Boston: Holbrook Press, Inc., 1976), p. 61.

[9] Hayakawa, *Language in Thought and Action*, pp. 8–17.

[10] In a study by S. Gray Garwood, reported in "The Importance of Not Being Ernestine or Egbert or Elmo or Beulah or Percival . . . ," *Detroit Free Press*, December 5, 1976, pp. 13–14 of the "Detroit" section.

[11] Gary Cronkhite and Jo Liska, "A Critique of Factor Analytic Approaches to the Study of Credibility," *Communication Monographs* 43 (June 1976), 101.

[12] See Joseph A. DeVito, *The Interpersonal Communication Book* (New York: Harper & Row, Publishers, 1976), pp. 242–246.

[13] From *The Supermarket Trap* by Jennifer Cross. (Bloomington: Indiana University Press, 1970), p. 75.

[14] Raymond Loewy Associates, *Super Market of the Sixties* (Chicago: Super Market Institute, 1960), p. 29.

[15] Cross, *The Supermarket Trap*, pp. 210–211.

[16] Ron Adler and Neil Towne, *Looking Out/Looking In: Interpersonal Communication* (San Francisco: Rinehart Press, 1975), pp. 277–279.

Chapter 6

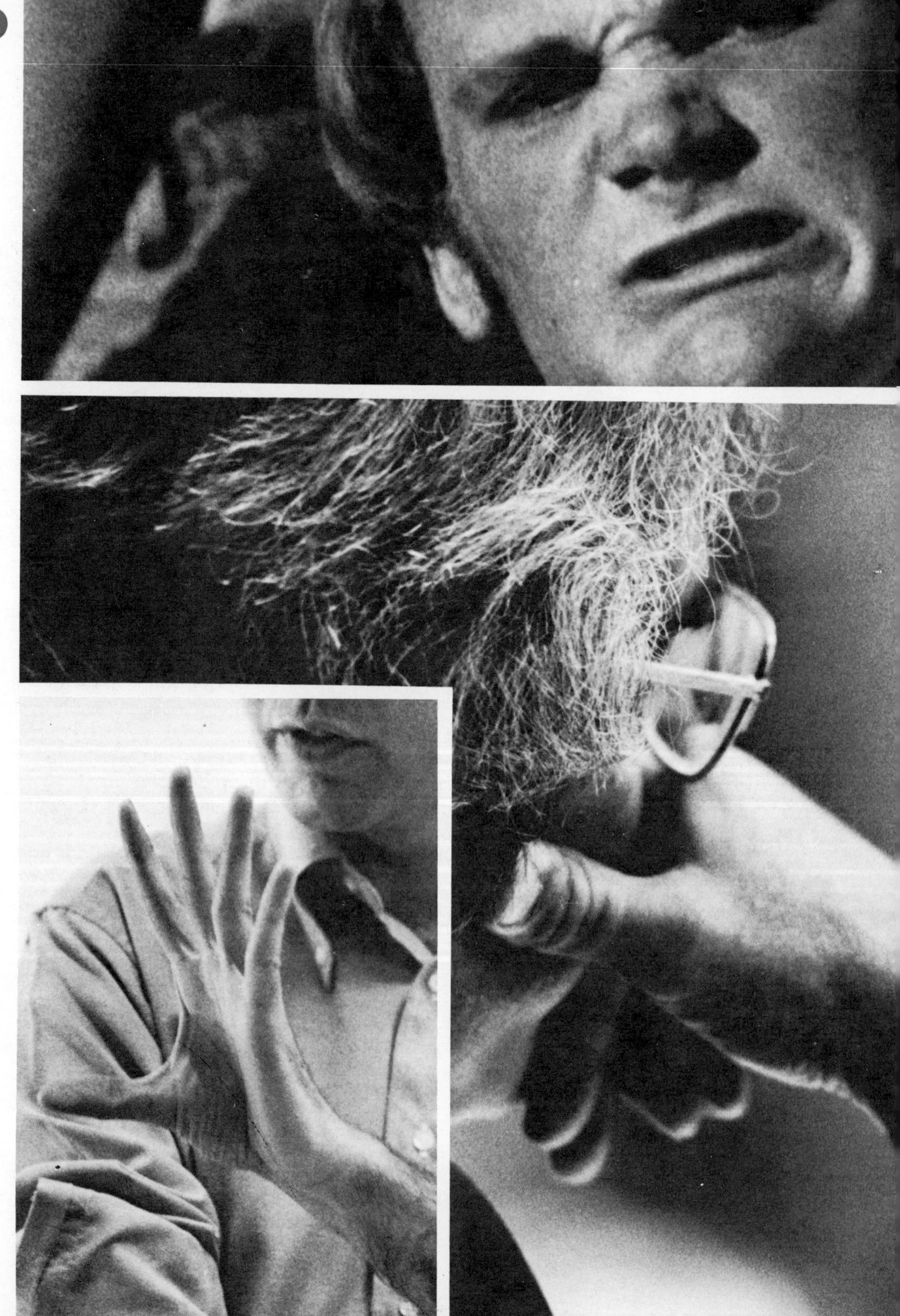

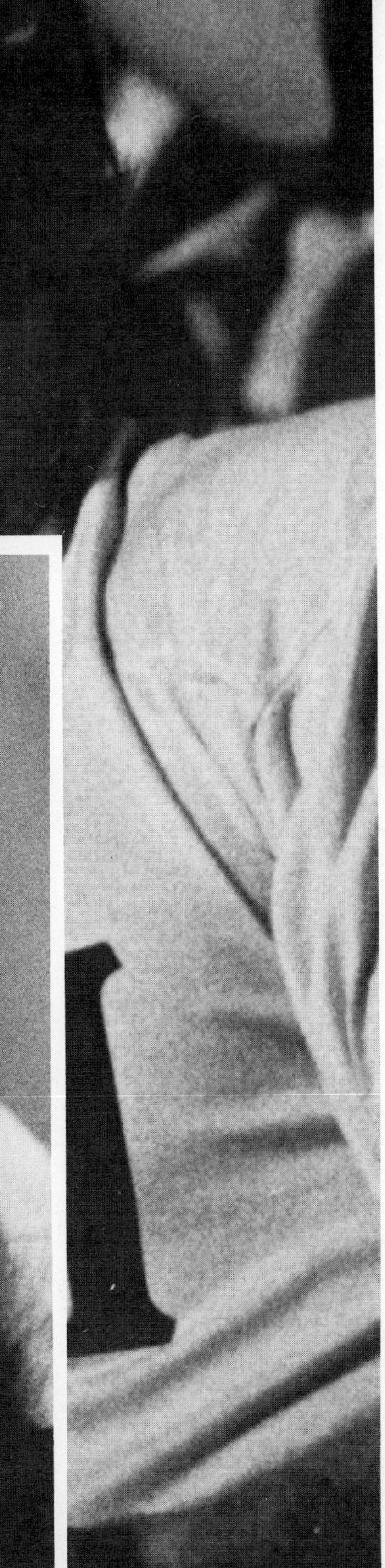

Communicating Without Words: Nonverbal Communication

Have you ever been in a public place and discovered someone was staring at you? You look away, but just to test your perceptions you look back at the person. "I wonder why he's staring at me," you think. You look away again, hoping his gaze will shift. This time when you look back at him, you do it quickly. If he continues to stare, you might become uncomfortable, angry, or even alarmed.

The direct, unwavering stare is a form of threat; it is an example of nonverbal communication.[1] Its meaning is clear and no words are necessary to drive the effect home. Too much eye contact, as with the unwavering stare, can serve to heighten intimacy, to express and intensify emotions, and in some cases to indicate possible sexual interest. What does it mean to "give someone the eye"? Americans often interpret prolonged eye contact as an indication of sexual attraction. You may have noticed a man give a woman a steady, challenging stare, with that stare followed by the woman lowering her eyes.[2] A great deal has been communicated without a word being spoken. Communicating without words is the subject of this chapter.

In this chapter I'm going to look at all the different ways we say things without using words. I'll discuss how our nonverbal communication conveys certain things better than verbal communication can—sometimes we reveal more about our selves than we may even want to! "Body language" is part of it. Vocal cues and spatial cues are just as important. Nonverbal language is not a precise language; we have to be careful we don't misinterpret nonverbal signals in our eagerness to understand what a person means by wearing those shoes or nodding that way or standing so close to us. But while we're not dealing with an exact science here, we can learn to send and interpret nonverbal messages in a way that enhances the total meaning exchanged in any communication.

THE RULES OF THE GAME

The stare is quite unusual in our society because of the connotations attached to it and because it is really opposite to the kind of behavior we have been programmed to accept. In the example just mentioned, the accepted rules require the woman to look away or lower her eyes. If she aggressively stares back or smiles or winks, the man might be pleased or frightened, but he would definitely know the usual rules were not in effect.

To be stared at is an invasion of privacy and can make us very uncomfortable. To be caught staring is an embarrassment. We've probably all at some time quickly looked away from someone we were staring at and pretended to be studying the clock or just the wall above the person's head. Erving Goffman, a sociologist who has investigated the behavior of human beings in public places, states that Americans meet one another with "civil inattention." Goffman means that we take enough visual notice of others to let them know that we know that they are there, but not enough notice to seem curious or to intrude.[3]

You may take offense at the phrase "behavior we have been programmed to accept;" we don't like to think we are predictable. But our culture does program us from childhood, teaching us what to do with our eyes and what to expect of other people. Think of what happens when we shift our eyes to look away from another person's gaze. We produce a response that is out of all proportion to the small muscular effort we made.[4] The response is somewhat predictable since we both know what we mean by our eye contact—the response may be one of anger or hurt if it is a friend we have chosen to look away from. It is amazing that such small muscular effort can arouse strong feelings!

Do you recall one of your parents or teachers ever admonishing you to "take that look off your face"? The slightest suggestion of a smile at an inappropriate time can draw a lot of attention! It's the same with eye movements and physical touching and other forms of nonverbal communication. We all know what it is to share an inside joke with a friend and to express our understanding of the joke with a timely nudge when other kinds of communication would be out of place. That nudge can say a great deal, considering how little effort we put into it. Nonverbal messages are like that; they can pack a lot of meaning into otherwise small looks and gestures.

All nonverbal communication is influenced by a variety of factors—our personality, the situations we are in, the attitudes we hold toward people, the pecking order we maintain with others, our cultural upbringing. Nonverbal components almost always operate in conjunction with each other. At the same time we are establishing eye contact, for example, we are also dealing with the nonverbal variables of facial expressions, gestures, and larger movements. We draw conclusions from numerous nonverbal signals at the same time and we do it very quickly. Whether accurate or inaccurate, we seldom have time to check. We respond hoping that we have perceived accurately and hoping, too, that we'll get further cues.

THE IMPORTANCE OF NONVERBAL COMMUNICATION

Communication researchers have shown that the words themselves carry only a small part of the information exchanged between people when they talk. In fact, it has been estimated that in face-to-face interaction, over ninety percent of the message we perceive is nonverbal, the rest being verbal.[5] It is easy to slip into the error of thinking that *all* communication must be verbal. But even when we think we are not consciously sending or receiving nonverbal messages, their influence is present and it is significant.

It Is Continuous

The more we think about nonverbal communication, the more we see how true it is that we cannot *not* communicate. Words come one at a time, but nonverbal cues come continuously. Several, even many, may exist and are perceived at the same time. All these nonverbal signals are used as a foundation for understanding the words. Nonverbal cues can be sent slowly or quickly, while words become distorted if spoken too slowly or too rapidly. We send *and* receive nonverbal messages in an uninterrupted, persistent, flow. All the time we are observing someone else's gestures and mannerisms, that person may also be observing ours.

It Conveys Emotions

When you think of it, objects and actions can generate more emotions than words because objects and actions are less abstract than words. To hear that someone cried or was injured is not nearly as powerful as seeing that person cry or get hurt. Words usually exert more of an intellectual appeal. If we want to convey sincerity, our facial and bodily gestures can probably do it better than our words, although words *reinforced* by nonverbal cues will convey the most unmistakable message.

Since nonverbal cues are so closely tied to the emotions, how well we understand nonverbal messages depends on how empathic we are. Everything I said earlier about empathic listening applies here as well. The empathic, alert perceiver will very likely understand (or at least be aware of) nonverbal cues. To understand verbal expression requires more skill. Nonverbal expression, learned much earlier and often closely tied to universal human emotions, is sometimes easier to attach meaning to, even though that meaning may be less than perfectly accurate.

It Is Rich in Meaning

Think of the last time you went to the doctor when you had certain symptoms but did not know what your illness was. You probably watched the doctor's face very carefully to see if you could detect how sick you really were. Ambiguous looks or "hmm-m-m" noises from the doctor could really make you uneasy. "My goodness, I'm dying!" you might think. In such situations, we look for even the most minute nonverbal signs to interpret.

Consider how the slightest sound or the most delicate movement can be fraught with meaning. Put these sounds and movements together into the larger context in which they occur and you realize how rich nonverbal communication can be. A raised eyebrow, a sly smile, a touch of the hand, can all say a lot in the right circumstances. Such nonverbal cues are especially useful when for some reason oral or written communication is inappropriate—during a concert or a lecture, perhaps, or even a movie. Nonverbal communication can be rich with meaning.

It Can Be Confusing

Although nonverbal communication may be rich with meaning, it can also be confusing. Certain cues may mean something entirely different than what we imagine. A man may be sitting on a sofa next to a woman with his legs crossed away from the woman. "Ahh-ha, obviously he has no interest in her, since his legs are crossed away from her," the enthusiastic reader of body language might think. "He is excluding her." Not necessarily. Some people *always* cross their legs right over left, no matter what. It's their habit, it's comfortable, and it doesn't mean a thing as far as nonverbal communication goes (except perhaps that they feel comfortable).

We can't assume that a woman with her arms folded in front of her is closed-minded and rigid—she may simply feel cold! We must be careful in interpreting nonverbal cues because they can be confusing. We do not always have enough information to make a judgment, and our guesses may be far from accurate.

DO YOUR ACTIONS MATCH YOUR WORDS?

One of the best and most logical ways to check our interpretation of somebody's nonverbal message is through that person's words. He or she might say, "I like you" or "You are a wonderful person to be with," confirming eye contact that seemed affectionate. But it's rare that people come right out and express their feelings so directly. Usually we have to pay attention to more subtle verbal cues. What we should watch for is whether there is congruency between act and word. Do this person's words match whatever he or she is doing? When there is congruency, it makes it easy for us because we can be surer of our interpretations. When there is incongruency, we either try to get more information, we suspend judgment, or we tend to believe either what we hear *or* what we see.

Nonverbal and verbal communication usually work together, even if not congruently.[6]

A nonverbal message may *repeat* what we say, reinforcing it. For example, it reinforces our message when we wave and say "good-by" at the same time. Nonverbal *replaces* verbal when we wave without saying "good-by" or when we nod in agreement to indicate "yes." Nonverbal communication may *underscore* the verbal portion of a message much the way italics strengthen the written word; leaning toward another person with concern reinforces "Tell me about it."

CONSIDER THIS

"We asked several people to act out six different moods on videotape. The moods were anger, fear, seductivity, indifference, happiness and sadness. Then we let our subjects review their portrayals and eliminate any that they felt were unrepresentative. The chosen portrayals, in other words, were emotionally authentic in the eyes of their creators.

When we played these videotapes to large audiences to discover if they could decode the moods intended, we found that most senders were able to project accurately only two **of the six moods. The particular moods, of course, varied from sender to sender, but in general we were surprised to learn that everyone appears to send out misinformation. Their portrayals often failed to represent their intentions. This finding lent strength to the hypothesis that the discordance between our emotional expressions and our intentions may represent conflicting impulses. It is possible, admittedly, that our audiences were unusually poor judges of nonverbal behavior; our senders, moreover, may have been better actors in less artificial settings. But at least we found evidence for the notion that there are many people whose emotional intentions and self-images are out of harmony with their actual behavior.**

I shall never forget two examples of this discordance. One girl, who tried like everyone else to appear angry, fearful, seductive, indifferent, happy and sad—and who subsequently edited her own performances for authenticity—appeared to her judges as angry in every case. Imagine what a difficult world she must have lived in. No matter where she set the thermostat of her emotional climate, everyone else always felt it as sweltering hot. Another girl in our experiment demonstrated a similar one-dimensionality; only in her case, whatever else she thought she was doing, she invariably impressed her judges as seductive. Even when she wanted to be angry, men whistled at her."

—Ernst G. Beier, *Psychology Today*, October 1974

Nonverbal behavior may *regulate* behavior, too. We often can tell when it is our turn to speak in a conversation through a nonverbal cue: the other person nods his or her head, changes position, or establishes strong eye contact with us. Similarly, we may show we wish to speak in a discussion group by leaning forward or suddenly looking very attentive—in so doing, we regulate the behavior of other people in the group to some extent. Finally, a nonverbal message can *contradict* the verbal message. We rarely send this kind of contradictory communication on purpose. Perhaps the most common example is when we look "down in the dumps" and someone asks us what's wrong and we reply, "Nothing." Albert Mehrabian suggests that when a person's actions and words contradict each other, we rely more on his or her actions to reveal true feelings.[7]

FORMS OF NONVERBAL COMMUNICATION

Nonverbal elements sometimes work separately from verbal communication; that is, we may receive a nonverbal message without any words whatsoever. The nonverbal component, in this case, is the entire message. But usually the nonverbal domain provides a framework for the words we use. If we think of nonverbal communication as including all forms of message transmission *not* represented by word symbols, we can divide it into the broad categories of sign language, action language, and object language.[8] These categories were first developed by Jurgen Ruesch, an early researcher in nonverbal communication.[9]

Sign Language

When we nod to signify agreement, when we shake a finger at someone as a threat, or when we raise our thumb to try to hitchhike, we are using a gesture in place of a word. If someone asks, "How many cards do you have?" and we show five fingers, we are using a gesture to replace a number—sign language. A smile is a form of sign language. If we pound our fist on the table at the end of a sentence, we are using sign language to show exclamation; we are using a gesture as a punctuation mark. Gestures used as sign language are generally unambiguous and readily understood.

Action Language

Have you ever thought much about the way you walk? When we are in a hurry or have an important appointment, our posture, motion, and pace reveal our excitement. If our mood, on the other hand, is sullen and blue—if we're worried about an exam we're not prepared for or a meeting we've been dreading—our posture, motion, and pace will reveal our concern.

Notice how much you can tell about someone's mood from observing his or her body movements. Although actions like walking and drinking are primarily functional activities, they also provide a kind of statement to others. Ruesch included such statements, even when unintended, in his category of action language. Intentional statements are just as common and they, too, are action language. We may intentionally stand near to someone at a party to show loyalty and affection for that person. We are making a nonverbal statement with action language.

Object Language

Think about what you are wearing right now—your hairstyle, glasses, jewelry, or other items. What do these things reveal about you? Ruesch labels as object language the statements we make with the books we carry, the car we drive, the clothes we wear, the furniture we have in our room. Whether we mean them to or not, these items transmit cues to observers. Our clothes, for example, will always reveal something about us. Even what we may consider a perfectly neutral set of clothes—jeans and a sweater, perhaps—says something about us, if only that we do not want our clothes to attract attention. Such statements made with *things* are object language.

TRY THIS

Classify each of the following into sign, action, or object language:

1. You jump out of bed in the morning.

2. You put on your best sweater.

3. You shake your head because your roommate borrowed the shoes that you wanted to wear today.

4. You storm out of the room slamming the door furiously.

5. You see your roommate in the cafeteria and shake your fist in anger.

6. You grab your books, walk slowly out of the building drooping with frustration.

Based on your own experience, is any one of these types of nonverbal communication more effective than any other in expressing how you really feel?

TYPES OF NONVERBAL CUES

Let's look more closely at these cues that tell others about us or that tell us about them. Our own self-awareness and empathic skills will increase as we become more sensitive to these different kinds of nonverbal cues. The broader our base for understanding, the more likely we are to have meaning for the cues we perceive. But we know that nonverbal communication can be ambiguous and we must be careful not to overgeneralize from the behavior we observe. We may feel hurt by the listless "hi" we receive from a good friend unless we remember that that listlessness could have been brought on by a headache, lack of sleep, preoccupation, or some other factor we don't know about. We would be unwise to assume we are being personally rejected if this friend doesn't smile and stop to talk with us every single morning.

We should always be alert to *all* cues and try to get as much information as possible on which to base our conclusions. One way to organize our thinking about nonverbal communication is to think in terms of spatial cues, visual cues, and vocal cues. In considering each of these, we should not overlook the fact that any communication occurs in a specific environmental setting. This setting will influence much of the nonverbal interaction that takes place. The weather can affect how we behave just as much as our actual setting—cafeteria, classroom, car, park bench, or whatever.

Spatial Cues

Everywhere we go we carry with us an area of personal space or territory—think of it as a bubble. As we speak with others, we protect this bubble, more or less. We tend to communicate with people at pretty much the same, fixed distance all the time. With good friends we are less concerned with preserving this bubble of space. Depending on the person we're with and the message we're exchanging, we may not guard our personal territory at all. Edward T. Hall, an anthropologist, has identified distances that we assume depending on the type of message we are sharing. He calls these distances intimate, personal, social, and public.[10]

TRY THIS

Would you like to know the size of "bubble" that a friend of yours carries around as his or her "personal space"? The next time you are involved in a conversation with your friend, get into a position where you are directly facing each other and there is nothing behind him or her. Then, as you talk, slowly inch closer and closer. As you infringe on the "bubble," your friend may begin to move backward. As the movement just begins, notice the size of the "personal space" that your friend is protecting. To test your perception of the size of the "bubble," slowly move closer yet. What distance did you find most comfortable for a casual conversation?

Intimate distance. At an intimate distance (0 to 18 inches), we often use a soft or barely audible whisper to share intimate or confidential information. Physical contact becomes easy at this distance. This is the distance we use for physical comforting, lovemaking, and physical fighting, among other things. At this distance, all of our senses can be activated—sight, scent, touch, sound, and even taste. Interestingly, we are forced in some situations to be with strangers at this intimate distance, in crowded buses or elevators, for example. At this range, sounds are intensified and even vision may be slightly distorted. However, vocalizations are minimal since most conversation need not be loud to be heard at this distance. The whisper can bring the participants closer together, reinforcing the psychological need to use this intimate distance even more.

Personal distance. Hall identified the range of 18 inches to 4 feet as "personal distance." When we disclose our selves to someone, we are likely to do it within this distance. The topics we discuss at this range may be more or less confidential, and usually are personal and mutually involving. At personal distance we are still able to touch each other if we want to. This is likely to be the distance between people conversing at a party, between classmates in a casual conversation, or within many work relationships. This distance assumes a well-established acquaintanceship. This is probably the most comfortable distance for free exchange of feedback.

Social distance. When we are talking at a normal level with another person, sharing concerns that are not of a personal nature, we usually use the social distance (4 to 12 feet). Many of our on-the-job conversations take place at this distance. Seating arrangements in living rooms may be based on "conversation groups" of chairs placed at a distance of 4 to 7 feet from each other. Hall calls 4 to 7 feet the close phase of social distance; from 7 to 12 feet, it is known as the far phase of social distance.

The greater the distance, the more formal the business or social discourse conducted is likely to be. Often, the desks of important people are broad enough to hold visitors at a distance of 7 to 12 feet. Eye contact at this distance becomes more important to the flow of communication; without visual contact one party will likely feel shut out and the conversation may come to a halt.

Public distance. Public distance (12 feet and farther) is well outside the range for close involvement with another person. It is impractical for interpersonal communication. Our senses are limited to seeing and hearing; topics for conversation are relatively impersonal and formal; and most of the communication that occurs is in the public-speaking style, with subjects planned in advance and limited feedback opportunities.

The important point regarding intimate, personal, and public distance is that space communicates. Our sense of what distance is natural for us for a specific kind of interaction is deeply ingrained in us by our culture. We automatically make spatial adjustments and interpret spatial cues. Can you imagine, for example, talking to one of your professors at the intimate distance? What would your most intimate friend say if you maintained the social distance for an entire evening? Try talking to people you interact with daily at a public distance. To be aware of how we and other people use space will improve our communication.

CONSIDER THIS

In an effort to force the British to give up Gibraltar, Spain has sealed its border with the peninsula—thereby dividing families and disrupting Gibraltar's commerce. But the people of Gibraltar, ever loyal to England, have learned to carry on.

Every Monday at 1:30 p.m., Frances Viagas goes down to the Frontier Fence and shouts at her mother.

It is a surrealistic family get-together, a gossip between a mother and daughter separated by iron gates, barbed wire, and 150 yards of no-man's land. They carry on their chat at the tops of their lungs while the police and soldiers of two nations listen in.

Visual Cues

Greater visibility increases our potential for communicating because the more we see and the more we can be seen, the more information we can send and receive. Mehrabian found that the more we direct our face toward the person we're talking to, the more we convey a positive feeling to this person.[11] Another researcher has confirmed something most of us discovered long ago, that looking directly at a

On one such Monday, Mrs. Viagas, standing in Gibraltar and squinting through binoculars, screams out news of the children. Her mother, Mrs. Josefa Morales, stands in Spain and shrieks back a wish that Frances would come see her. Mrs. Viagas shouts that she'll try. Both women know that the roundabout trip between their two homes, about a mile apart, will cost $100. . . .

So they come down to the Frontier Fence, each family at its allotted time. They bring the kids, and there usually is a lot of laughing and joshing, seldom tears; human beings, it seems, can get used to anything. On weekends, there may be up to 50 families on each side, screaming across the barrier and peering through binoculars in the glaring sun, trying to pick out relatives in the distance. The Gibraltarians claim to have trained themselves not to eavesdrop on people who may be roaring intimacies at their side.

—R. C. Longworth, *Chicago Tribune Magazine,* March 6, 1977

person, smiling, and leaning toward him or her conveys a feeling of warmth.[12]

When we look at someone, we get a total impression; we are reading numerous cues at the same time. Often the combination of cues provides the information, not a single cue by itself. As you think about the following types of visual cues, remember that we may discuss them separately but we send and receive all kinds of cues at the same time.

Facial expression. The face is probably the most expressive part of the human body. It can reveal complex and often confusing kinds of information. It commands attention because it is visible and omnipresent. It can move from signs of ecstasy to signs of despair within a matter of seconds. Research suggests that there are ten basic classes of meaning that can be communicated facially: happiness, surprise, fear, anger, sadness, disgust, contempt, interest, bewilderment, and determination.[13] Research has also shown that the face may communicate information other than the emotional state of the person—it may reveal his or her thought processes as well.[14] In addition, it has been shown that we are capable of facially conveying multiple emotions at the same time, not just a single emotional state.[15]

The face can communicate more emotional meanings more accurately than any other factor in our interpersonal communication. Dale G. Leathers has determined that the face:

1. Communicates *evaluative* judgments through pleasant and unpleasant expressions;
2. Reveals level of *interest* or lack of interest in others and in the environment;
3. Can exhibit level of *intensity* and thus show how involved we are in a situation;
4. Communicates the amount of *control* we have over our own expressions; and
5. Shows whether we *understand* something or not.[16]

Because faces are so visible and so sensitive, we pay more attention to people's faces than to any other nonverbal feature. The face is an efficient and high-speed means of conveying meaning. Gestures, posture, and larger bodily movements require some time to change in response to a changing stimulus, while facial expressions can change instantly, sometimes even at a rate imperceptible to the human eye. As an instantaneous response mechanism, it is *the* most effective way to provide feedback to an ongoing message. What better way do we have, for example, to stop a confusing, digressive, or irrelevant message than by a negative facial response? We can usually change what someone is about to say by squinting in a certain way or raising an eyebrow or tightening our lips noticeably. Such feedback is immediate and very influential.

Eye contact. A great deal can be conveyed through our eyes. If we seek feedback from another person, we usually maintain strong eye contact. We can open and close communication channels with our eyes as well. Think of a conversation involving more than two people. When we are interested in a certain person's opinion, we will look him or her in the eye, opening the channel for communication. Eye contact may be hard to maintain if we are too close to someone. We can use our eyes to create anxiety in another person. Eye contact also can show whether we feel rewarded by what we see, whether we are in competition with another person, and whether we have something to hide. Our eye contact habits may differ depending on the sex and status of the person we're talking to. If we are extroverted, in addition, our eye behavior is likely to be different than if we are introverted.[17]

Of all facial cues, eye contact is perhaps the single most important one. The fact that our culture has imposed so many rules on us

TRY THIS

Think of two people you have recently conversed with at each of the first three distances and two recent situations where you used the public distance.

1. **Intimate (0–18 inches)**
2. **Personal (18 inches—4 feet)**
3. **Social (4 feet—12 feet)**
4. **Public (12 feet or more)**

What kind of subject matter did you discuss at each of these distances? Was it different for each of the distances? How formal was each of the encounters? Next time you are talking with others, notice the distance you maintain with them, and think about the factors that led you to choose that distance.

regarding its use shows its significance. Think about your own patterns of eye contact. What rules do you follow? Until a certain age, children are rarely uncomfortable staring or being stared at. How long can you maintain eye contact with someone before it starts to feel awkward to you? It has been observed that as two people who do not wish to speak to each other approach, they will cast their eyes downward when they are about 8 feet apart, so they don't have to look at each other as they pass. Goffman calls this "dimming your lights."[18] Eye contact can have a major impact on both the quality and quantity of interpersonal communication.[19]

The body. The body reinforces facial communication. Recent research has discovered a number of interesting things about how we use our bodies to communicate:

1. The face may tell what emotion is being expressed, but the body can indicate how intense that emotion is.[20] For example, our message of anger will be reinforced if we become tense or rigid, clench a fist, or put our hands on our hips.
2. The body can also provide information of its own. Drive and defensiveness, as well as conscious or unconscious attempts to communicate with another person, may be revealed by the body.[21]
3. Bodily cues have been shown to be accurate indicators of our perceived genuineness as we engage in communication.[22]
4. As our educational level goes up, generally, our ability to interpret bodily movement also increases.[23]

People can learn quite a bit about us from the position of our body and limbs as a whole—our posture. If we slouch, we reveal our attitude toward the other person, the topic being discussed, and, perhaps, the situation. When we lean toward the person we are talking with, we indicate positive feelings toward that person.[24] Our posture can reveal warmth, status, inclusiveness, and deception. Our posture is likely to show such things as the amount of immediacy we feel with another person, the degree of responsiveness we feel, whether we agree or disagree, and the power or status we have in relation to this other person.[25]

Gestures. As a mode of nonverbal communication, hand gestures rank second in importance to facial cues. We use them with great frequency and intensity and they play a central role in interpersonal communication. We sometimes use gestures instead of words, as when we motion to another person where to move or sit or stand, without talking. Most of the time, however, our gestures reinforce a verbal message, as when we shake a fist and shout at a dangerous driver or show the shape of something with our hands as we speak.

CONSIDER THIS "**You've got to make posture and gesture work for you. The "thoughtful" attitude, for example, is going to take more than a thoughtful** face **to get anywhere. You can't have a thoughtful expression on your face, for example, and sit just any old way. Use the way you sit to help get your message across. Here are some specific suggestions:**

1. The thoughtful **pose: Legs crossed and tucked under desk or just to the side of desk. Chin resting on one hand. It's** this **that makes you look studious. And also props your face up. Gives your face a nice line. Don't put your head sideways and put your check on your hand, though. (You can vary these positions, but always ask yourself what the effect would be. Here, it would be poor. Cheek on hand would distort your profile and really hide your face.) Now, bend slightly forward over your desk . . . to show you're intent on what's going on.**

2. The casual **look: Legs crossed or toe of one foot behind heel of the other foot. One hand in lap. Torso bent slightly back, but not so your back has an unnatural arch. The idea of this posture is to look completely natural, completely relaxed. As relaxed as though you were on a beach. You're facing the front of the room, but this is the only clue that you're absorbed in the lecture. The rest of you gives the idea that you can turn in a split second if anything else is worth your attention.**

3. Sexy: **Sit almost sideways in your chair. Legs crossed. One elbow on back of your chair. See what this does to the line of your body? Interesting. Careful, though, or you'll be too obvious. Don't for example stick your feet** way **out in the aisle or thrust your chest out too far. Elbow on back of chair will usually give you just the right line. One more thing. You're sitting slantwise. So be sure your face is to the front of the room ninety-five percent of the time. If you're not careful about this, the teacher could get the idea you're not paying attention. And then you're on risky ground.**"

—Ellen Peck, *How to Get a Teen-Age Boy and What to Do with Him When You Get Him*

In our communication with others, our gestures show whether or not we are actively involved. They can convey our level of forcefulness and energy. The more committed we are to an idea and the more we wish to communicate this idea to another person, the more strength we are likely to put into stating the idea. We can demonstrate an evaluative quality with gestures as well. We can quickly show whether we think something is good or bad, right or wrong, or if we are not quite sure, using hand gestures. Gestures are also used as a control device. We can usually wave off a person who is coming up to talk to us with an appropriate gesture.

Although there is no consensus as to specifically how hand movements function in communication or how many meanings can be communicated, the hands are an important communicative instrument. When we find our selves needing to communicate with someone whose language we don't speak, we often end up using gestures to convey meaning. And many deaf people depend upon a complex set of hand gestures as a means of communicating; in this case the gestures are a highly developed language capable of conveying fine subtleties of meaning. People whose hearing is not impaired rarely need to depend on gestures for the exchange of precise meaning in the same way as deaf people, but it is interesting to think about how much *can* be communicated with gestures alone.

Personal appearance. Even if we believe the cliché that beauty is only skin deep, we must recognize that not only does our personal appearance have a profound effect on our self-image, but it also affects our behavior and the behavior of people around us. Our physical appearance provides a basis for first and sometimes long-lasting impressions. It also affects whom we talk to, date, or marry, how socially and sexually successful we will be, and even our potential for vocational success. It is unfair, but true.

The billion-dollar cosmetics industry provides testimony to the fact that people care about physical appearance and firmly believe it makes a difference. We apply all kinds of creams, lotions, and colorings to our skin. We may adorn our bodies in various ways with glasses, tinted contact lenses, ribbons, beards, hair ornaments, jewelry, and clothes. Body adornments are a big part of what Ruesch called object language.

Clothing is another communication medium over which we exert special control. Researchers have determined that our clothes provide three different kinds of information about us:[26]

1. Clothes reveal something about the *emotions* we are experiencing. This works both ways: how we feel affects what we wear and what we wear affects how we feel. We'll put on our most comfortable clothes in the morning if comfort is going to be our most important consideration that day. If we're going to speak as a student representative at a meeting of the board of regents of our college, chances are we'll choose our clothes less for comfort and more for the feeling we hope to convey at the meeting—confidence or maturity or whatever. In these cases we are dressing both for how we feel and how we intend to feel later on. We've all had the experience of

IS CONSIDER THIS

CONSIDER THIS CONSIDER THIS CONSIDER THIS CONSIDER TH

The darker the suit, the more authority it transmits. A black suit is more authoritative than a dark blue, although it is much too powerful for most men and should be rarely worn anyway because of its funeral overtones. The most authoritative pattern is the pinstripe, followed in descending order by the solid, the chalk stripe and the plaid. If you need to be more authoritative, stick with dark pinstripes. But if you are a very large man or if you already have a great sense of presence or if you have a gruff or swarthy appearance, it is best to trim down your authority so that people will not be frightened by you. This can be accomplished by wearing lighter shades of blue and grey and beiges.

Suits that will give you the most credibility with people of the upper-middle class are dark blue and dark gray solids and pinstripes of both colors. But note: Only the dark blue solid will give you high credibility with the lower-middle class.

If you must be authoritative and credible with both the upper-middle class and the lower-middle class at the same time—say you are a banker or a lawyer and must deal daily with a wide variety of people—light blue and light gray solids accomplish this, although the light blue is generally not considered an acceptable suit for the truly conservative businessman.

The suits in which men are more likely to be liked are again light gray and light blue solids and medium-range business plaids. Bright plaids sometimes turn off the upper-middle class.

—John T. Molloy, *Dress for Success*

feeling inappropriately dressed, either too formally or too informally, on some occasions, and we know how our clothes affect how we feel about those occasions.

2. Our clothes may disclose something about our *behavior.* If you have ever worn a uniform of any kind, you know how clothes can transform you and make you act differently than if you were not wearing those particular clothes. If we get dressed up for a job interview, we feel important; in our own mind our actions also take on importance. Because it occurs in our mind, it will also very likely affect how we actually behave. We will be more calculated, purposeful, and dynamic. We may stand rigid rather than slouched. We may tend to lower our voice, slow our rate of speaking, and use fewer nonfluencies ("uh"'s and "um"'s). Just as dress affects us, we are also likely to judge other people's behavior by the way *they* dress. What expectations do you have for a person dressed as a police officer, judge, nurse, or priest?

3. Our clothes function to *differentiate* us from other people. Twenty-year-old college students wear different clothes than twenty-

year-olds with jobs in the business world. Clothing also differs between age groups. A single man, for example, of 20–25 spends twice as much on clothes as a man of 45–50 and three times as much as a man of 65–70.[27] Clothing may also be used by people to raise themselves from a subordinate position, to raise self-esteem and apparent status.[28] Clothes serve to differentiate, too, between people who wish to be perceived as fashionable and those who don't care about fashion, between the formal and the informal, and between people with different social roles.

Vocal Cues

Vocal cues are all those attributes of sound that can convey meaning. Sounds (not words) are considered nonverbal communication. This includes how loudly or quickly we speak, how much we hesitate, how many nonfluencies we use. These vocal cues can convey our emotional state.

As we well know, all we have to do to reveal anger is change the *ways* we talk: we might talk louder, faster, and more articulately than usual. We may use our silences more pointedly. We can say exactly the same thing in a fit of anger as in a state of delight and change our meaning by how we say it. We can say "I hate you" to sound angry, teasing, or cruel. Vocal cues are what is lost when our words are writ-

"Dickie, I hardly recognized you! You've changed your format."

TRY THIS

Read the following sentence aloud seven times, each time emphasizing a different word in the sentence.

I hit him in the eye yesterday.

Notice how the meaning changes as you change your emphasis. You can get seven more variations by reading the sentence as a question instead of a statement.

ten down. The word often used to refer to this quality—what occurs beyond or in addition to the words we speak—is *paralanguage.*[29]

If you don't think paralanguage is very important, think of the impression made in a job interview by an applicant who pronounces words wrong or speaks too loudly or too fast or with too many hesitations. Such a person might find it hard to get employment in some prestigious business firms or to penetrate the upper strata of society in some circles. While a person's social or business acceptance will probably never depend *only* on vocal cues, there are times when it helps to have correct pronunciation and articulation as part of our credentials.

Research has shown that our vocal cues may accurately reveal the following emotions: contempt, indifference, grief, anger, anxiety, sadness, and happiness. How accurately these emotions are identified depends on the listener. Obviously, what a listener perceives can affect how he or she views our personality. Because we gain insights into our own personality through the feedback of others, listeners' views affect us directly.

It has been observed that if we use great variety in pitch (high or low), we are likely to be perceived as dynamic and extroverted. Males who vary their speaking rate are viewed as extroverted and animated. Interestingly, females demonstrating the same variety in rate are perceived as extroverted, but also high-strung, inartistic, and uncooperative. If our voice is flat, we may be thought of as sluggish, cold, and withdrawn. A person with a nasal voice is often perceived as unattractive, lethargic, and foolish.[30] Whether these perceptions are accurate or not, it's useful for us to know how we are likely to be perceived if we speak a certain way.

Certain vocal characteristics are perceived as revealing interpersonal trust, confidence, and sincerity: when trust or confidence is in jeopardy, excessive pauses and hesitations tend to increase. Also, the number of nonfluencies we use—stuttering, repetitions, slips of the tongue, incoherences—increases in situations where we are nervous or ill at ease.

READING NONVERBAL MESSAGES

One of the purposes of learning about nonverbal communication is to increase our understanding of our own actions and reduce the chances of someone misinterpreting us. It's easy to accidentally convey an attitude that may be misleading, inappropriate, or damaging to an interpersonal encounter.

According to Albert Mehrabian there are "only three primary

feeling dimensions that are involved in nonverbal behavior": *immediacy or liking, dominance or power,* and *change or responsiveness.*[31] This means of classifying nonverbal communication can be useful both in understanding our own and others' nonverbal behavior. In the following discussion, nonverbal behavior is categorized by emotional intent. That is, to understand nonverbal communication, we must consider the emotions from which certain behaviors spring.

Immediacy or liking. Mehrabian suggested that one of the main determinants in what our nonverbal behavior will be is our tendency to get involved with things we like and to avoid things we don't like. Touching, eye contact, and physical closeness characterize a feeling of immediacy with someone or something; distance, lack of eye contact, and absence of physical contact characterize dislike.

Dominance or power. According to Mehrabian, another factor that determines our nonverbal communications is our feeling of power or subordination in relation to a particular person or situation. If we feel dominant, we are likely to make large, expansive gestures, stand tall, and move in a relaxed way; we demonstrate submissiveness by avoiding eye contact, maintaining rigid, erect posture, and making small, tense movements.

Change or responsiveness. A third factor Mehrabian identified as crucial to our nonverbal expressions is our responsiveness to our environment. We respond either positively or negatively to all the stimuli we encounter—the weather, the food we eat, the people we run into, circumstances, events, etc. In every waking moment we are reacting to our environment in some way, and our nonverbal behavior will reflect these reactions.

There Are Limits

In reading the nonverbal cues that others send, we are automatically limited: our eyes can handle about five million bits of information per second but our brain can process only about 500 bits per second.[32] We must be selective. We are also limited by what we decide to look at, and what we can understand. If we can attach no meaning to cues we observe, we are obviously limited in those areas.

We are limited when we simply do not know someone well enough to know that whenever she is angry she makes certain gestures. We are limited when we do not know all the various meanings that may be attached to certain movements. How can we know what it means when a man moves his brow as he talks if we do not know

IS CONSIDER THIS CONSIDER THIS

Propriety of movement and general demeanor in company.—**To look steadily at any one, especially if you are a lady and are speaking to a gentleman; to turn the head frequently on one side and the other during conversation; to balance yourself upon your chair; to bend forward; to strike your hands upon your knees; to hold one of your knees between your hands locked together; to cross your legs; to extend your feet on the andirons; to admire yourself with complacency in a glass; to adjust, in an affected manner, your cravat, hair, dress, or handkerchief; to remain without gloves; to fold carefully your shawl, instead of throwing it with graceful negligence upon a table; to fret about a hat which you have just left off; to laugh immoderately; to place your hand upon the person with whom you are conversing; to take him by the buttons, the collar of his cloak, the cuffs, the waist, etc.; to seize any person by the waist or arm, or to touch their person; to roll the eyes or to raise them with affectation; to take snuff from the box of your neighbor, or to offer it to strangers, especially to ladies; to play continually with your chain or fan; to beat time with the feet and hands; to whirl round a chair with your hand; to shake with your feet the chair of your neighbor; to rub your face or your hands; wink your eyes; shrug up your shoulders; stamp with your feet, &c;—all these bad habits, of which we cannot speak to people, are in the highest degree displeasing.**

—Emily Thornwell, *The Lady's Guide to Complete Etiquette* (1884)

CONSIDER THIS CONSIDER THIS CONSIDER THIS CONSIDER TH

that different brow movements convey different meanings? Our own perceptual skills limit our ability to receive nonverbal cues. But while we must recognize our limits, we all can improve our skills in both sending and receiving nonverbal messages.

IMPROVING SKILLS IN NONVERBAL COMMUNICATION

As we try to improve our nonverbal communication skills there are three important ideas to keep in mind:

1. Nonverbal communication always occurs in a context. The meanings conveyed are intimately and directly tied to that context. If a man at a party stands with his hips thrust forward slightly, his legs apart, his thumbs locked in his belt, and his fingers pointing down toward his genitals, it may be considered a sexually provocative pose in that context.[33] If he stands the same way as he waits in line for a hamburger with his family, his pose may not carry the same message.

2. No nonverbal cue should be viewed in isolation. Cues must be observed as they interact with each other. In the instance just cited, it was not the man's posture alone that was suggestive, but that cue in combination with the position of his legs, thumbs, and fingers. Cues must be viewed in combination.

3. Although we can learn a great deal from observing nonverbal communication, our conclusions should always be tentative rather than final. Every individual is unique. There is always the possibility of actions occurring that are exceptions to any rule. We should view each behavior as existing at this time only, not assuming it exists permanently or always.

Some people have mannerisms that are habitual and are not meant to convey any special meaning. We must be careful not to read too much into the behavior of people we don't know well and can only guess about. A person's eye may twitch when he or she is nervous; the twitch could be interpreted by a stranger as an enticing wink. We don't have to refrain from making *any* observations, but it is good to be cautious. Remember, whatever meaning we assign to what we see is a meaning that exists *for us*. Meaning is not in the nonverbal cues we observe; meaning is *in us* and because it is in us, it will differ from the meaning other people assign.

Work on your self-awareness. The more we are able to express our selves clearly and accurately and the more in touch we are with our own feelings, the more likely we are to understand the nonverbal communication of others.[34] Our knowledge of our selves can be increased through self-disclosure and feedback. To open up, share, and request feedback from people we trust increases personal sensitivity. Opening channels for healthy, honest, open feedback can be of mutual benefit for us and for our friends. Our effectiveness in receiving nonverbal cues will be increased through self-awareness.

Monitor your own behavior. It's helpful to review our own communication experiences, whether positive or negative, to become aware of what we are doing. If we discover something we think might be important, we could solicit the help of friends to verify or deny our observations. We should think more about what we do. It is not easy to see our selves as others see us, but difficult or not, it is useful and worthwhile. It would be ideal if we could watch a videotape of our interactions with others over a period of twenty-four hours or so. Since this is not likely to come about, what we *can* do is enlist the cooperation of close friends to help us look for nonverbal cues that cause a disruptive function as we communicate.

TRY THIS

Watch parts of TV programs with the sound turned way down. Notice how skilled certain actors or entertainers are in enhancing their messages with nonverbal activity. Notice specifically if they:

1. use exaggerated facial expressions

2. touch other people in some way

3. make special use of hand gestures

4. use the space in which they are communicating (moving closer to or away from other people)

5. seem to move naturally and comfortably, like "real" people

You may find that some performers you thought were quite skilled turn out to depend almost entirely on their verbal messages to make a point. In which kinds of programs did you find the performers most adept at nonverbal communication—comedy? drama? action programs? news presentations? commercials?

Experiment with your behaviors. There are two reasons for trying out different behavior: to improve our communication and to break some of our routine, habitual ways of interacting. When we discover we have certain ineffective or distracting mannerisms, we should try to alter them in a meaningful way to increase our interpersonal effectiveness. If we force our selves to try new approaches, we'll increase the number of alternatives we have for behaving. We can "try on" new behaviors to see how they fit. This is part of the process of growing, changing, and becoming. If we find it very hard to break away from our usual routine, we can at least try to observe how other people handle themselves in similar circumstances. Such observations can give us a framework for monitoring our own behavior in the future.

Respond empathically. Our nonverbal sensitivity will increase as we train our selves to be empathic. Try to understand how the other person feels. Try to get "the big picture." We should always imagine how we would feel if we experienced the same thing. If we are the twentieth applicant for a job to be interviewed on a certain day and we see a tired, expressionless face on the interviewer, we should try to understand how we would feel if we had just been through a day of interviews. Again, this means always trying to see where the other person is coming from. This can explain a lot when we're trying to understand what a certain twitch or posture might signify. Our success in reading nonverbal messages will increase if we try to be *empathic*.

Look for patterns. The behavior we observe in others is usually reflected in their whole body and not just in their face or hands. We can usually recognize trembling hands as a sign of nervousness, but nervousness may be shown in other ways as well. Nervous people may bite their lips, speak too quickly, squirm in their chairs, always be ready to leave, avoid direct eye contact, or play with paper clips while talking. Too often we draw conclusions from too little evidence. The face and the hands are obvious and easy to observe, but we must also notice posture, bodily movement, dress, and talk, and try to see patterns of behavior as they relate to different social settings.

Check your perceptions. If we feel that a person's nonverbal behavior is influencing our reaction to that person, it may be wise to find out whether we have correctly understood that behavior. Just because people close their eyes does not mean they are not paying attention. Some people close their eyes to concentrate better on the

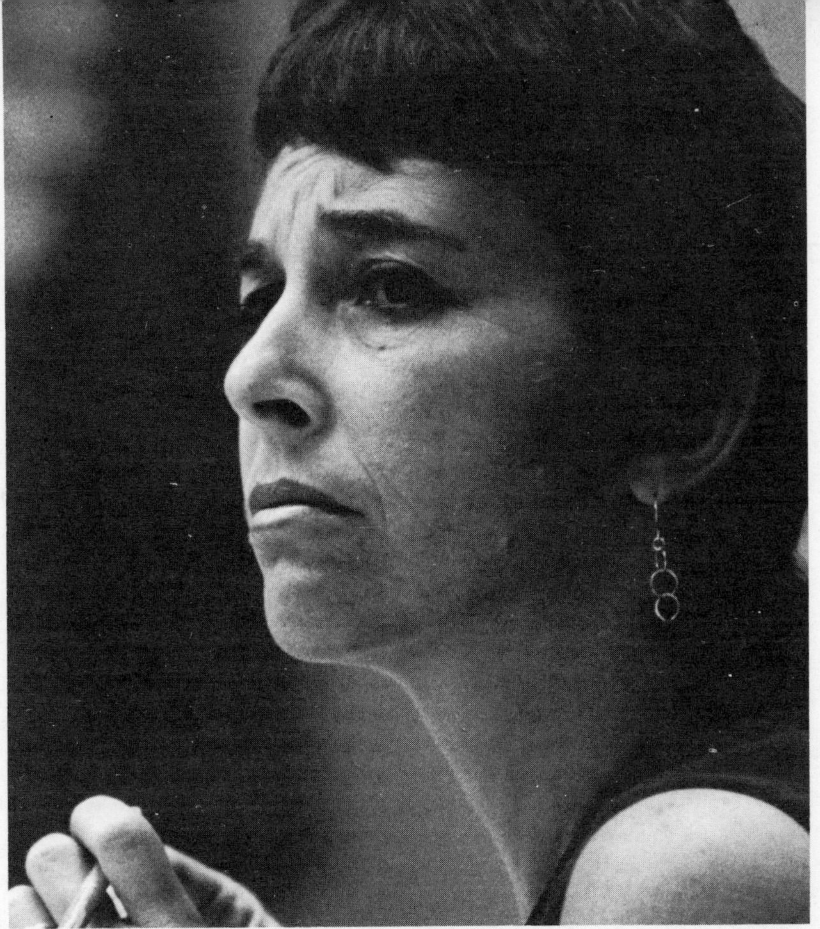

message by blocking out distractions. If we are talking to Jennifer and she keeps looking beyond us as we talk, we could check our perceptions by asking, "Do you care about this?" or "Are you listening to me?" Something may be occurring behind us that we should also see!

Express your feelings. The cultural norm that says people should not openly express their feelings is powerfully restricting. How can we accurately read other people's nonverbal cues if they are always feeling one thing and trying to show something else? All we can do is try to watch for congruency or noncongruency in the total communication. Some people smile constantly—a pleasant expression has become such a habit with them that they cannot clear their faces of pleasantness even when they are feeling frustration or despair. To understand a person's total message we need to put together the whole communication puzzle—including all verbal and nonverbal elements—and notice which pieces fit together and which don't.

Likewise, we must strive for congruency in our own communication. If we concentrate on not hiding what we feel, it will be much easier to make our nonverbal messages congruent with our verbal messages. In fact, if we are being perfectly honest, we shouldn't have to worry about sending consistent signals—they will take care of themselves. We must discover the potential of our body; what messages does it want to send? We tend to be too restrictive, too closed, and too inhibited in bodily expression. It's healthy to open the channels for sending honest messages.

People are often influenced more by our nonverbal messages than by our words. We tend to believe what we see and the tone of what we hear far more than the words we hear, and rightly so. People generally have more control over their verbal messages than over their nonverbal ones. True feelings, as revealed through nonverbal cues, are difficult to disguise. Becoming aware of our nonverbal communication habits will help us become more expressive. It will also increase our sensitivity to others.

In the next chapter, we will have an opportunity to increase our sensitivity in still another area. Tuning in to others means being aware of their verbal and nonverbal communication but also aware of the attitudes from which their words and actions flow.

OTHER READING

Flora Davis, *Inside Intuition* (New York: New American Library, 1973). Davis provides a comprehensive examination of nonverbal communication. This is a good starting point for learning about this important kind of communication.

Julius Fast, *Body Language* (New York: Pocket Books, 1970). This is the book that first created widespread popular interest in nonverbal communication. Fast briefly discusses the major areas of the field and gives a rather superficial glimpse of what it is all about. Easy-to-read and full of examples.

Erving Goffman, *Interaction Ritual: Essays on Face-to-Face Behavior* (Garden City, N.Y.: Anchor Books, 1967). Goffman presents six papers dealing with the social organization of spoken contacts. The focus is on social ritual. He discusses the kind of image people need to maintain to give and receive civilities, discourtesies, and other interpersonal gestures. An interesting sociological perspective.

Edward T. Hall, *The Hidden Dimension* (New York: Anchor Books, 1969). In this book Hall focuses on people's use of space—that invisible bubble that constitutes personal territory. He demonstrates how the use of space can affect personal and business relations. This is a well-written, entertaining book full of examples and illustrations.

Edward T. Hall, *The Silent Language* (New York: Premier Books, 1959). Behind the mystery, confusion, and disorganization of life, there is order. Hall urges a reexamination of much that passes as ordinary, acceptable behavior.

John T. Molloy, *Dress for Success* (New York: Peter H. Wyden, 1975). This book is meant for men in business. It is a guide for matching clothes, picking designs, colors, and fabrics, and dressing for leisure. In addition, Molloy provides advice on dressing up office space, and dressing successfully for job interviews. Written in a light, easy-to-read style.

Gerard I. Nierenberg and Henry H. Calero, *How to Read a Person Like a Book* (New York: Pocket Books, 1973). This is an illustrated handbook of types of nonverbal communication. Although it gives insights into the significance of gestures, one must remember that meaning lies in the speaker and in the listener—not in the gestures. This is a good starting point.

Robert L. Whiteside, *Face Language* (New York: Pocket Books, 1975), and Timothy T. Mar, *Face Reading: The Chinese Art of Physiognomy* (New York: New American Library, 1974). Both of these popularized approaches to this area of nonverbal communication suggest that reading faces insures expertise in getting at the true character of other people. Both books are working manuals that provide specific, simple techniques. Students of interpersonal communication can use these techniques to sharpen their perceptual skills.

NOTES

[1] Flora Davis, *Inside Intuition: What We Know About Nonverbal Communication* (New York: The New American Library, Inc., 1973), p. 55. The direct, unwavering stare is also a threat to some animals. See George Schallar, *The Year of the Gorilla* (Chicago: University of Chicago Press, 1964).

[2] Ibid., p. 58.

[3] Erving Goffman, *Behavior in Public Places* (New York: Free Press, 1963), pp. 83–88.

[4] Davis, *Inside Intuition,* p. 61.

[5] Albert Mehrabian, "Communication Without Words," *Psychology Today* (September 1968), p. 53. See also Randall Harrison, "Nonverbal Communication: Exploration into Time, Space, Action, and Object," in *Dimensions in Communication,* J. H. Campbell and H. W. Hepler, eds. (Belmont, Calif.: Wadsworth Publishing Co., 1965), p. 161.

[6] P. Ekman and W. V. Friesen, "Nonverbal Leakage and Clues to Deception," *Psychiatry* 32 (1969), 88–106. Also see P. Ekman and W. V. Friesen, "The Repertoire of Nonverbal Behavior: Categories, Origins, Usage and Coding," *Semiotica* 1 (1969), 49–98.

[7] Albert Mehrabian, *Silent Messages* (Belmont, Calif.: Wadsworth Publishing Co., Inc., 1971), p. 56. See especially Chapter 3, "The Double-Edged Message," pp. 40–56.

[8] Jurgen Ruesch and Weldon Kees, *Nonverbal Communication: Notes on the Visual Perception of Human Relations* (Los Angeles: University of California Press, 1956), p. 1.

[9] Jurgen Ruesch, "Nonverbal Language and Therapy," in *Communication and Culture,* Alfred G. Smith, ed. (New York: Holt, Rinehart and Winston,

1966), pp. 209–213.

[10] Edward T. Hall, *The Hidden Dimension* (Garden City, N.Y.: Doubleday & Company, Inc., 1966), pp. 114–129. In an earlier book, *The Silent Language,* (Greenwich, Conn.: Fawcett Publications, Inc., 1959) Hall identifies eight distances.

[11] Albert Mehrabian, "Orientation Behaviors and Nonverbal Attitude Communication," *Journal of Communication* 17 (1967), 324–332.

[12] Michael Reece and Robert N. Whitman, "Expressive Movements, Warmth, and Verbal Reinforcement," *Journal of Abnormal and Social Psychology* 64 (1962), 250.

[13] P. Ekman, W. V. Friesen, and P. Ellsworth, *Emotion in the Human Face; Guidelines for Research and an Integration of the Findings* (New York: Pergamon Press, 1972), pp. 57–65. These authors suggest eight categories. Dale G. Leathers adds the last two in *Nonverbal Communication Systems* (Boston: Allyn and Bacon, Inc., 1976), p. 24.

[14] C. E. Izard, *The Face of Emotion* (New York: Appleton-Century-Crofts, 1971), p. 216.

[15] P. Ekman and W. V. Friesen, "The Repertoire of Nonverbal Behavior: Categories, Origins, Usage and Coding," *Semiotica* 1 (1969), 75.

[16] Dale G. Leathers, *Nonverbal Communication Systems* (Boston: Allyn and Bacon, Inc., 1976), p. 34.

[17] Mark L. Knapp, *Nonverbal Communication* (New York: Holt, Rinehart, and Winston, 1972), p. 138.

[18] Erving Goffman, *Behavior in Public Places,* p. 84.

[19] See A. Kendon, "Some Functions of Gaze Direction in Social Interaction," *Acta Psychologica* 26 (1967), 46.

[20] Paul Ekman, "Differential Communication of Affect by Head and Body Cues," *Journal of Personality and Social Psychology* 2 (1965), 726–735.

[21] P. Wachtel, "An Approach to the Study of Body Language in Psychotherapy," *Psychotherapy* 4 (1967), 97–100.

[22] J. G. Shapiro, C. P. Foster, and T. Powell, "Facial and Bodily Cues of Genuineness, Empathy, and Warmth," *Journal of Clinical Psychology* 24 (1968), 233–36.

[23] G. Michael and N. Willis, Jr., "The Development of Gestures as a Function of Social Class, Education, and Sex," *Psychological Record* 18 (1968), 515.

[24] A. Mehrabian, "Communication Without Words," p. 54.

[25] Leathers, *Nonverbal Communication Systems,* p. 40.

[26] Mary Kefgen and Phyllis Touchie-Specht, *Individuality in Clothing Selection and Personal Appearance: A Guide for the Consumer* (New York: Macmillan, 1971), pp. 12–14.

[27] F. Zweig, "Clothing Standards and Habits," in *Dress, Adornment and the Social Order,* M. E. Roach and J. B. Eicher, eds. (New York: Wiley, 1965), p. 164.

[28] J. Schwartz, "Men's Clothing and the Negro," ibid., p. 164.

[29] See George L. Trager, "Paralanguage: A First Approximation," *Studies in Linguistics* 13 (1958), 1–12.

[30] D. W. Addington, "The Relationship of Certain Vocal Characteristics with Perceived Speaker Characteristics" (Ph.D. diss., University of Iowa, 1963), pp. 157–58. Also see D. W. Addington, "The Relationship of Selected Vocal Characteristics to Personality Perception," *Speech Monographs* 35 (1968), 492–503.

[31] Based on pgs. 113–118 from *Silent Messages* by Albert Mehrabian. © 1971 by Wadsworth Publishing Company, Inc., Belmont, California 94002. Reprinted by permission of the publisher.

[32] W. V. Haney, *Communication and Organization Behavior* (Homewood, Ill.: Richard D. Irwin, Inc., 1967), p. 53.

[33] Julius Fast, *Body Language* (New York: Pocket Books, 1971), p. 85.

[34] J. R. Davitz, *The Communication of Emotional Meaning* (New York: McGraw-Hill, 1964).

Chapter 7

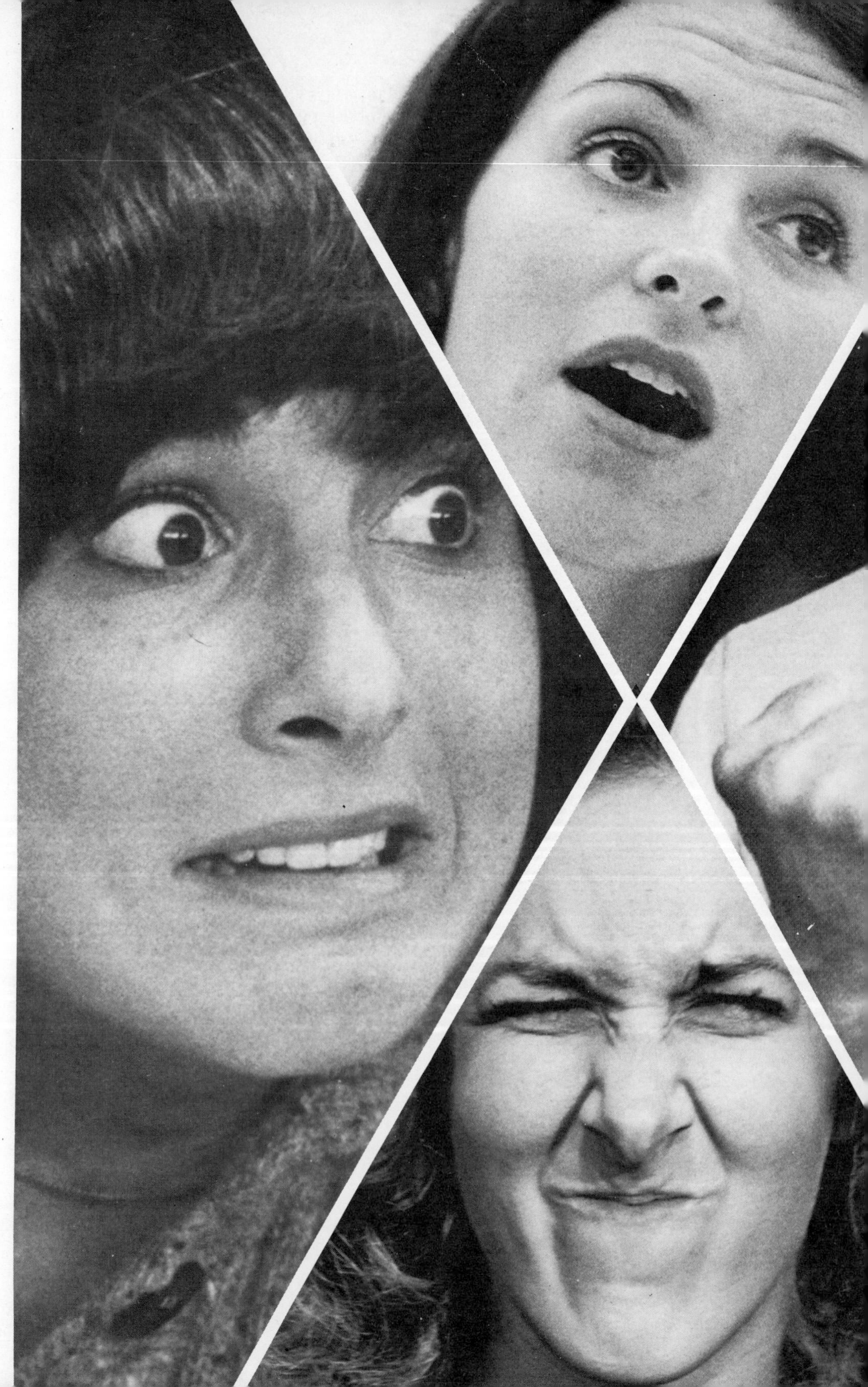

Tuning In: Attitudes

"I don't like your attitude!" "How long have you had that attitude?" "You'll never get anywhere with *that* attitude." Sound familiar? Our attitudes are an important part of who we are and how we interact with other people. Yet our own attitudes are often less apparent to us than the attitudes of people around us. That's because attitudes themselves are not observable, but the behavior stemming from attitudes *is*. And we are generally not very good observers of our own behavior.

What exactly is an "attitude"? The word is usually taken to mean a tendency to evaluate a person, thing, or idea either favorably or unfavorably.[1] It amounts to sorting our perceptions into two categories: relatively good and relatively bad. In Chapter 3 we saw how perception is the process of attaching meaning to information our senses take in. The attitude we form toward that information is an essential part of the meaning we assign to it.

Our behavior and communication habits are based, to a large extent, on our attitudes. In this chapter I'm going to discuss where these attitudes come from and what they are made of. I'll compare attitudes with beliefs and values. And I'll talk about attitude change and how we can improve our interpersonal persuasive skills.

ATTITUDES, BELIEFS, AND VALUES

A "belief" is a proposition that can be derived from what we say or do.[2] If we say we think something is true, we are saying we "believe" it. It may or may not be true in fact, but our thinking that it *is* true constitutes a belief. Our beliefs are not always logical. We may believe our father loves us and act both loved and loving because of our belief, even in the face of evidence to the contrary. Such beliefs are based on our own unique experiences: they may be confirmed or changed by the beliefs of people we care about and respect.

An "opinion" is usually narrower in focus than a belief. Opinions come and go. They tend to be situational. Our opinion of a certain kind of food may apply to that one particular food and to no other, and that opinion may change. Opinions can be thought of as tentative beliefs. They are our best judgment of a particular situation and they may, in time, come to be beliefs. That is, if we find we have a consistently low opinion of all the pickles we come in contact with, these opinions may evolve into a belief that pickles don't taste good and we will avoid eating them.

An "attitude" may be thought of as a system of beliefs organized around a common subject. We may believe that clothes are too expensive. We may believe that clothes we buy in stores are not well made. We may believe that clothes are just not made to fit us properly. As a result of these beliefs, we may develop a negative attitude toward store-bought clothes in general. We may decide we will not buy any new clothes for a while—we will either make our clothes or do with what we already have. Our attitude toward store-bought clothes is that they are relatively bad. An attitude is more general and, at the same time, more complex than a belief because it covers more areas. Attitudes usually develop over a long period of time and are not easy to change.

"Values" are still more general (and stable) than attitudes. A value is the common denominator in an attitude system. If we have an unfavorable attitude toward store-bought clothes and prepared convenience foods and manufactured furniture, it may be that we value self-reliance and personal creativity. We probably prefer to make our own clothes and furniture and to prepare our own food because we value our own industry. Values are usually very enduring because they relate to the way we conduct our lives and to the goals we set for our selves. Because our values are so central to who we are, they influence our communications and our behavior in many ways.

Given the relationship between beliefs, attitudes, and values shown in Figure 1, we can see how it is possible to infer that a person holds certain beliefs and attitudes because of the values we know he or she has. For example, if we know that Margaret values self-reliance and creativity, we might guess that she believes a gift of a ceramic pot made by a friend is preferable to a similar pot bought in a store. We may guess that she would rather plan a trip by herself than go on

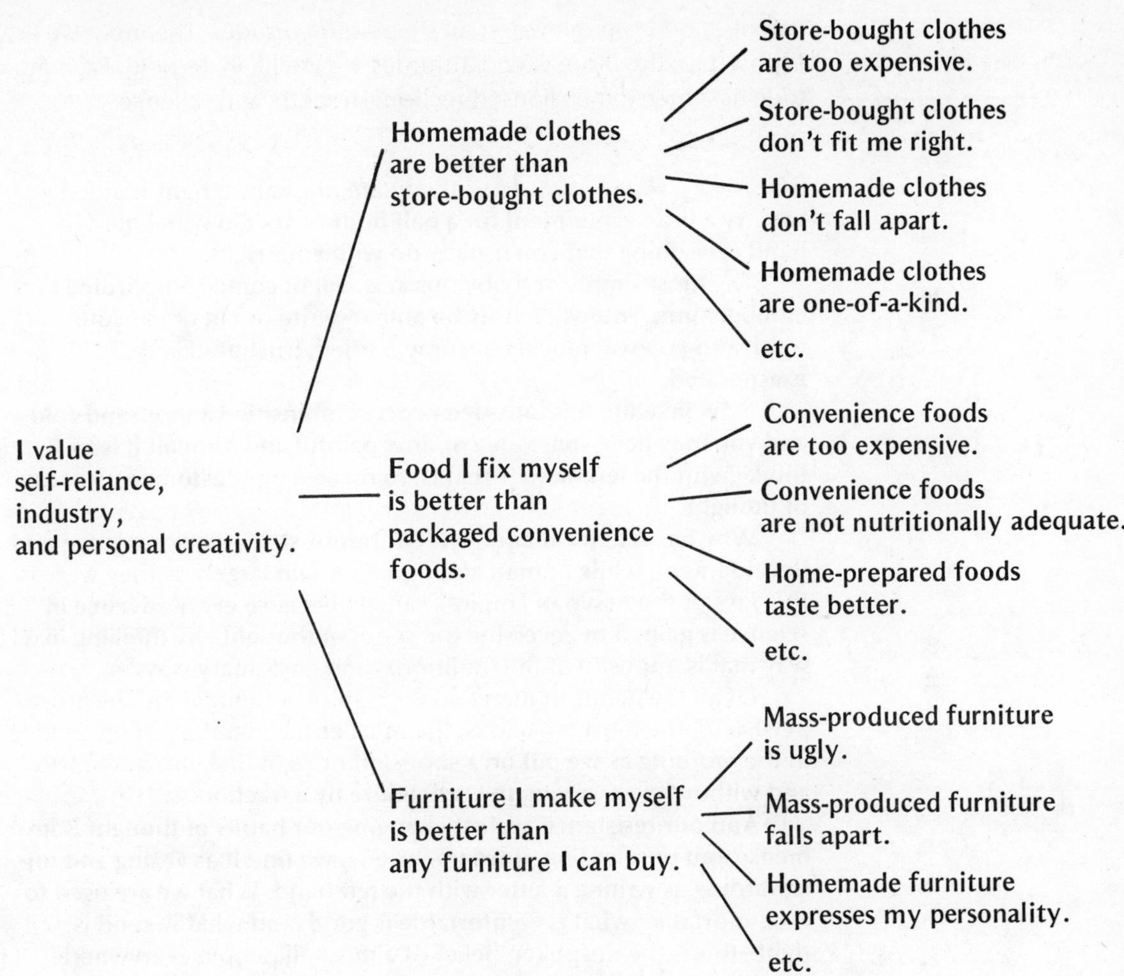

Figure 1. The relationship of values to attitudes and beliefs.

an organized tour. Guesses such as these can cause us to begin or end a relationship with Margaret. They may also determine how we communicate with her.

CHARACTERISTICS OF ATTITUDES

Attitudes exist internally. We derive them from different sources and hold them with different degrees of strength. Attitudes relate to things, people, and concepts. In general, we acquire them as a result of our experience: we may have a favorable attitude toward animals because our parents allowed us to have pets as children, or toward reading because our parents read to us often. Our peers, teachers, parents, and even television all shape our attitudes. The more we are exposed to, the more varied attitudes we are likely to hold. Each attitude has three dimensions: direction, strength, and salience.

CONSIDER THIS “**If you are normally a right-handed person, try a little experiment for a half hour or so: Do with your left hand everything that you usually do with your right.**

The most simple and obvious acts will become complicated and cumbersome. You will hardly be able to write or cut or eat your food; and you will quickly become baffled, frustrated and exasperated.

Now imagine this lopsided process intensified a thousand-fold, and you may have some idea of how painful and difficult it is to think "with the left hand"—that is, to reverse our customary process of thought.

Why has science made such enormous strides in knowledge and development, while human affairs still remain largely as they were in the days of the Assyrian Empire? Largely because every advance in science is gained by reversing the spool of thought—by thinking in a way that is opposite of the traditional and customary ways.

Of all the habits of mankind the habits of thought are the most persistent, the most tenacious, the most enslaving. We put on an idea in the morning as we put on a shoe, left or right first, unconsciously and without ever varying the procedure by a fraction.

And our resistance against changing our habits of thought is immense and unrelenting. If we try, briefly, we find it as vexing and unrewarding as writing a letter with the left hand. What we are used to is comfortable; what is comfortable is good; and what is good is right—this is the unspoken belief of almost all people everywhere.

When a scientist, however, tackles a problem that has hitherto seemed insoluble, he abandons all his preconceptions, and all the preconceptions of the past. Only when he begins to question the basic assumptions he has always held can he make an utterly fresh start, unencumbered by the intellectual baggage of the past.

I am not suggesting that a knowledge of the past is not useful, or that history and tradition have little to offer us—but they must be used as tools, not as points of departure. Our thinking about them must involve a painful revaluation of our most cherished ideas and ideals.

Not one person in a thousand is willing—although many are able—to think left-handed for more than a few minutes at a time. Yet every important discovery has been made in this way, from Harvey on circulation of the blood to Freud on the role of the unconscious. And we know what derision and abuse such men were subjected to for daring to violate the right-handedness of their times.”

—Sydney J. Harris, *The Best of Sydney J. Harris*

Direction

The *direction* of an attitude is simply whether we like something or not. Direction can be neutral: sometimes we do not care. A positive or negative evaluation reveals the direction of our attitude. Whether we like someone, do not like someone, or are indifferent toward someone, we have an attitude toward that person. We have attitudes on just about everything. When other people talk to us, we judge what they talk about according to our background of existing attitudes. If we do not know much about what they are talking about, we will probably form an opinion as a result of our conversation.

Strength

Direction refers to whether our attitude is favorable, unfavorable, or neutral; *strength* refers to how intense it is. We can like a person or we can love that person. We may not like one of our professors, but that dislike may be nothing compared with how we felt toward a high-school teacher whom we still "hate with a passion." In both cases, the direction of the attitude is the same but the strength is different.

Salience

When an attitude is important, it is likely to be prominent and conspicuous—*salient*. Since we have attitudes toward just about everything and many of them reflect the same direction, there must be some further way to distinguish among them. Strength is one way, salience is the other. Some things mean more to us than they do to other people. Some issues involve us more directly. Do not confuse strength and salience: we might really hate it when someone tells vulgar jokes around us—we have a very *strong* attitude toward vulgarity—but it is not terribly salient to us since the people we know do not tell vulgar jokes. A woman's attitude toward abortion would be much more salient than a man's because he could never experience pregnancy in the same way, though both their attitudes may have identical strength and direction.

TRY THIS

For each of the following topics, consider the attitude you hold. What is its direction (positive, negative, or neutral)? Its strength? Its salience?

money
gossip
competition
organized religion
conformity
school spirit
success
patriotism
cats
television
the library
football
hallucinogenic drugs
science fiction
natural foods
labor unions
big cities

FUNCTIONS OF ATTITUDES

We acquire attitudes for a number of reasons.[3] According to Daniel Katz, who provides one of the more popular, useful, and accurate approaches to attitudes, they serve four functions:

1. An *adjustment-utility* function, as when we like things that satisfy our needs;

2. An *ego-defense* function, as when we hold attitudes to cover up our insecurities or protect against external threats;
3. A *value-expression* function, as when we use attitudes to express our beliefs and values; and
4. A *knowledge* function, as when we use attitudes to help understand our environment by organizing and structuring it.

Adjustment-Utility

We tend to like those things we consider good for us and dislike those things we consider harmful. We hold certain attitudes just because we think they will help us gain our goals or help us maintain any present conditions that are similar to past favorable circumstances. If we know that businesses look at the college grades of job applicants, we may change our attitude toward the grading system when we realize that good grades increase our likelihood of being hired. We adjust our attitude to help us achieve our goal of getting a job. If we want our tastes to conform with our friends' tastes, we may adjust our attitudes to the point of liking the music they listen to, the books they read, the movies they see. We will tend to dislike or be apathetic toward things that we feel do not help us gain our goals or do not bring us pleasure.[4] We are more likely to change an attitude to fit a goal than change a goal to fit our current attitude. When Katz suggests that attitudes serve a utilitarian function, he simply means that we develop and hold certain ones because they are useful to us.

CONSIDER THIS “ **Then Tom turned the conversation again to my plight. I described some of the agonies of Watergate, the pressures I was under, how unfairly I thought the press was treating me. I was being defensive and when I ran out of explanations, Tom spoke gently but firmly.**

"You know that I supported Nixon in this past election, but you guys made a serious mistake. You would have won the election without any of the hanky-panky. Watergate and the dirty tricks were so unnecessary. And it was wrong, just plain wrong. You didn't have to do it."...

"Tom, one thing you don't understand. In politics it's dog-eat-dog; you simply can't survive otherwise. I've been in the political business for twenty years, including several campaigns right here in Massachusetts. I know how things are done. Politics is like war. If you don't keep the enemy on the defensive, you'll be on the defensive yourself. Tom, this man Nixon has been under constant attack all of his life. The only way he could make it was to fight back. Look at

the criticism he took over Vietnam. Yet he was right. We never would have made it if we hadn't fought the way we did, hitting our critics, never letting them get the best of us. We didn't have any choice."

Even as I talked, the words sounded more and more empty to me. Tired old lines, I realized. I was describing the ways of the political world, all right, while suddenly wondering if there could be a better way.

Tom believed so, anyway. He was so gentle I couldn't resent what he said as he cut right through it all: "Chuck, I hate to say this, but you guys brought it on yourselves. If you had put your faith in God, and if your cause were just, He would have guided you. And His help would have been a thousand times more powerful than all your phony ads and shady schemes put together."

With any other man the notion of relying on God would have seemed to me pure Pollyanna. Yet I had to be impressed with the way this man ran his company in the equally competitive world of business: ignoring his enemies, trying to follow God's ways. Since his conversion Raytheon had never done better, sales and profits soaring. Maybe there was something to it; anyway it's tough to argue with success. ”

—Charles W. Colson, *Born Again*

Attitudes can cause us to adjust our behavior. If we have a positive attitude toward academic work and we like to study, we may seek out jobs that involve some research and writing. We may adjust our behavior by joining groups that have an academic purpose, associating with other people who like to study, and accepting work that has an academic orientation. Our attitudes, in such instances, are useful to us because they help us attain our objectives.

How clear, consistent, or near to us the rewards for our activities are will be partly responsible for whether we hold an attitude or not. We may think of a good grade in a course as useful because it will satisfy our parents. Our parents have always smiled with pleasure when we got good grades—clearly a reward. When we were in high school, they might have let us use their car and removed curfews when our grades were good; this is consistent behavior. Also, vacation time is almost here and we may want the peace of mind that comes from having done well; the possible rewards are near. The consequences of our having a particular attitude toward grades are clear, consistent, and near.

Likewise, our attitude toward other people often depends on how we feel they can satisfy our specific needs. We might develop a favorable attitude toward a student who attends class every day and will be able to lend us notes when we miss the class. We may even

overlook some of his negative attributes because he can get us those class notes when we need them. True, this is manipulative. We sometimes do use our attitudes in manipulative ways. Katz suggests that the closer people are to satisfying our personal needs, the more likely we are to hold positive attitudes toward them.[5]

Ego Defense

According to Katz, attitudes also function to protect our self-image. It is no secret that we tend to hold attitudes that reinforce our own ideas about our selves. There is nothing wrong with this unless we do it at the expense of truth. Are you honest about your self? Look back at Chapter 2 where you made the "I am" statements. Did your answers accurately reflect who you really are or were you projecting an ideal self?

Sometimes when we cannot admit that we have a negative trait we project that trait onto a group or onto another person. It makes us feel levelheaded to think of other people as being too emotional. We may develop an attitude of "everyone is a gossip" in order to make us feel better about talking about other people. It makes us feel superior when we attach the label "inferior" to another person. Our perceiving of Susan as being manipulative may have less to do with how manipulative she actually is than with our own need to see her that way. These attitudes begin within us. The objects and people to which our attitudes are attached serve as convenient outlets for their

expression. The object or person has nothing to do with actually creating the attitude besides being available or convenient; the attitude stems from our own internal conflicts. If no outlet for expression is available, we may even create one.

We are hardly ever aware that we are using our attitudes to defend our egos. All people use them this way, to a certain degree. Some people are more defensive than others. And some people are more aware than others of their own reasons for holding certain attitudes. In some cases, we may know that we are doing it but we may not know why. In other cases, we may not even realize that we are deluding our selves.

Value Expression

The third function of attitudes identified by Katz is value expression. Even if some attitudes we hold keep us from revealing our true selves, other attitudes help us express positive things about our central values and about how we see our selves. In fact, an attitude can be said to be nothing more than an outlet for revealing our values—a means of self-expression. If we value honesty, our attitude toward cheating will reflect that value. We may tend to be very specific about the way we credit others with information we use from them; we may sit far away from others when we take an exam; we may be very careful about lending our lecture notes to people.

What rewards do we gain by sharing our attitudes and values with others? First, simply expressing such things gives clarity to our self-concept. Second, it may help us mold that self-concept so that it comes closer to what we want it to be. As an example, the way we dress reveals certain things about us. It shows the way we want to be revealed. If we dress and talk the same way as our friends do, we are clarifying our self-concept by establishing our identity with our peer group and rejecting, in part, the identity imposed upon us by other groups. Such clarity in our self-concept is important to growth and development and to a state of mental healthiness. It provides one more answer to the question, "Who am I?" As growth and development occur, it is also important to know that we are the type of person we want to be.

Sometimes we join groups so that we can reveal very personal, cherished attitudes without fear. Religious, political, and social action groups provide ideal environments for the expression of values. Such expression is satisfying and psychologically necessary.

Sometimes we join groups and then internalize the group's values. Our own attitudes may be strongly affected. This internalization is more likely to occur if 1) the group's values are already somewhat consistent with our own; 2) we are indoctrinated to do so; 3) we feel we are given an ample opportunity to participate; and 4) we are given an opportunity to share in the rewards of the group.

NSIDER THIS CONSIDER THIS

CONSIDER THIS CONSIDER THIS CONSIDER THIS CONSIDER THIS CONSIDER THIS CONSIDER THIS CO

"With the world in the mess it's in," she said, "it's a wonder we can enjoy anything. I tell you, the bottom rail is on the top."

Julian sighed.

"Of course," she said, "if you know who you are, you can go anywhere." She said this every time he took her to the reducing class. "Most of them in it are not our kind of people," she said, "but I can be gracious to anybody. I know who I am."

"They don't give a damn for your graciousness," Julian said savagely. "Knowing who you are is good for one generation only. You haven't the foggiest idea where you stand now or who you are."

She stopped and allowed her eyes to flash at him. "I most certainly do know who I am," she said, "and if you don't know who you are, I'm ashamed of you."

"Oh hell," Julian said.

"Your great-grandfather was a former governor of this state," she said. "Your grandfather was a prosperous landowner. Your grandmother was a Godhigh."

"Will you look around you," he said tensely, "and see where you are now?" and he swept his arm jerkily out to indicate the neighborhood, which the growing darkness at least made less dingy.

"You remain what you are," she said. "Your great-grandfather had a plantation and two hundred slaves."

"There are no more slaves," he said irritably.

"They were better off when they were," she said. He groaned to see that she was off on that topic. She rolled onto it every few days like a train on an open track. He knew every stop, every junction, every swamp along the way, and knew the exact point at which her conclusion would roll majestically into the station: "It's ridiculous. It's simply not realistic. They should rise, yes, but on their own side of the fence."

"Let's skip it," Julian said.

"The ones I feel sorry for," she said, "are the ones that are half white. They're tragic."

"Will you skip it?"

"Suppose we were half white. We would certainly have mixed feelings."

"I have mixed feelings now," he groaned.

—Flannery O'Connor, "Everything That Rises Must Converge"

When we join a political organization, we seek one that is somewhat consistent with our values. If the values are not entirely or exactly consistent with ours, political speeches, rallies, and discussions serve as an indoctrination program. Once a member of the group, we are given a chance to participate in business meetings and perhaps to join a committee. Finally, we share in the rewards of the group: the chance to interact with people who think as we do, the right to use the group's name, and the right to go to their sponsored activities. Our group affiliations can be extremely influential in determining the attitudes we come to hold.

Knowledge

The knowledge function of attitudes identified by Katz is one of the most important. Through this function we try to give meaning to an otherwise unorganized and chaotic world. Our attitudes help to provide a frame of reference for comprehending our environment. An attitude we hold becomes a standard against which we apply new information.

We need a certain amount of definition, distinction, consistency, and stability as a background for understanding. We use the attitudes we acquire for further organizing and structuring. A certain religion may help stabilize our world by giving us explanations and a rationale for the way things are. Science may do the same. Einstein's theory of relativity, for example, provided a structure and helped those in physics systematize many other conclusions related to his principle. We become favorably disposed toward a religion, science, or theory because it helps us give meaning to our world.

Probably the most common example of how attitudes serve the knowledge function is in our use of stereotypes. We adopt a stereotype to give us order and structure. We can make sense of a large number of items or random things by labeling and classifying. Notice the way this affects our interpersonal communication. We may have a stereotype about aggressive people that says such people tend to be shallow, fake, and in desperate need of attention. This stereotype might keep us from becoming involved with overbearing people. Similar stereotypes may help us categorize and respond to foreigners, old people, young people, fat people, thin people, etc. Although some of our reactions may be limiting or negative, we do need to find ways to make sense of our experience and stereotypical attitudes help us to do this. In this way, our attitudes serve the knowledge function by helping us organize and structure what we experience. They provide order and clarity from an overwhelming set of complexities.[6]

ATTITUDE CHANGE: FOR BETTER OR WORSE

When our attitudes are so deeply ingrained in us that we are hardly aware of them, it is very difficult to change them. And, similarly, it is difficult for us to cause attitude change in others. But there is a process by which attitude change takes place for most of us, especially if we are attempting to be more open and less rigid and more self-aware. This process can promote growth, as when we rid our selves of an unhealthy bias, or it can be manipulative, as when we try to persuade someone to hold the same attitude as we do. Let's look at how this process takes place.

As a communication source or receiver, we should be aware of what happens when we state an attitude to another person (or vice versa) and when we try to effect successful attitude change. At the outset, it should be clear that we always strive to maintain internal consistency, harmony, or balance among our personal beliefs, feelings, and actions.[7] What this means can be illustrated in one model of attitude change called Heider's Balance Theory.[8] Heider developed a model in which *P* refers to one person, *O* represents another person, and X stands for the topic being talked about. This is a useful way to picture the attitude change process.

Think of your self as person one, or *P*. The relationships between you and *O* and X will be represented by plus and minus signs. A plus sign indicates a positive attitude; a minus sign, a negative attitude.

Heider proposed that in interpersonal relations, you are in a state of balance if the people you like have the same attitudes you do. You are in a state of balance, too, if people you dislike hold different attitudes than you on the same topics. According to Heider, whenever you have three +'s or two −'s, the relationship will be balanced. (See Figure 2.)

In Figure 2, let X be a certain movie. In A, you like the other person and both of you like the movie (X). In B, you like the other person but neither of you likes the movie. In C, you like the movie and the other person does not, but you really do not care for him or her anyway. In D, you do not care for the other person or for the movie, even though the other person likes the movie. These are all what Heider would call states of balance. We feel comfortable in such situations because everything is stable or in equilibrium.

If, on the other hand, you have three −'s or two +'s, the relationship will be unbalanced. In E of Figure 3, you don't like the other person and neither of you likes the movie. In F, you both like the movie but you don't like the other person. In G, you like the movie and the other person, but the other person dislikes the movie. In H, you dislike the movie but you like the other person and he or she

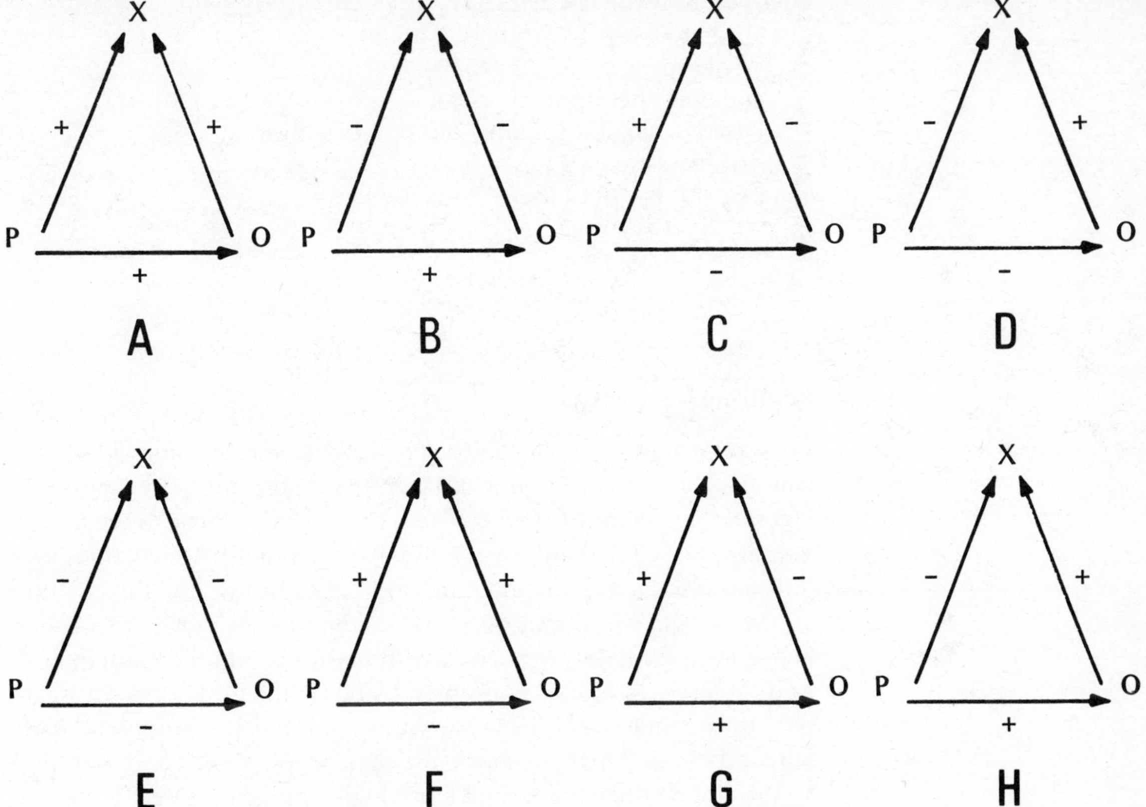

Figure 2. (P) *first person,* (O) *second person,* (X) *topic under discussion,* (+) *positive attitude,* (–) *negative attitude*

likes the movie. These are all what Heider would call states of imbalance. It's pretty obvious why. You are more comfortable when people you like think the same way you do.

Straining for Balance

When we are talking with a person we like very much and we realize that the two of us have different attitudes, we may try to bring our attitudes together.[9] How hard we try depends on how strong and how salient our own attitude is. It also depends on how much we like the other person and how important the relationship is to us.

Any strain for attitude balance will affect our interpersonal relationship with this other person. The more we want to make our attitudes like someone else's, the more likely we are to increase our communication with that person. And greater quantity of interaction—the sheer number of transactions—increases the probability that attitude change will occur.

CONSIDER THIS CONSIDER THIS CONSIDER THIS

i used to wrap my white doll up in
an old towel
and place her upon my chest
i used to sing those funny old school songs
god bless america
my country 'tis of thee
when i was young
and very colored

—Mae Jackson, "i used to wrap my white doll up in"

Resolving Imbalances

Because we prefer a state of balance, we perceive things in such a way that our balance is not disturbed. Suppose the X in E and F of Figure 2 is the movie *Duck Soup.* We see the movie with Arthur, whom we don't like. In E, we both hate the movie. In F, we both love it. In both cases we are uncomfortable because we don't like Arthur and we would prefer that our tastes were different from his. In G and H of Figure 2, we see *Duck Soup* with Barb, a good friend, but in both of these cases one of us likes the movie and the other doesn't. Again we are uncomfortable because we would like to agree with Barb. How do we resolve these states of imbalance?[10]

1. We could criticize the source of the disturbing message. We could think that Arthur and Barb don't mean what they say or simply don't know their own tastes.
2. We could say it doesn't matter. We may decide that disagreeing with Arthur or agreeing with Barb about this movie really isn't important.
3. We might go out and find additional information or other people to support us. This doesn't resolve the imbalance but it may make us more secure about our position. We could probably find movie reviews that reinforce our feelings whether they are positive or negative.
4. We might misperceive the other person's position. In the case of Arthur, this would mean thinking something like, "He said he didn't like it but really he just doesn't like black-and-white movies" or "He said he liked it but he laughed at all the stupid parts. He missed the really subtle humor." In the case of Barb our misperceptions might be more on the order of "She said she didn't like it but really she was just too tired to enjoy it. She wasn't in the mood" or "She said she liked it but she probably just thought I wanted her to say that."
5. We might tell our selves that our attitudes are not relevant to each

TRY THIS

For each of the following diagrams, think of an interpersonal situation you recall where the relationships were as shown here:

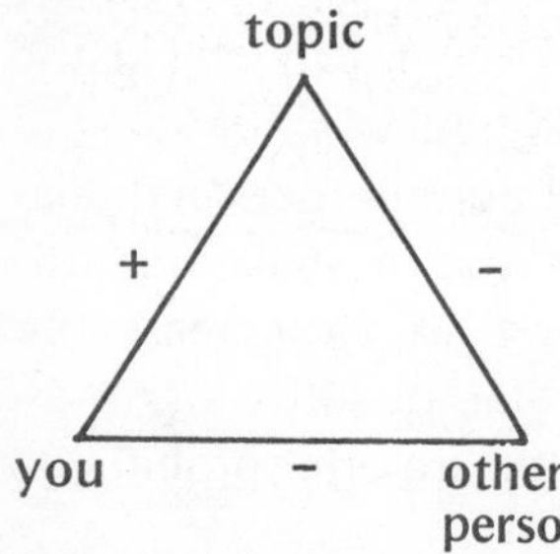

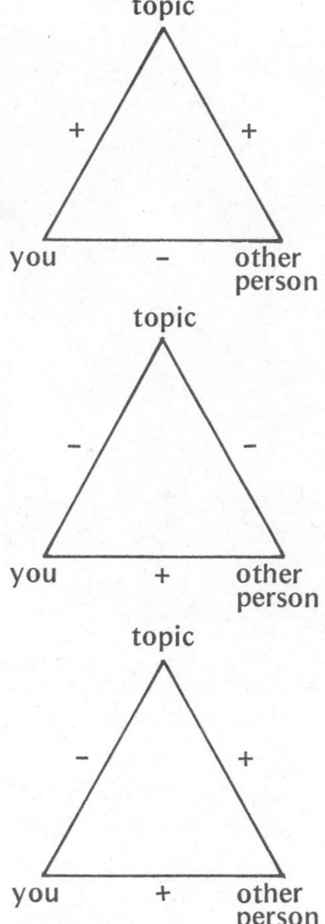

Which, if any, of these models are balanced? Do you agree that you feel more comfortable when your situation is in a state of balance?

other. For both Arthur and Barb, this might mean *we* were looking at the movie from the point of view of a film connoisseur, while *they* were casual moviegoers. Our perspectives are just too different to be relevant to each other.

6. We could try to convince Arthur or Barb that our attitude is the right one. This, of course, means convincing the others that they are wrong. We might try to do this by citing movie reviews or what we perceive as "popular opinion." Or we might simply describe in detail what we thought was good (or bad) about the film.
7. We could change our own attitude. We could say we'd reconsidered and really did think *Duck Soup* was great (or terrible).
8. We could consider the imbalance a virtue. We might convince our selves that it is healthy to admit we might agree with Arthur or disagree with Barb some of the time.

These methods of resolving imbalances show what we are up against when we set out to change someone's attitudes. We use some of these methods to protect our selves when we hear disturbing communications just as much as others do. But even if a change in attitude does occur, there is no guarantee that behavior will change correspondingly. Behavior changes will occur only if the direction, strength, and salience of the attitude are significant and if the context is appropriate. If Barb didn't like *Duck Soup* and we want to not only change her attitude but also to get her to go to more Marx Brothers movies, we'll have to convince her of the direction, strength, and salience of our own attitude.

The relationship between attitudes and behavior can be very loose. There is no reason to assume that because an attitude changes, a behavioral change will follow. People can be enthusiastic about something one minute and bored with it the next.

There are problems with looking at attitude change from Heider's perspective alone. The *P-O-X* model makes all attitudes look either positive or negative; of course we know that they vary not only in direction but also in strength and salience. We should realize that all options for resolving imbalance are equally possible; it is difficult to choose the most appropriate one. Finally, there are more alternatives available to us than simply changing one plus or one minus to bring a relationship into balance. We can alter as many elements as necessary to restore balance; the possibilities are infinite.

Temporary and Lasting Change

The point of discussing attitudes is to provide a base for understanding attitude change in our selves and thereby understanding what happens, in a unique way, for every individual. What causes us

to change our attitudes? Do we wake up one morning and say, "My attitude toward my family is poor. I think I'll replace it"? Not likely. We need time to realize the need for change and to make that change permanent.

We change our attitudes for a variety of reasons. Another person may give us a reward for changing our behavior or punish us for not changing it. This kind of change is called *compliance*. We may comply for the moment but really not change our attitudes. This kind of change is frequently only temporary. For example, we know we will be punished if we get caught disobeying the speed limit. We may comply with the law, even if we object to it, when the threat of punishment is near—we see a police car—but the compliance is temporary if we speed up when the threat disappears.

We may change our attitudes because of *identification*. If someone we admire holds a particular opinion, we may try to be like that person by adopting attitudes that are similar to his or hers. But when we are away from that person, our attitudes may change back to their original position. If we wanted to change another person's attitude through persuasion, one way to do it might be by using identification. We would try to present an honest, trustworthy, and credible image that the other person could identify with.

Internalization occurs when we adopt an attitude because we are truly convinced by it. If someone convinced us to quit smoking because it was harmful to our health, we might adopt the attitude because we were truly convinced we would suffer if we did not. We might be inclined to change our attitude toward a pass-fail grading system if someone convinced us that prospective employers prefer job candidates who took courses for a letter grade. Changes such as these are likely to be long lasting since they are based on intellectual and emotional agreement and do not depend on the presence of arbitrary reward or punishment or on another person.[11]

Up to this point, I've been talking about the ways we deal with challenges to our existing attitudes and how we adjust our thinking to maintain and protect those attitudes. However, we actually do change attitudes at times. There are reasons. For example, we might be coerced to change. If we do something illegal, law enforcement authorities may force us to change. Our attitude toward freedom may result in continual excessive speeding. The authorities may coerce us by 1) giving us a warning, 2) taking away our driver's license, or 3) putting us in jail. We might change our attitudes, too, because of more subtle coercion, or propaganda. An organization may get us to accept its doctrines through "mass hypnosis, constant repetition, loaded language, the subtle use of social pressures, or the appeal to irrelevant loves, hates, and fears."[12]

We might also change our attitudes because of manipulation. A manipulator may exploit us, use us, or control us.[13] This may be blatant control, as when a friend says, "If you have that attitude, you will no longer be my friend." Or it may be more subtle, as when advertisers try to change our attitude toward their product by suggesting it will make us happier and more popular.

The point is, there are many reasons for changing attitudes—some positive and some negative. We need to be aware of the forces at work on us. We also must try to avoid using coercion, propaganda, and manipulation in our interpersonal relations with other people. We should never use our knowledge of others for socially or self-destructive behavior.

It may sound as if attitude change occurs rapidly or as the result of a single conversation. With compliance, this may well be the case. But it takes considerable time and usually a number of interpersonal transactions for important changes to occur. Ongoing interpersonal communication is vitally important in changing another person's attitude.

Creating the Climate for Attitude Change

The problem in dealing with attitudes in any capacity is that we have so many different predispositions to act and so many influences operating. We can never know exactly what factors will work to change someone's attitude.

TRY THIS

All advertising is meant to be persuasive. Advertisers assume they have to change our attitude toward their product to get us to buy it. On a *P-O-X* model, we are *P*, the advertisers are *O*, and the product being advertised is *X*. We can assume *O* will always be favorable to *X*. Look at diagrams A, D, F, and H in Figure 2, where the *O-X* relationship is positive. Can you think of some television commercials which each of these diagrams describes? For example, diagram A describes a situation where we like both the product and the commercial itself. In D, we dislike both the product and the commercial. These are states of balance. Obviously, advertisers hope the A situation exists much of the time but we know that it doesn't. How do you resolve the attitudinal imbalance with advertisers represented by diagrams F and H? Think of the methods discussed in the text.

All we can say with certainty, with respect to changing an attitude, is that some need must be excited to cause attitudes to change. Some relevant cue in the environment must be touched. To do this successfully, we must know what is relevant as far as needs in general are concerned. If old attitudes do not keep up with current interests and needs, a person will be more likely to be open to someone who can suggest a new attitude. For example, if we are no longer happy with our choice of a major, we are susceptible to new attitudes because we are aspiring toward something else, even though we may not know what that something else is. But what does a new major need to offer us? What would make one major more attractive than another one? How could someone convince us to actually make a change? The following lists show some of the needs and environmental cues that might cause us to change our major:

Needs	**Environmental Cues**
our aptitude is more appropriate	better professors
better personality match	classes are nearby
interest will be greater	better social environment
more likelihood of getting a job	more variety in classes offered
more likelihood of success and security	better facilities

Some environmental cues might also be needs. It may be a function of the environment that another major offers more classes, but we may also want a major that offers more classes; thus, an environmental cue becomes a need fulfilled.

IMPROVING SKILLS IN PERSUASION

There are many situations in which we would like to make people think or act differently, where we would like to have an effect, where we would like to persuade another person. "Persuasion," in this discussion, will mean the interpersonal advice, urging, or inducements we use to get another person to think or act in a specific way. "Persuasion" is the label most commonly attributed to the tool used for bringing about changes in other people's attitudes.

The effect we will have on another person through persuasion depends on many variables. We must consider, for example, what the people we are trying to persuade think of us, whether they know we are trying to change them, how much exposure they are getting to our ideas, how committed they are to their present stance, whether they have expressed their position to others, and, obviously, how far apart our views are to begin with. These obstacles alone make our task difficult, but if we're really interested in changing an attitude, being aware of these elements can help us improve our odds. We should also consider how much time we will have to share our ideas and how many different contacts with the people we are likely to have—the sheer number of times we meet increases the likelihood of change. Affecting another person significantly is often a slow process, but if we want to be successful in changing attitudes, we must commit our selves to a long-term effort.

Show them that what you propose is approved by someone important to them. This is the concept I earlier labeled as "identification."[14] If others realize that people *they* consider important accept your ideas, your success will be more likely. Talking about friends, experts, or associates who already believe in the way you are suggesting helps others put their present beliefs or actions in perspective.

Show them that what you propose is consistent with their needs. What are the personal needs of the people you hope to persuade? Abraham Maslow categorized seven types of human needs: needs of physiology, safety, love, esteem, self-actualization, knowledge and understanding, and aesthetics.[15] Think of these as a hierarchy: each level, beginning with physiological needs, must be taken care of before going on to the next one. (See Figure 3.)

Actually, the hierarchy is not as rigid as it sounds. Most people have these basic needs in about the order Maslow suggests, but there are exceptions. For example, there are people who seek self-esteem above all else and highly creative people whose need to create is more important than any other need. Some people, too, have experienced long deprivation which may cause them to be content for the rest of their lives with just having their most elemental needs satisfied. There are also some people who were so deprived of love in the earliest months of their lives that their need to give and receive love as adults is distorted.

Physiological needs. These are the most basic needs having to do with our survival. We need food, water, and sleep to survive. These needs are the strongest because without satisfying them, we cannot pay attention to anything else.

Safety needs. Once our physiological needs are satisfied, our next concern is safety. Our concern for safety in our environment is reflected in our need for shelter, clothing, and protection from heat and cold. We want to prevent any kind of threat; we resist changes that jeopardize our safety.

Love needs. Family and friends help us satisfy our need to love

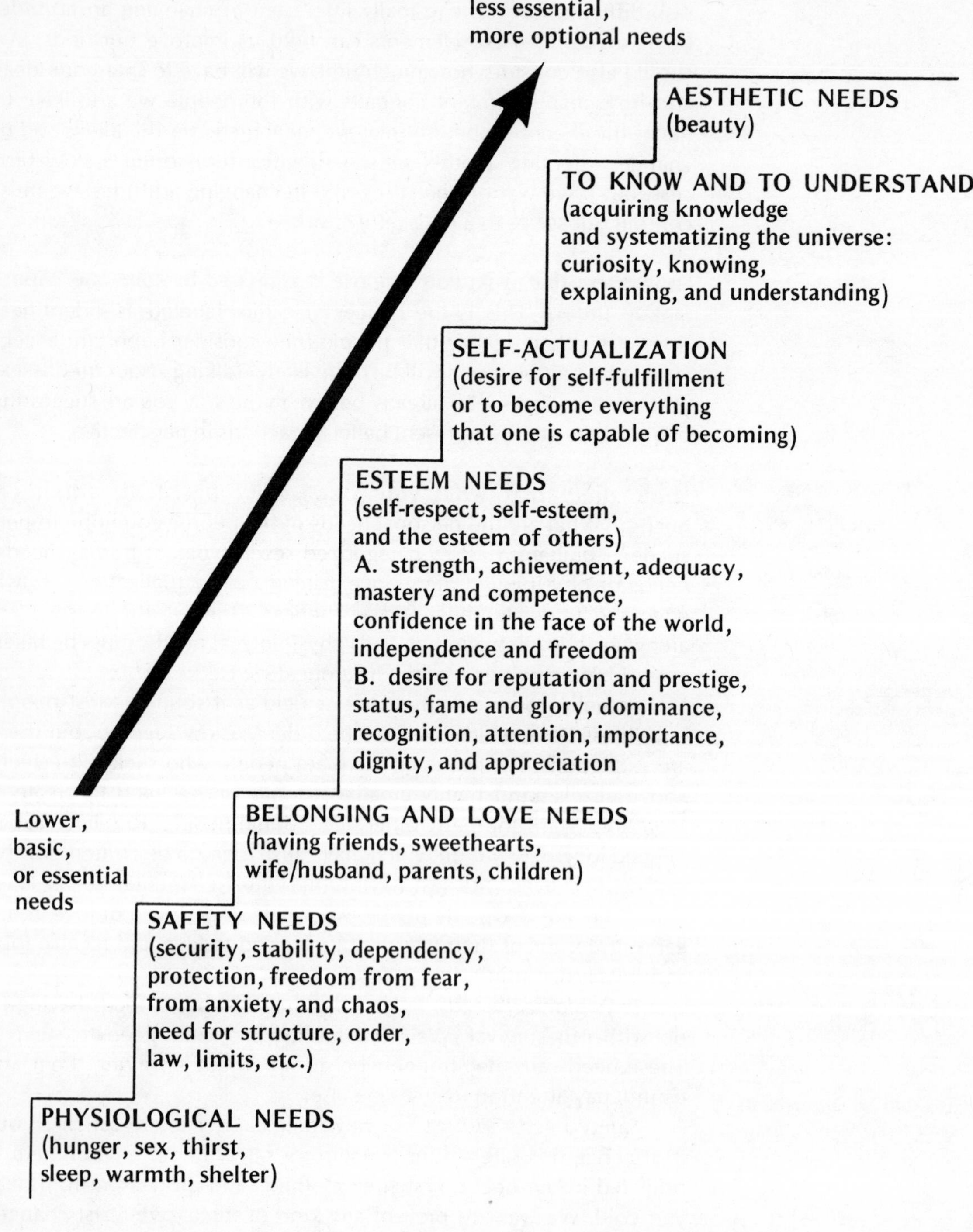

Figure 3. Maslow's hierarchy of needs.[21]

and to be loved. Also our membership in groups fulfills a need to belong, to be accepted, and to have friends. Marriage and professional associations also satisfy this social need.

Esteem needs. We need to be respected by others. This need has to do with our desire for status and a good reputation. If we seek recognition, aspire to leadership positions, desire awards, compliments, or acknowledgment for our work, our esteem need is operating. Our need for self-esteem is an important part of this need.

Self-actualization needs. When our more basic needs are satisfied, we can move toward self-actualization. This is our need to be everything we can be, to develop our selves to our highest abilities.

The need to know and to understand. We need to know and to understand in order to get along in society. For many people, knowledge and understanding are an important part of self-actualization. We need to inquire, to learn, to philosophize, to experiment, and to explain.

Aesthetic needs. Have you ever felt uncomfortable in a room where a picture was hanging crooked on the wall? For many people, such a situation is aesthetically displeasing and they need to remedy it. We have a wide range of aesthetic needs, but we all need to have things around us that we consider beautiful and orderly.

Exactly where our listener is in his or her development along this hierarchy and what he or she perceives to be the most pressing needs will make a difference in how we approach that person. Most college students, with the needs for physiological safety and security resolved for the time being by the fact that they are in school, can pay attention to love, esteem, and self-actualization needs. Achievement and success are values prominent in many college students' minds, but generally students have the same needs as other people.

If we want to persuade someone of something, we would do well to tie the attitude change we are seeking to those needs most salient to our listener. If a person is hungry and desperately trying to feed a family, it is absurd for us to try to persuade that person to get a job on the grounds that it would be self-actualizing. The person's most immediate need is for food, not self-actualization. If we really want to change that person's attitude toward "working," we had better relate "working" to his or her most pressing needs.

TRY THIS

Try to persuade someone of something you are not convinced of. Spend some time—even several days if necessary—continuing your effort.

Notice the effects you have on your listener. Were you successful? Why or why not? What kind of listener-needs did you appeal to in trying to persuade? Did you find some needs easier to work with than others?

Show that your proposal is consistent with alternative needs as well. If appealing to one need does not work, perhaps another one will. Do not assume that satisfying one need is necessarily enough. New times mean new needs; people are always changing. We may have misperceived the other person's needs to begin with.

CONSIDER THIS

Women are expected to behave differently from men in trying to get their way, and so they do, most of the time. Although feminine strategies often work, their use can seriously damage a woman's self-esteem and diminish the respect she gets from others. But if she adopts the more effective techniques used mostly by men, she may be called pushy or aggressive. . . . We asked over 250 college students, divided equally by sex, to write a paragraph on "how I get my way." The essays ranged from the use of blunt and simple argument to Machiavellian plots. . . .

Despite their diversity, the stories fall into certain patterns. First, we discovered that less than a third of the men (27 percent) but almost half of the women (45 percent) say they deliberately show emotion to get their way. They say things like, "I put on a happy face," or "I get mad." Women were responsible for over 75 percent of the negative emotions—sulking, pouting, crying. Fifty percent of the men who reported the use of negative emotion relied on anger; the others adopted a variant of the sad, sulking martyr role. Only 20 percent of the women who used negative emotion mentioned anger. Forty percent persuaded with sadness and sulkiness, and the rest with tears. . . .

To get their way, some

Know the power of fear in attitude change. Our subconscious fears are played upon all the time by people who want us to change our attitudes. Advertisers, for example, try to convince us that social or professional success hinges on our buying their product. A teacher may say that our grade depends on the successful completion of a project; we complete the project because we fear failure. We may be persuaded to carry a credit card out of fear of what would happen if we lost a large amount of cash.

Fear influences our attitudes and our behavior. There is nothing new or wrong with that—a certain amount of fear is necessary and healthy in many situations. But if we arouse fear to get another person to accept our ideas, we need to provide him or her with a means for removing the cause of the fear. Parents who persuade their children to wear their boots in the cold weather by telling them they will get sick if they don't should make sure their children understand what kind of sickness they mean. That is, they need not suggest pestilence and death will necessarily follow a few minutes with wet feet. And parents could say that the main point is not the boots themselves, but that the children are likely to stay healthier if they keep warm and dry.

There is an element of manipulativeness in using the fear approach. Be aware when someone is trying to use it with you. It is a fairly low-level appeal and generally suggests a low evaluation of the other person's intellectual powers. Still, a parent will use fear if necessary to keep a child from crossing a busy highway. You must decide for your self if you think arousing fear as a means of persuasion has any place in mature communication.

Offer a reward or incentive. How much of an incentive we need to offer to get a person to change an attitude depends upon the attitude, the listener, us, and the situation. There is no way this can be determined without knowing the variables that operate in a given case. Sometimes we may get another person to go along with an idea if our reward is as simple as saying, "If you do it, I'll go with you." Sometimes it is not so simple. But generally our society operates on a system of rewards and incentives; people want something in return for something. That "something" may be as small as a word of praise at the right time or it may be as elaborate as a large and expensive gift. The reward that will work best depends wholly on the circumstances.

Think small. Perhaps the most important suggestion for changing attitudes is to first try to change others in some small way that is consistent with their long-range goals.[16] Small changes are often more ac-

people rely on reasoned argument, or at least say they do. Others, slightly fewer in number and with considerable overlap, approach a power play with bargains, hints, deceit, rewards, and coercion. Those in the second group are more likely to be concerned with manipulating the emotional tone of the situation. And they are apt to be women.

—Paula B. Johnson and Jacqueline D. Goodchilds, *Psychology Today,* October 1976

ceptable and create less conflict and defensiveness than big changes. And small changes may show results more quickly, making bigger changes easier to come by later on.

Our attitudes are influenced by our experiences, including all the attachments we form with other people—people in our family, living area, schools, and social groups. Because of the ties we all have to reference groups and to other people, attitude change is a complicated process. We are likely to encounter opposition, conflict, and defensiveness as we deal with attitudes. Some disagreement is always likely. How to overcome the opposition, conflict, and defensiveness that stands in the way of successful interpersonal communication is the subject of the next chapter.

OTHER READING

John Powell, *The Secret of Staying in Love* (Niles, Ill.: Argus Communications, 1974). Powell discusses the human condition, human needs and the experience of love, love and communication, and the emotions. The author's warm, personal approach is interesting and enjoyable. The exercises provided include an emotional inventory that is effective for developing self-awareness.

Milton Rokeach, *Beliefs, Attitudes, and Values* (San Francisco, Calif.: Jossey-Bass, Inc., 1972). This textbook provides a philosophical and scientific approach to attitude and value formation. It is highly recommended to the student interested in an in-depth exploration of the development of attitudes, beliefs, and values.

Theodore Isaac Rubin, *The Angry Book* (New York: Collier Books, 1969). This is a book about anger. Rubin encourages readers to understand and work through their feelings about anger. This can lead to greater health, a fuller life, success, and happiness, Rubin contends. This is a down-to-earth presentation. The author's suggestions appear sound.

David Viscott, *The Language of Feelings* (New York: Arbor House, 1976). In straightforward, interesting language, Viscott demonstrates how feelings like hurt, anger, guilt, anxiety, and depression can be overcome by freeing the self of emotional debt.

John Wood, *How Do You Feel? A Guide to Your Emotions* (Englewood Cliffs, N.J.: Prentice-Hall, Inc., 1974). This is a book about people sharing their own feelings. It offers new possibilities, new ways to grow, new directions. Wood deals specifically with more than thirty emotions.

NOTES

[1] Irving Sarnoff, "Psychoanalytic Theory and Social Attitudes," *Public Opinion Quarterly* 24 (Summer 1960), 261.

[2] Milton Rokeach, *Beliefs, Attitudes and Values* (San Francisco: Jossey-Bass, 1968), p. 111.

[3] From "The Functional Approach to the Study of Attitudes" by Daniel Katz, *The Public Opinion Quarterly* 24 (1960), pp. 163–204. Reprinted by permission of Elsevier North-Holland, Inc.

[4] Attitudes acquired in the service of the adjustment function are either the means for reaching the desired goal or for avoiding the undesirable one. See Daniel Katz and Ezra Stotland, "A Preliminary Statement to a Theory of Attitude Structure and Change," in *Psychology: A Study of a Science*, Vol. 3, ed. by Sigmund Koch, (New York: McGraw-Hill, 1959), pp. 434–443.

[5] Katz, "The Functional Approach . . ."

[6] Walter Lippman, *Public Opinion* (New York: Macmillan, 1922), p. 95. Lippman's contribution to the study of attitudes was his description of stereotypes.

[7] William J. McGuire, "The Current Status of Cognitive Consistency Theories," in *Cognitive Consistency: Motivation Antecedents and Behavioral Consequences*, ed. by Shel Feldman (New York: Academic Press, 1966), p. 1.

[8] From "Attitudes and Cognitive Organization" by Fritz Heider, *The Journal of Psychology*, 1946, 21, 107–112. Reprinted by permission. The theory is developed more extensively in his *Psychology of Interpersonal Relations* (New York: John Wiley, 1958).

[9] This is called "symmetry theory," and is developed in Theodore M. Newcomb, "An Approach to the Study of Communicative Acts," *Psychological Review* 60 (1953), 393–404. Robert B. Zajonc, in "The Concepts of Balance, Congruity, and Dissonance," Kenneth K. Sereno and C. David Mortensen, *Foundations of Communication Theory*, (New York: Harper and Row, 1970) p. 185,

suggests that Newcomb's notion of "strain toward symmetry" will lead to a similarity of attitudes between *P* and *O* and X if *P* is attracted to *O*.

[10] Herbert W. Simons, "Persuasion and Attitude Change," in *Speech Communication Behavior: Perspectives and Principles,* ed. by Larry L. Barker and Robert J. Kibler, (Englewood Cliffs, N.J.: Prentice-Hall, 1971), p. 239.

[11] Herbert C. Kelman, "Processes of Opinion Change," *Public Opinion Quarterly* 25 (1961), 57–78.

[12] Franklyn S. Haiman, "Democratic Ethics and the Hidden Persuaders," in Haig A. Bosmajian, *Readings in Speech* (New York: Harper & Row, 1965), p. 196.

[13] Everett L. Shostrom, *Man, the Manipulator* (New York: Abingdon Press, 1967), p. 15.

[14] Herbert C. Kelman, "Compliance, Identification, and Internalization: Three Processes of Attitude Change," *Journal of Conflict Resolution* 2 (1958), 51–60.

[15] Data from pp. 35–52 "Hierarchy of Needs" in *Motivation and Personality,* 2nd Edition by Abraham H. Maslow. Copyright © 1970 by Abraham H. Maslow. By permission of Harper & Row, Publishers, Inc.

[16] A summary of the findings which support this generalization can be found in C. A. Kiesler, *The Psychology of Commitment* (New York: Academic Press, 1971), pp. 14–17.

Chapter 8

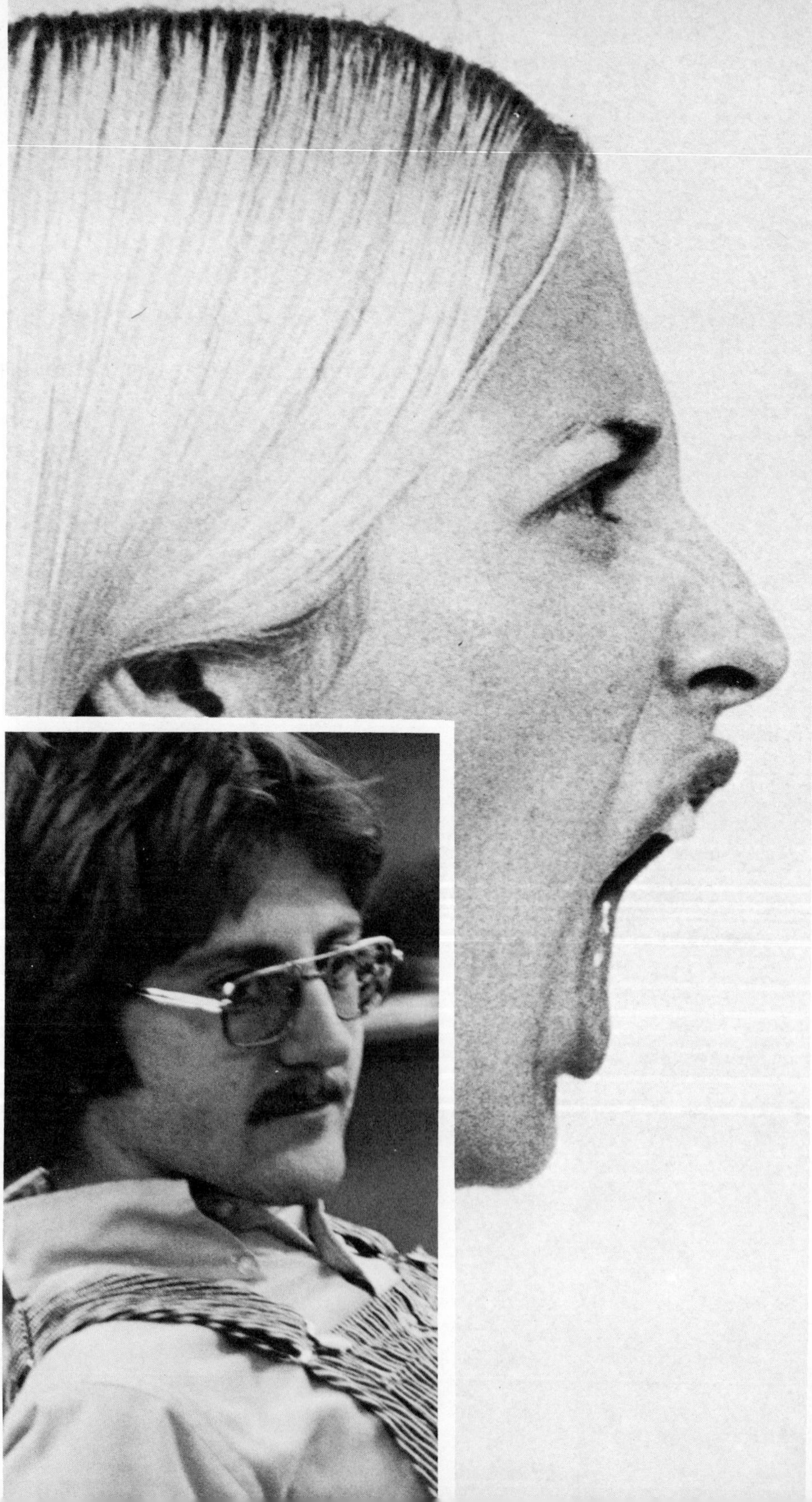

Overcoming Barriers: Coping with Conflict

So far I have talked a lot about openness, cooperation, and empathy in interpersonal communication. And those positive qualities are at the center of our success in communicating with others. In the last chapter I discussed attitudes and the nature of attitude change. As we attempt to change the attitudes of others, we often run into problems. We all face a certain amount of unpleasantness, hostility, conflict, and defensiveness in our relationships. What do we do about this? We can ignore it. Our society values cooperation and has not taught us how to deal with conflict or even to admit it exists in most cases. But ignoring conflict is not the solution. We can start to deal with conflict by accepting the idea that it is part of life. Next we can learn ways to manage it or cope with it. Finally we can practice those methods or skills.

We'll begin this chapter by considering how our society views conflict and how each of us reacts to it personally. Then I'll discuss ways of coping with conflict with suggestions for some skills to practice. Understanding the nature of conflict will help us to facilitate cooperative behavior, resolve problems, and enhance our interpersonal relationships and contacts. We can't eliminate conflict, but we can start to look at it as something we can handle.

HOW SOCIETY VIEWS CONFLICT

Conflict is considered bad in our society. You may have come to believe that conflicts are the cause for marriages to be dissolved, for employees to be fired, and for demotions, demerits, demoralization, and divisiveness. Certainly arguments, disagreements, and fights do

TRY THIS

Can you think of specific people who fit the following phrases?

1. **She really is kind.**
2. **Aren't they friendly?**
3. **They would do anything in the world for you.**
4. **He'd give you the shirt off his back.**
5. **She always has a smile on her face.**
6. **Isn't he sweet?**
7. **It wouldn't be a party without him.**
8. **She really is all heart.**

Can you think of other phrases that emphasize the nonaggressiveness we prize in our society?

CONSIDER THIS

What comes out of the whole range of questions about disagreements, however, is the strong sense that how **husbands and wives express their disagreement is much more important than** what **they disagree about. We asked**

force people apart and damage relationships. But more than likely it is not the conflict itself that causes the break in these relationships, but the poor handling of the conflict.

Anger, often one of the underlying causes of conflict, is also considered taboo in our society. This is supposed to be the age of reason and togetherness. Anger is not "gentlemanly," "ladylike," "nice" or "mature." The mere mention of fighting is enough to make some people uncomfortable. They may talk of their "differences" or of their "silly arguments" but not of "fights" because they feel "fight" implies a lack of maturity and self-control. Fighting here means verbal and nonverbal quarreling, not physical battle. Actually, not to admit to conflict or fighting implies a lack of maturity. People who are mature *do* fight. When we are on intimate terms with another person, our closeness may be characterized by quarreling and making up. We may try to live in harmony and agreement with another person but this desire alone creates a need for conflict—just to establish and maintain *our* notion of harmony and agreement.[1]

Our society has conditioned us to dislike and dread personal, aggressive openness. Well-liked people are described with such phrases as, "She is very kind; she'll do anything for anyone" or "He doesn't have a nasty bone in his body" or "She wouldn't raise her voice to anyone." Think of people you know who are admired and the phrases people use to describe them. Nonaggressiveness is praised and admired.[2] We are often taught that nobody will like us unless we are cheerful and that nice people do not fight.

Our society's attitude toward nonaggressiveness may be responsible for the vicarious pleasure many people get from watching the violent acts of other people. Sports such as hockey, football, and boxing include elements of violence; violence is also prominent in the news, in movies, and on television. Anger and aggressiveness are officially taboo, but as a society we are obsessed and fascinated with them and admire them. Our heroes and heroines are powerful, robust, forceful characters. There seems to be a difference between what we give lip service to and what we actually like. There is no doubt that conflict *can be* destructive. Whether it is harmful or helpful depends on how it is used.

HOW YOU VIEW CONFLICT

Healthy interpersonal communication is *not* conflict-free. Conflict is a part of all the relationships we have with other people. It can be constructive or destructive, depending on how we manage it.[3] Conflict is often the constructive means we use to challenge established

readers what they are most likely to do when they are displeased with their husbands and what their husbands are most likely to do—say nothing, brood about it, hint that they're unhappy, express their feelings or start an argument. We also asked how often they and their husbands behave in these different ways when they do argue—leave the room, sulk, sit in silence, swear, shout, hit out, cry or break things.

The most happily married wives are those who say that both **they and their husbands tell each other when they are displeased and thus try to work out their displeasure together by communicating in a calm and rational way. They also say that they and their husbands rarely or never fight in any of the different ways we listed; that is, they seldom resort either to the active-aggressive fighting (swearing, shouting, hitting out, crying or breaking things) or to passive-aggressive fighting (leaving the room, sulking or staying silent).**

The wives who are most unhappily married are in relationships where one or both partners can't talk calmly about what's bothering them or when one or both do a lot of fighting in the traditional ways. If one partner tends to avoid a fight and the other is a fighter, they're just as likely to be unhappy as if both were fighters.

—*Redbook,* June 1976

norms and practices and at times it is the means through which we are our most creative and innovative. Conflict often motivates us to summon up our untapped abilities. Some of our most eloquent moments result from impromptu situations that occur when we have been stopped from doing something or need to get our way. We should concentrate on managing interpersonal conflict to gain the maximum benefit, discovering our own best style of handling it in the process.

Any time we get together with another person for more than a short while, conflicts may arise that are serious enough to destroy our relationship if we do not know how to handle them. There are no magic formulas for overcoming barriers and resolving breakdowns. But we can look at those breakdowns in a fresh way. The fact that we are unique and that we experience the world in a unique way is enough to generate conflict because conflict occurs when human differences or uniquenesses meet. In addition to being unique, each of us is also able to make choices. We can decide how to handle the disagreements we encounter.

It may seem discouraging to think that even in the very best of relationships there is going to be conflict and that, on top of that, there is no guarantee that the conflict can be resolved. But we can change the way we deal with it. First we need to confront our own feelings. There are different styles of handling conflict. To know what happens when we disagree is a useful starting point.

WHAT HAPPENS WHEN YOU DISAGREE

Conflict is simply a situation in which we, our desires, or our intentions are in opposition to those of another person. Opposition means incompatibility: if our desires predominate, the other person's will not.[4] If we want to go to one movie and our friend wants to go to another one, a state of conflict results. If we feel we deserve an A and our instructor thinks a B is all we deserve, we are in conflict. If we believe that one interpretation of a poem is correct and our classmates think another one is more appropriate, we have another conflict situation. There are, of course, honest differences of opinion that lead to conflict. But there are also barriers and breakdowns in communication that create conflict and can be avoided.

Communication Barriers and Breakdowns

An atmosphere of acceptance is essential to preventing breakdowns in communication. Without acceptance, messages may not be re-

ceived at all or may be distorted if they are received. Not receiving a message or distorting it causes conflicts. An atmosphere of acceptance can be affected by contrary attitudes, newly acquired contrary opinions, jumping to conclusions, credibility, and hostility.[5]

Contrary attitudes. Our prejudices, biases, and predispositions affect the way we interact with and perceive others. When other people's views are contrary to ours, our reactions are aroused through a sense of irritation. This will become a barrier to communication unless we make a concerted attempt to be tolerant, understanding, and personally poised.

Newly acquired contrary opinions. Converts to a religious belief are generally thought to be stronger believers than those who have been brought up with the belief. The closer we are to the time we acquired a new opinion, attitude, or belief, the more rigid we will be in defending it. And the more rigid we are, the less vulnerable we are to change. Conflict is most frustrating when neither person is willing to be flexible. As time passes, we may begin to be more receptive to contrary ideas, even though we may still firmly hold our original belief. If we are conscious of the effects of the passage of time on creating an atmosphere of acceptance, we will be more careful about our timing when we need to present a new and potentially controversial idea to someone.

Jumping to conclusions. The problem with jumping to conclusions is that the climate of acceptance is destroyed when we rush to make a decision before we have enough facts on which to base the judgment. When we do not really listen, review the facts, or try to examine all the messages we are receiving, we create an atmosphere of misinformation and distrust which works against effective communication.

Credibility. Acceptance is affected if one of us perceives the other to be a person of low credibility. If we suspect someone of being unfair, biased, unreliable, hostile, or contradictory, we are not likely to hear what he or she says. This basic lack of acceptance creates a serious handicap to communication. To focus on the content of the message and not on the person will help, but a climate of low credibility is difficult to overcome.

Hostility. In the presence of outright hostility, it is very hard to achieve an atmosphere of acceptance. Hostility begets hostility. When we become aware of hostility directed toward us, we are likely to respond with a potentially hostile posture—prepared, alert, and equipped for a self-defensive action. Hostility then intensifies and communication is blocked.

TRY THIS

Every day we encounter many conflict situations. Of the following, which do you consider critically important? Which seem irrelevant to you?

1. Conflict with another person for control of your life

2. Conflict over what you should eat

3. Conflict about how you spend your money

4. Conflict about how you relate to other people

5. Conflict over how clean you keep your living area

6. Conflict about how you spend your time

7. Conflict over your lifetime goals

8. Conflict over whether or not you should get a job

9. Conflict about your driving habits

10. Conflict over what you want to believe in

11. Conflict over your use of tobacco, marijuana, alcohol, or drugs

12. Conflict about how you think of your self (your self-respect, self-esteem, or ego)

Styles of Handling Conflict

Conflict can evolve from situations that are critically important as well as from seemingly irrelevant ones. By "important" I mean situations where basic moral or ethical values are challenged. Such a situation might occur in a family where some members hold politically conservative views and other members have strong liberal tendencies—conflicts may spring up about military service, tax laws, and countless other subjects. Seemingly irrelevant situations occur daily as we must decide what to wear, whether or not to go to class, or where to eat lunch.

It is not for us to judge the importance of conflict to anyone else. What is a conflict situation to one person may not be for another person. Just as people view conflict differently, they deal with it differently. Some people tend to be more conflict-prone than others; they are sometimes less adaptable and their points of view tend to oppose other people's. Some people, too, get certain satisfactions from setting up competitive, win-lose situations. I won't explore all the psychological reasons, but this is a type of person most of us have known. When someone else takes a stand, you can almost predict that this conflict-prone person will stand squarely against that position and an argument will ensue.

Whether we are conflict-prone or not, we can ignore conflict by actively denying that it exists or by running away from it. We can attack the other person directly by challenging his or her credibility. Direct attacks can take many forms; all are destructive to effective communication. There are, fortunately, some other alternatives:

1. We can give in or agree to meet the other person halfway.
2. We can postpone the confrontation, hoping that the passage of

time will eliminate the conflict, shed new light on the situation, make one side in the conflict predominate, or cause the other person to forget about it.

3. We can work through the problem until differences are resolved or both of us agree to disagree.

Using the wrong approach can do irreparable damage to a relationship. On the other hand, interpersonal communication can be enhanced if the conflict is handled effectively. People essentially take one of two positions: they may "erupt" or they may "withhold."[6]

"Erupters" tend to enter a conflict situation with vigor. They might lash out at the opposition, bystanders, and whoever else is available, venting their emotions. When these people believe they are right, they may be unwilling to compromise. They may find it hard to apologize or to forgive. They use this means of reacting because they know of no other alternatives, or they know them but do not practice them.

"Withholders" tend to be afraid of conflict. Because of exposure to highly emotional people, because of upbringing, or because of certain personality characteristics, these people may avoid expressing any conflict-oriented feelings. They withhold their frustrations, anger, hate, resentment, irritations, and annoyances. Sometimes these feelings build up and are let out all in one emotional avalanche, but more often they build up inside, causing mental and physical harm. Self-hate is just one of the possible side effects resulting from the containment of strong feelings.

Neither of these ways leads to satisfactory solutions. Only the third way—working through the problem until differences are resolved—makes any sense for strengthening interpersonal relationships, yet this alternative is not often used. I will label people who take this approach "confronters" or "copers."

COPING WITH CONFLICT: A SUCCESSFUL APPROACH

An approach has been designed for managing all stressful conflict situations that puts a high priority on creative coping and on maintaining self-esteem. How successfully we use these coping behaviors depends on our recognition of a conflict situation and on our ability to keep our wits about us as we put this approach into action. The four main elements of this approach to coping are gaining information, organizing our selves, striving for independence, and anticipating conflict situations.[7]

"We all realize that violence should never take the place of reasoned discussion in the settlement of most disputes."

Information: Get Enough of the Right Kind

In any communication setting, whether conflict-laden or not, we act best when we are well informed. In a conflict situation, we need to find out all we can about the problem to assure our selves that we have more than one way to deal with it. The information we pick up may involve the nature of the communication itself or it may involve the other person. Problems with information may develop in three major ways: through overload, manipulation, and ambiguity.

Communication overload. If one person provides another person with more information than he or she can handle, a problem will arise.[8] We call this "overload." The information I am referring to here has to do with the content of a communicator's message to a listener, not with information of a general nature about a conflict situation, as discussed above.

A human being can handle only so much information at one time. This has to do with the capability of the human brain to decipher material but also with the various ways the emotions get bound to certain experiences. Often the root causes for conflict are closely tied to our emotional response pattern. In such cases, as sure as conflicts are bound to come up, so are the emotions that go along with them. If we are having an emotionally involving experience, it is difficult to take on and fully comprehend a new "load" of information at the same time. Our senses are preoccupied. If someone else tries to share some vital news with us while our feelings are thus tied up, interpersonal conflicts may result. We may experience this when we try to listen to a classroom lecture just after we've heard some upsetting news. The intensity of the emotional experience overshadows any material the teacher could offer. We simply don't have room for any more information; trying to fit it in would be overloading.

Manipulative communication. Communication breakdowns are likely to occur when a listener feels information is being offered with manipulative intent. You may have experienced manipulation at one time or another when you felt someone was using you or trying to control you. People manipulate other people for various reasons. In some cases, a person looks to others *for support.* Not trusting them to give it, he or she manipulates them to steer them in the right direction. Manipulation may also result *from love.* The problem is described by Everett Shostrom:

> We seem to assume that the more perfect we appear—the more flawless—the more we will be loved. Actually, the reverse is more apt to be true. The more willing we are to admit our weaknesses as human beings, the more lovable we are. Nevertheless, love is an achievement not easy to attain, and thus the alternative that the manipulator has is a desperate one—that of complete power over the other person, the power that makes him do what *we* want, feel what *we* want, think what *we* want, and which transforms him into a thing, *our* thing.[9]

Erich Fromm has said that the ultimate relationship between human beings is that of love—knowing a human being as he or she is and loving that person's ultimate essence.[10] Loving someone's "ultimate essence" is just the opposite of manipulation.

A third reason that manipulation occurs is *out of frustration with life.* People who feel overwhelmed may decide that since they cannot control everything, they will control nothing. They become passive manipulators. They may use various devices and tricks to accentuate their helplessness. They will try to get other people to make decisions for them and carry part of their burden, manipulating through their own feeling of powerlessness.

CONSIDER THIS "**Next time you are angry with your husband, why not try some childlike mannerisms: Stomp your foot, lift your chin high and square your shoulders. Then, if the situation merits it, turn and walk briskly to the door, pause and look back over your shoulder. Or you can put both hands on your hips and open**

your eyes wide. Or, beat your fists on your husband's chest. Men love this! Or, there is the timid, frustrated manner of pouting, looking woeful or looking with downcast eyes while mumbling under your breath, or putting both hands to your face, saying "Oh, dear!" These are only a few of the childlike mannerisms you can adopt.

Some of these actions may seem unnatural to you, at first. If they do, you will have to be an actress to succeed in childlike anger, even if only a ham actress. But, remember, you will be launching an acting career which will save you pain, tension, frustration, a damaged relationship and perhaps even save a marriage. Is any acting career of greater importance? So, turn on the drama. It is guaranteed to ease tension and bring humor into your life instead of pain.

. . . Acquire a list of expressions or words which compliment masculinity, such as "you big, tough brute," or "you stubborn, obstinate man," or "you hairy beast." Other appropriate adjectives are—unyielding, determined, difficult, hard-hearted, inflexible, unruly, stiff-necked, indomitable and invincible. Be certain that your words compliment masculinity and will not belittle his ego, such as the words little, imp, pip-squeak, insignificant, weak, simple-minded, etc. ”

—Helen B. Andelin, *Fascinating Womanhood*

There are two other reasons that people manipulate that appear to be near opposites. People may deal with others ritualistically in an effort *to avoid intimacy or involvement.* An example of ritualistic communication is the teacher who cannot deal with students in other than strictly teacher-student terms. The same type of ritualistic behavior might be seen in employer-employee and doctor-patient relationships.

Another reason people manipulate is *to gain the approval of others.* There are people who think they need to be approved of by everyone. They may be untruthful, trying to please everyone in their quest for acceptance. An example of this behavior is the friend who tells us everything we do is "great" just to keep us as a friend.

Ambiguous communication. Ambiguous information may contribute to a conflict situation because ambiguity almost always leads to misunderstanding.[11] Ambiguity can result when not enough information is provided or when it is too general. If one of your friends told you that everyone was going to the show tonight and that you should meet them downtown, you might easily misunderstand. Who is "everyone"? Where exactly should you meet them? What time? Also, the more abstract our language is, the more likely it is to be ambiguous and conflict-promoting.

Whenever we find our selves in a conflict situation, we should pay special attention to the kind of information we are exchanging: Is there enough? Is there too much? Is it manipulative? Is it ambiguous? It will be helpful to remember that every receiver of messages creates his or her own meaning for that communication based upon what he or she perceives. We can never know exactly which stimulus aroused meaning in someone else's head. The kinds of phenomena that can provoke meaning are limitless—there is no way anyone can control with certainty all the variables that will eliminate potential conflict situations.

Finally, remember that the message a receiver gets is the only one that counts in a conflict situation. The message that he or she acts upon may be quite different from the information that was sent. To discover precisely what message was received is useful in coping with conflict. We may need to ask the other person, "Now, what did you hear?" or "What is it that you understand?" or "What are you going to do?" As far as possible, we need to know where the other person is coming from if we are to deal successfully with conflict.[12]

Organization: Sort Things Out

Think of a situation to which you had a powerful emotional response: fear, anger, grief, or passion. If you needed to cope with conflict at that time, you may have found your judgment was affected. To reestablish stability and a sense of right and wrong we need to organize our selves within our selves—we need to get our selves together.[13]

This is not to say we should avoid emotional experiences. Feelings of fear, anger, grief, and passion are healthy and normal and should not be repressed. But when in the throes of extreme emotional experiences, we must remember that our senses are affected, that we cannot depend on our perceptions. This is why, for example, people are wise to make funeral arrangements *before* a person dies. In the emotional aftermath of the death of a loved one, decision making is difficult and judgments are not as rational as they are at other times.

When our perceptions are distorted, conflict is likely to escalate because of the misunderstandings exchanged. One such misunderstanding has been labeled by David W. Johnson as "mirror image." In conflict, "mirror image" occurs when both people think they are right, both think they were the one maligned, both think the other person is wrong, and both think they are the only one who wants a just solution.

Another kind of misunderstanding occurs when one person sees

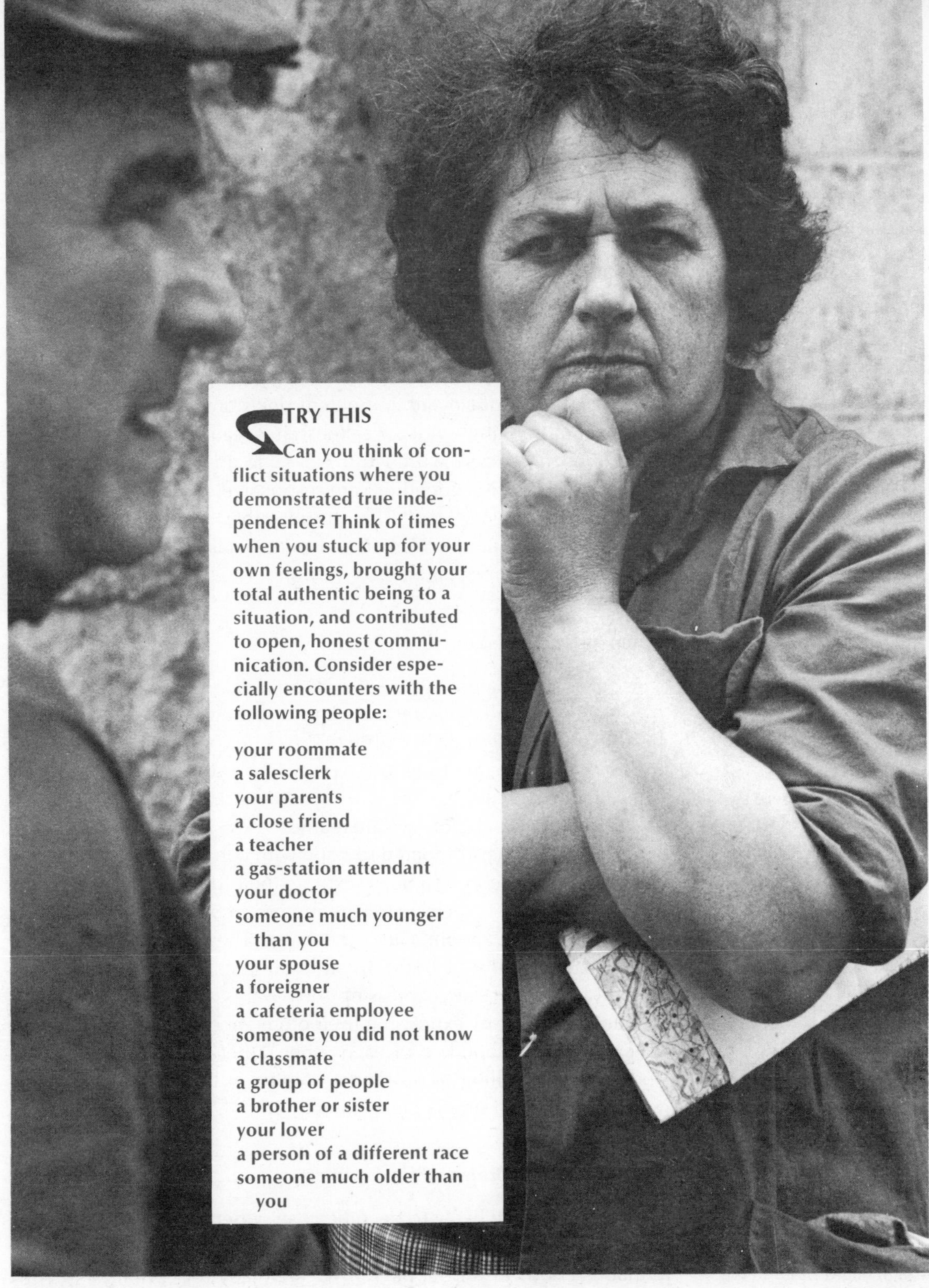

TRY THIS

Can you think of conflict situations where you demonstrated true independence? Think of times when you stuck up for your own feelings, brought your total authentic being to a situation, and contributed to open, honest communication. Consider especially encounters with the following people:

your roommate
a salesclerk
your parents
a close friend
a teacher
a gas-station attendant
your doctor
someone much younger than you
your spouse
a foreigner
a cafeteria employee
someone you did not know
a classmate
a group of people
a brother or sister
your lover
a person of a different race
someone much older than you

identical acts committed by both sides but considers those of the other person illegitimate, unfair, unjust, and unreasonable while viewing his or her own as legitimate, fair, just, and reasonable considering the circumstances. This is known as the "double standard."

In conflict situations, too, thinking becomes polarized. Both individuals might come to have an oversimplified view of the conflict. In this uncomplicated view, anything the other person does is bad and everything we do is good. Obviously, when such misunderstandings are at work, it is difficult to organize our thinking.

When we are aware that we are not coping rationally, we would do well to seek help from others. It's a good idea to go to trusted friends for help in making decisions and carrying out plans. To recognize that we cannot make competent decisions until we have reorganized our thinking is not a weakness; it is realistic and mature.

To be organized within our selves is an awareness function. People who "have it together" are responsive, alive, and interested. They listen to themselves.[14] The attitudes they express are based on firmly rooted values. An organized person takes time to think, to monitor, and to reevaluate before responding.

CONSIDER THIS

"Listen to that rain!" said the woman to her husband. "Will it never stop?"

"What harm is a sup of rain?" he said.

"That's you all over again," she said. "What harm is anything, as long as it doesn't affect yourself?"

"How do you mean, when it doesn't affect me? Look at my feet. They're sopping. And look at my hat. It's soused," He took the hat off, and shook the rain from it onto the spitting bars of the grate.

"Quit that," said the woman. "Can't you see you're raising ashes?"

"What harm is ashes?"

"I'll show you what harm," she said, taking down a plate of cabbage and potato from the shelf over the fire. "There's your dinner destroyed with them." The yellow cabbage was lightly sprayed with ash.

"Ashes is healthy, I often heard said. Put it here!" He sat down at the table, taking up his knife and fork, and indicating where the plate was to be put by tapping the table with the handle of the knife. "Is there no bit of meat?" he asked, prodding the potato critically.

"There's plenty in the town, I suppose."

"In the town? And why didn't somebody go to the town, might I ask?"

Independence: Be Your Own Person

Most conflict situations we deal with on a daily basis are not the extremely taxing kind. The better we know our selves, the better we will be able to cope with daily conflict. The better organized we are, too, the more likely we are to be our own person—autonomous. We need to be free to act and to deal with conflict and we must avoid being pushed into action before we are ready.[15]

The people best prepared to cope with conflict are spontaneous. They have the freedom to be, to express their full range of potentials, to be the masters of their own lives and not to be easily manipulated. Successful copers are open and responsive. They can assert their own independence without trying to stifle another person's. They show their independence by expressing their wants and needs instead of demanding them, by expressing their preferences instead of ordering, by expressing acceptance of each other rather than mere tolerance, and by being willing to surrender genuinely to the other person's wishes rather than simply pretending to submit.[16]

Anticipation: Be Prepared for Conflict

Conflicts are more likely to become crises when they catch us totally unaware. Try to anticipate conflict situations. Try to cut your emotional reactions off at the pass. If we are ready for conflict and con-

"Who was there to go? You know as well as I do there's no one here to be traipsing in and out every time there's something wanted from the town."

"I suppose one of our fine daughters would think it the end of the world if she was asked to go for a bit of a message? Let me tell you they'd get husbands for themselves quicker if they were seen doing a bit of work once in a while."

"Who said anything about getting husbands for them?" said the woman. "They're time enough getting married."

"Is that so? Mind you now, anyone would think that you were anxious to get them off your hands with the way every penny that comes into the house goes out again on bits of silks and ribbons for them."

"I'm not going to let them be without their bit of fun just because you have other uses for your money than spending it on your own children!"

"What other uses have I? Do I smoke? Do I drink? Do I play cards?"

"You know what I mean."

"I suppose I do."

—Mary Lavin, "Brigid"

fident in our ability to deal with it, we'll be much less anxious if and when conflict develops.

By anticipating a conflict situation, we will be more likely to have some control over the context in which it occurs. Instead of focusing, for example, on whose fault the conflict is, we can try to get in touch with where we and the other person are and attempt to work from there.

In addition, with some anticipation, we can take responsibility for our feelings and actions. We can plan, in advance, to say such things as "I am angry" instead of "You make me angry," or "I feel rejected" instead of "You are excluding me again," or "I am confused" instead of "You don't make sense." In this way, we own our feelings—we take full responsibility for them. And we convey our feelings to others, creating trust in the process.

Finally, anticipation can cause us to be more aware. Resolving interpersonal conflict is easiest when we listen to the other person and respond to him or her with feedback. Conflict is likely to be reduced when we try to support and understand the other person.

IMPROVING SKILLS IN CONFLICT MANAGEMENT

The following ideas will aid in developing a constructive approach to dealing with conflict situations.[17] Remember that there are no guaranteed solutions or sure-fire approaches. Remember, too, that not all conflicts can be resolved but that we can always choose how to handle them.

Define the conflict.[18] How we view the cause, size, and type of conflict affects how we manage it. If we know what events led up to the conflict and especially the specific event that triggered it, we may be able to anticipate and avoid future conflicts. We should learn to see the true size of a conflict: the smaller and more specific it is, the easier it will be to resolve. When a large, vague issue or principle is involved, the conflict itself is often escalated and enlarged. We can get very upset over how the system of higher education stifles individual initiative and growth, but that is a large, vague issue. To narrow the cause of the conflict, we might focus directly on a particular professor we are having problems with.

View the conflict as a joint problem. There are two general ways of looking at a conflict: as a win-or-lose situation or as a joint problem. If we look at a conflict as a joint problem, there is a greater possibility for a creative solution which results in both of us being satisfied. If

CONSIDER THIS CONSIDER THIS CONSIDER THIS CONSIDER THIS CONSIDER THIS

When a child exceeds a limit, his anxiety mounts because he expects retaliation and punishment. The parent need not increase the child's anxiety at this time. If the parent talks too much, he conveys weakness—at a time when he must convey strength. It is at times like this that the child needs an adult ally to help him control his impulses without loss of face. The following example illustrates an undesirable approach to limits:

Mother: I see that you won't be satisfied until you hear me yelling. O.K. [Loud and shrilly] **stop it—or I'll beat the living daylights out of you! If you throw one more thing, I'll do something drastic!**

Instead of using threats and promises, mother could have expressed her very real anger more effectively:

"It makes me mad to see that!"

"It makes me angry!"

"It makes me furious!"

"These things are not for throwing! The ball is for throwing!"

In enforcing a limit, a parent must be careful not to initiate a battle of wills.

—Haim G. Ginott, *Between Parent and Child*

we are having trouble with our English professor, we could easily turn the situation into a win-lose confrontation. We might say, "She thinks she's so great, I'm going to show her. I'll go to the department head. . . ." If we perceive the conflict as a joint problem, we might say, "Perhaps she has a point; maybe if I go in to see her, we could talk about this." The way we label a conflict partly determines the way we resolve it.

Defining conflict as a joint problem means trying to discover the differences and samenesses between our selves and the other person. There is always the question of not just how *we* define the problem but also of how the *other person* defines the problem and how our definitions differ.

State the problem. We'll have a better chance of resolving a potential conflict quickly if we have a clear idea of what behavior is acceptable or unacceptable to us and if we express our position to the other person. When we say to another person, "When you interrupt me when we are talking to other people, I feel put down and unimportant" or "Every time you publicly criticize how I dress, I get angry with you," we explain specific behaviors that are unacceptable to us. And we can then discuss or change those behaviors.

When we focus on a specific bothersome behavior, we reveal what is going on inside us. We take responsibility for our feelings by using "I" language instead of "you" language. This lessens the likelihood of defensiveness by not placing the blame on the other person as we would if we said, "You insult me" or "You make me angry."

Check your perceptions. Under any circumstances, it is easy to be misunderstood, misquoted, or misinterpreted. Especially in a conflict situation, we should always check to make certain our message has been received accurately. We should also make sure we understand the other person's responses by paraphrasing them before we answer. Because our emotions quicken in times of conflict, further hurt

S CONSIDER THIS

CONSIDER THIS CONSIDER THIS CONSIDER THIS CONSIDER THIS CONSIDER THI

Some people get savage and bitter when to backbiters they re-
fer, But I just purr.
Yes, some people consider backbiters to be rankest of the rank,
But frankly, I prefer them to people who go around being frank,
Because usually when you are backbitten behind your back you
don't know about it and it doesn't leave a trace,
But frankness consists of having your back bitten right to your
face,
And as if that weren't enough to scar you,
Why you are right there in person to scotch the defamation,
and if you don't happen to be able to scotch it, why where
are you?
Frank people are grim, but genuine backbiters are delightful to
have around,
Because they are so anxious that if what they have been saying
about you has reached your ears you shouldn't believe it,
that they are the most amiable companions to be found;
They will entertain you from sunset to dawn,
And cater encouragingly to all your weaknesses so that they can
broadcast them later on,
So what if they do gnaw on your spine after enjoying your beer
and skittles?
I don't blame them the least of jots or tittles,
Because certainly no pastime such diversion lends
As talking friends over analytically with friends,
So what if as they leave your house or you leave theirs back-
biters strip your flesh and your clothes off,
At least it is your back that they bite, and not your nose off.
I believe in a place for everything and everything in its place,
And I don't care how unkind the things people say about me so
long as they don't say them to my face.

—Ogden Nash, "Hush, Here They Come"

or resentment can occur quickly through distortions caused by expectations or predispositions. Empathic listening is essential. We can determine where we are in our conversation with another person through paraphrases and summaries.

TRY THIS

How would you cope with each of the following situations? Would your reaction help to maintain a positive interpersonal relationship? Your goal should be to effectively cope with the situation without generating new or unnecessary conflict.

1. You have just been accused of cheating and you are not guilty.

2. You have been told that a trusted friend is sharing your intimate secrets with a person you despise.

3. Your roommate is telling you that you cannot use your room at certain times.

4. You have just bought a new car and one of your friends wants to borrow it for the weekend.

5. Some people you like want you to go drinking with them tonight and you have a tough exam in the morning.

6. Your parents have just told you they do not like the people you hang around with.

7. Your closest friend wants to break off your relationship.

8. You have been given what you consider an unfairly low grade by a teacher you have no respect for.

Generate possible solutions. It is important, once we have shared what is bothering us, to consider how change can occur. We need not come up with all the solutions ourselves. A joint, cooperative solution is more likely to work. Flexibility is important in this process. Julius Fast views flexibility as extremely valuable, calling it "an awareness of alternative solutions as well as the ability to discard one solution if it doesn't work and select another."[19] What is needed? What can the other person do? What can we do? What can be done together? These are realistic questions that should be raised. As we get possible answers to these questions, we should paraphrase and summarize them so that we are certain that both of us know what has been suggested and what alternatives exist.

Reach a mutually acceptable solution. When we have considered all the possible alternatives we and the other person could generate, we should decide which of them would be mutually acceptable. It is important that we find an answer somewhat agreeable to everyone involved. But we cannot stop there. We all should understand the possible outcomes of implementing the solution. What is likely to happen? We should also understand what needs exist for cooperative interaction. In what ways, for example, will a particular solution require us to work together? When we have come to a final agreement on how to settle our conflict, we should make certain everyone fully understands what we agreed on by paraphrasing and summarizing the results.

If we cannot reach an agreement we should stop. Plan another meeting. Try again later. To get away from the problem for a while may result in new insights being generated.

Implement and evaluate the solution. Before we put the proposed solution into effect, we should try to agree on how we will check it later to see if it solved the problem. Plan a check-up meeting to evaluate progress. After we implement the solution, we'll want to find out if the results are mutually satisfying. If they aren't, we might have to go back to the beginning, possibly to our original definition of the conflict. We should have some way of knowing how to tell if the implemented solution worked well or did not work at all. If we have moved through the conflict successfully or are at least making progress, some gesture of appreciation might be appropriate.

Conflict in interpersonal communication is an inevitable human experience. We are unique, the next person is unique; when these uniquenesses meet, conflict can occur. Conflict does not need to fracture friendships, split marriages, or break up other interpersonal relationships. There is nothing inherently destructive, threatening, or mysterious about conflict. How well we handle it while maintaining our values and our self-esteem and, at the same time, protecting the values and self-esteem of other people will help determine our effectiveness in interpersonal relationships. We are often called to stand up for our rights, values, and beliefs—to be assertive. Assertiveness is the subject of the next chapter.

OTHER READING

George R. Bach and Peter Wyden, *The Intimate Enemy: How to Fight Fair in Love and Marriage* (New York: Avon Books, 1968). Fighting is good for you, the authors contend. They provide constructive ways to use fights. This is an excellent book on how to use conflict and defensiveness positively. Many examples and illustrations demonstrate the significance and importance of their suggestions.

Ernst G. Beier and Evans G. Valens, *People-Reading: How We Control Others, How They Control Us* (New York: Warner Books, 1975). This book focuses on what the authors label "unaware communication"—cues delivered without awareness. The authors attempt to answer the questions, "Why do we behave as we do?" and "What kind of information do we have to look for and work with to change behavior?" Beier and Valens encourage the reader to examine and try to improve the whole fabric of unsettling relationships.

Eric Berne, *Games People Play: The Psychology of Human Relationships* (New York: Grove Press, Inc., 1964). Berne's catalog of games that people play in their family and business relationships is designed to heighten awareness. Berne contends that in playing games people are striving for an emotional payoff.

Julius Fast, *Creative Coping: Your Guide to Positive Living* (New York: Perennial Library, 1976). This is a survival manual on how to get along with our fellow human beings. We all use such coping elements as aggression, flexibility, empathy, reason, masking, and control. The iethods and examples in this book provide further alternatives and approaches.

Robert J. Ringer, *Winning Through Intimidation* (Greenwich, Conn.: A Fawcett Crest Book, 1974). The purpose of this book, like many of the others, is to promote awareness. To know what intimidation is, how people become intimidated, and how to avoid falling victim to intimidation can be helpful in avoiding conflict situations.

Everett L. Shostrom, *Man, the Manipulator: The Inner Journey from Manipulation to Actualization* (New York: Bantam Books, 1967). All people are manipulators. Many of us do not recognize the manipulation we use and are exposed to. Shostrom explains both the manipulations and the alternatives. There is an excellent chapter on "Teachers and Students."

NOTES

[1] George R. Bach and Peter Wyden, *The Intimate Enemy: How to Fight Fair in Love and Marriage* (New York: Avon Books, 1968), pp. 25–26.

[2] George R. Bach and Herb Goldberg, *Creative Aggression: The Art of Assertive Living* (New York: Avon Books, 1974), p. 82.

[3] Robert J. Doolittle, "Conflicting Views of Conflict: An Analysis of Basic Communication Textbooks," *Communication Education* 26 (March 1977) 121.

[4] Kenneth E. Boulding, *Conflict and Defense* (New York: Harper and Row, 1962), p. 5.

[5] Based on pgs. 172–176 from *Elements of Interpersonal Communication* by John W. Keltner. © 1973 by Wadsworth Publishing Company, Inc., Belmont, California 94002. Reprinted by permission of the publisher.

[6] Ron Adler and Neil Towne, *Looking Out/Looking In: Interpersonal Communication* (San Francisco: Rinehart Press, 1975), p. 303.

[7] Julius Fast, *Creative Coping: A Guide to Positive Living* (New York: William Morrow and Co., Inc., 1976), pp. 187–188.

[8] W. Charles Redding, *Communication Within the Organization* (New York: Industrial Communication Council, 1972), p. 87.

[9] Adapted from *Man, the Manipulator* by Everett Shostrom. Copyright © 1967 by Abingdon Press. Used by permission of Abingdon Press.

[10] Erich Fromm, "Man Is Not a Thing," *Saturday Review* (March 16, 1957), pp. 9–11.

[11] Richard C. Huseman, James M. Lahiff, and John D. Hatfield, *Interpersonal Communication in Organizations: A Perceptual Approach* (Boston: Holbrook Press, Inc., 1976), p. 99.

[12] Redding, *Communication Within the Organization*, pp. 28, 30, and 37.

[13] Fast, *Creative Coping*, p. 187.

[14] Ibid., pp. 187–188.

[15] Shostrom, *Man, the Manipulator*, p. 50.

[16] Ibid., p. 53.

[17] David W. Johnson, *Reaching Out* (Englewood Cliffs, N.J.: Prentice-Hall, Inc., 1972), pp. 217–219.

[18] This approach is a variation of Dewey's problem-solving method. See John Dewey, *How We Think* (Chicago: D. C. Heath, 1910).

[19] Fast, *Creative Coping*, p. 53.

Chapter 9

Getting There from Here: Assertiveness

You are sitting alone in your room one evening. You've done all your assignments and readings for the next day. Everything is quiet. "Now, finally," you think, "I have some time just for my self—to do what *I* want to do." Just then there is a knock at the door. A close friend asks you if you would, as a special favor, go to a meeting with her. You get a sinking feeling in your stomach. You really wanted this time to be alone and yet, after all, this is one of your closest friends! What do you do? How do you feel about your self and your friend as a result of your choice?

We've all had the experience of needing to assert our selves with loved ones, teachers, doctors, salesclerks, and public employees. With friends and with strangers. With children and with people much older than we are. How do we handle it? In this chapter I'm going to consider different ways of coping with situations that too often end up awkward and leave us with bad feelings about our selves and other people. I'm going to look at how our attitudes, ideas, and values affect our choices. I hope to give you information that will help you pinpoint your real feelings and improve your skills in direct, honest, and appropriate communication.

WHAT IS ASSERTIVENESS?

What do we mean by "assertiveness"? Self-assertion usually begins with saying, "I am." It's a hard thing for many of us to say. Equally hard is "I want." Assertiveness means thinking, saying, and acting on the fact that each of us *is* and *wants* certain things. We can be assertive without infringing on the rights of others and feel comfortable about our behavior.[1]

What is being encouraged here is a degree of selfishness, but not the extreme kind of selfishness that is self-seeking, self-satisfying, and egotistical to the exclusion of all else. Most people are taught from childhood that selfishness is wrong, but there is a level of selfishness that is healthy and productive. Caring for one's self is not only good; it is necessary. Like anything else, selfishness can be carried too far, as when we care *only* about our selves or try to satisfy *only* our own desires and the rest of the world be damned. But keep in mind throughout this discussion of assertiveness that selfishness in the sense of self-affirmation is healthy. We must maintain and defend our basic human rights. We have to put our selves forward boldly, at times, to show concern for our selves, to protect our selves, and to *be* our selves.

We have the right to be and to express our selves and to feel good about doing so as long as we do not hurt others in the process.[2] No matter how confident or successful we feel, there are still areas in our lives where we may hesitate to claim our rights, where we are anxious about our feelings, where we are unable to respond to anger, or where we feel powerless in our relations with people. But each of us has the right to be treated with respect. Each of us has the right to have and to express feelings, opinions, and wants; to be listened to and taken seriously by others; to set our own priorities; to be able to say no without feeling guilty; and to get what we pay for. These are some of our fundamental rights.[3]

You might wonder what's wrong with *not* being assertive. I can think of several things wrong with it. By not asserting our selves:

1. we may end up with shoddy merchandise and service;
2. we bottle up our real feelings;
3. we don't do anything to improve a bad situation that already exists and needs improvement;
4. we are cheating another person out of a chance to air the real issues;
5. we get involved in situations we would rather not be in;
6. we end up being a "yes" person—having to do all the work while others sit by and watch;
7. we run into communication barriers because nobody is willing to say what he or she *really* wants.

ASSERTIVENESS AND COMMUNICATION RELATIONSHIPS

Our society tends to evaluate human beings on scales which make some people "better" than others. In some situations, the "right" person to be is a 40-year-old WASP male. In another situation, the

THIS CONSIDER THIS

If you are reticent about asking for a raise or telling neighbors that their stereo music is shaking the pictures on your walls, bite your tongue no longer. . . .

There is someone who will ask for that raise for you, will tell your best friend that it would be an asset to him if he started using deodorant, and will even tell your loved one that you're in love with someone else.

This someone, with all the gusto and assertiveness that many of us lack, is a 30-year-old Western Springs housewife and mother of two who, for a $5 fee and the cost of making a long-distance phone call, will deliver your message.

Marti Hough began operating her "Speak Up Service" from her home in November after taking an eight-week assertiveness training course.

"Many people in the course would say 'I can't do it, why don't you do it for me' and out of this I saw there was a need for someone to speak for others," she said.

"I've been averaging about six calls per day and have received calls from all over the Chicago area and even calls from as far away as Connecticut and Virginia."

She says that 75 per cent of her callers are men.

Hough will receive calls between 9 a.m. and 5 p.m. Monday through Friday but will deliver messages whenever it's best to reach the designated person.

"The only information I take is the caller's name and number, the name and number of the person to be contacted, when this person can be reached, and the message," she said. . . .

Most just say thanks when they receive the calls, but Hough says a few get furious.

"One man's boss had refused to give him severance pay, and when I called the employer he went crazy and started yelling," said Hough. "Another woman, who lived in an apartment building, was annoying her neighbors because she would get up at 8 o'clock every Sunday morning and make a lot of noise with her heavy soled shoes. She got furious when I phoned and said the neighbors have asked her to wear soft-soled slippers."

—Carole Carmichael, *Chicago Tribune*, January 23, 1977

CONSIDER THIS CONSIDER THIS CONSIDER THIS CONSIDER THIS CONSIDER THIS CONSIDER

"right" people are black, teen-aged girls. In another, a middle-aged mother is the "right" person to be. Outsiders (anyone else!) can very easily be made to feel out of place by the "better" people in any given situation. Social structures perpetuate this treatment of people in these roles; in them, some people are treated as if they are actually of greater value than others.[4] While society is not likely to change overnight, we can change our perspective about communication relationships. If we see that all human beings are equal and if we recognize that we have the same fundamental rights as the other person in interpersonal relationships, despite roles and titles, we will find it easier to assert our selves and feel comfortable doing it.

What, in any given situation, might make us hold back from asserting our selves? A few possibilities:

1. laziness
2. apathy
3. feelings of inadequacy
4. fear of being considered unworthy, unloved, or unacceptable
5. fear of hurting the other person or making him or her angry
6. fear of getting no reinforcement
7. fear of not knowing how to accomplish our desired goal
8. feeling that if we don't do it, someone else will

TRY THIS

For each of the following situations, think of how you would respond. Be honest. Are you as assertive as you would like to be?

1. You were passed over for a raise.

2. Your grade on your paper was much lower than you expected.

3. A friend wants to use the research you did for a history paper.

4. You have been nominated for a job you do not have time to do.

5. You have been selected to serve on a prestigious faculty-student committee that you have little interest in.

6. You have a friend with a constant problem of body odor.

7. Your friends want you to borrow something from your roommate without telling him or her.

8. You find your seat taken at a ball game but there is one that is not as good several rows higher.

9. A police officer says you were going ten miles an hour over the speed limit when you know you were not.

No One Is More Equal than Anyone Else

There is a difference between the legitimate exercise of authority and the infringement of another person's rights. Consider an employer-employee relationship. Certain defined, often well-understood relationships exist between an employee and a boss. In a job situation, an employer can literally tell the employee what to do—type this, read that, add this, move that over here. That is not to say a boss might not try to infringe on the rights of an employee and overstep his or her legitimate authority. A boss's authority usually does not extend to telling an employee how carefully to drive or where to go for dinner or interfering in other personal affairs. It does not extend to telling the employee to use personal time on the boss's behalf or to fudge the record books. The illegitimate use of authority, in these situations, becomes an infringement of rights.

Acting in our own best interests is a matter of personal choice. Who knows better than we do what is best for us? The key to assertiveness *is* choice. There are rarely any single ways that we *must* act in particular situations. True, some situations have prescribed or "proper" ways of acting, but even within such guidelines, there is often great latitude for individuality and variety. For example, we know that we would act with a certain amount of deference if we were introduced to the President of the United States—that is a generally prescribed guideline—but within the realm of deference, we can still be our selves. The main point is that we need not be manipulated by circumstances or by people. We must choose for our selves how to act.

10. Your parents make some derogatory remarks about your friends.

11. You just got a box of popcorn that is only three-quarters full but there is a line of people waiting for service.

12. You have just been introduced to a person who did not hear your name correctly and has just called you by the incorrect name.

13. You are in line waiting to get a drink of water and someone has inadvertently stepped directly in front of you.

Did you find you would be assertive in each case? If not, why not? Is there a pattern to your assertive/non-assertive behavior?

ASSERTIVENESS, NON-ASSERTIVENESS, AND AGGRESSION

You have come to meet with an instructor to discuss a research paper you wrote and that she recently returned. She is a strict teacher who scares you a little in her manner and approach. You put a great deal of time and effort into your paper and you feel the grade is not justified. A girl you know wrote the paper the night before and got an A on hers; you spent the better part of a week on yours and received a low C. She has just begun the conversation with, "Well, I'm glad we are going to have a chance to discuss your paper. . . ."

You have many different options as far as your response to this instructor is concerned. You might reply: (1) "I'm sorry the paper didn't live up to your expectations. I really tried, but . . . you know . . . I guess I just didn't give the paper enough time. . . ." or (2) "You have no right to give me a C on my paper! I worked harder than the girl down the hall and she got an A. Teachers are really unfair; they never give you credit for the work you do. If you don't change my grade, I'm going to see the dean" or (3) "I think you should know how hard I worked on this paper. I spent most of last week researching and writing. I really thought the paper deserved more than a C. Will you tell me your reasons for the grade? Then at least I would know how to approach your next assignment."

These three alternatives are oversimplified for the purposes of explanation. You would, of course, have other options as well. You could discuss the grade and the reasons for it without becoming apologetic or defensive at the outset. Discussion unencumbered by apology or defensiveness is likely to create a positive climate and yield satisfying results as well. Discussion should be conducted in an atmosphere of strength and conviction. That is, you should not sacrifice your values or compromise your standards; you should be able to defend your work and support your overall effort. Discussion is a mutual process of give-and-take that involves *mutual* compromise—not self-sacrifice, apology, or defensiveness. Effective discussion can and should take place in a climate of assertiveness.

Clearly, the (1) and (2) responses above are inadequate. In (1) you apologized and used the "excuse" technique. This non-assertive behavior is both dishonest and unfair. You did not really express your feelings and you denied your teacher honest feedback to her evaluation of the paper. In (2) you showed little sensitivity to the instructor's feelings and used aggressive language that would probably put her off. Only in (3) could you save your self and the instructor embarrassment, hurt, or awkwardness by a straightforward, assertive response.[5] Your initial response sets the tone for all the communication to follow.

A person who is too politely restrained, tactful, diplomatic, modest, and self-denying—whose behavior falls at the extreme *non-assertive* end of the continuum—may be unable to make the choice to act. To act is to be assertive. A non-assertive person says, in effect, he or she will let someone else decide what will happen to him or her. Not to decide is to decide. Freedom of choice and self-control are possible when we develop assertive responses. Being assertive lets others know where we stand. It gives us choices because we are not allowing others to act for us; we act in our own behalf. We reveal a non-assertive style, on the other hand, when we do the following things:

1. stay in the back of groups
2. always stick to the middle-of-the-road position or refrain from taking a stand
3. allow others to make decisions for us
4. pass by potential friendships because they seem like too much effort
5. always keep our voice low or avoid eye contact to keep from calling attention to our selves
6. verbally agree with others despite our real feelings
7. bring harm or inconvenience to our selves to avoid harming or inconveniencing others
8. procrastinate to avoid problems and to keep from making decisions
9. always consider our selves weaker and less capable than others
10. always escape responsibility with excuses and "good" reasons

Non-assertiveness can cause the beginning of a negative cycle. For example, we may get a paper back from a teacher with a lower grade on it than we feel the paper deserves. If we go along with the teacher's evaluation without question or discussion, we may acquire a whole new set of doubts—"What is wrong with me? I am not cut out for this. I cannot compete. I'll never succeed." These doubts can lead to further and sometimes intensified inadequate behaviors. (See Figure 1.) We may come to think of our selves as wholly inadequate when, in fact, we may simply have misunderstood the assignment.

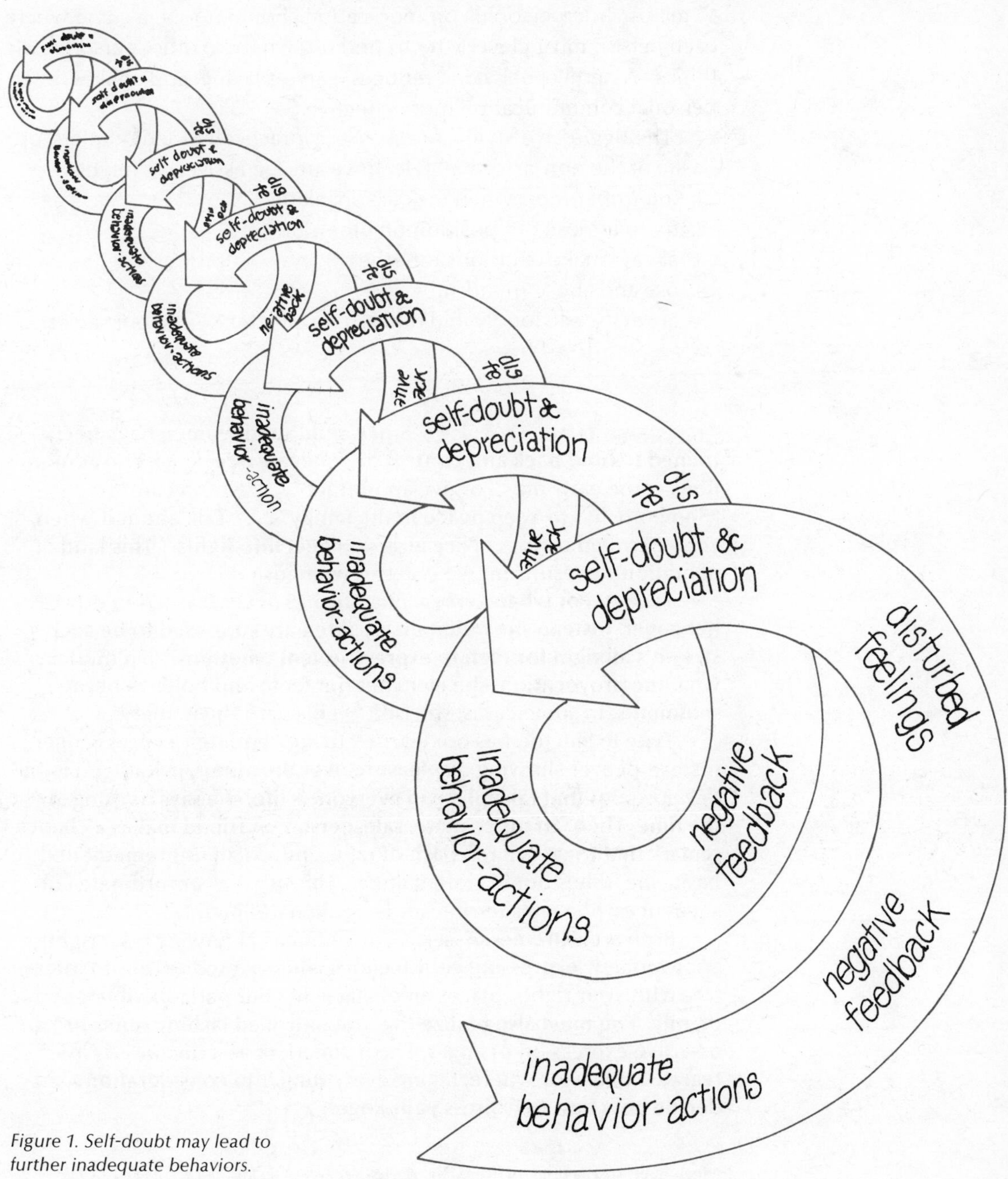

Figure 1. Self-doubt may lead to further inadequate behaviors.

If we are non-assertive we deny our selves and fail to express our actual feelings. We leave it to someone else to decide what's to happen to us and we may *never* reach our desired goals. This places an unnatural and uncomfortable burden on our interpersonal communications. How do we know how others feel unless they are willing to tell us? Interpersonal communication should not be a game where each person must cleverly try to find out what the other person *really* thinks. Assertive behavior reduces game-playing and makes interpersonal communication more effective.

The *aggressive* style of response is practically the complete opposite of the non-assertive style. If we are aggressive, we might:

1. interrupt others when they are speaking
2. try to impose our position on others
3. always make decisions for others
4. use and abuse friendships
5. always speak loudly and otherwise call attention to our selves

CONSIDER THIS **"Since childhood women have been trained to hold back and control their negative feelings. The admonitions come early on: "Forgive and forget" . . . "Not to care" . . . "Someone has to keep peace in the family" . . . "Talk about it when you've cooled off" . . . "Nice girls don't get into fights." This kind of conditioning results in two types of women:**

Type A: For whatever reasons, she has never learned to express her anger. Instead she rationalizes, "Men are supposed to be aggressive—it's all right for men to express violent emotions." No matter what the provocation, she clenches her teeth and holds in her resentments. In some cases, she isn't even aware she is angry.

Type B: She too has not learned to appropriately express anger. Instead of ever showing displeasure over the minor, irritating day-by-day episodes that take place in everyone's life, she says nothing at the time. Then, an office mate, salesperson, or friend makes a chance remark that triggers a red flash of rage, and, on an unpremeditated basis, she lashes out in violent anger. This fury has unfortunate consequences: She feels terrible and she alienates people.

Both are extremes. Assertive anger means knowing your rights, appropriately expressing your feelings when someone tries to interfere with your rights, places an obstacle in your path, or violates your dignity. You must also realize that uncontrolled lashing out is not an assertive expression of anger. The hallmark of assertiveness is integrated behavior where, taking everything into consideration, you **decide how best to express your anger."**

—Jean Baer, *How to Be an Assertive (Not Aggressive) Woman in Life, in Love, and on the Job*

TRY THIS

Make up an aggressive, an assertive, and a non-assertive response to each of the following questions and statements. This will help you become familiar with the differences between these response styles.

1. Can I nominate you for our organization's president?

2. Would you carry in the things from the car?

3. Prepare a speech for us on why we should abolish grades.

4. Help me with my homework.

5. Could you take me downtown?

6. Would you babysit Saturday night while we go to a movie?

7. Go to the lecture and take notes for all of us.

8. Would you tell him for me?

9. We're all going. Aren't you going to join us?

10. Tell him he expects too much.

With which of the response styles do you feel most comfortable? Most uncomfortable? What other conditions would it be helpful to know in the above examples that would indicate which of the three response styles is most appropriate?

6. accuse, blame, and find fault with others despite their feelings
7. bring harm or cause inconvenience to others rather than bring harm or cause inconvenience to our selves
8. speak beside the issue, distort the facts, or misconstrue the truth to get our solutions accepted quickly
9. always consider our selves stronger and more capable than others
10. accept responsibility and positions of authority for the purposes of manipulation or to give us a means of vehemently expressing our selves

If we use aggressive behavior we try to accomplish our life goals at the expense of others. Although we may find this behavior expresses our feelings, we may also hurt others in the process by making choices for them and by implying they are worth less than we are as people.

The *assertive* style, in contrast, is self-enhancing because it shows a positive firmness. The assertive style is revealed when we:

1. allow others to complete their thoughts before we speak
2. stand up for the position that matches our feelings or the evidence
3. make our own decisions based on what we think is right
4. look to friendships as opportunities to learn more about our selves and others and to share ideas
5. can spontaneously and naturally enter into conversations using a moderate tone and volume of voice
6. try to understand the feelings of others before describing our own
7. try to avoid harm and inconvenience by talking out problems before they occur or finding rational means for coping with unavoidable harm or inconvenience
8. face problems and decisions squarely
9. consider our selves strong and capable, but generally equal to most other people
10. face responsibility with respect to our situation, needs, and rights

As truly assertive people, we feel free to reveal our selves. We communicate in an open, direct, honest, and appropriate manner. We go after what we want and make things happen. Finally, we act in a way that we, our selves, can respect. We know that we cannot always win. We accept our limitations but no matter what the situation, we always make a good try so that we will maintain our self-respect.[6]

At different times we may be non-assertive or aggressive or assertive. The problems occur when we are non-assertive or aggressive too often—when it is a *habit* for us to be one way or the other. The idea is to be assertive when we want to be—not controlled by the habits of others or by situations. When we can no longer choose for our selves how we will act, the trouble begins.

COPING WITH MANIPULATION: GETTING OUT FROM UNDER

There is some manipulator in all of us, but it might be easier to recognize manipulative behavior if we look at some of the many ways we are manipulated. How can we identify what is being done to us by subtle and overt manipulators so that we can take sensible steps to correct it? There are, of course, times when authority may be legitimately exercised over us. Just because we sometimes have to do things we do not like to do does not necessarily mean we are being manipulated. When we talk about being manipulated we mean those times when we are exploited, used, or controlled or when we are treated as a thing rather than as a person. Some signs of manipulation are:[7]

1. When people in positions of authority pull rank on us—rely wholly on their position to get us to do something. "Do this for me because I'm your boss" or "It's right because I say it's right and I'm your_______" may indicate when this is occurring.

2. When people give in to us too readily, feign extreme sensitivity, or withdraw from the slightest confrontation. "Sorry, I forgot" or "I couldn't hear you" or "I just could not understand" may be examples of this passivity. Sometimes people manipulate by backing off.

3. When people have all the answers, are too quick with their response to any objection, or seem to be outwitting and controlling us at every turn. We see this happening when people only pretend to listen to us but really have already made up their minds and are not about to change them.

4. When people become too dependent on us, wanting constant guidance and asking to be taken care of. "Would you mind doing this for me" or "I just can't seem to figure this out" may signify this kind of behavior is going on. Some people who seem to be always apologizing for their own inadequacy and asking for favors are really trying to manipulate us.

5. When people are overtly aggressive, unkind, or threatening to us. "If you don't do this, I'm going to . . ." or "You'll be sorry. . . ." are their ways of controlling us.

6. When people are excessively, unreasonably affectionate. Some people kill us with kindness. It is difficult to spot this kind of manipulation because these people make things so easy for us and

are often very pleasant to be with. They win arguments and achieve their goals through sheer affection and kindness which we can never wholly reciprocate.

7. When people are extremely critical. These people manipulate by bulldozing everyone into accepting their critical standards. They blame others, distrust everyone, and are often resentful. "You can't trust Mark, remember when he . . ." or "Of course, that's all right if you like third-rate schools . . ." are the kinds of statements they might make.

8. When people are overly supportive. They manipulate us with their undying protection. We can always count on them to step in to our defense whether we ask them to or not. "I'll talk to her for you . . ." or "Let me take care of it for you . . ." are the statements they use to reveal their commitment to us.

In situations of manipulation, the kinds of cues listed above are

R THIS CONSIDER THIS

CONSIDER THIS CONSIDER THIS CONSIDER THIS CONSIDE

The ability to say No can be pyramided into a position of unique influence and authority. This power is usually financial, and manifests itself as a kind of "Scrooge power" in most organizations, in which every request for money, whether it is an investment, an expenditure or a raise, is automatically turned down at least twice, however reasonable, even profitable, the request may be.

Power and money await anyone who can manage to say No all the time, nor are such people easy to find. Almost everybody likes to be thanked and loved, no matter how powerful they are, and saying Yes is therefore a constant temptation for most people. The true "no-sayers" . . . are incorruptible and invaluable, nor do they mind looking ridiculous. Their mode of operation is simple: they say No to everything until overruled, secure in the knowledge that they are likely to be right at least sixty percent of the time and forgiven for the other forty percent. . . .

The most important thing for those who want to play the "no-game" is to be consistent—the moment you start saying Yes to some things, making value judgments, acceding to certain requests because they're reasonable, you've become simply another decision-maker.

—Michael Korda, *POWER! How to Get It, How to Use It*

often combined and exaggerated or are revealed consistently only over a period of time. Sometimes they are subtle, sometimes obvious. We, the manipulated, must be cautious in how we respond to them. Too often we see only one side of a person or only what we want to see, but just because we don't like a person it doesn't mean he or she is manipulating us. The crucial thing to watch for is whether our basic rights are being jeopardized or abused.

To get out from under a manipulator requires some understanding of the communication concepts we've been looking at throughout this book. In Chapter 2 we saw how important it is to trust our selves and others. To be assertive requires some basic faith in our selves and in our ability to cope with life. Trust is essential in coping with manipulation. Our perceptual skills are also important in learning how to assert our selves in manipulative situations. We need to be alive, interested, and responsive to our selves and to others. Becoming more aware helps us to make certain we are not just seeing what we want to see and hearing what we want to hear. It is easy for a manipulator to project faults and weaknesses on others without realizing that he or she is guilty of those very faults.

How effectively we listen to others directly affects how well we deal with manipulation. We should listen to discover whether the person has made an error, is misinformed, or is trying to manipulate us. If we suspect manipulation, we must try to discover where the other person is coming from.

It isn't always easy to cope with manipulation and we can't always do it successfully. Trying to be direct and straightforward with others helps. Refraining from hostility also eases the situation. If we approach others confidently yet in a friendly way, we will serve as a model for the manipulator. We can try not to be judgmental and yet feel free to express our own convictions strongly. This is assertive behavior that will help us get out from under those who attempt to manipulate us.

IMPROVING SKILLS IN ASSERTIVENESS

Where do we begin? If we are serious about learning to assert our selves we must understand our rights—the ground on which we can stand and which we can defend just by being a human being. Our assertive rights are the framework upon which we build positive interpersonal relationships. If our rights are often violated, we will begin to find it difficult to express our individual selves to others. Trust may give way to suspicion, compassion may evolve into cynicism, warmth and closeness may disappear, and love (if it exists at all) may acquire an acid bite. The assertive rights that follow are statements about our humanness, about our true responsibilities for our selves and our own well-being, and about what other people should be able to expect of us.[8]

TRY THIS
Think of people who you feel have manipulated you. Can you picture specific instances where manipulation occurred? Was it with a:

1. **boss**
2. **worrier**
3. **seducer**
4. **parasite**
5. **hater**
6. **pleaser**
7. **blamer**
8. **martyr**
9. **dictator**
10. **quitter**
11. **con artist**
12. **crier**
13. **shamer**
14. **helper**

Can you now think of ways to cope with this manipulation? Are there things that you would do now to cope with this manipulation that you did not do at the time that it occurred?

Take responsibility for your self. This is our primary assertive right from which all the others are derived. If we take the responsibility for our own existence, then we are in control of our thinking, feeling and behavior. When someone, for whatever reason, reduces our ability to be the judge of what we do, we are being manipulated and our most basic right is in jeopardy.

When we can put this primary assertive right into practice, we will learn how to work out ways to judge our own behavior. Just through trial and error we will discover standards of behavior that fit our own personality and life-style. These standards need not be logical, consistent, or permanent; in fact, they may make no sense to anyone else. But our own judgment is *our* guide and it is important to us. This means we take full responsibility for our own happiness and well-being.

We derive our other rights from this one. In a sense, they are everyday applications of this prime right. They provide the foundation for assertive behavior.

Don't over-apologize. When we return merchandise, we are accustomed to explaining what is wrong with it. When we cannot go somewhere with a friend, we usually explain why we cannot go. But we often tend to over-explain. We offer lengthy apologies when a brief one would do. While some word of explanation is both polite and helpful, people are hardly ever interested in long, involved excuses. When others demand our explanation to convince us that we are wrong, they are manipulating our behavior and feelings. No friendship should be based upon the requirement that we explain our behavior at every turn. In asserting this right, we should, of course, observe common courtesy. Not to give a reason when one would be helpful may be seen as a negative reaction, especially if we

"I don't want a raise, Mr. Harlingen. I just want bouquets and accolades and tokens of esteem and bravos and huzzahs and a piece of the action."

are accustomed to giving reasons and if others expect them from us. But it's best to be brief.

Don't try to rearrange someone else's life. A friend may come to us wanting us to help him or her become healthy and happy. We may be compassionate and we may give advice and counsel, but the person with the problems has the responsibility of solving them. Our best guide in such situations is to assert who *we* are and the limits of what we're able to do. We should help the other person to do the same. As much as we might wish good things for our friends, we really do not have the ability to create mental stability, well-being, or happiness for anyone else. We might temporarily be of some help, but real change requires hard work from the person who wants to change. The reality of the human condition is that everyone must learn to cope on his or her own.

Feel free to change your mind. There is a myth in our society that holds that if we change our minds we are irresponsible, two-faced, scatterbrained, and unreliable. The belief says if we do change our minds, we must justify our new choice or say that we were in error before. We don't want to appear to be wishy-washy because this can affect our credibility: "Don't trust him, he'll just turn around and change his mind!"

Human beings do, however, change their minds. We might make a decision about how to do something, and no sooner do we get started with it than we find a better way. Our goals and interests are constantly changing. Our choices may work for us in one situation, but there is no reason to believe they will work for us in another. To keep in touch with reality, to promote our own well-being and happiness, we must believe that changing our minds is both healthy and normal.

Feel free to make mistakes. Nobody is perfect; everyone makes mistakes. If we think errors are wrong or should not be made, we leave our selves open to manipulation every time we make one. Often when we make costly errors we feel compelled to retreat and not call attention to our selves for awhile. In that submissive posture, we leave our selves open to people who want to make us pay for our error or who want to put us down for it.

If you make an error of judgment at work, for example, admit the mistake as soon as you realize it. Apologize to anybody who may have been hurt, then forget it. "It seemed like a good idea at the time" is often the most honest, simplest explanation. You may well be genuinely sorry if others were hurt by your mistake; the important

thing is not to feel subhuman for having made it. When you realize you've erred, simply show that you are responsible. In this way, you admit that you made the mistake, that it made trouble for the other person, and that, like everyone else, you make mistakes.

Learn to recognize unanswerable questions. Some questions are unanswerable. Some you may have heard are: "Didn't you know that would happen?" "Why didn't you remember to . . . ?" "What would this world be like if everyone . . . ?" What can we say? "I don't know! I don't know!" We do not need to have immediate answers for questions people ask us.

It is a fact news reporters depend on—most people are very uncomfortable leaving questions dangling, unanswered. Almost everyone will give *some* kind of answer, no matter how preposterous the question. But we should learn to see that questions in themselves do not demand answers. We need not be intimidated by inquiries.

We can recognize other people's attempts to manipulate us by phrases that begin with "What kind of a friend (or son or daughter) would do . . . ?" To deal with questions like this, we simply need to say, "I don't know. What kind of a friend (or son or daughter) would do . . . ?" No one can know all the possible consequences of his or her own behavior. If someone else wants to know, let him or her speculate! This is not a defense of irresponsibility, but there *are* limits to how much we can know.

Feel free to say "I don't know." There are legitimate, answerable questions that we just do not have the answer to. Either we don't have the facts or we have not had time to think about them or we do not have enough evidence to make a judgment. Whatever, the best response to questions like these is, "I don't know." Sometimes others will try to commit us to a premature response or to quickly answer a question that is complex or confusing. It is better to say "I don't know" than to make the commitment. We should feel free to say we want more time to think about it.

Don't depend on the goodwill of others. Everyone likes to be liked. Everyone needs to be liked. But although we all need other people, they don't all need to be our brothers and sisters. No matter what we do, someone is not going to like it or is going to get his or her feelings hurt. If we feel that we must have another person's goodwill before dealing with him or her, we become open to manipulation. All the other person would need to do is to remove his or her goodwill and we are stopped.

Why do you suppose we have the stereotype of the smiling, friendly used-car dealer? Because the assumption is that we will feel liked and will want to keep the dealer's goodwill by buying a car. There are many examples of the "I like you" smile used for manipulative purposes. Parents control children by withholding smiles, politicians win friends with a broad grin, and advertisers generate sales by showing happy, smiling faces.

TRY THIS

Take a moment right now to practice alone saying "Yes, I agree" and "No, I don't think so." Say these phrases over several times just to hear how they sound.

With someone else, practice really listening to what he or she is saying. Don't just nod or smile indiscriminately at whatever is said. After listening, ask your self, "Do I really agree with what is being said?" Use the phrases, "Yes, I agree" and "No, I don't think so" or other emphatic statements. Say them like you really mean them. Let your reaction grow out of your genuine feelings and don't hesitate to speak up.

We are mistaken if we believe we must have the goodwill of anyone we relate with or we cannot deal with them. The belief continues that we need the cooperation of *all* others to survive and it is vital that everyone likes us. The next time you catch your self thinking like this, think again. Do you really care if this salesclerk (or whoever) likes you and the way you live your life? Would you accept this person's judgment on what you should or shouldn't have for lunch? Of course not! So why let him or her judge *you?* We may have great difficulty saying no if we assume that a relationship is impossible to maintain without 100% mutual agreement. We cannot live in terror of hurting other people's feelings. Sometimes we may offend others. Such is life.

Feel free to be illogical. Logic is not always the answer in dealing with wants, motivations, and feelings. Our emotions occur in different degrees at different times. Logical reasoning may not help in understanding why we want what we want or in solving problems created by conflicting motivations.

Logic is not without its place, of course. We turn a paper in on

DEAR ANN LANDERS: I am engaged to a very beautiful, very fine and (I thought) very pure young woman. She comes from a religious, politically conservative family. We've been going together (exclusively) for four years. During all this time we have rarely gotten into heavy petting, much less slept together.

Last week my friends threw a rather far-out, raunchy bachelor party for me. There was too much drinking and of course the customary "stag" films.

I could be making a terrible mistake but I swear to God that my lovely, ladylike fiancee was the star performer in one of the films. I know she was a working girl before I met her and pulling down some pretty heavy bread.

My question is this: Should I confront her with my suspicions and risk losing her, or should I keep silent and tell myself I've got to be wrong?—GOING NUTS IN GAINESVILLE

—syndicated in *The Blade: Toledo, Ohio,* August 23, 1976

DEAR ANN LANDERS: I'm a 16-year-old girl who smiles a lot but I'm so miserable I can't describe it in words. My problem: A fear of talking. I used to be afraid to talk in front of boys. Now I can't even talk in front of girls. After a night out I always tell my parents I had a good time, then I run to bed and cry—letting out all the anger. Is this normal?

I try to plan topics to talk about beforehand but I always fade into the background and the same kids take over and become the life of the party.

I'm attractive and talented but I hate myself for being so quiet. I'll look back at my high school days with regret because I never have any fun. Is there any hope for me?—CHOKED UP

—syndicated in *The Blade: Toledo, Ohio,* December 31, 1976

time because we know if we don't we will lose a grade. We fill up the gas tank when it's nearly empty because we know that if we don't, we could get stranded. But being logical works best when we are dealing with things we completely understand, and often solutions to problems lie outside these limits. In some cases we just have to guess, no matter how crude that is or how inelegant the results. It is our right to be illogical.

Feel free to say "I don't understand." It is impossible to understand much of what goes on around us but we survive nevertheless. We understand as a result of experience. But experience teaches us that we do not always understand what another person means or wants. We simply do not understand. People may try to manipulate us by implying we are expected to know something or to do something for

DEAR MAXINE: My daughter Connie is midway through her freshman year at college. So far as I can tell, she has been unhappy every since she went away.

All her troubles seem to stem from her roommate. I grew suspicious after I tried to call my daughter several times late in the evening and her roommate never knew where she was.

Reluctantly, my daughter admitted that her roommate often has her boyfriend stay in the room with her and my daughter has to find somewhere else to stay for the night. Usually she ends up on the floor in a friend's room.

My daughter is broadminded, but I know she isn't happy. I have waited for three months for her to go to a counselor in the dorm and demand a new roommate. Every time I bring up the subject, she puts me off.

My husband says Connie must learn on her own how to handle her problems. I say that if she doesn't do something soon, I should contact the college myself. What do you say?—SITTING AND STEWING.

—*Chicago Daily News*, February 8, 1973

them. We may not understand a teacher's explanation of a concept, or a gas station attendant's directions, or any everyday confusing situation. Rather than blame our selves automatically for not "getting" something, we should ask for clarification or restatement. Who says the other person is being as clear as possible?

We can hardly be expected to always understand what other people's needs are. Sometimes when we don't guess correctly, people think we are irresponsible or ignorant. Often, this manipulation occurs after a conflict. People who believe they have been wronged may expect us to understand that they are displeased with our behavior, that we should know what behavior displeases them, and that we should change so that they will no longer be hurt or angry. If we allow this manipulation, we end up blocked from what we want to do and often do something else to make up for wanting to do it in the first place. We have difficulty enough trying to read our own minds, without trying to perform this service for others.

Feel free to say "I don't care." If we set our selves up to be perfectly informed and concerned in all matters, we will be disappointed and frustrated. It can't be done. Some things will matter more to us, others less. We have the assertive right to say that we do not care about certain things. We do not need perfect knowledge in what someone else has determined to be *the* important category. Some people may try to manipulate us into thinking we need to improve until we are perfect in all things.

The teacher who says, "How can you call your self a history major when you know nothing about medieval England?" and the athletic coach who says, "How do you expect to run the 440 when you eat sugar instead of honey?" are trying to impose their standards on us. If we submit, we fall into the trap of being affected by someone else's arbitrary choice of what constitutes perfection. We end up apologizing for failing in our obligation to become perfect in all things. The only certain way to stop this manipulation is by asking our selves, "Am I satisfied with my own performance and with my self?" We should be free to make our own judgment (remember the first assertive right) about whether or not we wish to make a change.

Being assertive will help us communicate directly, honestly, and appropriately with people we meet in dyadic communication situations. Assertiveness encourages goodwill and self-confidence and aids in pinpointing our real feelings. It is a means of self-expression and has the added advantage of making us feel good about our selves. Asserting our selves is how we get from here to there, from being an object or a pawn to being a human being with rights that should be recognized.

This freedom of positive expression will result in greater openness in the communication of genuine, positive feelings toward other people. Those who are most likely to benefit from our new behavior are those who are closest to us most of the time: our family, our friends, and our work associates. Developing more effective interpersonal communication with these people is the subject of the next chapter.

OTHER READING

Robert E. Alberti and Michael L. Emmons, *Stand Up, Speak Out, Talk Back!* (New York: Pocket Books, 1975). This is the same material as in *Your Perfect Right,* rewritten in some parts for general readership. This book has more examples and illustrations to which students will be able to relate.

Robert E. Alberti and Michael L. Emmons, *Your Perfect Right: A Guide to Assertive Behavior* (San Luis Obispo, Calif.: Impact, 1974). This is the book that started it all. An excellent, easy-to-follow explanation of how to become an assertive person.

George R. Bach and Herb Goldberg, *Creative Aggression* (New York: Avon Books, 1974). "Creative aggression" is simply a method for expressing natural anger constructively. In this lengthy discussion, the authors present sound, provocative, workable ways to stop the tyranny of unreal "nice" behavior. They offer constructive suggestions on how to live with aggression.

Lynn Z. Bloom, Karen Coburn, and Joan Pearlman, *The New Assertive Woman* (New York: Dell Publishing Co., Inc., 1975), and Bryna Taubman, *How To Become an Assertive Woman* (New York: Pocket Books, 1976). Highly readable, practical books. The former tends to be more scholarly, thorough, and in-depth; the latter is simpler, more superficial, and is based on popular sources.

Herbert Fensterheim and Jean Baer, *Don't Say Yes When You Want to Say No* (New York: Dell Publishing Co., Inc., 1975). Numerous specific suggestions for improving behavior and relationships supported by abbreviated case studies. Interesting and specific. A broad range of applications are provided: eating habits, sexual variants, and assertion on the job are some.

Jerry Greenwald, *Be the Person You Were Meant to Be (Antidotes to Toxic Living)* (New York: Dell Publishing Co., Inc., 1973). When Greenwald talks of emotionally nourishing behavior, he is talking about assertive behavior. Toxic behavior is non-assertive or aggressive. The point of this book is not to offer answers to specific dilemmas but to help everyone utilize his or her own potentials for standing up and discovering what is needed to live a nourishing life.

Stanlee Phelps and Nancy Austin, *The Assertive Woman* (San Luis Obispo, Calif.: Impact, 1975). Same fundamental content as Alberti and Emmons. Many opportunities provided here for analyzing our own behavior. This was the first assertiveness book written by women for women. Well constructed and easy to follow.

Carl Rogers. *On Personal Power: Inner Strength and Its Revolutionary Impact.* (New York: Delacorte Press, 1977). Rogers urges "unconditional positive regard" for the self and for other people as a means of releasing the "constructive power of the organism." An important author writing on an important subject.

Manuel J. Smith, *When I Say No, I Feel Guilty: How to Cope—Using the Skills of Systematic Assertive Therapy* (New York: Bantam Books, 1975). This is a "how to" book on dealing effectively with the conflicts people have in living with each other. Smith is especially strong in his presentation and explanation of assertive human rights. A well-constructed, thorough, and easy-to-read book.

NOTES

[1] Lynn Z. Bloom, Karen Coburn, and Joan Pearlman, *The New Assertive Woman* (New York: Dell Publishing Co., Inc., 1975), p. 15.

[2] Robert E. Alberti and Michael L. Emmons, *Your Perfect Right: A Guide to Assertive Behavior* (San Luis Obispo, Calif.: Impact, 1974), p. 6.

[3] Bloom, Coburn, and Pearlman, *The New Assertive Woman,* pp. 11–12.

[4] Robert E. Alberti and Michael L. Emmons, *Stand Up, Speak Out, Talk Back!* (New York: Pocket Books, 1975), p. 14.

[5] Ibid., pp. 36–37.

[6] Herbert Fensterheim and Jean Baer, *Don't Say Yes When You Want to Say No* (New York: Dell Publishing Co., Inc., 1975), p. 20.

[7] Everett L. Shostrom, *Man, the Manipulator* (New York: Abingdon Press, 1967), pp. 35–39.

[8] From *When I Say No, I Feel Guilty* by Manuel J. Smith. Copyright © 1975 by Manuel J. Smith. Published by The Dial Press. Reprinted by permission.

Chapter 10

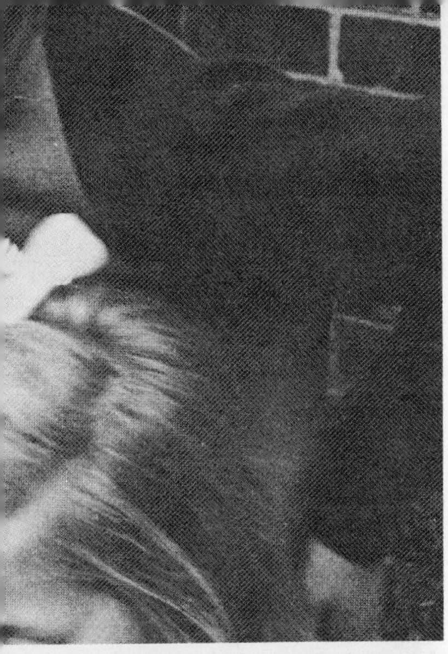

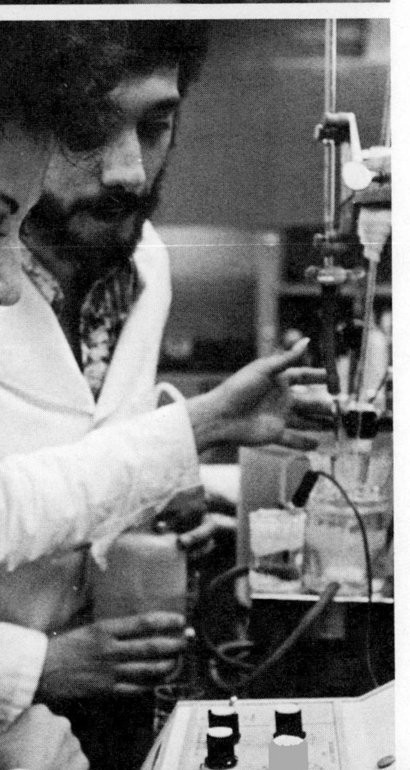

Experiencing Life:
Family, Friends, and Work

We exist only through our relationship to the world around us. Our relationships with family, friends, work associates, and others provide context and meaning for our lives. Growth without these relationships is not likely; it is through them that we learn, share insights, and develop our full potential. It is through them that life takes on meaning.

This chapter is structured differently than those preceding. In other chapters, I developed a concept and then presented specific skills for dealing with it. Obviously the concepts like perception, self-disclosure, listening, and verbal and nonverbal communication are meaningful only in the context of interaction with others. In this chapter we put it all together and discuss the special needs and demands of communicating interpersonally in three vital areas of our lives: family, friends, and work. We all have certain conceptions and expectations for our family, friends, and work relationships. What are they based on? What are our values in these areas?

There are some additional skills we need to gain the most from these important relationships. These additional skills are really emphases rather than ideas I haven't mentioned before. This chapter will focus on these emphases, not specifically on concepts and skills.

FAMILY

"The greatest happiness and the deepest satisfaction in life, the most intense enthusiasm and the most profound inner peace," says Sven Wahlroos in *Family Communication,* "all come from being a member of a loving family." [1] The reverse side of the coin is also true: some of the greatest pain can come from family relationships. But while we

choose our friends, we do not choose our family. We can move in and out of relationships with most people, but it is often more difficult with family members. Our choices and our freedom are more limited within family relationships. Family relationships present unique problems and unique satisfactions in interpersonal communication.

The Familiar Question: Who Am I?

Communication within the family is the subject of complete books and is a very complex area of study. Within a few pages here I want to encourage you to consider your place in your own family and some of the barriers to communication you may experience and contribute to with your parents or brothers and sisters.

A useful way to begin to think about communicating with our families is to think about the various family roles we all may have assumed or been assigned. "Sister" or "daughter" are some obvious roles, but for most of us things are more complicated than that. There are other influences that decide our roles for us. Whether we are male or female may have determined whether we mowed the lawn or did the dishes, carried out the garbage or cleaned the house, were given freedom in dating or were more controlled—just to cite some obvious examples. Our sex may have affected how we were perceived: forthright, aggressive, athletic, awkward, friendly, or mis-

chievous. Birth order strongly influences family roles. First-born children are often more restricted than those born afterward. Older children, too, are often treated as more mature and responsible; younger children may be spoiled or treated as irresponsible, delicate, or dependent.

Physical and mental attributes also affect the role we may have assumed or been assigned. The physically biggest child in a family may be perceived as the clumsiest or may be given the most responsibility. The smartest may have had "success" in school drilled into him or her since kindergarten. Family members may peg a highly emotional child as the family troublemaker, the one who starts arguments. These qualities (and there are many more) do determine our roles to a great extent. Because they tend to be constantly reinforced, they come to be the roles with which we feel most comfortable. Being perceived as a clown or a peacemaker, moody or jolly, gentle or cruel in family relationships will strongly affect how we relate to people outside the family. It is important to understand where we fit and what our role may be. It is important, too, not to be locked into these roles.

Communication Barriers in the Family

Although the emphasis here is on the family in which you grew up, because of its importance in establishing many of your patterns for communication, some of these things will operate in a family you may form for your self later on. You will be establishing another pattern of roles in that family. These roles will be based, in part, on what your growing-up experience was.

Family roles provide a subtle but continuing influence on our lives. One of the first communication barriers that may develop out of family roles is the tendency for family members to see a person *only* in one role. This does not allow for growth or change. Despite the fact that we may have become an outgoing person or more independent, family members may still treat us as if we are shy or dependent. We may become a corporation president but family members may still perceive us as a helpless kid sister. This not only may limit our own possibilities for change but may cause breakdowns in communication resulting from misperceptions and false assumptions. Our needs, attitudes, beliefs, values, and goals change.

TRY THIS

Which adjectives best describe how you were perceived by other family members as you grew up?[2]

active
affectionate
agreeable
aggressive
alert
antisocial
apathetic
awkward
cautious
cheerful
complaining
confident
cooperative
cruel
demanding
disorderly
dumb
emotional
friendly
generous
gentle
gloomy
happy
high-strung
hostile
impatient
impulsive
independent
irresponsible
irritable
kind

The second problem results from our assumption that everyone already knows everything about us. We have grown up in the family, a situation where everyone knows us. Communication breakdowns occur when we assume people outside the family know us as thoroughly. We may respond to others with very brief answers to questions, expecting them to fill in the gaps.

There is a related communication problem which is the assumption that no matter *what* we actually say, the other members of our family will understand us.[3] Though family members do often communicate with each other very efficiently by means of a kind of communication shorthand, sometimes we come to depend too much on this system of signals and implied meanings. An example of the barrier involved is the fellow who agreed with his father that whenever he wanted to use the family car, he would make arrangements with him in advance. The son used the car and the father accused him of violating the agreement. The son insisted he had told him: "You saw me washing and waxing the car, and you know I never do that unless I'm planning to use it." Our meaning is not always as clear as we might think, even within our family.

In the family relationship, much mutual "picture taking" goes on. That is, members are often involved in forming mental pictures of how others are feeling, reacting, or thinking. As Virginia Satir, a leader in the field of family therapy, states in *Peoplemaking,* "The people involved may not share their pictures, the meanings they give the pictures, nor the feelings the pictures arouse." Those involved guess at meaning and then assume those guesses are facts. This guessing procedure results in a great many unnecessary family communication barriers.

We simply cannot assume the other person always knows what

lazy
mischievous
naughty
noisy
odd
outgoing
peculiar
persistent
pleasant
quarrelsome
quiet
rebellious
reliable
responsible
self-centered
self-confident
selfish
shy
slow
smart
sociable
stable
stingy
strong
stubborn
talkative
timid
tolerant
unattractive

How have these perceptions affected you? Have you seen their influence on your relationships with others? Are there other adjectives that better describe how you were perceived by other family members as you grew up?

we mean, even if we have grown up with that person. The reason this assumption causes special problems in the family is that people who share such a close relationship feel they *should* be able to read each other's minds. Everyone is supposed to know how everyone else feels—no one needs to say or show what he or she feels. Serious misunderstandings can result when this doesn't work. Think of a time when you felt *very strongly* that the family should take a specific vacation, make a certain purchase, or eat at a certain restaurant. Did you reveal this strong feeling to other family members? Just because you felt it does not mean you showed it to others. We are not as transparent to others as we are to our selves.

This extends to our policy of criticizing and complimenting other family members, too. Whether we're very aware of it or not, we look to our families for reinforcement and rewards. We may not voice praise or gratitude because we expect people to know our feelings without our spelling them out. But our message doesn't always get through, and it should. Not surprisingly, family members are often less inclined to hold back criticisms of each other. When the free and heavy flow of criticism gets to be too much, family relationships may turn into nothing more than opportunities for negative exchanges, with estrangement and resentment resulting. A pat on the head is not only liked but needed from time to time. Wahlroos even goes so far as to say that "the main reason for . . . discord [in families] is simply that the consciously felt love and the good intentions harbored by the family members are not *communicated* in such a way that they are recognized." [4]

Communication Patterns That Fail

Because we see so much of other members of our family, and because we are likely to feel freer and less inhibited with them, stressful situations are more likely to occur in these relationships than in others. Satir discovered certain "universal patterns in the way people communicate" when faced with stressful situations: placating, blaming, computing, and distracting.[5] Leveling, a fifth possible response pattern, is discussed as a remedy or solution.

Placating. If there is a member of your family who never takes a stand, always goes along with what other people say, continually tries to make others happy, and never gets mad, you know how frustrating it can be. This person is a placater. Some people have the notion that the way to keep people happy is never to disagree. They may also feel that in this way everyone will like them; they placate as a means to gain approval.

CONSIDER THIS CONSIDER THIS

CONSIDER THIS CONSIDER THIS CONSIDER THIS CONSIDER THIS CONSIDER THIS CONSIDER THIS

My child arrived just the other day.
He came to the world in the usual way.
But there were planes to catch, and bills to pay;
He learned to walk while I was away.
And he was talkin' 'fore I knew it, and as he grew, he'd say,
I'm gonna be like you, Dad. You know I'm gonna be like you.

And the cat's in the cradle and the silver spoon.
Little boy blue and the man in the moon.
When you comin' home, Dad? I don't know when,
But we'll get together then;
You know we'll have a good time then.

My son turned ten just the other day.
He said, "Thanks for the ball, Dad.
Come on, let's play.
Can you teach me to throw?"
I said, "Not today. I got a lot to do."
He said, "That's ok," and he walked away,
But his smile never dimmed and said,
"I'm gonna be like him, yeah,
You know I'm gonna be like him."

Well, he came from college just the other day,
So much like a man, I just had to say,
"Son, I'm proud of you. Can you sit for a while?"
He shook his head, and he said with a smile,
"What I'd really like Dad is to borrow the car keys.
See you later. Can I have them, please?"

I've long since retired. My son's moved away.
I called him up just the other day.
I said, "I'd like to see you if you don't mind."
He said, "I'd love to Dad, if I can find the time.
You see my new job's a hassle, and the kids have the flu,
But it's sure nice talking to you, Dad.
It's sure nice talking to you.
And as I hung up the phone, it occurred to me,
He'd grown up just like me.
My son was just like me.

—Harry Chapin and Sandy Chapin, "Cat's in the Cradle"

The person who plays this role to any great extent may find it hard to communicate openly. He or she often reveals an impression of no self-worth or self-esteem. The placater accepts any criticism as if it is deserved; it is as if he or she feels fortunate to have someone communicating with him or her at all. The placater, Satir states, is a "syrupy, martyrish, bootlicking person."

The placater doesn't realize that the most fulfilling relationships are those where ideas, emotions, and opinions are allowed to occasionally clash. Resolving mutual problems and sharing a variety of viewpoints reflect healthy communication. Unfortunately, the placater cannot hold up his or her end of such a relationship. No matter what the placater really feels, his or her response is always an accepting one that offers no opposition or opportunity for growth and change.

Blaming. The blamer is the family member who wants always to look strong in the eyes of others. To show that they are boss, blamers find fault and command others to do their bidding. They always try to reveal superiority, strength, and even perfection. Blamers usually feel that if it were not for everyone else, the world would be perfect. In the eyes and mind of the blamer, nothing is right. It is most important for the blamer to "be somebody," to "act important," to "cut someone down to size," and, thus, to "count for something."[6]

It is difficult to deal with blamers because we can do nothing right. They accuse us of doing things that we did not do. Essentially, the blamer operates from a stance of no self-worth, attempting to lower others, not to raise himself or herself. There are few ways to remedy such a situation; but recognizing that a person is a blamer will help us to understand the communication relationships that involve him or her and the reasons that communication may be blocked.

Computing. There may be a member of your family out of whom you would like to shake some emotion, some feeling, some strength of conviction. The computer, according to Satir, always deals with experience in a logical and reasoned manner. "Calm, cool, and collected," he or she attempts to "sound intelligent." Computers try to impress upon people that they are deep and thoughtful and correct. The display of feelings or emotions would destroy the effect.

Many people assume this posture is ideal. They feel human beings are rational and must deal with information in a cold and calculated manner. They feel it would significantly improve the human condition if interactions could take place in a context devoid of feelings. But humans do have feelings, and when those feelings are suppressed, the communication that results is incomplete. The sharing of feelings brings people closer together—it allows for a more complete communication experience—but most of all it allows people to be people.

The computer attempts to deal with all messages, whether harmful or harmless, in the same manner. He or she may try to reveal self-worth by using large words—even meaningless words—to establish credibility and rationality. It is difficult to deal with such people because they seem to be unfeeling; they react in much the same way to things that affect them deeply and things that they consider trivial.

Distracting. The distracter in the family will ignore threats. Involved in an argument, distracters will change the subject to avoid a confrontation. Rather than respond to the controversial point, they will say something totally irrelevant. Such a role provides relief from responsibility. Although distracters can escape obligations by heading off in an irrelevant new direction each time they are faced with the slightest challenge, their purposelessness can result in loneliness and frustration. They accomplish little, seldom achieve satisfaction, and can maintain only superficial relationships.

Basically, distracters lack a sense of seriousness. Have you ever tried to carry out a serious conversation with a person who assumes a "who cares?" posture? To such a person, all the world's problems are equally meaningless and nonexistent.

Leveling: A Possible Remedy

TRY THIS

We have all known people who fit the roles Satir identified. Try to think of one person you have known who best fits each of these communication patterns. What kind of behavior characterizes each of the people?

1. **placater**
2. **blamer**
3. **computer**
4. **distracter**
5. **leveler**

Fortunately, there is a fifth pattern of communication that is positive and that provides an ideal which family members can work toward. Open, genuine communication between family members is its primary characteristic. Leveling is a means of resolving discord, breaking deadlocks, and restoring communication between people. "In any relationship," states David Viscott in *How to Live with Another Person,* "we need people to wish us well just the way we are and in pursuit of the goals we have chosen for our selves."[7] When we level, we offer another person love and acceptance based on the way he or she is, not on how he or she fits our mold or notion of the world.

Leveling requires honesty. If we make an error, we must be willing to apologize for it. If something happens that we do not intend, we must own up to the situation and admit our predicament. The focus of the apology is on the error or act, not on us as a person. A leveler never apologizes for his or her existence. Leveling responses are content-bound rather than person-bound.

The leveling response allows us freedom to act and to respond as human beings. It provides for the true and open expression of feelings. It provides for change without the need for jumping from one topic to another. It is a genuine response in which nonverbal elements reinforce verbal statements accurately so that the messages conveyed are direct and true. In the ideal leveler, the body, mind, and emotions are balanced and harmonious. Satir says that in addition to this integration, there is "a flowing, an aliveness, an openness and what I call a *juiciness* about a person who is leveling." [8] We feel safe in the presence of a leveler, able to express our true feelings and reactions.

Levelers are assertive. They are not afraid to make a mistake, to accept criticism from others, to impose on others when necessary, to look inferior or imperfect, or to allow others to leave a relationship. As levelers we respond to people *as they are,* not as we think they should be; we disagree with them because *we* want to; we are responsive, alert, aware—assertive.

If you are a leveler, according to Satir, you are "in touch with your head, your heart, your feelings, and your body." The results, as she presents them, are certainly worth any effort you can exert in this direction. Becoming a leveler "enables you to have integrity, commitment, honesty, intimacy, competence, creativity, and the ability to work with real problems in a real way." [9] In short, a leveler embodies all the values we have emphasized throughout this book for the effective interpersonal communicator.

The point of discussing these various roles is explained by Watzlawick, Beavin, and Jackson in *Pragmatics of Human Communication* when they state that "the behavior of every individual within the family is related to and dependent upon the behavior of all the others." [10] Our attempts at leveling will have a direct influence on other family members. The better we are at leveling, the more likely harmonious and cooperative family interaction will occur.

Maintaining Family Relationships

Most of us would like to maintain or improve our family relationships. Chances of our doing this are good if we practice *all* the interpersonal skills we have discussed, but especially these: self-awareness and self-disclosure, perception of changing relationships and roles, ability to listen to others and to provide feedback, noticing the attitudes and beliefs of others, attempting to overcome barriers when they occur, and protecting our basic human rights—being assertive.

Changing or Breaking Off Relationships

One major problem that can arise in family communication stems from the fact that we tend to see each other as unchanging, as having an assigned place in the family. The failure to recognize constant change in these relationships can cause great trouble. In particular, failing to see and to accept change in our selves and in other family members makes it difficult to grow in a relationship. It becomes cast in bronze and about as alive.

There are times we must change a relationship or break one off. Relationships can become troublesome. People grow apart; they no

CONSIDER THIS "**Looking at human behavior with all that we know—and can infer—about the life of our human species from earliest times, we have to realize that the family, as an association between a man and a woman and the children she bears, has been universal. As far as we know, both primitive "group" marriage and primitive matriarchy are daydreams—or nightmares, depending on one's point of view—without basis in historical reality. On the contrary, the evidence indicates that the couple, together with their children, biological or adopted, are everywhere at the core of human societies, even though this "little family" (as the Chinese called the nuclear family) may be embedded in joint families, extended families of great size, clans, manorial systems, courts, harems or other institutions that elaborate on kin and marital relations.**

Almost up to the present, women on the whole have kept close to home and domestic tasks because of the demands of pregnancy and the nursing of infants, the rearing of children and the care of the disabled and the elderly. They have been concerned primarily with the conservation of intimate values and human relations from one generation to another over immense reaches of time. In contrast, men have performed tasks that require freer movement over greater distances, more intense physical effort and exposure to greater immediate danger; and everywhere men have developed the formal institutions of public life and the values on which these are based. However differently organized, the tasks of women and men have been complementary, mutually supportive. And where either the family or the wider social institutions have broken down, the society as a whole has been endangered.

In fact, almost everywhere in the world today societies are **endangered. The difficulties that beset families in the United States are by no means unique. Families are in trouble everywhere in a world in which change—kinds of change that in many cases we ourselves proudly initiated—has been massive and rapid, and innovations have proliferated with only the most superficial concern for their effect on human lives and the earth itself. One difference between the United States and many other countries is that, caring so much about progress, Americans have moved faster. But we may also have arrived sooner at a turning point at which it becomes crucial to redefine what we most value and where we are headed.**"

—From "Can the American Family Survive?" by Margaret Mead. Reprinted from *Redbook* Magazine, February 1977.

longer have anything in common. One person may try to suffocate another—to take total, controlling interest. One person may no longer care to work at sustaining a relationship. These may be reasons for terminating relationships.

If the people involved have tried and failed to remedy their problems and are sure that their perceptions are accurate, the best way to break the relationship is through honesty and openness. Without willingness to share true feelings, both people's motives may become open to conjecture and misinterpretation. Self-disclosure is a mature and responsible approach to solving the problem. Honest self-disclosure may expose what turn out to be misperceptions—what we had construed as apathy may turn out to be fear of failure. Such honesty at this point leaves the door open for change and growth.

Just because we perceive the need to change a relationship or break it off does not mean that others perceive it in the same way. It is good to get other points of view.

When we speak of changing relationships, we include many

sorts of circumstances. There are important changes that occur in a relationship when two people choose to marry or to divorce or to have a child. There are changes that occur when a parent becomes too old to take care of herself or himself and needs looking after. Other sorts of changes take place as a child, once dependent, becomes an independent adult. There is no way to discuss in this space all the psychological and emotional effects of such change, but there are some guidelines for communicating through what can be an exciting but difficult time:

1. Keep flexible. Realize that tastes, perspectives, ideas, and feelings *do* change.
2. Be open and communicative. Do not cut off contact with others.
3. Listen. The best information on your own growth and development will come from others.
4. Accept change. Do not hold on to rigid perceptions of your self or others.
5. Take command. Begin to make decisions and solve problems for your self. Take charge of your life.
6. Stand by your decisions. Support what you do, believe, and feel. Do not be quick to back down at the slightest contradiction or challenge.
7. Seek help from others. You may be surprised how willing others are to provide advice and counsel. Since you are part of a network of interactions, use the network to your advantage.
8. Develop a purpose. Try to accomplish something you can be proud of. Do not spend your time worrying about what others say of you.
9. Be persistent. Life is just as full of setbacks as it is of successes. Persistence produces results.
10. Have a confident, positive attitude. As a free person in a free society, you can excel, find solutions, develop a purpose greater than your self. Act like the person you want to be. Get excited.

TRY THIS

It is important to monitor the relationships we have with our family to help us know when they need attention and/or mending. In monitoring a family relationship, ask the following questions:

1. **Are you reasonable in your demands on others?**
2. **Are you clear, specific, open, and honest in making your feelings known?**
3. **Do you take the feelings of others into account?**
4. **Do you continually play games with others, using unfair communication techniques?**
5. **Do you accept the feelings of others and really try to understand them?**
6. **Are you tactful, considerate, courteous?**
7. **Are you constantly nagging, yelling, or whining?**
8. **Are you always joking around? Do you know when to be serious?**
9. **Are you a good listener?**
10. **Are you guided by values and principles more important than your self?**

These questions get at some of the basic communication barriers that may arise from your side of the relationship. Can you think of other barriers? The decline of a relationship is usually a two-sided problem.

FRIENDS

As we saw in the earlier chapters of this book, a great deal of personal growth is possible within our friendships. There are thousands of large and small reasons for forming friendships, for choosing the friends we do. Each friendship is unique since each person is unique. We are a slightly different person in each relationship, thus, the interpersonal communication skills we need in one friendship may not be the same skills we need in another one.

Communication Barriers in Friendship

Many of the same barriers that occur in family relationships are likely also to come up in friendships. Some of these stem from freezing-in of roles—from each of us perceiving the other in one role that never changes. Too, we may assume our friend already knows everything about us. We may make guesses about each other and assume those guesses are fact. We may assume our friends know what we mean without our telling them, and hold back from expressing our feelings.

Perhaps the biggest barrier to communication within friendships is the inability of those involved to accommodate change. Too often, friendships are static. They may survive on the circumstances and feelings expressed at the beginning of the friendship. As quickly as these factors become stale, so does the friendship. When friends are unwilling to grow beyond this initial base, communication becomes tired and expressionless. No development occurs.

Another barrier shows up when friends cannot or will not break out of their defense systems, when neither wants to risk anymore. They go as far with each other as they want to and do not open up to further trust. They become prisoners of the relationship and gain little or nothing from it. Communication in such situations is cliché-level and superficial.

CONSIDER THIS

I must feel pride in my friend's accomplishments as if they were mine, and a property in his virtues. I feel as warmly when he is praised, as the lover when he hears applause of his engaged maiden. We over-estimate the conscience of our friend. His goodness seems better than our goodness, his nature finer, his temptations less. Every thing that is his—his name, his form, his dress, books and instruments—fancy enhances. Our own thought sounds new and larger from his mouth.

—Ralph Waldo Emerson, "Friendship"

Forming and Maintaining Relationships

As we become wiser in the ways of human beings, more sensitive to our selves and more perceptive about others, we become more careful about the kinds of friendships we begin. The more we know about the types of personalities with whom we should or should not become involved, the more likely we are to choose friends with whom a relationship will last a long time.

Often people view the art of acquiring and holding friends as a passive process. They feel fortunate when they find a friend and are happy when that friendship lasts, but they do not realize that friendship involves commitment, giving, and energy. Often people are too lazy to make friendships work. These people never discover what friendships can be and do, and the mutual needs that can be fulfilled. Andrew Greeley, in *The Friendship Game,* calls friendship "the most pleasurable and most difficult of specifically human activities."[11]

In forming and maintaining relationships, all our interpersonal skills come into play. Friendship involves risk, disclosure of self, finding a "rhythm," and practice. It also involves making choices that are not always based on logic. There is a chemistry that occurs between good friends. Sometimes an instant rapport is deceptive and dangerous; we learn to distinguish this from that which is authentic. The skills described here for forming and maintaining relationships assume that you know someone with whom friendship seems likely and you wish to proceed. The purpose of this section is to help you think more clearly about the problems and challenges of friendship.

Taking risks. To develop a friendship we must be willing to run a risk. If we are unwilling to offer our selves to another person, there can be no mutual bond. Offering our selves to another person is the riskiest of all human endeavors because we tend to be ill at ease with people we don't know well. We wonder, for example, if others will like us. The fear that results when we are afraid others will not think well of us may be strong enough to prevent us from taking a risk. Friendship means breaking through this fear of rejection; it means successfully conquering this basic and fundamental barrier.

It is not easy to tear down the walls that separate. For some people it is impossible. But if we view friendship as an invitation, some of the risk may be diminished. As an invitation, we extend to another person a polite request to join us in casting aside fears. We express a desire to comfort, challenge, and support through honest and open conversation. We establish bonds that will hold us and the other person together and that will clearly identify the conditions we both must honor if our friendship is to succeed.

It is easier to do this if we have a strong self-concept. It is easier, too, if we have done it before. Friendship is not something we establish once and then never again worry about—we use our friendship skills over and over. Even in ongoing relationships based on love, in which giving of the self has already occurred, further giving is still challenging and risky and necessary. There would be no challenge or risk if there were no fear, but friendship would be worth neither challenge nor risk if it were not for the satisfactions it holds.

TRY THIS

To find out whether you have the base for a fruitful and productive friendship, ask your self the following questions. If you can answer yes to most of the questions, it is likely that the friendship will grow and develop; if not, it is likely to become troublesome.

1. Are you willing to risk—to overcome fear of the unknown?

2. Are you attracted to the other person?

3. Do you share values and goals with the other person?

4. Do you have some of the same interests, commitments, and expectations?

Disclosing the self. Friendship is not possible unless you offer your self. You must, first, have respect for the self you offer. There is a catch here because you must be strong to be able to offer your self and yet it is through friendship that you become strong. But you cannot rely on the other person for strength. *You* must be strong; to give your self to a relationship does not mean sacrificing your dignity and integrity.

Giving your self to a relationship does not mean throwing your self at another person, either. To do this is to ask for rejection, disapproval, or avoidance. People shy away from sudden, seemingly unexplained change or bombardment. Revealing your self in a relationship must be a slow, steady process which builds on previous

5. Are you willing to be open and honest?—to acknowledge your part in the relationship?—to respond to the other person authentically?

6. Can you count on each other to be responsible and reliable?

7. Can you play together—to let your self go and have fun without feeling embarrassed or ill at ease?

8. Does the relationship enable you to see your self more clearly?

9. Does the relationship allow you to remain open to other kinds of relationships with other people?

10. Does the relationship feel good?

If your answers here are predominantly no, then you should probably either get out of the relationship or begin at once looking for ways to improve it. Neither solution will be painless, but the longer you wait, the harder it will get.

revelations. You cannot hurry it, force it, or display it all at once. Through this sometimes painful, sometimes delightful process, you not only expand your self, you also learn about the self that is the other person.

As the other person responds to your self-disclosure with warmth and encouragement, you will discover things about your self that you didn't know before. Self-disclosure is not one-way. If you expect warmth, acceptance, and encouragement, you must be open to the other person's self-revelations as well. But just because you allow some of your self to show does not mean you can expect reciprocal display from the other: one revelation need not evoke an equal or complementary revelation from the other person. Self-disclosure occurs at different times and speeds and requires constant adjustment. Sometimes slow, sometimes fast, the pace is determined by a variety of factors unique to your particular relationship with this other person.

Finding a "rhythm." "Playful rhythm," according to Greeley, is necessary for mutual growth in a relationship. He defines this rhythm as the willingness to lead or be led:

> At one moment we surrender, and at another moment we conquer. At one moment we seduce; at another moment we let ourselves be seduced. At one moment we support; at another moment we seek support. At one moment we are very fragile and vulnerable; at another moment, very strong and firm. . . . At one moment we dominate; at another moment we are passive. At one moment we challenge, and at another moment we respond to challenge. The ecstasy of the relationship is perhaps to be found most completely in the very fact of the alternation of roles.[12]

To allow the alternation to occur, we must be able to see friendship as freedom for play. With this attitude, friends can overcome difficulties and problems together and know they are richer for the effort. Such a situation is growth-promoting. It reveals rhythm.

Practicing the art. If you look at friendship as an art, you will notice that, like any other art, it has some general characteristics. Erich Fromm, in *The Art of Loving* lists four: discipline, concentration, patience, and supreme concern.[13] By practicing these requirements we may be able to move from amateur to artist in our relationships with others.

Discipline. We need a lot of self-control to secure and to hold true friends. Often we treat our friends carelessly; friendships cannot survive a great deal of carelessness. While we may be able to sustain a certain level of friendship if we work at it only when we are in the

mood, to become a master at the art of friendship we need to rebel against laziness.

Concentration. Have you ever allowed a friendship to be the focus of your attention? We tend to not concentrate on our friendships unless there is something obviously wrong with them. But maintaining a healthy, growing relationship requires attention, too. No friendship can become the center of our attention when we are distracted by trying to do too many things at once. Our friend is only one of many stimuli competing for our attention at any given moment.

Sometimes it seems that surface contacts are what this society is built upon, yet surface contacts are not friendships. Friendships require some intensity. They require an active commitment of both thought and feelings. We need to put distractions aside and make time for friendship.

Patience. Friendship takes time—often so much time that people do not like to wait for it to develop. They are impatient. We live in a society that is always in a hurry. We want to get where we are going quickly. Just as learning to play the piano, paint, dance, or write takes time, so does building friendships. If we want quick results we will neither establish a friendship nor learn an art.

TRY THIS

Think of a friendship that has been worthwhile and meaningful for you. How has it required discipline, concentration, and patience? Have you noticed times during the development and maintenance of the friendship where you or the other person showed supreme concern? Think of some specific examples. Would you say that you have shown deep love for each other in this friendship? In what ways?

If we rush into intimate disclosures with another person, it is unlikely that the friendship will last. Just as we cannot force a plant to grow by adding more and more water, we cannot force a friendship to flourish by excessive contact or self-disclosure. A plant is likely to live longer if its root system is deep. Friendship needs a well-developed root system as well, and we need to patiently allow time for such growth. Only then can the friendship endure the trials and tribulations that will surely come.

Supreme concern. Supreme concern, according to Fromm, means beginning "by *practicing* discipline, concentration and patience throughout every phase of [your] life." Every dyad really has three parts: you, me, and us. To reveal supreme concern is to focus attention on the "us" of a relationship—the third self. It is not easy because it requires 1) faith, 2) courage, and 3) risk. You need to be faithful to your self and to the other person; you need to demonstrate a spirit of boldness and venturesomeness; and you must realize that in pursuing friendship, you have no guarantee you won't ever be hurt or disappointed.[14]

How do we show supreme concern? We might see evidence of it when a person is unwilling to take a new and better dormitory room because to do so would mean leaving a friend behind. We see supreme concern and sacrifice where one person is willing to give a kidney to save the life of a relative. Extreme sacrifice involves giving up something we want *very* badly so that a friend might be able to have what he or she wants instead. Supreme concern is an expression of deep love for another person.

Changing or Breaking Off Relationships

Friendships are based, in large part, on shared needs or interests. When those needs and interests change, the basis for friendship may disappear. We have all had the experience of having a best friend in grade school and having little in common with him or her by the time we reached high school. The questions arise:

1. When does change or break-up come?
2. What justifies it?
3. How do we do it?
4. How do we feel about it?

When does change or break-up come? Friendship is closely tied to freedom. It is a freedom that involves responsibility, and recognizes the possibility of the end of the friendship. Not to recognize that a friendship can be terminated at any time by either party is unrealistic, naive, and restrictive. In most friendships there will always be certain elements that are imperfect. These need not be causes for break-ups unless they become pervasive or extreme.

Friendships end for the same reasons that family relationships end. People find they are no longer willing to risk, find nothing attractive about each other, acquire different values and goals, develop interests, commitments, and expectations that are different, or no longer wish to work at the relationship.

What justifies it? Whether or not the termination of a friendship is justified depends on the particular people and circumstances involved. It is different in every case. If we are aware, for any reason, that a relationship is destroying one or both of us, we must get out of it—even if we have been forced into the situation by the other person. We must carefully take stock of where we are and where we're going in the relationship and make our decision based on whether there is any possibility left for change.

How do you do it? It is wise to realize that just because we terminate a friendship, the world does not stop revolving. We must go on. Though to end a relationship abruptly is the quickest way to terminate friendship, it is not always the easiest to accomplish. It may mean that we stop seeing each other, terminate all forms of contact, and put geographical distance between us.

The premise here is that we have correctly analyzed the situation and decided that abrupt termination is best. Such abruptness may preclude a variety of other more moderate remedies such as trying to work at some alternatives or compromises:

1. Could you see less of each other?
2. Could you change your behavior or feelings?
3. Could both of you alter your goals or expectations somewhat to bring them into harmony?
4. Are there other ways to change your relationship?

How do you feel about it? Breaking out of a relationship can be either painful or exhilarating or both. The pain comes from leaving something secure and known—from tearing out the roots that are the foundation of the tree. The exhilaration comes from experiencing the novel and unknown—from taking the roots and planting them in a new location. Can we outlive the pain to experience the exhilaration? Is the temporary discomfort worth the risk? Too often people do not accept the risk because of their fear of the unknown.

CONSIDER THIS

Men tend to focus on their bosses' expectations of them, while women tend to concentrate on their own concept of themselves. The difference can be critical. It means that men will necessarily be more alert to cues and signals from their superiors. The signals may concern very small things such as how one speaks or dresses; whether one appears quick and clever or slow and reflective. Most men ask themselves, "What does this boss want?" They know he can probably make or break them for the next job.

Women place much less weight on the demands and expectations of others. Women tend to say, "This is who I am—like it or leave it." They generally have little sense of playing the game, little willingness to temporarily adopt a different style for reasons of self-interest.

How and when do men develop their apparently greater flexibility of

personality, and their greater capacity for dissembling? In their youthful team play, boys learn how to put up with each other, to tolerate each other and to use each other in ways that girls do not find as necessary. Later on, with this background of shared assumptions and team experience, men learn to sit in corporate meetings and to put up with each other to a degree that women often find incomprehensible. As one asked us, "How can two men who dislike each other intensely sit in a meeting and pretend to be considerate and helpful to each other, while everyone else knows what the situation is? How can they be such hypocrites?"

That's a revealing question. Corporate manners tend to be the manners of a society whose members are bent both on winning and on sheer survival. Until one has won, discretion is advisable. At the age of 12, little boys already know they need 10 others to make a football team, whether or not they like them all.

Women bring with them the manners of another society, one in which relationships tend to be ends in themselves. As a result, women tend to fall into the trap of emotional intolerance as typified by a remark such as "I don't like him, and I can't work with him."

—Margaret Hennig and Anne Jardim, *The Managerial Woman*

WORK

The interpersonal skills we have talked about in this chapter and throughout the book are vital to our satisfaction and success in our work. They do not apply just to the close personal relations we have with family and friends.

What do we look for in a job? We often define what we want in a job very much in terms of our value system: money, fame, service to others, etc. Aubrey Sanford, writing on human relations, says that the conditions which most often lead to job satisfaction include experiencing a sense of achievement; deserving and receiving recognition for the work we do; finding our work interesting, challenging, and varied; taking responsibility for outcomes; and discovering potential for growth and advancement.[15]

There is often a close relationship between how we feel about our work and how we feel about our associates at work. If we like the people we work with, it can make even unpleasant work tolerable. If we find our work confusing or if we are frightened by the demands, deadlines, and dilemmas that we must face daily, it may be that we don't see our need for the people around us. We *do* need them. They are an important part of our ultimate job satisfaction. Ideally, the person who finds his or her work thoroughly enjoyable and fulfilling will be unable to distinguish it from play, and will find work pleasurable and happy.[16] Understandably, this attitude results in more effective relationships with the people we work with.

Communication Barriers on the Job

Our attitude toward work can be one barrier. People who love their work are rare. It would be nice if we could all have the luxury and the opportunity of doing creative, fulfilling work in the field of our choice. As we well know, life is not like that. Most people will tell us that the main reason they go to their jobs every day is that they are paid to do so. We work for many reasons, but one of the biggest is that working is *the* socially approved way of getting money, and in our society we need money to live. That is not to say that a job cannot hold other satisfactions, too. It is not uncommon to hear of people winning a huge sum of money in a contest or lottery and continuing to work at the same low-paying job as before, even though they could retire comfortably on their winnings. They are getting paid for their work but obviously they are getting other benefits, too: companionship, a chance to do something they're good at, the satisfaction that comes from accomplishing necessary work, and possibly a sense of dignity.

"Dignity of the work," says Jess Lair, "comes from inside the person doing the work."[17] It's a known fact that people work more productively when they are proud of themselves and the job they're doing. It's when people feel they are performing a meaningless task

CONSIDER THIS CONSIDER THIS CONSIDER THIS CONSIDER THIS CONSIDER THIS CONSIDER THIS

Once you get your interview, your next tactical objective is to convince the recruiter that you are the person for the job. To do that, you have to get four ideas across to him: that you are competent, that you are intelligent, that you are honest, that you are likable. . . .

Competence encompasses everything it takes to do the job: the right background and credentials, natural ability, reliability, the right amount of aggressiveness for the job, and the proper appearance and attitude. It also includes such traits as ability to work under pressure and decisiveness. The quality of your resumé and the testimony of the people you use as references are important factors in convincing the recruiter that you are competent.

Honesty is essential. It would be naive to suggest that there are not employers who would expect you to cheat someone else. But no employer is going to hire you if he thinks you might cheat or deceive him. The recruiter is not going to have anything to do with anyone who comes off as shifty. Never lie in a job interview. Not only is it foul, but you can also get caught. And if you get caught, you won't get hired. What if you got fired from your last job for stealing? Well, you're in trouble. But your best bet is to be forthright about it. It will certainly keep you from getting many jobs, but there are plenty of people in business who strongly believe that anybody deserves a second chance—and they are willing to back up that belief by hiring you.

Intelligence is required for almost any job. Would you hire a stupid coal miner? No. One foolish action underground could jeopardize the lives of hundreds of people. The recruiter measures your intelligence according to how articulate, thoughtful, persuasive, and agreeable you are in answering his questions and asking him your questions.

Likability is crucial. If you are an obnoxious, disagreeable, argumentative show-off, you should suppress your basic nature. That shouldn't be too hard to do for only a half-hour interview.

—Kirby W. Stanat with Patrick Reardon, *Job Hunting Secrets & Tactics* in a meaningless organization that they experience real job dissatisfaction.

While some people have the idea that work is *inherently* dignified or fulfilling, actually work is simply part of the process of life. It is what we bring to it that is rewarding, exciting, and challenging, or punishing, boring, and demeaning. Our attitude toward work affects what we put into it and what we get out of it. If we simply tolerate our work, enduring it as a necessary evil, we are not likely to see the potential that it holds, the joy that might possibly result from it. We need to stay open to *all* experience, work included. This attitude can open communication channels and broaden our range of experience.

Another communication barrier arises if we use our work as an escape, to insulate us from our selves and from reality. Our society is work-oriented. Lair facetiously says one of the commandments of our society is, "Thou shalt work thyself to death." When we assume our role of "worker" to the exclusion of all others, it lets us escape from discovering information about our selves. It allows us, too, to flee from our friends, family, community, and from many responsibilities. Lair adds that "work is an escape only if it is on top of us and we can bitch and moan and groan and feel miserable and yet occupy ourselves with our grief all day long."[18]

When we find our selves assuming the following things, it may be that the work ethic has become ingrained in us to the detriment of our interpersonal relationships and communications:

1. Everything in our job revolves around us; without us nothing would get done.
2. To say no to additional jobs or responsibilities is a sign of weakness.
3. Work comes first; whatever time is left is given to family and friends.
4. Getting the good things in life is solely dependent on work.

When work is everything, we experience the frustration of being a "workaholic" and we share this pain with our work associates. They are likely to respond by rejecting us—workaholics do not make the best companions. Communication is ended.

We must turn escape around. If we are so immersed in our work that we have no time for anything else, we limit our own future. Since we find out about our selves through other people, if our work takes us away from them, we remove the mirror of information. But if we hate our work, too, we tend to be preoccupied with our intense emotions of dislike and to use up emotional energies that we might have applied in a more productive direction. Then communication breakdowns occur.

We *can* do something about the barriers we create for our selves.

We can do less about those others create. Perhaps we work in an atmosphere that does not encourage self-expression. We can try to find a job that allows self-expression. As much as we are able, we must try to find situations where we are free to develop our own potential.

Using Your Interpersonal Skills on the Job

Let's look briefly at the roles self-concept, perception, listening and feedback, language, conflict, and assertiveness play in a work situation.

Self-concept and work. It is obviously preferable to find a job that will help us grow rather than stifle our growth. It should be challenging and enriching. Not only does our self-concept help dictate the kind of job that would be appropriate, but the kind of job we choose has a direct bearing on our self-concept. Have you ever had a job where you had a job title you weren't proud of? It's not uncommon for people to think more of themselves or less of themselves depending on their current job status. A job where we have a great deal of latitude, responsibility, and room for creative development will make us feel good about our selves and our potential. We will want to progress because we will feel strong about what we do and who we are.

TRY THIS

Consider each of the following occupations. Which of them do you feel you could work well at? Which do you think you would not be suited for? (There may be some jobs listed here with which you don't have enough experience to guess about your suitability.)
chiropractor
airplane pilot
secretary
cabinetmaker
teacher
beautician
engineer
psychologist
nurse
store manager
artist
pharmacist
auto mechanic
disc jockey
cook
farmer

Letting a negative self-concept get the upper hand is self-defeating. A low opinion of our selves can lead to a low opinion of our boss, our co-workers, and our whole job situation. We *do* have some control over our situation insofar as we can change a negative self-concept to positive. This isn't easy, as we saw in Chapter 2, but it can be done. The advantage of a positive self-concept extends beyond just the obvious. Sometimes we look at our job as a separate part of life, and yet we tend to spend more time on the job than we do in most other pursuits. A positive self-concept will help us get as much out of the work situation as we can. It will improve communication channels as well so that the feedback and reinforcement we get is continuous and open. To review, what can we do to develop a positive self-concept?

1. Assess our strengths and weaknesses.
2. Act on our needs for self-improvement.
3. Handle our feelings constructively.
4. Initiate change as well as accept change.
5. Assess situations and design approaches to them.
6. Revise our values and establish new goals.
7. Cope with problems inventively and realistically.
8. Stockpile successes as guides to future self-direction.

business executive
accountant
interior decorator
lawyer
golf pro
contractor
electrician
dentist
bank teller
salesperson
optometrist
mortician
telephone operator
radio/TV announcer
barber
mail carrier
plumber
musician
coal miner
researcher
architect
writer
social worker
doctor
truck driver
public relations director
real estate agent
minister/priest/rabbi
insurance agent
law enforcement officer
school principal
designer

You will notice that you feel comfortable with some occupations and not with others. Why is this? Are there occupations not listed here which you are interested in? Being in touch with your self gives you a better base for making these judgments.

9. Set and accept reasonable, realistic situational limits.
10. Keep growing steadily in the direction we want to go.
11. Reach out and up for peak experiences in the process of being and becoming.[19]

Perception and work. Remember as we briefly discuss perception here that the way we perceive is directly related to our self-concept because our self-concept helps determine what we process. Remember, too, that perception is simply the process of gathering information and giving it meaning. It is through perception that we gain a meaningful picture of our job and our work associates.

We function best in any situation when we have sufficient information. Too often we operate with blinders on. We perceive our selves as a tiny cog in a very large machine, as if we don't make a difference. With such a perception, we close our selves off to the big picture—we see our personal cog but not the whole machine. In so doing we protect our selves but we limit the amount of information we attain and become rigid and inflexible. *We* become machinelike and not like an active, responding, involved human being.

Our job restricts our perceptions because it affects what we expect, need, and believe. If we get a job with great potential for upward mobility, we might start thinking about our future more concretely than we ever have before. Jobs can affect perceptions even more directly than that. If we teach, we might start perceiving people according to the kind of student we guess they are or were. If we sell insurance, we might start thinking of people we meet as possible clients. If we sell, we might start seeing the world as consisting of two kinds of people: buyers and nonbuyers. If we work as a waiter or waitress, we might start thinking of people as potentially big tippers or potentially small tippers. The list could go on and on.

There's nothing wrong with letting a job affect how we perceive the world. It can give us insights into people and behavior we could not have gotten any other way. The problem comes when perceptions acquired in this way come to dominate our thinking. People we meet may *well* be possible clients, big tippers, etc., but they have many other aspects we don't know about. We shouldn't presume to know them based on our limited view.

Listening/feedback at work. Many instructions get misinterpreted and many directives are never carried out because people fail to listen on the job. Work-listening usually requires more concentration than social listening because work situations tend to be oriented toward action and productivity where social situations are not. Our su-

pervisor may say something to us only once—if we don't get it the first time, we don't get it at all. We can't afford to let our mind wander. Especially if our work involves dealing with the public, we must listen well to understand requests and instructions quickly in order to perform efficiently.

The important thing about listening is that we must consider it an active process. We have to make an emotional and intellectual commitment as well as arrange the best opportunity for the physical process to occur. Many on-the-job communication breakdowns result from halfhearted and lackadaisical responsiveness. People who get ahead in business are alert and responsive; they listen effectively.

Alertness requires getting instructions and directives correct. As an employee, we may feel subservient to our employer. Because of this difference in status, we might adjust our communication patterns to fit the situation. We may accept rather than question and challenge things our employer tells us. But we shouldn't abandon what we know to be good listening habits that work well for us in non-job circumstances. To check our listening, we can still question and paraphrase. Feedback is the way to make certain mutual understanding has occurred in any situation. It results in more accurate message transmission. It lets us know we are understanding our instructions as we are meant to understand them.

In providing feedback to a boss or co-worker, work to make your message complete. Do not assume they know what you mean. Monitor the responses you get to determine if you are being understood. Do not assume others know all the facts you do.

Language and work. We may find that our job has a vocabulary all its own. One of our first tasks, on taking a new job, is to learn the special meanings that certain words have in that workplace. We want words to mean the same things to us as they mean to the people we work with.

The most important part of language as it relates to a work situation is that we need to get others involved in our frame of reference. This means asking them questions—how do they feel about what we say? Doing this opens channels for the give-and-take necessary for effective communication. It is the best way to catch misunderstanding before it results in loss of time, energy, or money.

Conflict at work. There are many work situations that produce conflict. How we deal with that conflict can determine how happy we are at work, with our work associates, and with people outside the work environment. We need to deal successfully with conflict because our peace of mind, not to mention our efficiency, depends on it. In some cases our security on the job may even be at stake.

The best way of establishing a base for coping with conflict situations is to make sure we have enough information. We need all the options and alternatives we can get. We need to find out all we can about potential problems and solutions.

The second thing to realize about conflict situations is that there is no way we can keep them from occurring. There are simply too many variables over which we have no control. There is no reason to become discouraged just because you see a conflict shaping up in the future. Conflicts will happen. We have to be ready for them so we can cope in a mature way.

In any situation, but especially in on-the-job conflicts, we need to determine the nature of the situation from the other person's vantage point. How is that person coming at the message or situation? What did he or she hear, perceive, and understand? What are his or her plans? Conflict is reduced when all the people involved see the situation in the same way, as much as this is possible.

It's important to stay calm in conflict situations. Relax. The emotion generated by the current conflict is already enough to distort perceptions, meanings, and understandings. Further emotion will just add fuel to the fire.

Finally, try to anticipate conflict situations. We put our selves in a difficult situation when we have to act hastily or respond on the spur of the moment. We may make an impulsive decision we later regret. To avoid impulsive behavior entirely is impossible, but to eliminate many such situations is possible if we think ahead. Anticipation

TRY THIS

What is your first reaction to the following potential conflict situations?

1. The boss has accused you of coming to work late and leaving early.

2. A co-worker has become angry because you are working too hard and thus raising the boss's expectations.

3. The boss has suggested your unit is taking too long at coffee breaks.

4. Somebody has suggested that you and he are doing the same work but that you are getting paid much more for it than he.

5. Your boss is suggesting you take on some new duties that you feel are beneath you.

6. A co-worker accuses you of "brown-nosing" and becoming too good friends with the boss.

is the difference between a mature, well-thought-out response, and an immature, careless one.

Assertiveness and work. The work situation, often by definition, encourages superior-inferior relationships. We are often reluctant to assert our selves in such circumstances. It is especially important in the work environment to not be manipulated by circumstances or by people. We must choose for our selves how to act, knowing that there is probably no one right way.

The best guidelines for assertive behavior at work are:

1. Feel free to reveal your self to your co-workers and boss.
2. Communicate with them in an open, honest, and appropriate manner.
3. Act in a way *you* can respect.
4. Be aware of your own limitations—what you can and cannot do.
5. Maintain an active and aware orientation to life. Be interested.

Remember the basic assertive rights outlined in Chapter 9. They will remind us we are human beings with rights that must be protected.

I have included this chapter on family, friends, and work because it is within such relationships that so much of our interpersonal communication occurs. Our success in these relationships depends largely on how much we care about succeeding. No growth or change can occur if we do not care.

In work and school situations especially, we find our selves needing to deal with problems involving a group of people. In such cases, communication characteristics special to small groups are important. These will be developed and explained in the next chapter.

OTHER READING

George R. Bach and Ronald M. Deutsch, *Pairing* (New York: Avon Books, 1970). This is a book about intimacy: how to establish it and how to keep it going. The authors contend that anyone who can be open and genuine can approach anyone else with a probability of some success. This probability, they add, frees people to explore the potentials of any number of relationships.

Mack R. Douglas, *How to Make a Habit of Succeeding* (Grand Rapids, Mich.: Zondervan Publishing House, 1966). Building on his own background as an executive, Douglas provides specific suggestions and inspiring commentary in the following categories: purpose, goals, imagination, confidence, persistence, motivation, desire, and action. This is an enjoyable book full of examples and illustrations.

Julius Fast, *The Incompatibility of Men and Women and How to Overcome It* (New York: Avon Books, 1971). In a simple writing style supported with numerous examples, Fast explains the nature of compatibility and incompatibility between men and women. His purpose is to formulate ways that men and women can rid themselves of frustration and achieve total personal fulfillment.

Andrew M. Greeley, *The Friendship Game* (Garden City, N.Y.: Image Books, 1971). Greeley examines friendship in relation to love, self-revelation, shame, play, selfhood, freedom, patience, tenderness, and society. Openness and honesty are stressed. Friendship, he contends, is a challenging and demanding game that requires the sharing of common efforts, joys, sorrows, and fears.

Napoleon Hill, *Think and Grow Rich* (Greenwich, Conn.: Fawcett Publications, Inc., 1960). Hill is talking about more than just monetary rewards. The ideas he offers here can bring great riches in lasting friendships, harmonious family relationships, sympathy and understanding between business associates, and also inner harmony. This is a "how to" book full of basic techniques designed especially for people who want to enter the business world.

Barrie Hopson and Charlotte Hopson, *Intimate Feedback: A Lovers' Guide to Getting in Touch with Each Other* (New York: New American Library, 1973). Intimate feedback, the authors state, is what takes place when we open vital lines of communication. This is a book of games designed to help people tackle commonplace problems. This book touches on basic communication awarenesses and skills.

Nena O'Neill and George O'Neill, *Open Marriage: A New Life Style for Couples* (New York: Avon Books, 1972). The O'Neills discuss verbal and nonverbal communication as well as self-disclosure, feedback, productive fighting, and fantasy sharing. This bestseller is stimulating and thought provoking.

Nena O'Neill and George O'Neill, *Shifting Gears* (New York: Avon Books, 1974). Continuing in their warm, personal style, the O'Neills offer practical guidelines for achieving full personal potential—centering on identifying real needs, turning crises into opportunities, breaking out of the traps of self-belittlement, and developing a creative life strategy. Their section on creative maturity is especially strong.

Stanton Peele, *Love and Addiction* (New York: New American Library, 1975). Interpersonal relationships are the focus of this book. Peele presents guidelines for analyzing existing relationships. The goal is mutual growth—to be able to share all that people find best in themselves and each other. A well-written, comprehensive book.

Letty Cottin Pogrebin, *Getting Yours: How to Make the System Work for the Working Woman* (New York: Avon Books, 1975). This is a guidebook on the pitfalls and possibilities of the working world. Although designed for the career-minded woman looking for a job opportunity, it is useful for anyone who wants to get ahead in a career. The book is filled with facts, advice, and solid information.

Virginia Satir, *Peoplemaking* (Palo Alto, Calif.: Science and Behavior Books, Inc., 1972). Provides basic ideas for helping families discover the causes of some of their problems and offers creative ways of working through them. This is a clear and comprehensive treatment of family living—a workbook designed to enhance self-awareness, to stimulate partner conversation, and to induce new levels of family communication.

Gail Sheehy, *Passages: Predictable Crises of Adult Life* (New York: E. P. Dutton & Co., Inc., 1976). In her thorough and well-documented book, Sheehy describes the personality changes common to each stage of life as people pull up roots, pass through the twenties and thirties, and approach midlife. She compares the development of men and women, talks of couples, and examines the strains that occur in relationships.

Sven Wahlroos, *Family Communication: A Guide to Emotional Health* (New York: New American Library, 1974). This book stresses the importance of communication in both creating and solving problems between human beings. Wahlroos presents twenty communication rules to improve relationships and ten characteristics of emotional health and how to achieve them. This is a useful guide.

NOTES

[1] Sven Wahlroos, *Family Communication: A Guide to Emotional Health* (New York: New American Library, 1974), p. xi.

[2] This list of adjectives was borrowed, in part, from David W. Johnson, *Reaching Out: Interpersonal Effectiveness and Self-Actualization.* © 1972, pp. 29-30. Reprinted by permission of Prentice-Hall, Inc., Englewood Cliffs, New Jersey.

[3] Virginia Satir, *Peoplemaking* (Palo Alto, Calif.: Science and Behavior Books, Inc., 1972), pp. 51-56.

[4] Wahlroos, *Family Communication,* p. xii.

[5] Satir, *Peoplemaking,* pp. 59-79.

[6] Ibid., p. 67.

[7] David Viscott, *How to Live With Another Person* (New York: Arbor House, 1974), p. 143. See especially Chapter 12, "Living with Your Family."

[8] Satir, *Peoplemaking,* p. 74.

[9] Ibid., p. 77.

[10] Paul Watzlawick, Janet Helmick Beavin, and Don D. Jackson, *Pragmatics of Human Communication: A Study of Interactional Patterns, Pathologies, and Paradoxes* (New York: W. W. Norton & Co., Inc., 1968), p. 134.

[11] From *The Friendship Game* by Andrew M. Greeley. Published by Image Books, a division of Doubleday & Company, Inc., 1971, p. 15. See also pp. 25-32, 46-56, 74-83, and 135.

[12] Ibid., p. 80.

[13] Erich Fromm, *The Art of Loving* (New York: Harper & Row, 1956), pp. 108-110.

[14] Muriel James and Louis M. Savary, *The Heart of Friendship* (New York: Harper & Row, 1976), p. 155.

[15] Aubrey C. Sanford, *Human Relations: Theory and Practice* (Columbus, Ohio: Charles E. Merrill, 1973), pp. 175-176.

[16] Abraham H. Maslow, *Motivation and Personality,* 2nd ed. (New York: Harper & Row, 1970), p. 179.

[17] Jess Lair, *I Ain't Well—But I Sure Am Better* (Garden City, N.Y.: Doubleday & Company, Inc., 1975), pp. 171-172. See Chapter 10, "Loving our Work."

[18] Ibid., p. 175.

[19] Raymond F. Gale, *Who Are You? The Psychology of Being Yourself* (Englewood Cliffs, N.J.: Prentice-Hall, Inc., 1974), p. 68.

Chapter 11

Joining Together:
Small-Group Problem Solving

You have undoubtedly at one time or another belonged to a group that needed to arrive at some decision or solve a problem. What part did you play in the group's interaction? In the final decision? Do you remember how you felt when a solution or proposed course of action had been decided on? You may have left the group thinking it had done nothing to improve the situation, thinking it had been a waste of time. You might have thought you or someone else could have come up with a better answer by acting alone. Or were you encouraged by the outcome? You may have left the group convinced that the best and most workable solution had been discovered, thanks to input received from many members of the group.

Your satisfaction with the group's deliberations and with the way the problem was finally solved was probably closely related to how well the group worked together and to how closely the group's final decision paralleled what you personally considered the best approach. If you were lucky, you came out of the group knowing your opinion had counted, or at least that you had been fairly heard. And you would feel that, thanks to input from other people, the problem had been weighed from angles that might never have occurred to you. "I never thought of that" is a good thing to be thinking (and saying out loud!) as you leave a successful problem-solving session. Putting together ideas that other people may not have thought of is the whole idea of group problem-solving. In this chapter I'm going to be talking about ways for this to happen. I'm going to look at ways of improving a group's chances for meaningful exchange and for coming up with the best possible solution to its problem.

Have you ever heard it said that a camel is just a horse put together by a committee? How about: "A group is a bunch of people who singly can do nothing, but together decide that nothing can be done"? We have all tasted the broth spoiled by too many cooks. The cliché of the inefficient, bumbling, procrastinating committee is always good for a laugh (or a groan) because we've all had experience with just that kind of committee, the committee that didn't work. Why are so many groups nonproductive in this way? It shouldn't happen.

ADVANTAGES OF THE GROUP METHOD: WHEN TWO HEADS ARE BETTER THAN ONE

In many situations, a group of people working together to solve a problem is the best and most logical way to approach it. Obviously, more possibilities can occur to two people than can occur to one, more to three than to two. And the broader the base of information available, the more likely it is that a good solution can be arrived at. Committees *can* work. Groups, by their very definition, should be able to change attitudes and behavior. That is, we may come to agree with a proposition we formerly disagreed with just because we have had access to the ideas and attitudes of the other members of a small group. We might also tend to do something we might not have done otherwise because other group members do it.

The point here is that individuals affect and are affected by the group. Small-group judgment tends to be better than individual judgment. Groups often are able to foresee more difficulties than individuals working alone can; they explore more facets and avenues; they visualize more outcomes; and, thus, they produce better solutions. Discussion can also improve the spirit of those participating. There is a psychological satisfaction we gain from participating with other members of a group. A final value is that group solutions often obtain more support. Because many of the "bugs" have been removed during the discussion, the solution is generally more supportable. And because there are a number of people involved in arriving at the solution, there already are a number of people available to support it, to exert the extra effort required to make the solution a success.

Lawrence Rosenfeld provides several guidelines for determining whether or not to use a group to solve a problem.[1] Certainly, the nature of the task, the members, and the situation will help determine which of the following guidelines are most important. If you must answer yes to many of the following questions, a group might be a good idea; many no's indicate an individual would be better:

1. Are many steps required to solve the problem?
2. Are there many parts to the problem?

3. Will the solution be difficult to verify?
4. Are the individuals involved likely to perceive the problem as an impersonal one?
5. Will the problem be of moderate difficulty for the individuals who constitute the group?
6. Is a great deal of information required to solve the problem? Would a single individual be unlikely to possess it?
7. Does the problem demand a division of labor?
8. Are many solutions desired?
9. Are many man-hours required for the problem's solution?
10. Will individuals have to assume a great deal of responsibility for the solution?
11. Are the proposed solutions likely to be diverse?
12. Are the attitudes concerning the problem likely to be diverse?
13. Is it unlikely that group members will engage in non-task-oriented behavior?

TRY THIS

Select a crossword puzzle from your local newspaper. Duplicate it. Give one copy to each of several groups. Also give a copy of it to several individuals working alone. Who finished first? Who completed the most items correctly? What kinds of problems were encountered? Are there some kinds of problems that are better handled alone? In groups?

Small-group interaction is one of the important contexts of interpersonal communication. But just because a number of people come together does not mean a group is formed. Think of six people riding in an elevator together. This is a collection of people—not a small group. It is not a small group because the people are not engaged in interaction, are not reacting to each other as individuals, are not interacting with one another face-to-face, and, finally, are not interdependent in any way. If, however, the elevator got stuck between floors and the six people needed to work together to find a solution to their problem, they would become a problem-solving group. Thus, we have a definition of what we refer to when we speak of *small-group* communication: three or more interdependent people involved in face-to-face interaction with each other. The ideal group size is five to seven members. The interdependency may range from a simple need to be with the others to having to solve a problem together.

This need for interdependency points up an important distinction with respect to small groups. There are generally two kinds of activities that relate to small-group process: problem solving and relating interpersonally. These activities are not mutually exclusive; however, there are some groups that meet to accomplish a task, and some that meet just to get together for the social benefits. Social groups are generally viewed as friendship groups. Although these groups are important, interaction in them seldom concerns a task and will not be the focus of this chapter.

The problem-solving group may include social interaction, but the achievement of a goal through verbal interaction is the group's primary objective—solving a specific problem. This chapter will be primarily concerned with small-group behavior as it occurs in problem-solving groups. We encounter such groups when a number of students in one dormitory decide they want to change the regulations and get together to accomplish their goal; when students want to pool their efforts to solve a problem posed by an instructor; or when students who wish to change a university policy form a group to decide the best means for presenting their case.

There are also work groups that are formed by people whose jobs overlap or whose closeness with fellow workers causes them to interact to complete an on-the-job task. There are therapy groups where the focus is on human-relations training—members share their reactions to the immediate experience to help improve their insight and self-awareness. We will not deal specifically with such groups in this chapter. We encounter the small group in all life situations, whether it be in college, on the job, in organizations, or in the community. Understanding small-group procedures will help us to participate effectively in all sorts of groups. Problem solving in group situations is a characteristic of a democratic society.

Small-group communication is considered a form of interpersonal communication because even though there are more than two people involved, much of the communication that occurs takes place between only two people at a time. Of course there are other times in the small-group setting when a group member does not speak directly to one other group member, but delivers a comment to which anyone else in the group may respond. Instead of saying, "Can *you* cite an example of this?" we would say, "Can *anyone* cite an example of this?" and *anyone* is more likely to respond to our question.

There are certain characteristics of the small-group situation that distinguish it from other kinds of communication. These characteristics describe a task-oriented group rather than a social group. Members of an ideal problem-solving group:

1. Prepare thoroughly for discussion;
2. Follow a plan or agenda;
3. Participate effectively;
4. Maintain a healthy atmosphere; and
5. Respond to appropriate leadership.

CONSIDER THIS "**Why are groups so important? As humans we are social animals and have an inherent social nature. It is not in our nature to live alone. We are born into a group called the family and would not survive the first few minutes, the first few weeks, or the first few years of our lives without membership in this**

group. Our personal survival as well as the survival of our species has always been linked to the interrelationships formed among human beings. It is within the family and peer groups that we are socialized into ways of behaving and thinking, educated, and taught to have a certain outlook on the world and ourselves. Our personal identity is derived from the way in which we are perceived and treated by other members of our groups. Almost all of our time is spent interacting in groups; we are educated in groups, we work in groups, we worship in groups, we play in groups. Our whole life is spent in a variety of group memberships. Even our species identity as a human is developed in our interactions with others within groups. What makes us human is the way in which we interact with other persons, and we learn how to interact within the groups in which we are socialized and educated. At all stages of our lives we need **to belong to groups.** ”

—David W. Johnson and Frank P. Johnson, *Joining Together: Group Theory and Group Skills*

PREPARING TO DISCUSS: LAYING THE GROUNDWORK

The first obvious difference between effective group problem-solving and simply "shooting the bull" is that group members serious about solving a problem will *prepare* for the discussion. Without this preparation, we can end up simply with a pooling of ignorance. For example, if you and a group of people decided to discuss student-faculty relationships to determine how you could improve them, you would quickly run out of information if you depended solely on the limited personal experiences of the members of the group. Besides, you can never be sure that the experience of a single group member is typical of other students' experiences. Without some background information, the group is really ignorant of the problem. Most people are not experts in a number of different fields, and relying on their own knowledge will not get them very far. Such knowledge cannot sustain group discussion. For discussion to be really good, all the available ideas, facts, and opinions that bear in any way on the topic must be considered. Members need more than their own personal backlog of knowledge and experience in order to bring all the available facts to bear on the topic at hand.

Group discussion requires advance study and preparation. Discussion breaks down when the participants have not put in the time or effort required. In addition, the more information gathering we do, the more likely it is that we will free our selves from bias. The more sources we go to, the more objective our information becomes. Staying with a single source makes us the victim of one person's biases and makes our information subjective—characteristic of that one individual's thinking.

As we study and prepare for a small-group discussion, we would do well to cultivate an attitude of suspended judgment. This kind of reservation will help us both during research and during discussion. No one can entirely suspend his or her judgment, but if we are aware of our own biases, we can compensate for them by consciously seeking out information to support the position opposing our own.

Our own study and preparation should include the careful testing of any hypotheses we may have formed on the subject. Since hypotheses are dependent on good evidence, we should be particularly interested in testing the evidence. Is it current? Are the authorities acceptable? Biased? Confirmed by other sources or authorities? Too often people believe that because something is published, it is valid and reliable. It's good to have a healthy skepticism as we consider the evidence. If a group's deliberations are based on a poor substructure of information, the group's final decision will be suspect. Poor preparation can render a great deal of group effort and interaction meaningless.

Finally, study and preparation require the exploration of all possible solutions. Be ready to dig beyond the obvious alternatives. Digging may require using sources other than the more popular magazines and journals; we may need to interview people closer to and more informed on the topic than we are. To limit our sources to the day's newspaper and a couple of weekly news magazines is usually inadequate.

FOLLOWING A PLAN: ONE STEP AT A TIME

If you could choose between informal, sociable interchange with a group of people and meeting with that same group to share ideas and arrive at conclusions on a specific topic, which would you choose? Most people would prefer the former; they would prefer it so much that, placed into the latter, task-oriented type of group, they will do everything in their power to turn it into a social encounter. They may digress, talk about their own personal experiences, shift the focus, or tell stories. They often will do anything and almost everything except talk about the agreed-upon purpose.

To approach a proposition in a systematic and logical manner gives us a place to start and a place to finish. Having a system puts a light at the end of the tunnel—not only a way of getting through the tunnel but a way of knowing when we've reached the end. You might think simply using common sense will get us to the same place. In some cases you might be right. But more often the unstructured approach results in merely "muddling through." Moving with directness, forthrightness, and a sense of purpose is almost always a more likely way to get where we're going. To have a method at our fingertips saves precious time in trying to determine what to do next or "where to go from here." It is not a weakness to use an already developed approach to solving a problem. Why not use an approach that has been tried and tested and found to be workable?

There are, of course, a variety of systems that can be used. One may be better than another for certain groups or certain problems. Based upon usage, flexibility, and easy comprehension, John Dewey's "Reflective Pattern" is often the best. It is probably the most popular pattern for problem-solving discussions.[2] It consists of the following five distinct steps: 1) perceiving a difficulty; 2) locating and defining the problem; 3) suggesting possible solutions; 4) developing the suggested solutions; and 5) further observing and experimenting, leading to the acceptance or rejection of some solution.

Perceiving a Difficulty

The group must first express its reasons for coming together at all. It should ask questions like, "Is this a new problem?" "How serious is it?" "What attempts have been made previously to help solve it?" and "What is likely to happen if nothing is done?" The group must try to determine the exact difficulty and degree of importance of the problem. If a difficulty cannot be determined or its importance cannot be identified, why waste time on it?

Sometimes some members of a group may discover a difficulty but not all members agree that it is a difficulty. Then what? These disagreements, of course, are part of what the process of discussion is all about. The first thing that must be done is to allow full and free discussion to take place. Group members must be free to tell why they feel the way they do. Once all the ideas are out, then the merit of the ideas must be considered. Based on the merit of the ideas, perhaps agreement can be reached. If not, it may mean members will have to vote to resolve the problem. This should be a last resort, but it may be necessary so that a decision can be reached and the group can proceed.

People in a community might perceive a difficulty regarding the school system. Specifically, they might feel that students lack individual attention because of crowded conditions. They perceive that students could become more tense because of crowding, illnesses might spread more rapidly, and teachers might become frustrated. A real difficulty is perceived.

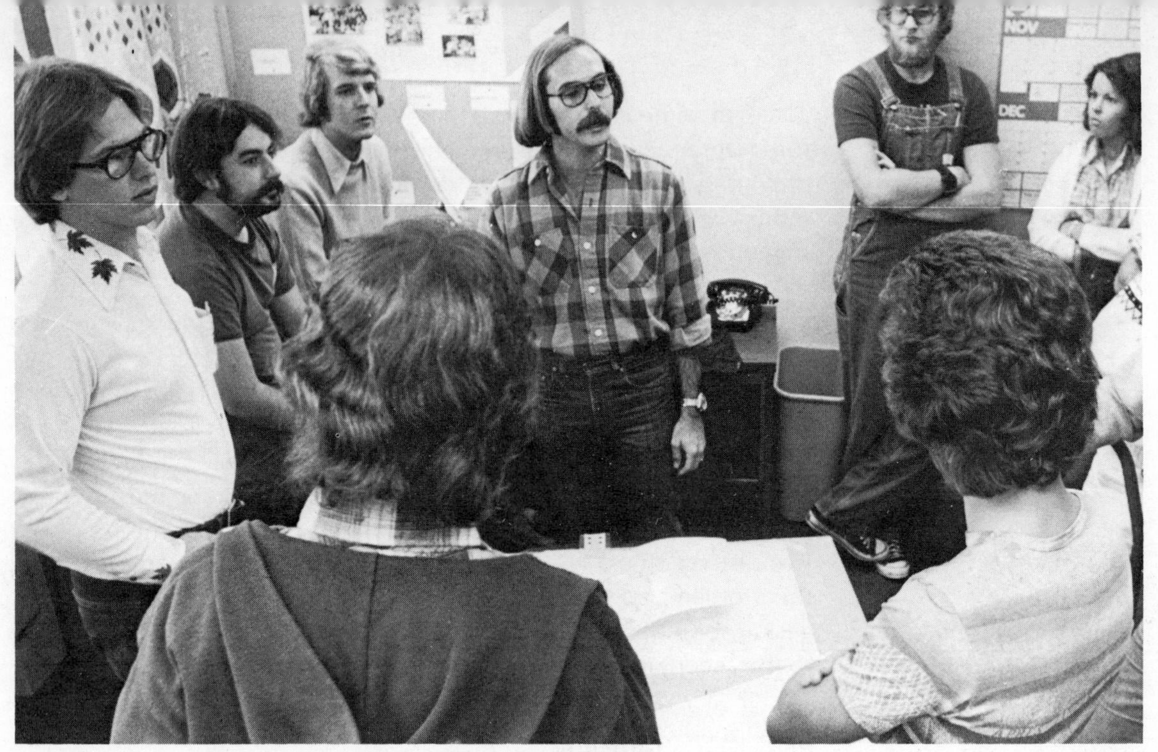

Locating and Defining the Problem

Once a difficulty has been identified and all members agree that it is important, we must locate and define the problem. This is one of the most important steps in the problem-solving sequence. To skip this step makes for chaotic discussion later on. With no definite boundaries to the problem, discussion could wander almost anywhere.

Locating a problem means determining its scope, specificity, and limits. Does the problem have a history? How much of one? How much of the topic can the group hope to cover? What is the range of the problem? Exactly what does it include? How does it relate to other areas? These questions relate to the scope of the problem. Determining its specificity means identifying characteristics peculiar to this problem and to no other. What are the boundaries of the problem? What will we include and what will we exclude in our discussion?

Building on the answers to these questions, our group can construct a specific statement or proposition in the form of either a declarative or an interrogative sentence. Be certain the statement includes a subject and a predicate. If our group's general topic is rape, for example, our proposition might be, "How should rape be prevented in our community?" This question provides a focus on one specific aspect of the topic. Too broad a topic can cause problems: group members tend to give short, unrelated speeches presenting their information. There is no real discussion. Too narrow a topic, on the other hand, may limit how much information we can find on it and, thus, the amount of discussion that will be possible.

A proposition is simply a problem that is formally stated. It should be similar in structure to these statements:

> To what extent should students control their own educational destinies?
>
> The university's grading system should be changed.
>
> Should required courses be abolished?
>
> Has the university a right to impose graduation standards on its students?
>
> Students ought to have to pass minimal reading, writing, and speaking standards before entering a college or university.
>
> Should the community support the building of a new school?
>
> To what extent should our area of this business take on more responsibilities?

While mere statement of the problem does not solve definitional problems, it makes it easier to focus on specific words that should be questioned. What do we mean by "control"? What is an "educational destiny"? What is the background or history of the problem? To have something in words gives group members a place to begin. Forcing the group to put the problem in precise words can stimulate precision of thought later on in the discussion as well.

Referring back to the community group that perceived a difficulty in their school system, that group might locate and define the problem by considering the following issues:

1. How long has overcrowding been a problem?
2. Is it perceived as a problem by all concerned: parents, teachers, administrators, school board?
3. How extreme is the problem of overcrowding?
   a. What is the proper, reasonable teacher-student ratio?
   b. What is the current teacher-student ratio?
4. Can the problem be solved? Can a group of concerned citizens expect to accomplish anything?
5. What other problems might be encountered in trying to solve this one? What new problems might the solution of this one cause?
6. What characteristics are peculiar to *this* problem?
7. What are the boundaries of *this* problem? What other school systems might be affected by our problem and/or solution?

At this point the citizens might want to phrase a specific proposition: "How should the problem of overcrowding in our schools be solved?" or "To what extent can we solve the problem of overcrowding in our schools?"

TRY THIS

Practice suggesting possible solutions by coming up with at least three of them for each of the following concerns:

1. lack of student interest in campus politics

2. lack of support by students of campus athletics

3. general boredom of students

4. alcoholism on campus

5. poor quality of dormitory food

6. need to stimulate bright students

7. too many required courses

8. lack of rapport between students and the administration

9. need to bring entertainment to campus

10. poor quality of teaching

To eliminate this step of definition is to proceed without knowing as much as we can about what we are doing. We may be trying to find a solution and, once we find it, discover that it does not directly apply. Most groups fall short here because they do not perceive the importance of definition and do not want to take the time. Locating and defining serve several important functions:

1. Making the problem clear.
2. Determining that everyone knows what is included in the topic.
3. Making certain everyone knows how each term is being used.
4. Ensuring that the focus and direction of the discussion are concrete and specific.
5. Simplifying beginning research and preparation for the discussion.

We must spend time at this stage if future discussion of the topic is to be purposeful. Locating and defining a problem are too important to slight.

Suggesting Possible Solutions

Most groups want to jump right into this step with no preliminaries. And no wonder! Often this is an exciting and vital part of the discussion. People like to say what they think ought to be done. Based upon the analysis and exploration of the problem that has preceded and keeping limitations in mind, the group must try to propose as many alternatives for solving the problem as it can. The more alternatives we can suggest, the more likely that we will find one (or a combination) that specifically satisfies our exact problem. It is helpful here to have someone in the group write down all the possible solutions.

No alternatives should be ridiculed or ruled out at this point. People should be encouraged not to censor or ridicule themselves, either. Too often people prejudge their own ideas; it is better to let the group judge. It's always better to get an idea into the discussion than to suppress it. One idea, even if farfetched, may bring to mind something else more possible. The pooling of all ideas is essential because often we can reach a solution through the combination of ideas offered, rather than by using one *or* another. The group should encourage suggestions, saving evaluative judgments until later. The goal of the group in this step should be to lay out as many courses or directions as possible. These ideas lay the foundation for later examination and evaluation.

The group considering overcrowded schools might offer some of the following alternatives for solution of the problem:

1. Staggered school schedule with some students attending early in

the morning, some late in the afternoon.
2. Additional rooms added to present buildings.
3. Adding space by converting presently unused space to classrooms: storage rooms, lounges, lobbies, or basements.
4. Converting, remodeling, or reconditioning other buildings not currently being used.
5. Building a new facility.

Developing Suggested Solutions

This stage involves developing possible courses of action and testing their adequacy. This can be one of the truly exciting parts of group discussion. This is where the reasoning capability of the group members shows up as they try to discover and test the implications of the solutions suggested. This is the most crucial stage of the group discussion: the group must now come up with a solution that justifies all of the previous handling of the problem. This is when the group must become evaluative, making judgments about how much the implementation of each proposed solution is likely to cost, and how feasible each solution appears to be.

TRY THIS

Make plans now to observe a small-group discussion in action. Analyze how well the group follows a plan. Answer the following questions:

1. Did they perceive a difficulty?

2. Did they locate and define the problem?

3. Did they suggest possible solutions?

4. Did they develop the suggested solutions?

5. Did they plan to do any further observing and experimenting?

Were certain steps skipped or overlooked? Did the group add steps not included above? How efficient were the members of this group? Were there ways you could suggest for them to increase their efficiency?

At this point the group should be very conscious of the exact wording of its proposition, taking care that each proposed solution satisfies it precisely. We must be objective in considering the alternatives and try not to close our minds to others' proposals. Basic questions such as "Will it work?" or "Is it possible?" relate to feasibility. Questions about the practicality of the solution might be: How soon could it be put into operation? How long will it take altogether? What people need to be involved? Who will be affected by this course of action? Is it legal? It is very easy to become too idealistic. Pie-in-the-sky solutions can provoke interest and discussion, but sooner or later the group must become realistic about what can actually be carried out.

As a group, all members share in reaching the decision, but they all share in any consequences as well. As part of a group, we are not free from responsibility because *we* did not come up with the solution or *we* did not agree with it. As part of the group, we must accept full responsibility for the results; that's why we try to make certain the group decision is one we personally can support.

It is at this stage of developing suggested solutions that the potential exists for a group to become greater than the sum of its parts. If each member not only shares his or her own information but also builds on that provided by others, solutions and ideas that would not occur to any one single individual result. As members add on to the contributions of others, a dynamic interaction can occur that is an

outcome of this particular group of people and would probably not result if one person tried to solve the same problem or if another group of people attacked the identical subject. Solutions and ideas develop as a result of the interaction—a unique product of this group's effort. The group's having reached a decision signals the completion of this step.

The group working on the overcrowded-school problem might decide that because the community is expected to continue to grow at its present rapid pace, the most feasible solution is to build a new school *and* to add rooms to existing facilities. The addition of rooms would help keep down the cost of the new facility. Certainly, the overall cost of the solution would be a major consideration. Another would be public acceptance, since the public would pay most of the cost through increased taxes. Other concerns would be:

How soon could a new school be built and classrooms added on to the existing facilities?

What other people need to be involved?

Who else might be affected by the decision?

Is it legal to do this? What are the legal guidelines regarding this?

Can the necessary funding proposal be passed in this community?

How much funding is needed? How long will it take to pay for this project?

Further Observing and Experimenting

This is the step where we measure the solution against reality. The group must see if the proposed solution works when actually implemented. The group now goes beyond the hypothetical into the area of testing. This involves *trying it out.* How do we recognize a success? A failure? When do we stop and start over? How do we know which of our steps was faulty? These are questions we must be alert to as we observe and experiment.

In trying to solve the overcrowding situation in the schools, the group may discover that the situation is not as bad as in other communities, or that the public feels that a new school is not merited, or that a great deal of money will be needed just to publicize the need for the school bond issue. The group must look at the problem realistically in terms of the community attitude. It might have to go back and reconsider other alternatives. The group would want to consider the history of successes or failures on past school bond issues: what were the problems or why were they successful?

PARTICIPATING EFFECTIVELY: A TIME TO TALK, A TIME TO LISTEN

For problem solving in the small group to work best, some kind of participation is needed from each member. The person who says nothing at all might just as well not be part of the group. The person who says too much can destroy group effectiveness and group interaction totally. A proper balance must be achieved, and this requires a determination from each of us to be sensitive to our own level of participation.

The Non-Talker

People who do not actively participate in small-group deliberations may have one of a variety of reasons for their behavior. They may not wish to talk because they don't like another group member, the topic, the group as a whole, or the way they see things working out. Often the reasons go much deeper than that. We might sometimes suppress our opinions if we:

1. *think our opinion conflicts with the majority.* Maybe it does. Maybe it doesn't. More people might agree with us than we think. The only way to find out is to express our opinion. Other people may be glad we've expressed for them something they were reluctant to say.

2. *think we are not as sure of the correctness of our opinion as other group members.* Maybe we are. Maybe we aren't. But we are probably just as certain as everyone else. If we are really uncertain, we may offer our opinion tentatively: "I'm not sure this is correct, but what if . . ." or "Not to play the role of devil's advocate here, but. . . ."

3. *think the group's decision affects us less than it does other members.* Although some members may be more affected by the decision of the group than others, we will be held just as responsible for it as the others by our presence in the group. It pays to contribute to make sure that our insights are part of the whole effort and that we can somewhat support the findings of the group.

4. *want to avoid disagreeing with a friend.* As long as our disagreement is not with him or her as a person but with his or her ideas, we can disagree within the group in a mature and rational manner. If we cannot disagree with an opinion or idea of a friend without being afraid of destroying the friendship, what kind of a friend is he or she anyway?

5. *have too strong a desire for group unity.* Group unity includes us as part of the group. Group unity will be even stronger if we present our ideas and let them be discussed. We will feel better about

TRY THIS

Want to see if you are a good group participant? Ask the following questions with respect to your participation in a specific group:

1. Did I propose new ideas, activities, and procedures? Or did I just sit and listen?

2. Did I ask questions? Was I shy about admitting that I did not understand?

3. Did I share my knowledge? Or did I keep it in?

4. Did I speak up if I felt strongly about something? Was I shy about giving an opinion?

5. Did I try to synthesize ideas? Or did I concentrate only on details under immediate discussion?

6. Did I understand the goals of the group and try to direct the discussion toward them? Or did I get off the track easily?

7. Did I question the practicality or the logic of what was happening, and did I help evaluate the group process? Or did I always accept unquestioningly the things being done?

8. Did I encourage fellow group members to do well? Or was I indifferent to their efforts and achievements?

9. Did I serve as a mediator and a peacemaker? Or did I allow ill feelings to develop?

10. Was I willing to compromise? Or did I remain inflexible?

11. Did I encourage others to participate and did I give everyone else a fair chance to speak? Or did I sit by while some people hogged the floor? Did I sometimes dominate the discussion?[3]

the discussion as a result. Besides, it might just be our comment that welds the group together more tightly!

6. *lack skill in expressing our ideas.* The way to gain skill is through experience. Problem-solving groups need information and ideas—not necessarily eloquence. If our ideas are good, it will more than make up for a weak delivery.

7. *feel inferior to other members.* Feelings of inferiority, too, can be overcome if we have done our homework. If we've prepared well for discussion and can offer useful information, we will be able to work on an equal level with other group members.

8. *become too emotionally involved in the topic.* We should make every attempt to reserve judgment, to be objective, and to monitor our own behavior. Examine the facts and the reasons for arguments. Be open-minded.

Group problem-solving means participation by *all* members. If you know in advance that you tend to be shy or introverted in groups, there are several things you can do. First, *be thoroughly prepared.* To do extensive research and preparation will help build your self-confidence and will provide you the information you need to contribute. Second, *find questions or problems* regarding the topic that you can write down and ask others during the discussion. To be an opinion- or information-seeker often shifts the participation "burden" enough to relax you, and it allows sufficient time for orientation and acclimation. Having a prepared question also gives you a vehicle for entering the conversation. Third, *know your material well.* Go over your evidence so that you are familiar with it and do not need to fish for it during the discussion. Fourth, *inject your self into the discussion.* Maintain a strong and responsive posture. This means that you should be physically and mentally alert. Sit up in your chair and keep your mind on what is going on. When opportunities arise, do not shrink back or hesitate—assert your self directly and forthrightly. (See Chapter 9 for ideas that will help you assert your self in group situations.) Fifth, *keep up with what is going on.* Try not to get sidetracked in group discussions. If you become distracted by something one person has said and you let ten minutes go by while you mentally work out a reply to it, the discussion will pass you by! Be a good listener. (See Chapter 4.) Knowing your material well will help you make your comments at the appropriate time.

The Excessive Talker

This is the other side of the participation coin: people who talk too much are also a problem in small-group discussion. They can be even more disruptive of the group process than the non-talker because they don't give anyone else a chance.

In a group situation, the excessive talker is revealing three negative characteristics. First, he or she is being selfish—oblivious to the needs and desires of the other members of the group. Second, he or she is being uncooperative—being unwilling to share ideas with others in a reciprocal fashion. Sharing ideas involves both giving and getting. Third, the talkative person is a barrier to open communication. He or she is an obstacle to creating spontaneity—a situation where everyone feels free to contribute to the group.

The excessive talker, just as the non-talker, has many reasons for his or her behavior. If you are an excessive talker, it may be that you:

1. *want attention.* If other group members recognize this, they can help by rewarding your efforts and complimenting you on your contributions. Thus, you will gain attention for the quality, not quantity, of your ideas.

2. *want to make up for weak evidence or bad preparation.* It may be that you just did not do the amount of work you should have in preparing, and with a verbal barrage you plan to conceal this fact. There is, obviously, little excuse for this. Perceptive group members will see through your facade; they cannot allow an ill-prepared member to dominate the discussion.

3. *do not recognize your problem.* Some people just talk too much. They forget themselves in conversation. Strong group members must try to include others in the discussion, refocus attention on the problem, or in some way capitalize on your ability by asking others to respond to your comments.

4. *think your ideas are more important than those of others.* A group effort is a *group* effort. There is little purpose in group discussion if all members do not have an *equal* chance to voice their ideas. Their ideas are just as important as yours, and they have a right to express them.

The talkative person must change if he or she wishes to improve group behavior. The first thing you can do if you suspect you dominate too often is to *monitor your own behavior.* You probably have some idea how talkative you tend to be. If you talk too much, be alert to this. The second thing you can do is to *try to let others talk.* Practice providing a channel for letting others get their comments into the discussion. This will give you a way to participate without saying too much. For example, you could say, "Susan, didn't you find some information on this?" or "Dan, what do you think of this idea?" or "Does anyone have any other suggestions?" Practice going to the group first before offering your own information. This discourages selfishness and excessive participation. The third thing you can do is to reduce the amount you need to talk by working to *condense your thoughts.* Be brief. The final thing you can do is to *listen.* One of the worst things about excessive talkers is that they assume no one else has anything worth saying. They need to consider seriously what others say, not just pretend to open up discussion.

Participating effectively also involves knowing when to state a position on an issue. You should hold off describing your position until the most appropriate time. This has several advantages:

1. It keeps you from being the central focus of attention. Often when a position is made public, opponents may argue or try to convince you to change instead of getting on with the discussion.

2. It allows you the possibility of changing your mind as a result of the evidence presented by others during the discussion. A position made public is harder to change; such a change may strike others as indecisiveness, or being two-faced.

3. It emphasizes your awareness of good group-discussion procedures. Group discussion does not require argument or confrontation. The emphasis should be on the amount and quality of ideas presented. The opinions need not even be those of the participants but, rather, of experts in the field under discussion.

INTERPERSONAL COMMUNICATION IN THE SMALL GROUP: MAKING IT WORK

CONSIDER THIS

I myself have always believed that the kibbutz is the one place in the world where people are judged, accepted and given a chance to participate fully in the community to which they belong not in accordance with the kind of work they do or how well they do it, but for their intrinsic value as human beings. Not that kibbutz life is never flawed by envy, dishonesty or laziness. Kibbutz members are not angels, but they are the only people, as far as I know, who truly share almost everything—problems, rewards, responsibilities and satisfactions.

—Golda Meir, *My Life*

Bearing in mind the values of group discussion, how can we turn our attention to the other members of the group? How can we have and reveal concern for the interpersonal relations of others in the group? The concepts we are talking about for small-group communication are largely the concepts developed earlier in the book: perception, listening, feedback, language, attitude change, resolving conflicts, and assertiveness. To become an effective small-group leader or participant requires knowledge of these concepts and practice of the corresponding skills. Remembering the cliché that "a prudent person profits from personal experience; a wise one from the experience of others," we can show concern for others by actively working to create a healthy small-group atmosphere.

There are a number of things we can do to create a healthy small-group atmosphere:

1. *Encourage everyone to view the situation as a problem-solving one.* We all have something at stake or we wouldn't be there. We have something in common—we'll all benefit by resolution of the problem. This way of thinking has several advantages: First, it keeps people focused on the task rather than on personal concerns. Second, it helps prevent the situation from becoming merely a rap ses-

sion composed of one digression or "interesting" story after another. Third, it is efficient because it uses time in the most profitable manner.

2. *Encourage feelings of acceptance.* Since all members depend on each other and since the best discussion results when everyone contributes, it is important that everyone feels that his or her presence makes a difference, that contribution is worthwhile, and that continued participation is valued.

3. *Foster feelings of empathic understanding.* We will avoid many arguments and unnecessary quibbling if we can encourage everyone to try to see where others are coming from before attacking their evidence or opinion. Empathy involves trying to feel what the other person feels and trying to see what the other person sees. We can never accomplish this entirely, but the closer we can approach it, the more understanding we will tend to be. There is always the danger of carrying this to an extreme—"chumminess" can distract the group and can lessen objectivity. But most groups do not suffer from this problem.

4. *Encourage a listening environment.* Go back and review the listening skills listed in Chapter 4. We cannot merely hear what others say, we must also bring our own intellect and emotions to bear on ideas. True, genuine, and open responsiveness is not just pleasant—it is necessary.

5. *Develop a climate of spontaneity.* This means encouraging a climate where everyone feels free to contribute, and does. Certainly, courtesy and tact must also exist or there will be total chaos, but the rules of courtesy and tact are slightly different in a task-oriented group than in normal conversation:

A. Make all comments fairly brief. Contributions longer than thirty seconds seem like little speeches which slow down the pace of the group and limit the number of contributions that can be made.

B. Be willing to interrupt others and be willing to be interrupted. First hear out what a person wants to say on a point, but if he or she is already moving on to another point and we have a question or comment on the last one, we have not only a right but an obligation to interrupt. Unwillingness to interrupt can cause several problems:

   a. It can allow one person to dominate the discussion.
   b. It can allow important points to go by without discussion.
   c. It can turn discussion into a series of short speeches rather than a situation where anyone may respond to any comment.

C. Let non-talkers go first. If we are ready to contribute and we notice that a person who has not been saying as much as we have wants to say something at the same time, we must be willing to back off and open a channel for his or her participation.

D. Try to stay energetic, enthusiastic, and interested. It is in this atmosphere that we find excitement and the group is more likely to be productive.

The interpersonal relations of group participants find their most positive and genuine expression in an environment of spontaneity. When spontaneity occurs we will know it because its results are general satisfaction and happiness with the small-group effort.

KEEPING A SENSE OF DIRECTION: WHAT NEXT?

To get from a starting point to the completion of its task, a group functions best when there is some form of leadership. The leadership style most appropriate for a particular group depends on the task, the

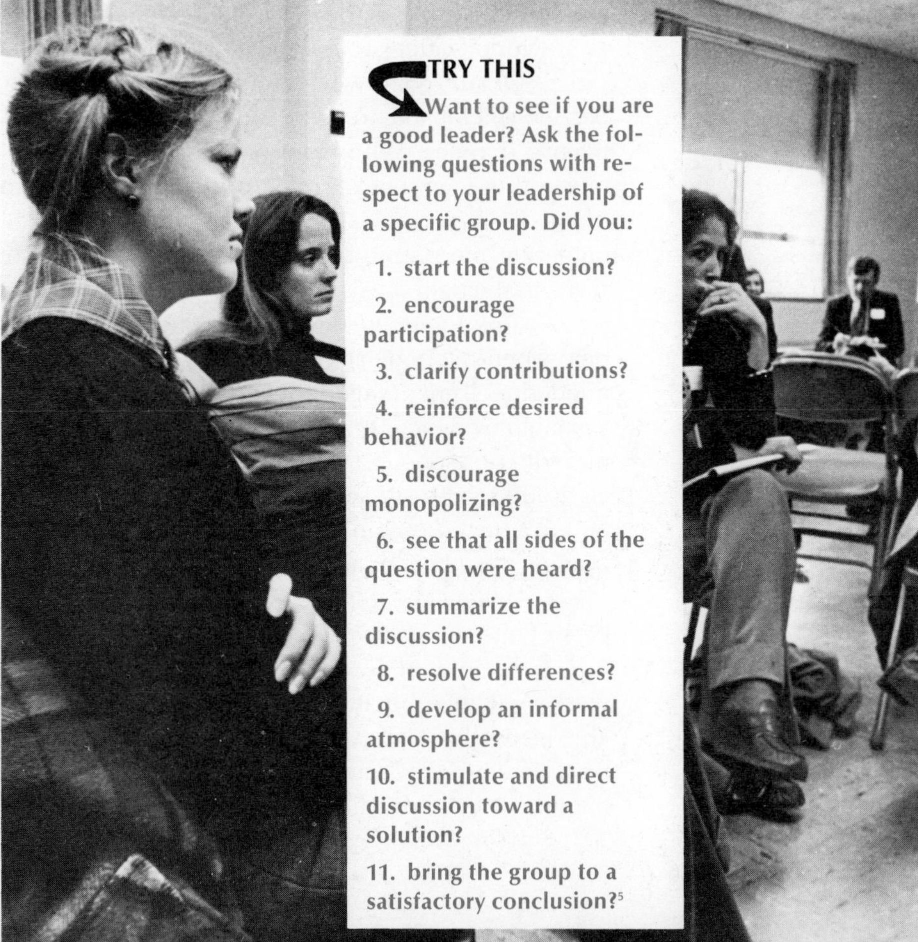

TRY THIS

Want to see if you are a good leader? Ask the following questions with respect to your leadership of a specific group. Did you:

1. start the discussion?

2. encourage participation?

3. clarify contributions?

4. reinforce desired behavior?

5. discourage monopolizing?

6. see that all sides of the question were heard?

7. summarize the discussion?

8. resolve differences?

9. develop an informal atmosphere?

10. stimulate and direct discussion toward a solution?

11. bring the group to a satisfactory conclusion?[5]

situation, the members, what the members desire or need, and the amount of time the group has available. An informal task, like deciding what movie a group would like to see, may require little or no leadership. Trying to develop a series of official rules or regulations may require a stronger form of leadership. A social group trying to determine some activities for the coming year might require little or no leadership. An academic situation may be different. Members who have had training in group work may need little or no formal leadership; members who have had little experience in group work often need the direction a leader can provide. Time is also a factor. The less time a group has to complete its task, the greater the need for structure and leadership. These requirements vary from group to group.

Leadership Functions

In any problem-solving group there are some fundamental roles that help the group move toward its goals. These are leadership functions, but they can be performed by any group member. These are skills that, if learned and practiced, will make us more willing and more comfortable rising to the occasion when it calls for leadership:[4]

A good leader is:

1. *Organized.* If we commit Dewey's Reflective Pattern to memory, we will be able to help lead the group through the process of reflective thinking. We would probably show greater knowledge than most other members on how to move the group from the beginning of the discussion to a specific goal. We would be able to help coordinate movement from one step to the next and insure that the group stays on the right track.

2. *Open-minded.* If we can suspend our judgment, we will appear open-minded—another quality of an effective leader. Open-mindedness encourages the presentation and consideration of all available evidence. It also shows a willingness to hear and consider minority opinions. An effective leader is aware of the participation of all group members, and politely draws out members who are reluctant to offer an opinion. Only in this way can all the facts, ideas, and opinions that bear in any way on the topic be considered.

3. *Willing to listen.* Being ready to hear the opinions of all members of the group reveals respect for them. To react to others with tact, concern, and acceptance shows the other group members that we are willing to treat all members with equal dignity—another valuable leadership trait. This is the kind of person who is most likely to be accepted as a leader by the group because he or she can bring harmony to group deliberations.

IS CONSIDER THIS

"We've got to decide about being rescued."

There was a buzz. One of the small boys, Henry, said that he wanted to go home.

"Shut up," said Ralph absently. He lifted the conch. "Seems to me we ought to have a chief to decide things."

"A chief! A chief!"

"I ought to be chief," said Jack with simple arrogance, "because I'm chapter chorister and head boy. I can sing C sharp."

Another buzz.

"Well then," said Jack, "I—"

He hesitated. The dark boy, Roger, stirred at last and spoke up.

"Let's have a vote."

"Yes!"

"Vote for chief!"

"Let's vote—"

This toy of voting was almost as pleasing as the conch. Jack started to protest but the clamor changed from the general wish for a chief to an election by acclaim of Ralph himself. None of the boys could have found good reason for this; what intelligence had been shown was traceable to Piggy while the most obvious leader was Jack. But there was a stillness about Ralph as he sat that marked him out: there was his size, and attractive appearance; and most obscurely, yet most powerfully, there was the conch. The being that had blown that, had sat waiting for them on the platform with the delicate thing balanced on his knees, was set apart.

"Him with the shell."

"Ralph! Ralph!"

"Let him be chief with the trumpet-thing."

Ralph raised a hand for silence.

"All right. Who wants Jack for chief?"

With dreary obedience the choir raised their hands.

"Who wants me?"

Every hand outside the choir except Piggy's was raised immediately. Then Piggy, too, raised his hand grudgingly into the air.

Ralph counted.

"I'm chief then."

The circle of boys broke into applause. Even the choir applauded; and the freckles on Jack's face disappeared under a blush of mortification. He started up, then changed his mind and sat down again while the air rang.

—William Golding, *Lord of the Flies*

CONSIDER THIS CONSIDER THIS CONSIDER THIS CONSIDER THIS CONSIDER THIS CONSIDER THIS CONSIDER TH

4. *Knowledgeable.* Familiarity with the subject is also very important. Being well prepared on the topic means that we are sensitive to relevant issues and implications. It is easy to go out and amass a large body of research; it is not easy to synthesize the research into relevant issues and then to try to determine the implications of those issues. This means we have to go beyond the research, to step back from the research process and examine the accumulation of data with some objectivity. Knowledgeability also means that we can distinguish essential, trustworthy opinions and facts from those that are questionable. Dumping a lot of research in an unexamined, raw form onto the group discussion serves little purpose. We have a responsibility to test our own evidence just as we have a responsibility to examine the evidence presented by others.

Other leadership functions are more obvious but no less important. Often those who rise to the occasion when leadership is necessary are those who can express themselves well orally. Improving our oral-communication skills will aid us in leading small-group discussions. Flexibility and self-control will also help us in demonstrating leadership functions.

Who's in Charge?

TRY THIS

Observe (on television, perhaps) a small-group discussion of an issue of current interest. Keep track of who talks the most and the least. If there is no appointed leader, does one emerge? What specifically does he or she do to keep the group on track?

There are three major leadership styles in addition to groups that have no leader at all. Different groups, because of different situations, need different kinds of leadership. There is *democratic* leadership, *authoritarian* leadership, and *functional* leadership. These are not mutually exclusive styles. One person may exhibit all of these, or the leadership of a group may move from one style to another. They can also exist in degrees: one person may be a strong democratic leader, another may be a laissez-faire democratic leader. No single style is necessarily best, but under certain conditions, a group may operate best with one style rather than another.

Democratic leadership. The democratic leader encourages all members to be as valuable to the group as possible. The leader protects the worth and dignity of all members, allows all to show initiative, encourages a free exchange of ideas through full intragroup communication, and strives for consensus so that all decisions are a result of *group* achievement.

Authoritarian leadership. The authoritarian leader takes full control of the group. Control is rigid and strong and is shared with no one. The authoritarian leader insists on some deference and respect from others. He or she plans well, makes decisions, gives orders, and as-

CONSIDER THIS "**Eugene Donnelly, a veteran of Battery D and a Kansas City lawyer: "We were a pretty rough bunch of boys; anyway, we thought we were. We'd already got rid of four commanding officers when Harry came along. He looked like a sitting duck to us. He was sort of small and with four eyes.**

"And then he called all the noncoms together, and he said, 'Now, look, I didn't come here to get along with you guys. You're going to have to get along with me, and if any of you thinks he can't, why, speak right up, and I'll give you a punch in the nose.'

"He was tough, but he was fair; he was a good officer.

"I remember once a bunch of us were going to Paris on a furlough, and we didn't have any money. Harry found out about it, and he lent us the money we needed. We'd have done anything for him then, and nobody that I know has changed his mind.""

—Merle Miller, *Plain Speaking: An Oral Biography of Harry S. Truman*

sumes responsibility for the progress and procedure of the group. Usually, this person will dominate the participation of the group and will be the focal point for all contributions; that is, all comments will be directed to him or her. Authoritarian leadership is appropriate in certain circumstances: in the operating room, in war, or in the kitchen (you can't cook by committee!).

Functional leadership. This style of leadership does not differ from the preceding two styles in terms of degree of freedom or control—rather, functional leadership is a method. In both preceding styles, leadership belongs, essentially, to a single person. In functional leadership, it changes from one person to another. It is the kind of leadership in which anyone can take over the group process at any time and help move the group forward.

Functional leadership is effective in small problem-solving groups where the talent is fairly evenly spread among all members and where *all* members are willing to assume some responsibility for the success of the group as a whole. Since all members possess some information that will help the group achieve its goal, often they, not someone else, are the ones who can best discover at what point their information will serve the group purposes best.

Although a group always retains the right to resist leadership functions expressed by members at any time, accepting the notion of functional leadership will help the group in several ways:

1. It will make it clear that leadership is not the property of any

single individual. Leadership, to be most effective, is a function of the group as a whole.

2. Accepting functional leadership will also help group members by showing that they are all equally responsible for resolution of the group's problem. When one member's ability, interest, or knowledge can be most useful to the group, leadership is conferred, often unknowingly, on him or her during the group process. The information an individual has or the insight he or she can give makes him or her a leader at any point in time.

3. Leadership is not static. It varies with the task of the group, the issue being discussed, and with the peculiar skills of the group members and how these skills relate to the functioning of the group. Leadership may move from individual to individual; it may not. It is unpredictable, but its lack of predictability makes it flexible and workable, as well as adaptable to most small-group problem-solving situations.

Functional leadership allows members to be self-directive, to set their own goals, to create a non-threatening group atmosphere, and to initiate change. The group members should become so capable and self-sufficient that a leader, in the literal sense of the word, would not be necessary at all. All members would be equally goal oriented, and the word "leader" could disappear from their thinking.

Functional leadership is often effective, but you might wonder what happens when a leader is imposed on a group by some outside force like a teacher, supervisor, facilitator, or executive. The most ef-

HIS CONSIDER THIS

CONSIDER THIS CONSIDER THIS CONSIDER T

It would be difficult to describe the subtle brotherhood of men that was here established on the seas. No one said that it was so. No one mentioned it. But it dwelt in the boat, and each man felt it warm him. They were a captain, an oiler, a cook, and a correspondent, and they were friends, friends in a more curiously iron-bound degree than may be common. The hurt captain, lying against the water-jar in the bow, spoke always in a low voice and calmly, but he could never command a more ready and swiftly obedient crew than the motley three of the dingey. It was more than a mere recognition of what was best for the common safety. There was surely in it a quality that was personal and heartfelt. And after this devotion to the commander of the boat there was this comradeship that the correspondent, for instance, who had been taught to be cynical of men, knew even at the time was the best experience of his life. But no one said that it was so. No one mentioned it.

—Stephen Crane, "The Open Boat"

fective imposed leader will create an atmosphere in which functional leadership can emerge. Leaders are sometimes imposed to avoid awkward, sometimes embarrassing, moments of silence. They are sometimes imposed so that someone has the responsibility for guiding the group and giving it purpose. Whatever the reason, imposed leadership and functional leadership need not be contradictory.

There are specific things an imposed leader can do to aid group discussion. Given the position of "imposed leader," a person should move quickly to do the following:

1. encourage a cooperative atmosphere
2. be an active but not domineering participant
3. be democratic
4. show sensitivity to and respect for others
5. show self-control
6. be open-minded
7. attempt to organize group thinking through group participation
8. have a good grasp of the problem
9. give credit to the group and share rewards with them
10. promote spontaneity

These things are expected of any leader using any style of leadership. The main problem with imposed leadership is that it may go to a person who would never have chosen the role for himself or herself and who, for one reason or another, does not have the best interests of the group at heart.

With increased effectiveness and skill in each of these important areas, each of us can become a more effective group member. We will know how to efficiently help our selves and other members prepare to discuss, follow a plan, participate effectively, create a healthy small-group atmosphere, and lead the group. These are not the only concepts and skills on which successful group problem-solving is based. Small-group interaction is an interpersonal experience. All the concepts and skills developed in this book are important and are brought into play as the process continues.

OTHER READING

Eric Berne, *The Structure and Dynamics of Organizations and Groups* (New York: Ballantine Books, 1963). In this book Berne provides an illustrative analysis of a group meeting, discusses the group as a whole, examines the individual in the group, and, finally, offers a systematic framework for the therapy of "ailing" groups and organizations. It is useful and provocative.

Ernest G. Bormann and Nancy C. Bormann, *Effective Small Group Communication,* 2nd ed. (Minneapolis, Minn.: Burgess Publishing Company, 1976). This book provides a practical, working knowledge of the topic without an in-depth study of all the recent research. Following a clear and well-organized approach that is free of jargon, the authors offer a brief but complete description of small-group dynamics with numerous examples.

John K. Brilhart, *Effective Group Discussion,* Second Edition (Dubuque, Iowa: Wm. C. Brown Company Publishers, 1974). A comprehensive examination of group discussion with a thorough bibliography and stimulating exercises. Contains an excellent chapter on leadership. Well written and illustrated.

Edward De Bono, *New Think: The Use of Lateral Thinking in the Generation of New Ideas* (New York: Avon Books, 1968). De Bono provides a method of breaking the habit of logical thinking that opens the mind to creative, uninhibited thought. It is written in a clear, easy-to-follow style.

John Hasling, *Group Discussion and Decision Making* (New York: Thomas Y. Crowell Company, 1975). This is a brief guide to successful group discussion. Hasling discusses barriers to communication and conflict management in addition to finding solutions, structuring the discussion, and testing decisions. This is a straightforward, well-written textbook.

William S. Smith, *Group Problem-Solving Through Discussion: A Process Essential to Democracy* (Indianapolis, Ind.: The Bobbs-Merrill Company, Inc., 1965). Discussion is approached as a practical, empirical process based upon the scientific method of making inquiries and evaluations and drawing conclusions. Smith's chapters explore the uses, methods, and results of group problem-solving.

NOTES

[1] From *Human Interaction in the Small Group Setting* by Lawrence B. Rosenfeld, pp. 91–92. Copyright © 1973 by Bell & Howell Company. Reprinted by permission of Charles E. Merrill Publishing Co.

[2] John Dewey, *How We Think* (Chicago: D. C. Heath, 1910).

[3] From "Am I a Good Group Participant?" by Leland P. Bradford, *Today's Education: NEA Journal,* March 1956. Reprinted by permission.

[4] Adapted from John K. Brilhart, *Effective Group Discussion,* Second Edition, (Dubuque, Iowa: Wm. C. Brown Company Publishers, 1974), pp. 130–132.

[5] Richard L. Weaver, II, *Speech Communication: A Student Manual* (Columbus, Ohio: Collegiate Publishing, Inc., 1976), pp. 116–117.

INDEX